D1266358

The ATLAS of MIND BODY AND SPIRIT

The ATLAS of
MIND
BODY
AND
SPIRIT

PAUL HOUGHAM

Gaia Books

For Nila

**Reconnect with yourself
and the planet**

First published in Great Britain in 2006 by Gaia Books
a division of Octopus Publishing Group Ltd
2–4 Heron Quays, London, E14 4JP.

Copyright © Octopus Publishing Group Ltd 2006
Text copyright © Paul Hougham 2006

Distributed in the United States and Canada by
Sterling Publishing Co., Inc.
387 Park Avenue South, New York, NY 10016–8810

All rights reserved. No part of this work may
be reproduced or utilized in any form or by
any means, electronic or mechanical, including
photocopying, recording or by any information
storage and retrieval system, without the prior
written permission of the publisher.

Paul Hougham asserts the moral right to be identified
as the author of this book.

ISBN-13: 978-185675-247-3
ISBN-10: 1-85675-247-X

A CIP catalogue record of this book is available from
the British Library.

Printed and bound in China

10 9 8 7 6 5 4 3 2 1

Publisher's note The publisher and author
specifically disclaim any responsibility for any liability,
loss or risk that may be claimed or incurred as a
consequence, directly or indirectly, of the use of
any of the contents of this publication.

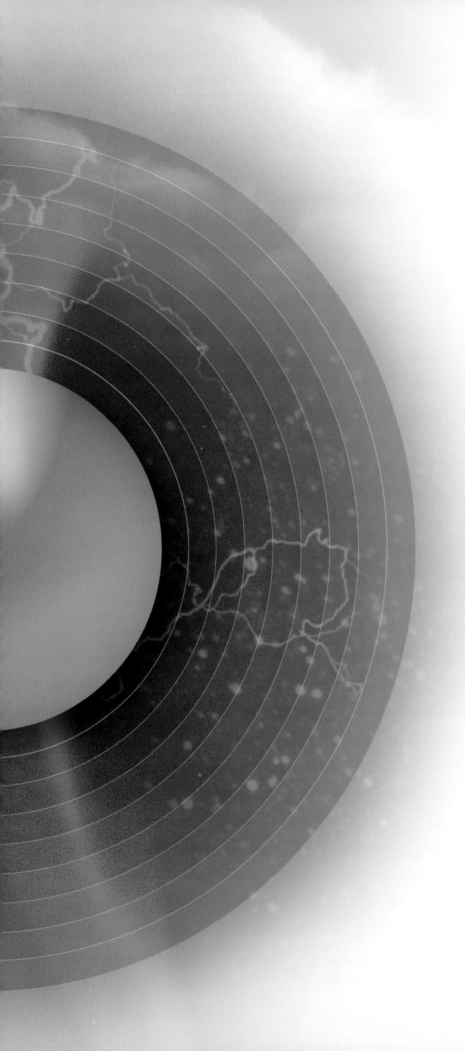

Contents

Foreword

The subject of this remarkable work is one that has preoccupied me throughout my life – our hidden human potential. From my first book, *The Outsider*, onward, I have been fascinated by those strange moments in which we experience a curious sense of power and happiness – what one philosopher called 'contact with the source of power, meaning and purpose'. It is rather like wandering along a familiar road and finding a door in a wall that leads into some amazing garden – in fact, H G Wells created that image in *The Door in the Wall*.

Where is this magical door? The answer is quite clear: somewhere inside us. But why is it so hard to find, and how can we find our way back to it? This is the subject of the book you are now holding. It is a kind of atlas of our inner being.

This search for 'the door in the wall' has been known to every nation and culture on earth, and Paul Hougham is more qualified than most to talk about it, since he has an encyclopaedic knowledge of world cultures.

I became interested in the problem of the door in the wall as a child, for it presented itself to me every Christmas. There was a marvellous sense of inner peace, as if the world had made a truce and promised to smooth out all the difficulties of life. And as we walked down to my grandparents for tea, the streets I knew so well somehow looked different. And when Christmas was over, and 'reality' gradually returned, I found myself wondering, without putting it into words: Was that marvellous feeling an illusion? Or was it – as I felt strongly at the time – the 'real' reality behind the face of this difficult and often boring everyday life?

Here is an example that will underline my point, from a book called *Seeing the Invisible*, a collection of accounts of 'visionary' experiences submitted by ordinary people to the Alister Hardy Foundation:

'At the age of 22–23 I remember standing in my room when suddenly I felt "dizzy" – overwhelmed by a sensation of "light" – it felt as if flame was around me. It seemed as if I was transported on to another plane of consciousness, shot through with an almost unbearable Joy. I don't know how long this experience lasted, maybe a few minutes or even only a few seconds: it did not belong to a time–space world. The sensation of joy and inexplicable happiness lasted two or three days, gradually fading. It happened at a time in my life when I was enjoying things enormously in a normal way.'

I cannot claim to have experienced the same kind of ecstasy. But I felt that the Christmas feeling, 'when I was enjoying things enormously', was a kind of prelude to it. And I suspect that every one of us could tell a similar story, for we all have a natural insight that feelings of delight and intensity are somehow a natural human birthright.

Now, as you will see from this book, many cultures have their own methods of approaching 'the door in the wall'. In fact, the Kabbalah describes several different doors, each approached by a different path. Paul Hougham's chapter on it is one of the best short accounts I have ever read.

Although I wrote a rather large book – called *The Occult* – that included an account of the Kabbalah, I have never given precedence to this approach. My own approach has always been psychological, and based upon the observation of the American psychologist Abraham Maslow, to the effect that *all* healthy people have, with a fair degree of frequency, what he called 'peak experiences' – experiences of sudden bubbling happiness, when we experience what G K Chesterton called 'absurd good news'.

Such experiences happen, of course, when we experience sudden relief from anxiety. And when we are oppressed with some worry, we have the feeling that *if only* this would go away, we would be able to feel happy for days or weeks. In fact, the former head of the BBC music programming, Hans Keller, once described how, when he was in Hitler's Germany and saw fellow Jews disappearing into concentration camps, he reflected:

'If only I could get out of Germany I would never be unhappy again.' Of course, he didn't succeed in living up to his promise. But it is easy for all of us to identify with the feeling that it would be quite easy to live up to it.

Now for years I pursued my investigation into that question of the peak experience and how it comes about. And then, towards the end of 1979, I had a major breakthrough. This is how I describe it in a book called *The Devil's Party*:

'On New Year's Day, 1979, I was trapped by snow in a remote Devon farmhouse, where I had gone to lecture to extra-mural students. After 24 hours we decided we had to make an effort to escape. It so happened that my car was the only one that would climb the slope out of the farmyard. After several hours' hard work with shovels, we finally reached the main road.

'The snow on the narrow country road had been churned up by traffic, but was still treacherous. And in places where the snow was still untouched, it was hard to see where the road ended and the ditch began. So as I began to make my way home, I was forced to drive with total, obsessive attention. Finally back on the main Exeter road, where I was able to relax, I noticed that everything I looked at seemed curiously real and interesting. The hours of concentrated attention had somehow 'fixed' my consciousness in a higher state of alertness. There was also an immense feeling of optimism, a conviction that most of our problems are due to vagueness, slackness, inattention, and that they are all perfectly easy to overcome with determined effort. This state lasted throughout the rest of the drive home. Even now, merely thinking about the experience is enough to bring back the insight and renew the certainty.'

This experience of a 'more powerful' consciousness seemed a revelation, because it was not some sudden mystical 'flash'; *I had done it myself*. So it ought to be possible to do again.

I found it far more difficult than I had anticipated. I often tried it when driving, and achieved it briefly, but never for long. I did, in fact, succeed again on a long train journey. But when I tried again the next day, on the return journey, I found it impossible. Obviously, the effort had exhausted some inner energy. I began to suspect that it was the sense of emergency that had brought about my first success, and that this was difficult to create at will.

But over the years I have gone on trying. And finally, about two years ago, I found I was succeeding. I was succeeding in achieving the 'trick' that would result in the type of focused attention required to release a sense of access to some kind of brain-energy. This focused attention brings with it an insight: that one of the by-products of the quest for insight is our tendency for what might be called 'negative feedback'.

The author puts his finger on the nature of the problem in his introduction, when he says:

'Ten years after Schrödinger's first meeting with his cat, the philosopher Maurice Merleau-Ponty published *The Phenomenology of Perception*, in which he described greater possibilities of how we know things. Perception, he suggested, is neither the subjectivity of personal perception nor any objective reading of objects beyond our sphere, but rather a blended phenomena of experience itself, constantly affecting itself. It is often argued that such qualities of subject contamination in the processes of perception occur only at a theoretical and quantum level of reality. But in each question we ask of the world, in the hypotheses of scientific experiment and our expectations as to what we see, we irrevocably shape what we find. This is the intersubjective basis for every aspect of being-ness within the universe. And as we will discover, we are powerful beings both at a global and a personal level. What we seek we will find in the effect of our choices on the health of our planet, our cultures, and our personal wellbeing.'

It was when I was reading this passage that I suddenly realized just what an important book The Atlas of Mind, Body and Spirit is.

Another brilliant insight can be found in the closing epigraph to the final chapter:

'We don't discover, we create. The neutrality of our participation in life is a mere limiting ruse; we inevitably create the texture of our lives.'

It is natural to see ourselves as passive because we spend so many years as children, accepting that adults know what is going on and what it is all about. Then we achieve adulthood and discover that this was untrue. Adults don't know, any more than children do.

But some adults, just a few, understand. Merleau-Ponty understood, and he learned it from his master, the philosopher Edmund Husserl. He knew that perception is active, not passive – he called it 'intentional' – and that if we could learn to grasp that perception is an *unconsciously creative act*, we would have taken a vital step up the evolutionary ladder.

Colin Wilson

A body of knowledge

The body as spiritual landscape

William Blake described us as the 'human form divine'. This Atlas is an odyssey through the holistic sciences that have tracked such a landscape and speculated about its potential. It is the notion of the body as a landscape that is the central theme of this work, placing alongside each other traditions that do not separate different areas of experience, of body, mind and spirit. The body as a spiritual landscape; the spirit embodied in our physical form; the mind and emotions as other facets of our individual uniqueness.

Such holistic sciences have been found across many lands and in many cultures at different times. Here, they are named as traditions, as lineages, as schools: bodies of knowledge that have not always used the written word, but transmitted learning through oral traditions, through dreams, and within the 'virtual' halls and temples of meditation and prayer.

Given the gulf between some of these sciences, let alone within their many schools, the telling of them here attempts to convey something of their uniqueness as they come up against a universal experience of what it means to be human. The assumption is that each tradition has insights to offer regarding the nature of life.

This chapter moves through themes that enable us to navigate such a panoramic perspective to the Body/Mind/Spirit without losing our balance on uneven and shifting surfaces as we encounter ideas that might otherwise contradict each other. These are the 'surveyors' skills' that will equip us with the philosophical equilibrium necessary to abandon certainties we are attached to and take one step back. These skills will equip us to see things in context, to survey our own experiences, bodies, minds and spirits as we encounter the human form divine . . . as it has been surveyed by the schools and traditions of our ancestors . . . as it is being explored by our contemporary visionaries. The astrolabe (left) was once the global-positioning system of sailors, placing each adventurer in relation to the sun and stars. It is similar skills that we are seeking here to guide us through spiritual landscape of the body:

- What we see depends on where we stand
- Just by looking at or thinking about something, we change it
- Nothing is solid
- Energy is life
- We are powerful

Just as we are about to explore the various experiences of Mind/Body/Spirit, we are also about to traverse realms of consciousness. In the ways of such traditions, some images and words here might linger long after we have read them, as keys of insight taking us further into the material presented, deeper into the treasure house of our own individual expressions of mind, body and spirit. For, as is suggested to us in the Taoist classic, the *Tao Te Ching*: 'Without stirring abroad, one can know the whole world; without looking out of the window, one can see the way of Heaven.'

What we know

kaleidoscopic worldviews and a fluid epistemology

Warning: You are in the process of being indoctrinated . . . What you are being taught here is an amalgam of current prejudice and the choices of this particular culture. The slightest look at history will show how impermanent these must be. You are being taught by people who have been able to accommodate themselves to a regime of thought laid down by their predecessors . . . Those of you who are more robust and individual than others, will be encouraged to leave and find ways of educating yourself . . . Those that stay must remember, always and all the time, that they are being moulded and patterned to fit into the narrow and particular needs of this society.

Doris Lessing

What we know very often depends on where and when we were born. For there is an inevitable historical and cultural perspective to what we know about the world. Whatever the relationship is between ourselves and any objective reality, there is a confounding diversity of ways in which we perceive the world. This is further dependent initially on our experience as humans and the physiology of our particular senses. We don't consciously register seismic rhythms in the planet's crust; we don't see light beyond the wavelengths our physiology determines for us. From within the basic formation of these senses, our perception is shaped.

A PROPER CONTEXT

Western culture has long sought a 'grand theory of everything', an all-encompassing description of our world and experience that reconciles all of the inconsistencies and contradictions of what we believe we know. It may be that this has precipitated an imperialist approach to science and culture that has also hobbled any attempt at true science in which we take off the brakes and explore our world.

In the 1950s, William Perry carried out research at Harvard University into how students learn. He found that most of us engage in a period of study in order to confirm what we already know and seek ammunition to help other people realize that they are wrong. As we begin to appreciate the vastness of intellectual and spiritual varieties across both history and geography, we then tend to see that there is a context to what we know and believe, that relativism has a place within the infrastructure of who we are.

WORLDVIEWS

For many of us, this can be a catastrophic blow to our internal edifices of belief and, as a result, we usually fall into a black hole of believing nothing or revert to a dogmatic absolutism. But Perry did observe that there was another potential stage of intellectual development after relativism had scuppered our Icarean rise towards absolute knowledge. This was the skill to be able to accept the shifting sands of any knowledge that we are able to attain. We would then make a conscious choice to sculpt a particular set of intellectual perspectives as our own working model of reality, fully aware of their potential relativity in any absolute sense, but also fully enamoured of their value and meaning in our lives.

This is the mastery of a philosophical double vision. I see what I see because of where I stand, and I see the many other views of life from where I have been, from what others tell me, and from what I can imagine. But this is what I choose at this moment to believe for myself.

We need to train our consciousness so we are flexible enough to conceive of different ways of viewing the Body/Mind/Spirit without a compulsive need for any single perspective to be the only way. Epistemology is how we know things. We need a fluid epistemology so that we can change our approach when we need to, move from microscope to meditation, from trance dance to evidence-based medicine without so much as a whimper. These are the kaleidoscopic worldviews of scientific necessity and suspended disbelief – of placing in parallel the contrasting evidence of our experience and developing a fly eye's vision of life.

There is very little hope for a singular worldview able to reach up and over the contradictions of localized theories of how our world works and gather them into a more enlightened and mature perspective. Here, however, we suggest a different kind of globalism that doesn't seek to equalize and converge, but retains the integrity of each science and tradition, knowing that the dynamics between them is the lifeblood of our ongoing creativity.

THE GIFTS OF HERESY

Those who are convinced they have a monopoly on The Truth always feel that they are only saving the world when they slaughter the heretics.

Arthur Schlesinger

Within most cultures, both secular and religious, heretics provide the lifeblood of change that nourishes the very vibrancy of the traditions themselves. While often pilloried and frequently executed, they offer the essential antithesis of a collective consciousness, that is at times honoured, at times cast out. Here also is the uncomfortable presence in the wisdom held by the soldiers of all lands that in coming to fight their nemesis find an uncomfortable similarity. The necessary brutality of war is primarily a brutality of the spirit, where we force those who fight for us to dehumanize the enemy enough to be able to kill them. The pinnacle of the warriors' way across all the world's traditions is the power of the kill with no such dehumanizing justification. This is the honour of the samurai, the chivalry of the knight, the integrity of the Hashshashin. And as so often happens in such extremes of warfare and meeting, the culture of the warrior is shared, leaving an inevitable blending in the manner that was probably the worst fear of those who instigated the war in the first place. People speak to each other, thankfully.

What we see depends on where we stand.

~

It is wise to stand in at least two places in relation to any knowledge, so that a third position can naturally arise.

The real world

an empty, malleable universe

It is a question of not putting the perceptual faith in place of reflection, but on the contrary of taking into account the total situation, which involves reference from the one to the other. What is given is not a massive and opaque world, or a universe of adequate thought; it is a reflection which turns back over the density of the world in order to clarify it, but which, coming second, reflects back to it only its own light.

Maurice Merleau-Ponty

Our general perception is that there is a level of objectivity to science's progress. This objectivity is, however, probably very seldom achieved from economic or cultural perspectives, let alone from the challenges within science itself. In 1935, physicist Erwin Schrödinger posed a problem that forever challenged any hope of objectivity. He suggested a mind experiment where a cat was placed in a steel box with a phial of poison that may or may not be activated by a random generator. We would only ever know whether the cat was alive or dead once we looked in the box, illustrating that the world is as we perceive it only once we choose to look at it. This cat still poses challenges in the field of quantum science.

THE NATURE OF THE UNIVERSE

This fundamental malleability of experience takes place within yet another of quantum physics' great challenges to our common sense – that the universe is predominantly empty. As we will see overleaf, the building blocks of life are less the solid-state myths of the periodic table or the traditional wisdom of the elements, and more a complex interconnected web of information and attraction. The universe is not solid and each newly discovered 'smallest bit' is continuously revealed as hollow, empty space.

Such inner hollowness at the smallest scale of sub-atomic particles is mirrored by the vacuums within the largest scale of space itself. Just as we normally expect the solidity of our ground to be solid, so, too, do we expect the solidity of our assumptions to be equally firm. If we are to stray into any accuracy of how we might view the Body/ Mind/Spirit, it may serve us to accept its basic emptiness, and that every aspect of who we are is an intrinsic part of the reality

of the world. We can no more separate our subjectivity from the world than we can remove the water from the ocean, but to notice the ripples in the surface as we dive into the vastness of the world, that is possible.

THE RANGE OF HUMAN EXPERIENCE

There has ever been a battle to define the world we live in. It is an essential human function to engage with and understand our experience, and often this will entail struggling with anomalies – places where our experience does not fit within the bounds of our current view of the world. This may be as straightforward as a family member acting out of character in a way that rocks our world and causes us to question our assumptions. Or we might have an experience in the laboratory or on the mountain top that cannot be explained by what we currently know.

Historically, one worldview has tumbled as another fills its place, replacing its predecessor with the new knowledge that is, in fact, incontrovertible. Absolutely true. No question about it. Until the next time, when evidence mounts and causes us to update our knowledge once more. And there can be resistance to new knowledge and a compulsive addiction to jettison all of the old worldview, as if betrayed by its fallibility.

As our knowledge progresses, we can use philosophical stabilizers to minimize the impact of our historical immaturity. On one side, there is the humbling knowledge that our current fashion of reality is still only a stage in our discovery of the universe. On the other, there is the realization that the 'obsolete' superstitions of our ancestors hold a wisdom inaccessible to us if we assume the superiority of the questions we now ask of the world. So we look forward and backward and develop the perspective of the two-faced Janus. Such perspective in itself then has an opportunity to become a gateway, somewhere we are not bound by the limitations of the past, present or future, and where we can begin to touch a consciousness beyond time.

INTERSUBJECTIVITY

Maurice Merleau-Ponty

Ten years after Schrödinger's first meeting with his cat, the philosopher Maurice Merleau-Ponty published *The Phenomenology of Perception*, in which he described greater possibilities of how we know things. Perception, he suggested, is neither the subjectivity of personal perception nor any objective reading of objects beyond our sphere, but rather a blended phenomena of experience itself, constantly affecting itself.

It is frequently argued that such qualities of subject contamination in the processes of perception occur only at a theoretical and quantum level of reality. However, in each question we ask of the world, in the hypotheses of scientific experiment and our expectations as to what we see, we irrevocably shape what we find. This is the intersubjective basis for every aspect of beingness within the universe.

And, as we will discover, we are powerful beings, both at a global and at a personal level. What we seek we will find in the effect of our choices on the health of our planet, our cultures, and our personal wellbeing.

Just by looking at or thinking about something, we change it.

~

Our very existence creates ripples within reality.

It makes more sense to look at the shape of the ripples

rather than any mythical nature of reality.

Building blocks and rhythm
the elements of life

*It is the girding paradox of the Arch of Time, the
undisciplined restraint of the Earth's creation,
the absent bone of the EarthPower, the rigidness of
water and the flux of rock. It articulates the wild
magic which destroys peace. It is the abyss and the
peak of destiny. It is brought into use like any other
power – through passion and mystery, the honest
subterfuge of the heart.*
Stephen Donaldson

Just as we see with the seemingly perpetual
paradoxes of light (is it a wave or particle?),
our quest for the basic building blocks of our
universe goes on and on. The atom, once the
culmination of this search, comes from *atomos*,
Greek for 'indivisible'. And just as the atom
lost its title as the smallest 'bit' to the electron,
so that, too, has yielded to more 'indivisible'
particles, ones that move in other dimensions.

Once Einstein had opened the door to
quantum theory, scientists began to discover
paradoxes about how the universe seemed
to work, how light could be both wave and
particle, how two distant and seemingly
unconnected particles could communicate
instantaneously, and how observation was
a key part of the very construction of the
universe itself.

While these developments have not
invalidated the discoveries of the periodic
table, they have introduced new concepts
into the quest for the basic substance of the
universe, especially the notion that our
brains may store information in ways akin to
a hologram, the interference patterns of
lightwaves that go beyond the usual restric-

tions that we place on what we think of as
physical matter. It is into this environment
that the alchemical understandings of the
elements contribute their wisdom of the
interface between consciousness, intention,
and the substance of the worlds. For as we
dive into the substrata of matter with our
physical sciences we find ourselves staring
back at us, asking what mechanisms we
have now for sculpting this world of
intention and form.

Our skills of navigation are constructed
as we go – the great scientific criterion of
the pragmatic model at the heart of our
endeavours. In such an environment it may
yet be that the traditional structures of the
elements of Chinese medicine, Western
magic or druidic ceremony still have some
purchase in the slippery world of reality.

NATIVE TRADITIONS
The elements associated with native traditions commonly number 4 or 5 and do not
restrict themselves to being the 'stuff' of the
universe, but classically ally themselves with
one of the directions of the compass, and a
class of being that encompasses the calendar,
phases of the moon and aspects of the
manifest worlds. That each civilization yields
a different map of the elements can be understood if we consider the different locations
each inhabits on the Grandmother, and
that the elements were invariably linked
to the directions.

At a very basic level, the nature of the
elements is the tuning of the human energy
field in relation to that of the Earthstar, the

planetary and celestial bodies. In this way,
the cultural filters of each tradition's words,
ceremony and symbol will both mask and
reveal the essence of the element in its path
towards the centre, where all elements find
their union in their own essence and as a
unified path to the void of pure consciousness.

Magic emerges as the foundation of the
elements when they are engaged with by
any consciousness as a mechanism by which
to surf consciousness itself. When such an
initiation takes place, a pathway is formed
for the path of the soul to establish itself
further with this incarnation. As this occurs,
the building of a relationship between the
elements and the energy field serves to
refine the song of our elemental interface
with the world. The constant inversion of
perspective that this yields serves to open
the elements as gateways to other realms.
This is the path of transformation rather
than ascension, and it happens within the
embrace of the Earth Alliance and the World
Soul, rather than as an evacuee's escape
route from the wheel of death and rebirth.

The elements are the beginning and
the end of magic, the vehicle and grail of the
spiritual journey. While there might linger a
hangover from traditions that have tried to
separate the quest of the soul from the
arena of the world, each of the five elements
provides the song, avenue and substance of
the Great Work.

TRADITIONAL ELEMENTS

Our search for the smallest 'bit' of life has much to
say about the dimension within which it may exist,
the information it carries and even its behaviour.
Characteristics such as 'quark', 'strangeness' and

'charm' have more relevance at this level of sub-
atomic physics than any sense of substantiality.
These themes resemble the elements as they were
described by the ancient traditions, such as the

Druids, Chinese and Greeks. The elements noted
below are listed in the order they are considered
most significant by each culture.

Celtic	Fire	Water	Earth	Wind	Aether
Chinese	Wood	Fire	Earth	Metal	Water
Greek	Fire	Earth	Water	Air	Aether
Hindu	Earth	Water	Fire	Air	Space
Medicine Wheel	Fire	Earth	Water	Air	Void
Japanese	Earth	Water	Fire	Wind	Void

Nothing is solid.

~

There are no actual building blocks of the universe or matter,
just streams of information and energy we classify as elements.
Humans don't so much stand on the web of life as surf it.

Energy
the language of life

Words are not just wind. Words have something to say. But if what they have to say is not fixed, then do they really say something? Or do they say nothing? . . . Where can I find a man who has forgotten words so I can have a conversation with him?

The Inner Chapters, Chuang Tzu

Throughout this atlas, the terminology of energy is used widely, with a broad range of meanings that are at times not clearly defined. This is necessary in order to absorb some of the cross-cultural slack in trying such a scale of endeavour. Within each chapter, the context and narrative of a tradition's understanding of energy emerges as the landscape within which it resides is surveyed. But even accounting for such relativity, a dedicated exploration of its unifying notions will help construct the starting point of our quest.

QUESTIONS OF LANGUAGE

As we employ terminology and ascribe a similarity of translation to terms that arise within different cultures, we encounter the challenges of whether we can ever find a universal translator of meaning. Philosophers of language have tackled the questions of language ever since we began using words to frame our experience. Questions arise as to how words execute the function of referring to the world and shaping it at the same time. Of how any term can ever escape the cultural contexts of its origins and achieve translation into another language.

The basic characteristic of energy from a scientific perspective is the capacity for any of its forms to undergo transformation to another. At a simple level, this can be seen in the transformation of electrical energy in the mains supply to the thermal energy in a cooker.

Energy can be seen in many ways, but its basic manifestations will be kinetic, potential or internal. Kinetic energy is the momentum possessed by any body. Potential energy is the interactive potency of a system's component parts, whether the poles of a battery or the gravitational forces of the planets. Internal energy is that held within molecules by the interactions of their atoms.

Each manifestation of energy constantly changes its various states at vastly different rates. The themes of transformation and interaction are shared in some capacity by both prana and chi, the two principal translations of energy as it is used within this atlas and the wider communities of energy medicine and science. Even in their native etymologies, the construction of the terms within their cultural contexts, these themes of transformation and interaction arise.

It is essential to maintain the richness of diversity within ourselves and our cultures that might spawn the creativity to produce new words, dialects and slang, lest we rest in the uncomfortable cul-de-sac of a language or science that is fundamentally dead.

LAO ZI AND THE NAMELESS

You cannot be told. Words spoil the knowledge. Language was returned to humans thousands of years ago, but it was never explained how it could destroy.

Greg Bear

Together with Chuang Tzu's ridiculous quest to find someone who was beyond words in order to have a conversation with him, many cultures have their own ways with words, and how they shape and construct reality. In her science fiction books on the history of the Elvenkind, Mercedes Lackey describes the relationship that Elves have with words, hearing one say that: 'Words are very

direct. We of leaf and star consider them a form of coercion.' Given that the 'immortals' of Taoist culture are sometimes penned as 'elves' in translation, such customs hold a natural sympathy with the Taoist wisdom of fluidity and softness in approaching life. It may yet be that such wisdom holds true for the questions we ask of the universe, and the words we ask them with. Perhaps if we persist in too harsh an enquiry we determine the nature of its reply.

Energy is life.

~

The cascading chaos of the primal soup and the big bang

are still with us, however we name and shape them.

Such creativity remains available to us.

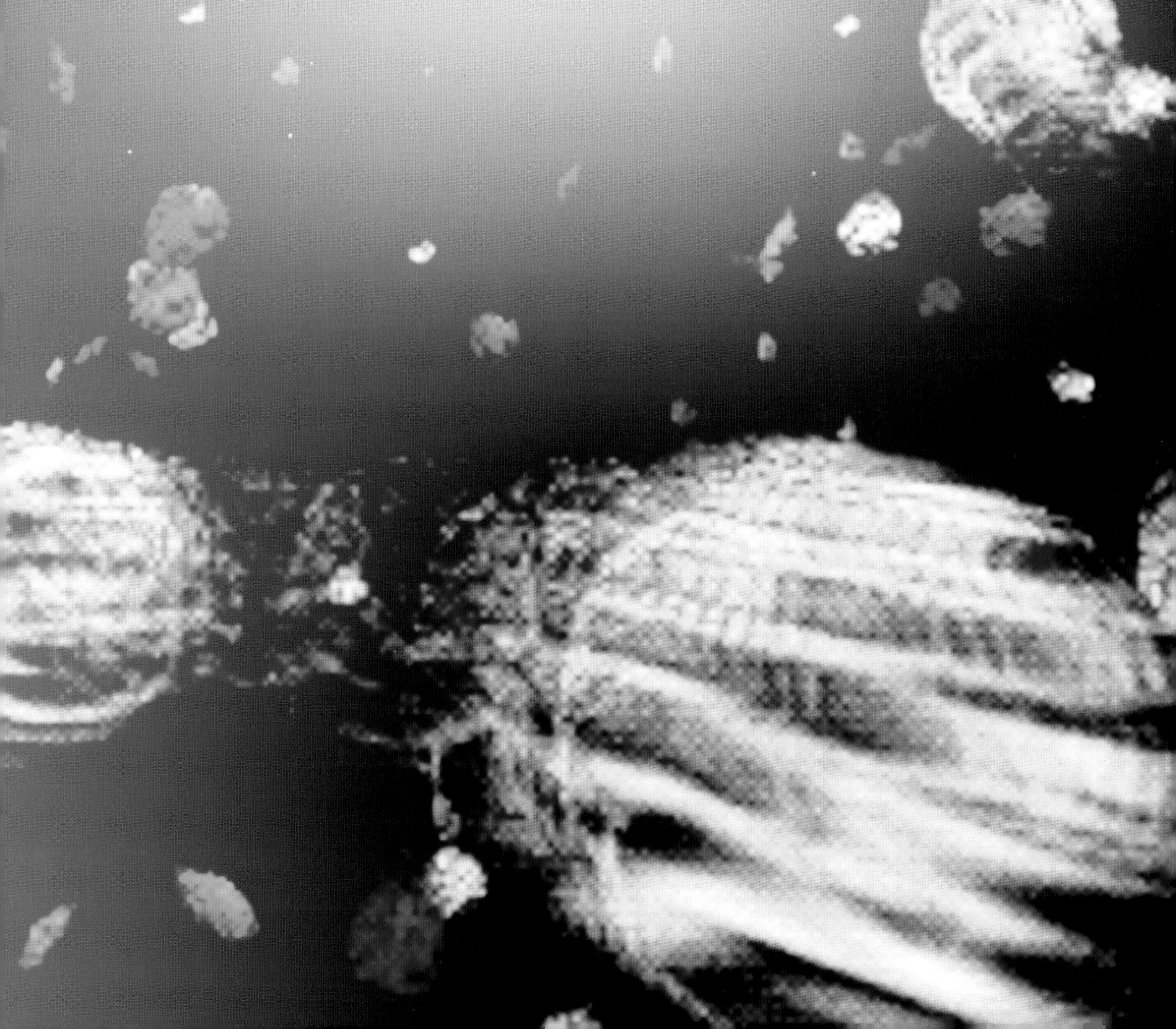

Intention
the future of consciousness

Education either functions as an instrument which is used to facilitate the integration of the younger generation into the logic of the present system and bring about conformity to it, or it becomes the 'practice of freedom', the means by which men and women deal critically and creatively with reality and discover how to participate in the transformation of their world.
Richard Shaull

Within acupuncture traditions there is a teaching that often completely confounds new students as they begin to learn the art of the practice. The Chinese phrase is *yi yi yin chi*, and its translation is 'energy follows intention' or, occasionally, the more lyrical version 'where intention goes there energy flows'.

In practice, this is often experienced as the focus of the practitioner being important to the successful needling of the point, in the necessary connection being made with the chi of the meridian in such a way that it successfully changes the overall energy of the patient. For students, this can be extremely off-putting, especially within an environment where the accuracy of their acupuncture point location determines their progress, and where they are also exposed to the seeming infinity of adaptations and developments of a medicine where the hands, feet, ears, and even knuckle joints all seem to yield areas that offer access to the whole of the body's energy field.

It is also argued that since research has pointed to such a high placebo content for acupuncture's success, its mechanics are therefore superfluous and could easily be disposed of. But such reasoning holds water only in the limited and causal world that has stunted our intellectual growth for centuries.

SEARCH FOR TRUTH
Addicted to a model of the world that can be replicated by anyone, science has refused to accept its own highest ethic to explore and research what actually happens, rather than try to cram the evidence into an ill-fitting set of assumptions.

The mastery of acupuncture arises from its ability consciously to sculpt the mystery of healing. The future of research for consciousness is exactly this interface of how we can change our world, manage the unruly passions within us in order to change the Body/Mind/Spirit. We may even need to stretch to the notion that each person may be different, and apply appropriate methods of discipline in supporting their development.

A MATTER OF FAITH
For too long we have laboured under the impression that faith was a lingering tail of superstition, forcing it into a corner in which it festered and rebelled into fundamentalism. Faith is intelligence of the spirit, no less important in the scientific quest as it is in the religious passion, although equally dangerous should it calcify in either. For faith can bring the inner peace that allows us to consider love in the universe, to know it in our hearts, and have the spiritual centredness that allows another being their truth. We may happen to conflict and even war over our territorial claims of land and resources, human rights and welfare, but it will not be the righteous crusade of an evangelist, rather the inevitable honesty of the pragmatist.

It is the centring within each person of their own power that enables us to continue to sculpt the form that serves us best in navigating the universe. This is not necessarily the education of reading, writing and arithmetic, but the intrinsic trust self-instilled in a growing child fostered by love, play and the existential space within which to discover the full extent of who they are.

From this foundation of faith will come the core of intention that is able to sculpt an experience of the world that can absorb the shock and beauty of life and find an approach that best serves the inner experience. And for the one who holds such a centredness of personality comes the openness to other forms of life, other realms of life. It is such equilibrium that the astrolabe seeks to conjure – and suggests that each one of us is part of the onward journey.

THOUGHT IS A LIVING LANGUAGE

Evelyn Carter had been clairvoyant since childhood, but during the 1940s began to enter into periods of trance mediumship. In some ways she was a traditional mill worker and mother from Lancashire, northern England. In others, she held a gateway of hope and inspiration during the mid 20th century where other beacons were less obvious.

Central to her teachings was a vision of 'the Work'. This vision echoed the aspirations within Hermeticism and the Western mystery traditions, where the 'Great Work' is regarded as the transformation of humanity through the transformation of the individual. Evelyn's vision of the Work shared this core ethic of changing the world through changing ourselves, but her particular expression held more in common with the Mayan teachings of the planetary transitions of 2013 (see page 204).

Evelyn taught that currently isolated aspects of reality become commonplace, where telepathy, the skills of reading auras, ley lines, and the energies of rocks, trees, and other people emerge as agents of massive social change. Her wisdom held at its heart an understanding of ourselves as spiritual beings and how our thoughts are the foundations of our world.

She never joined the circuit of professional mediums and the simplicity of her teachings together with the power of her presence and guides leap-frogged the many traps that ensnare more sophisticated depictions of the Work.

We are powerful.

~

We can purposefully alter our state of mind, the health
of our bodies and the insight of our spirits.
The Body/Mind/Spirit is our vehicle of experience,
exploring and changing the universe.

Form

The human maps of anatomy

He concentrated the very vibrations of the weather within himself, holding them within him in such a way that out of the very intimacy he had with them he could stand rapt, with all his pores open and not only feel the life of the winds and the clouds within his own self, but also direct and engender it.

Herman Hesse

The first levels of awareness we have of our bodies is of their extension in space – they have height, depth and breadth and retain a constant physical form. The cohesion of their basic substance, how we are enclosed in our skin, held upright by our skeleton, articulated by our joints and ligaments, fuelled by our blood and networked by our nerves, all contribute to this structural integrity. And such form is the stuff of our planet, we correspond in each aspect of our being with the life of the earth.

Our bones are rocks, calcium and phosphorus, chalk cliffs of our internal scaffolding. Our body fluids are 70 per cent of our weight, just as the oceans cover 70 per cent of the planet's surface. Our breath is matched with incredible accuracy to the specific compositions of the planet's atmosphere.

We rarely stop to think of the sheer strangeness of physical existence. The focus of our concern often ranges from everyday issues to ongoing dilemmas and challenges. In order to appreciate the nature of the human form, it is useful to contemplate its wonder and absurdity. If we step outside of an acceptance that two-legged, carbon-based life forms are the standard vehicles of consciousness, then we not only begin to think about what other, different varieties there might be, but also become able to take a fresh look at our own physical form.

With our imagination refreshed by a dose of absurdity, we can also contemplate how unique our forms are in terms of their suitability for this planet. Each aspect of our infrastructure is intimately connected with a corresponding aspect of our planet's make-up. This is seen by Darwinists as a long, slow accident of life, and by creationists as the seven-day plan of a supreme being. What we are gradually seeing within our global culture is a beautifully disorganized expansion of what we know about how our bodies and planet interact.

As superstition, fundamentalism and a narrowness of scientific hypotheses increasingly engage one another, our imagination irrepressibly blunders into new explorations of who and what we are. At times, such explorations of form are merely cosmetic and do not expand our collective sense of identity and possibility. Botox isn't ground-breaking, but a quadriplegic moving an index finger after years of paralysis is – and sets us off on new avenues of considering what the limits of our physical expansion might be. But we need the fun and uselessness of most of our explorations to allow us fertile cultural ground for such miracles, discoveries of what is beyond the limit of what we currently know.

Bones

gravity and alignment

Bone is the basic substance of our skeletal system, the hard internal scaffolding that enables us to remain upright and to hold a constant form. It provides the structure for all the strength of the body, allowing hard pivots and fulcrums for the muscles to pull against. It also offers protection for the most vulnerable vital organs (brain, spinal cord, heart and lungs) and houses the marrow within which red blood cells begin their creation cycle.

The microscopic composition of bone is tubular, resembling the rings on a tree, far stronger than any simple, solid structure. It is interlaced with both blood and lymph vessels and informed by nerves. Even though bone is incredibly hard, it is also alive.

BONE CREATION

Bones begin to develop while we are in the womb and do not stop growing until our mid 20s, from which point they are renewed and nourished. In both development and regeneration, each component of their making is essential. Bones comprise water, minerals and the cellular matrix that binds them together. Bone-making cells, called osteoblasts, deposit a collagen-fibre matrix onto these structures of tendon, membrane and cartilage. As soon as this matrix is laid down, it is calcified by the calcium carried in the blood. This process is primarily governed by our hormones and diet.

The current phase of our hormonal life-cycle (infancy/puberty/menopause) will determine the particular characteristics of our bone growth and the challenges that can arise. Two of the more common bone problems are osteoporosis and Paget's disease. Osteoporosis often occurs in post-menopausal women, when the reduction in oestrogen production affects the regenerative laying down of calcium. Paget's disease often occurs in adults over 40 years of age, when the cycle of bone regeneration becomes hyperactive and this causes the bones to become thick and soft.

Almost half of our bone structure is rock – primarily calcium and phosphorus – that is derived from the vegetables and nuts we consume, absorbed with the help of the vitamin D that is manufactured just under the skin in response to the sun's rays. The calcium component of bones is particularly important in maintaining their strength. But calcium is also a resource, used to transport digested proteins around the body. A high-protein diet can cause us to deplete our calcium stores more than would otherwise be the case, and if the calcium levels in the blood are not high enough to facilitate the transportation of protein, then it will be drawn from bone tissue. In this way, milk (with its high protein levels) may not be the best source of calcium compared with certain greens and seeds, such as kale, watercress, parsley, almonds, brazil nuts (and sardines).

BONE DENSITY

While bone density varies, according to health and age, it tends to remain within parameters suitable for the Earth's gravitational field. One of the side-effects for astronauts living without the effects of gravity is that their bone density begins to drop. Athletes who train hard develop increasingly strong bones. Both of these scenarios arise as the natural refurbishment of bone responds to the gravitational and impact stresses it finds itself under. The suspected mechanical impossibility of dinosaurs to support their own weight is probably explained by a reduction in gravity during the Jurassic period, which then contributed to their extinction when it rose once more.

As bones hold our core stability and strength, so too do they hold our ancestral patterns. Whether from the central role of bone marrow in determining the uniqueness of our DNA and genetic heritage to our instinctual association of bones with ancestors, bone is the foundation of our world, both planet and body.

OSTEOPATHY

Osteopathic manipulation to the neck

The word 'osteopathy' comes from the Greek *osteon*, meaning 'bone', and *pathos* meaning 'suffering'. Together they give us the concept of the 'suffering of bone'.

Osteopathy was developed as a distinct branch of modern medicine by an American, Andrew Taylor Still, in the 1870s. Still recognized that the correct functioning of the body's structure was absolutely essential to good health.

The treatment offered by osteopathy is holistic, in that it focuses on the whole of a patient's experience and wellbeing rather than just the presenting symptoms. Revolutionary at its time within Western medicine, osteopathy seeks actively to promote interaction between each of the body's individual systems.

Diagnostic techniques are based on hands-on detection of injury and illness, often supported by x-rays and other laboratory-based tests. In the United States, osteopaths also sometimes perform surgery and prescribe medication, while in other countries they concentrate on manipulation alone.

Osteopathic manipulation is the adjustment of the bones and muscles using a variety of techniques. Typically, these involve rhythmic and graceful thrusts that promote a greater alignment within the body, and it is this adjustment that encourages the body's own healing powers. Osteopathic manipulation is often accompanied by massage, muscle release, dietary advice, physical exercises and health education.

Authors Peta Sneddon and Paolo Coseschi, who operate a joint osteopathic practice in Chianti, Italy, write that: 'Rather than bone specialists, osteopaths are in fact masters in the biomechanics of the human machine.'

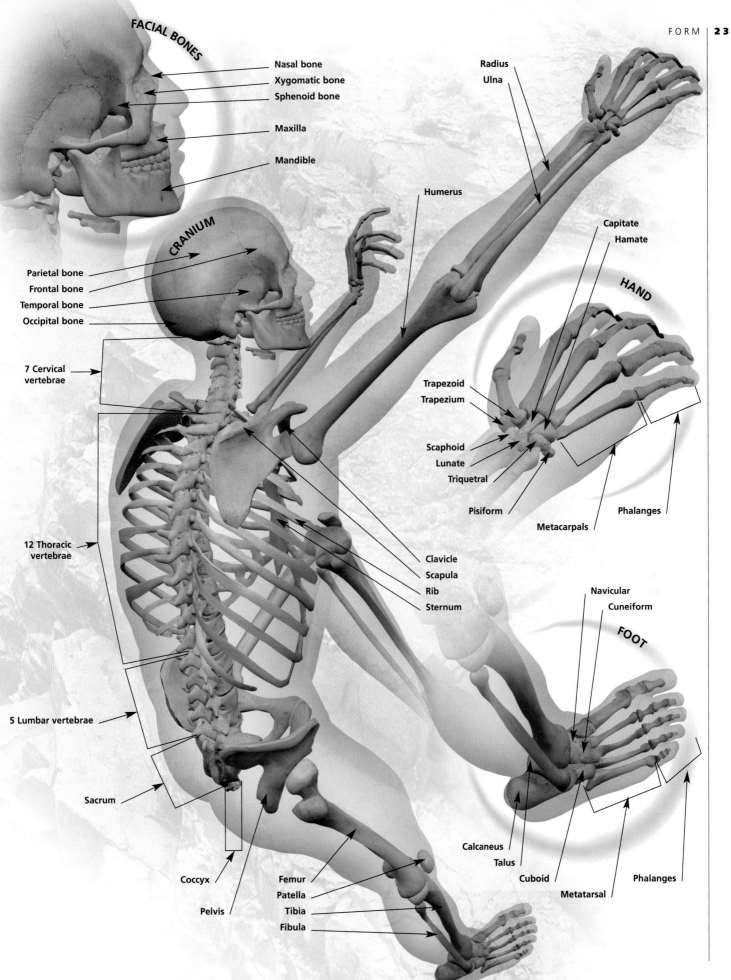

FACIAL BONES

Nasal bone
Xygomatic bone
Sphenoid bone

Maxilla

Mandible

CRANIUM

Parietal bone
Frontal bone
Temporal bone
Occipital bone

7 Cervical vertebrae

12 Thoracic vertebrae

5 Lumbar vertebrae

Sacrum

Coccyx

Pelvis

Femur
Patella
Tibia
Fibula

Radius
Ulna

Humerus

Clavicle
Scapula
Rib
Sternum

Capitate
Hamate

HAND

Trapezoid
Trapezium

Scaphoid
Lunate
Triquetral

Pisiform

Metacarpals

Phalanges

Navicular
Cuneiform

FOOT

Calcaneus
Talus

Cuboid
Metatarsal

Phalanges

Muscle
our expansion into the world

Muscle is our power of movement, the potency of our action within the world in an expression of conscious will. It provides the unconscious rhythms of our heartbeat and the balance of tensions within internal structures. Each muscle is an elastic band of flesh that contracts and relaxes in response to both voluntary and automatic triggers.

Muscles begin to develop from the start of pregnancy. Embryonic cells, mesoderms, begin life clustered around the growing nervous system, multiplying and transforming into bones, muscles and connective tissue. After the first year of life, all our muscle cells have formed and the subsequent growth of muscle is just the lengthening of existing cells.

From the age of about 30, a reduction in physical activity leads to muscle tissue being replaced by fat. Regeneration of muscle occurs only in response to the activation of dormant cells alongside muscle fibres. Any injury that leads to a loss of muscle also reduces these dormant cells, with the result that injured muscle is replaced by scar tissue. The exception is the regenerative power of muscle fibres within the uterus, blood capillaries and veins, which can subdivide and restore themselves.

MUSCLE TYPES
There are three types of muscle within the body: striped, cardiac and smooth.

Striped muscle is under voluntary control and moves and holds bones. Each muscle comprises nerve and blood supplies supporting groups of banded fibres whose elongated cells lie parallel to each other. Within each band of fibres, the nerve and blood supplies become motor neurons and blood capillaries. At a microscopic level the muscle fibre is made up of protein filaments. Thick dark filaments (myosin) and thin light filaments (actin) slide over each other as the fibre contracts in response to its neurochemical trigger.

Cardiac (heart) muscle shares characteristics of both striped and smooth muscle. It is activated by electrical impulses from its own pacemaker (the sinuatrial node) which then ripple down throughout the heart. This coordinated cascade is possible due to the interlacing of muscle fibres within the heart rather than them being distinct and separate and needing to be triggered individually.

Smooth muscle lines the walls of hollow vessels, such as those carrying blood and lymph. It is also found in the respiratory tract and bladder, as well as in the skin at the base of hair follicles. This type of muscle cell is small and slow compared with striped and cardiac muscle cells, but has the distinction of being able to regenerate itself.

FUELLING MUSCLES
Muscle contracts and relaxes in response to chemical and neurological stimuli. Messages are carried along the nerves from either our somatic nervous system (conscious mind) or autonomic nervous system (involuntary body-mind). Once delivered by motor neurons, these messages transform into chemical triggers within the muscle cells. Specifically the neurotransmitter acetylcholine activates a release of calcium ions into the belly of a muscle fibre and locks onto the thin actin filaments, exposing them to ATP (see below), the fuel for the actin to swing into an active power stroke of contraction. Once the exertion is over, more energy (ATP) is actively used to reduce the levels of calcium ions within the fibres, and so relax the muscle.

The fuel used by muscles is ATP (adenosine triphosphate), the principal energy-carrying molecule in the body. In the conversion of ATP's latent energy into physical movement, some energy is lost to heat – indeed, 85 per cent of body heat is derived from muscle contractions. If there is not enough oxygen in the blood, the efficiency of energy conversion dips and by-products are produced, such as unprocessed lactic acid, which makes muscles hurt after a sprint.

Muscles enable us to hold posture and internal equilibrium. It is their tone and nourishment, rather than size, that determine physical potency. But beyond both of these is the power of the neurological trigger. 'Mind over matter' – how we coordinate the physiological equilibrium – is perhaps the most significant component of a healthy and effective musculature.

Bowen Technique
RESETTING MUSCLE BALANCE

The Bowen Technique is a bodywork therapy developed in the 1950s by a self-taught Australian healer, Tom Bowen. It predominantly treats pain and musculoskeletal conditions, although, as with many holistic disciplines, it often affects other systemic imbalances. During a Bowen session, light pressure is applied in rolling 'moves' across muscles and tendons. This is done with the intention of 'disturbing' the body-mind in order to trigger its own innate knowledge of how it needs to organize itself. Moves are applied in a sequence to the whole of the body, with specific sequences for certain areas. Most moves relate to muscles and where they either overlap with other muscle groups or where they begin and end. Moves also related to the belly of the muscle itself.

The Bowen Technique is a therapeutic procedure rather than an integrated system of medicine with a full diagnostic framework. There is no preconceived assessment as to what is wrong with patients beyond their own reporting of symptoms. There is no conclusive understanding as to how the Bowen Technique works, but its effect on the structural integrity of the body through minimal intervention does suggest that it operates as a trigger for the body's own physical intelligence. During a session, the therapist leaves the room between moves in order to allow the body to process the impact of the interaction in an unimpeded fashion. The capacity to prompt the body's innate knowledge of its own health has led to the technique being described as 'resetting' the balance of who we are.

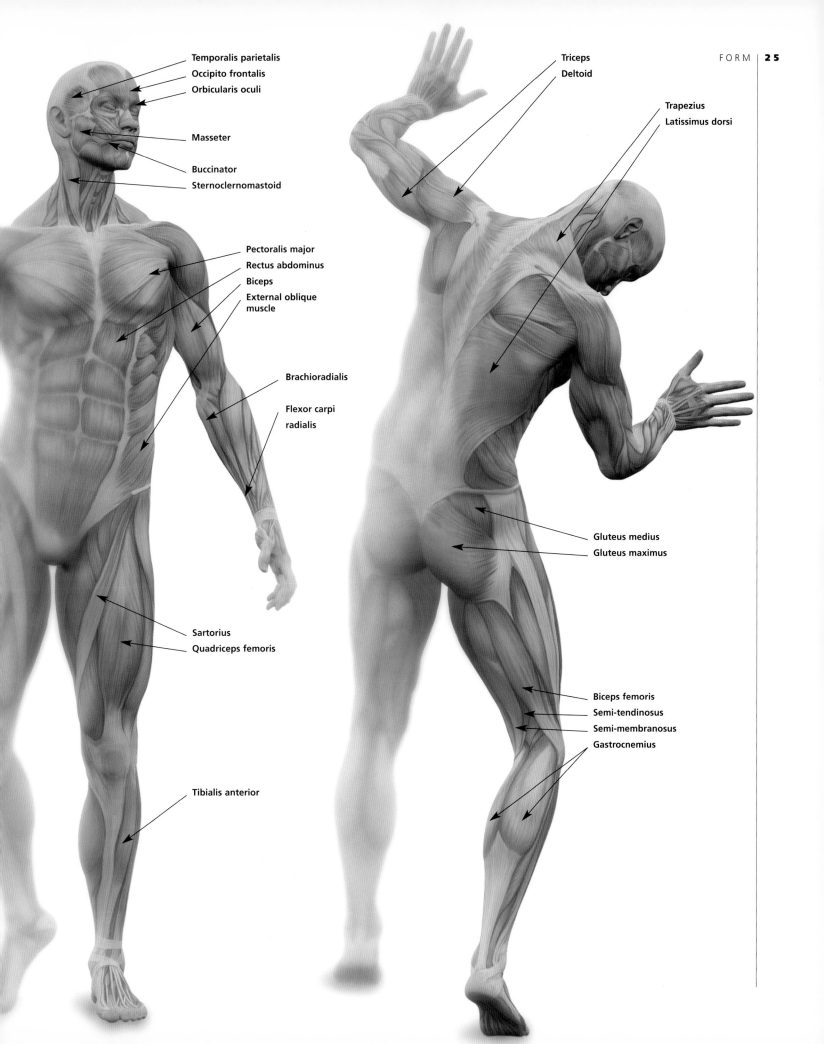

Temporalis parietalis

Occipito frontalis

Orbicularis oculi

Masseter

Buccinator

Sternoclernomastoid

Pectoralis major

Rectus abdominus

Biceps

External oblique
muscle

Brachioradialis

Flexor carpi
radialis

Sartorius

Quadriceps femoris

Tibialis anterior

Triceps

Deltoid

Trapezius

Latissimus dorsi

Gluteus medius

Gluteus maximus

Biceps femoris

Semi-tendinosus

Semi-membranosus

Gastrocnemius

Ligaments
connective tissue and the body's rigging

Ligaments are the strong, flexible fibres that hold our bones together. They are part of the whole class of connective tissue that is the internal rigging of the body.

Connective tissue as a whole is responsible for holding organs and tissues to each other as well as protecting vulnerable areas of the body. This tissue also insulates the body and specific organs and transports nutrients and energy.

TISSUE TYPES
Connective tissue is found in all areas of the body. It is derived from embryonic cells that soon differentiate into various tissue types. In addition to bone and blood – a fluid connective tissue that is the main transport system within the body – it also appears as areolar tissue, which provides elastic tension throughout the body.

Adipose tissue, or fat cells, make up about 20–25 per cent of the average weight of a healthy adult and act as an important insulation, a suspension system for the eyes and kidneys and an energy store.

Elastic tissue provides flexibility within blood vessels, and also forms the earlobe.

Cartilage is the rubbery gristle that forms as vertebral discs and ligaments, and contributes to the shape of certain organs.

SKELETAL INTEGRITY
The principal job of connective tissue is to bind the skeleton together. Ligaments link bones to each other, providing stability and preventing joints from extending beyond a certain range. Microscopically, they comprise closely packed bundles of protein fibres called collagen, which forms a protective covering for bones and some internal organs, as well as an enclosing sheath for muscles.

CELL TYPES
Within the molecular matrix of connective tissue are various types of cell, arranged and proportioned according to the type and function of the connective tissue.

Fibroblasts produce the basic molecules of the matrix, while macrophages are white blood cells that track and destroy bacteria as well as clearing up as cells break down.

Plasma cells are small cells that secrete antibodies, particularly in the breasts and gut. Mast cells work with blood cells, mainly producing histamine, which relaxes blood vessels around inflammation.

TISSUE COMPOSITION
Each type of connective tissue comprises a combination of fibrous tissue as well as a molecular matrix that acts as a liquid glue and source of replenishment.

Ligaments have a preponderance of collagen fibres lying very close to each other, while areolar tissue in the skin and blood vessels is semi-solid, with a looser arrangement of fibres. Fat (adipose tissue) has even fewer fibres, and these are arranged as a malleable, floating matrix.

The predominant component of ligaments is a substance called collagen. This is a fibrous protein, the most prolific in the body and comprising a quarter of all the body's protein.

Chiropractic RIGGING THE BODY'S INNATE INTELLIGENCE

Chiropractic is based on the premise that the body possesses an internal system that strives for balance. This internal system is called your 'innate intelligence'.

Robert Berkowitz

(chiropractic educator)

Chiropractic is a holistic therapy that promotes neurological balance by realigning the deviations of the joints in the body, particularly the vertebrae. The word 'chiropractic' comes from the Greek *cheiros*, which means 'hand', and *praktos*, which translates as 'done by'.

Chiropractic was developed as a modern therapy by Daniel David Palmer in the 1890s in Iowa, USA. Palmer was a self-taught healer who sought to alleviate pain without the use of drugs and who pioneered the relief of the nervous system through attending to spinal alignment.

Spinal manipulation has been practised widely throughout history (Hippocrates wrote extensively on spinal curvature and deviations of bones). Palmer's innovation was a therapeutic focus on the relationship between the body's overall health and how this is mediated by the nervous system as it branches from between each of the vertebrae. Problems arise when a vertebra moves out of its correct position and thus exerts pressure on the spinal nerves, causing either pain or interference with the messages travelling along the nerve. These vertebral deviations are called 'subluxations' and are similar to dislocations in other joints.

In healthy joints, ligaments hold the bones together, allowing movement only within normal limits. With both dislocations and subluxations, the ligaments are either stretched or torn. Chiropractic seeks to support the role of the ligaments in holding together the flexible but strong infrastructure of each joint.

Chiropractic diagnosis is achieved predominantly by palpation (hands-on detection). Some common adjustment techniques are:

- The toggle drop – a firm pressing and then a quick thrust cause one of the vertebral joints to be adjusted.
- A lumbar roll – with the patient on his or her side, a misaligned vertebra is restored to its correct position.
- Release work – the fingertips are gently used to separate the vertebrae and restore their correct position and alignment.
- Twilight sedation manipulations – where normal adjustments have not taken and manipulations need to be done under anaesthetic.

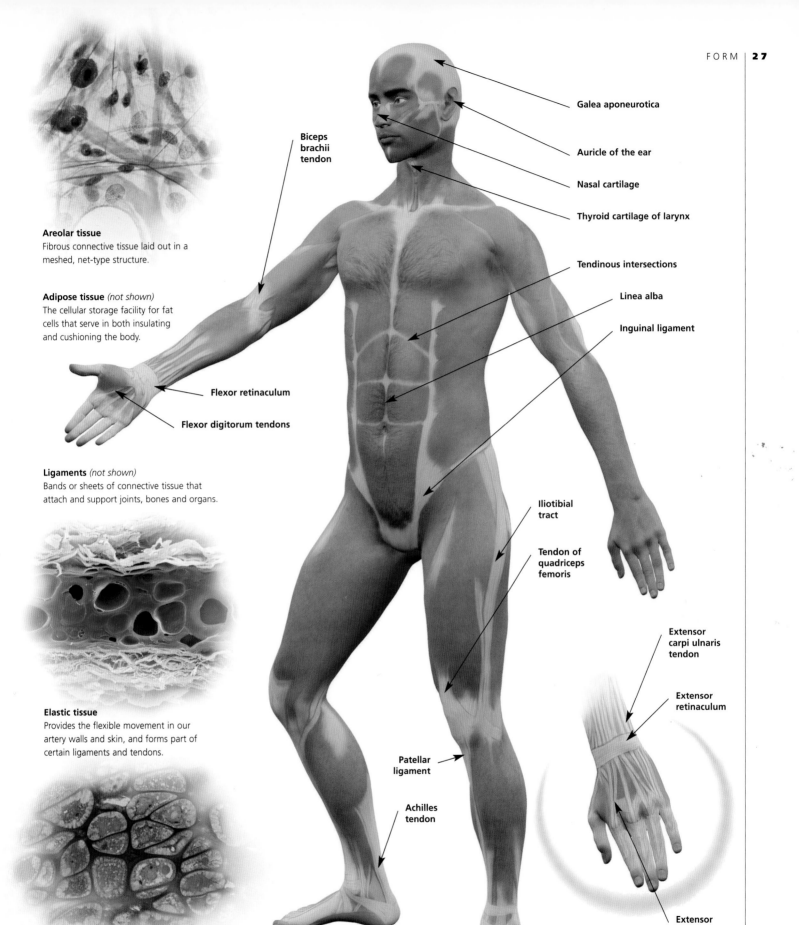

Areolar tissue
Fibrous connective tissue laid out in a meshed, net-type structure.

Adipose tissue (not shown)
The cellular storage facility for fat cells that serve in both insulating and cushioning the body.

Ligaments (not shown)
Bands or sheets of connective tissue that attach and support joints, bones and organs.

Elastic tissue
Provides the flexible movement in our artery walls and skin, and forms part of certain ligaments and tendons.

Cartilage
Forms most of the young skeleton. In the adult, forms part of larynx, nose and outer ear.

Biceps brachii tendon

Galea aponeurotica

Auricle of the ear

Nasal cartilage

Thyroid cartilage of larynx

Tendinous intersections

Linea alba

Inguinal ligament

Flexor retinaculum

Flexor digitorum tendons

Iliotibial tract

Tendon of quadriceps femoris

Extensor carpi ulnaris tendon

Extensor retinaculum

Patellar ligament

Achilles tendon

Extensor digitorum tendons

Skin
our interface and barrier

Skin is the protective, waterproof barrier enclosing our body. It is our boundary and shield, protecting our internal environment. Not only does it form a boundary between us and our immediate environment, it also operates as a two-way exchange of heat and information. Heat is absorbed and released by the skin to keep the body's temperature within operable limits.

REGULATOR AND SENSORY RECEPTOR

In low temperatures, blood is withdrawn from the surface of the body to preserve heat and prioritize life support for the internal organs. We also shiver to generate heat. In high temperatures, blood vessels relax, bringing internal body heat to the surface to be lost to the air. In addition, sweating covers the skin with moisture, which, as it evaporates, cools the body. Hypothermia and sunstroke occur when these temperature-regulating mechanisms fail to keep body temperature within tolerable limits.

While the sun is our ultimate source of energy, filtering its radiation is essential. Too much or too little sunlight is damaging to health, causing either skin cancer or vitamin D deficiency. A deficiency in vitamin D can lead to the weak, soft or deformed bones of osteoporosis and rickets and leave us more prone to some forms of cancer.

So, as the skin regulates temperature, it also mediates the sun's fire as it contributes to the maintenance of our bone structure. Such a regulation has its own side effects, however, in the form of the risk of skin cancer. Despite this, we do need about 20 minutes of sun exposure each day. But skin is also our sensory mechanism and the primary receptor of wind, heat and even sound. The whole of the peripheral nervous system terminates at the skin. We locate ourselves in the world through the sensitivity of our skin, and if our skin sensitivity is reduced or even non-existent for some reason, we lose the constant update of our health and wellbeing in our hands, feet and every part of the body we cannot see with our eyes.

HEALTH AND MOOD

Skin is also interactive as the mechanism by which we excrete hormones, which are transferred to the atmosphere primarily by our body hair (see pages 36–7). The flush that occurs during sexual activity, reddening the face and genitals with fresh blood, also occurs as facial blushing, indicating anger, excitement or embarrassment. And the tension or flaccidity of the musculature just under our skin can communicate wellbeing and mood.

As well as excreting hormones, skin, as our largest organ, provides a valuable detoxification of chemicals that we have ingested or metabolized. In this way, we can often identify illness through body odour.

The moulting human

While some creatures, such as snakes, shed their whole skin many times each year, humans constantly renew their outer covering through the paced loss and regeneration of individual skin cells. New cells take between two and four weeks to be born and reach the surface of the skin, where what we see and feel of as our skin actually comprises dead skin cells waiting to take their place among household dust, of which they form around 70%.

THE ANOINTED BODY

The plug has been lifted from the unguent jar.
Oh, cascade of black hair, perfume of the hour.
The past has been written, rolled and sealed in a
scroll I'll not see again.
The eye of the hawk ranges the sky unblinking.
Open. Shut. Perfect.
The Papyrus of Ani
(a copy of the Egyptian *Book of the Dead*)

Skin is perhaps one of the most important aspects of how we view ourselves. Throughout our history we have adorned, tattooed, modified and tried to preserve the youthful appearance of our face to the world. How we tend our skin, in terms of what we expose it to, substantially affects both its health and its appearance. Each people have developed anointments and salves to heal, beautify or sanctify the skin. The blessing of our bodies as we come into the world and leave it are often done with unguents and oils, and in between we mediate and mark our environment. The Hopi elder Grandmother Caroline has spoken of how odours in themselves can both cause illness and, sometimes, even death.

Our symbolic associations with oils often follow through in their healing potential: rose blesses, mint purifies, musk stimulates and sage clears. In 17th-century France, four men were hanged for looting the houses of plague victims, but not before giving up the secret of their protective ointment, which contained vinegar, wormwood, meadowsweet, juniper, cloves, rosemary, marjoram and sage.

Odours can protect as well as harm, sacred space often being demarcated by the presence of sweet smells. This is an aspect employed by the burning of censers, incense and herbs and it is also applied within aromatherapy as a contemporary therapeutic discipline.

Nerves

message and sensation

Our nervous system is a sophisticated relay station of sensations and responses, mediated by our conscious awareness. Nerves themselves are incredibly long structures, with their cell bodies tethered in the brain or spinal cord and their tails extending throughout the body. They are invisible to the naked eye, but the bunching of cell bodies in the brain appears as 'little grey cells'.

ELECTRICAL/CHEMICAL RESPONSES

Cell bodies mostly form relay teams of three neurons that pass chemical 'batons' to each other at synapses, thereby transmitting messages and instructions around the body in a constant translation of chemical and electrical information. Some neurons pass electrical messages to each other through their close proximity and the minuscule tunnels formed between their cells. This occurs predominantly in embryos or heart muscle, where the greater coordination and speed of direct electrical communication over chemical/electrical relays is an advantage.

The chemical/electrical relay takes place at the intersections of nerves as their opposite ends link with each other. This need for translation enables the body to filter and assess information rather than just reacting to stimuli. The chemical batons they pass are neurotransmitters, such as noradrenaline and serotonin. A great many pharmaco-logical and recreational medicines are based on inhibiting or imitating the role of these neurotransmitters.

THE NERVOUS SYSTEM

The nervous system is organized into specific categories – the central nervous system of the brain and spinal cord and the peripheral nervous system comprising the nerves that branch out of the spinal column towards the organs and other tissues served by them.

Peripheral nerves both initiate and perceive changes within and outside the body. This loop of stimulus and response operates at various levels of consciousness, leading to the other main classification of the nervous system – the voluntary and involuntary (autonomic). The extent to which any sensation/movement cycle is voluntary depends on the height within the brain and spinal cord that the cycle occurs. If we receive a visual stimulus that we wish to speak about, the signals will pass through the visual and speech centres of the brain in the cerebrum. These signals are highly conscious as they are mediated by the higher brain centres. If, however, we burn our hand, we do not tend to deliberate too long before removing it from the heat source. Such a reflex stimulus/response can happen within the spinal cord itself without reference to our conscious will. The brain can override the impulse if necessary: say, for example, if we are holding a child.

Included in the autonomic nervous system are the regulation of internal secretions and rhythms, such as gastric juices and heart rate. Certain disciplines, such as biofeedback training (see right), seek to push back the limits of what might be considered voluntary.

Referred pain arises when pain signals from a particular area of the body come in to the spinal cord, stimulating the incoming sensory nerve as well as a neighbouring nerve and causing it to send a pain signal. In this way, pain in the liver is perceived as pain in the right shoulder. Each part of the body's surface is served by sensory nerves that all link ultimately to one of the spinal or cranial nerves.

Pain (neuralgia = nerve pain) can occur if there is pressure or trauma within the spinal cord. Paralysis will occur if there is severe damage, with broken backs or necks leading potentially to paraplegia (paralysis of the legs) or quadriplegia (paralysis of the arms and legs). The actor Christopher Reeve, who died in 2004, became quadriplegic in 1995 after being involved in a riding accident. He proceeded to challenge medical orthodoxy when, five years later, he purposefully moved the tip of his left index finger. This feat was achieved after dedicated training that attempted to remind his neural pathways how to move. This was biofeedback training at the most extraordinary levels of will and stamina (see right).

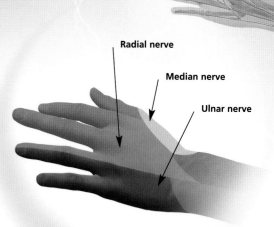

Radial nerve

Median nerve

Ulnar nerve

Peripheral nerve distribution
Each of the nerves rising through the arm governs the movement of the arm and hand. Peripheral nerves govern certain dermatomes – surface areas of skin that give rise to sensation.

BIOFEEDBACK TRAINING

Biofeedback training includes a whole range of techniques aimed at increasing our conscious control over seemingly unconscious physical processes. It involves the disciplined connection between what we intend to do and how our muscles and glands respond.

Biofeedback training can be split into two main categories: those that rely on the subject's own sensory observations of how they are consciously affecting their own bodies, and those that use instrumentation, such as EEG machines.

The whole approach of biofeedback also seems to harness the active potential of our own healing powers. It is not merely a method of changing one isolated aspect of physical functioning, but promotes the experience of self-autonomy. This has wide implications in terms of accessing our own volition and, through promoting self-empowerment, accessing that whole cascade of neuro-socio-psycho-biological factors that promote health, wellbeing and the unfolding of our potential.

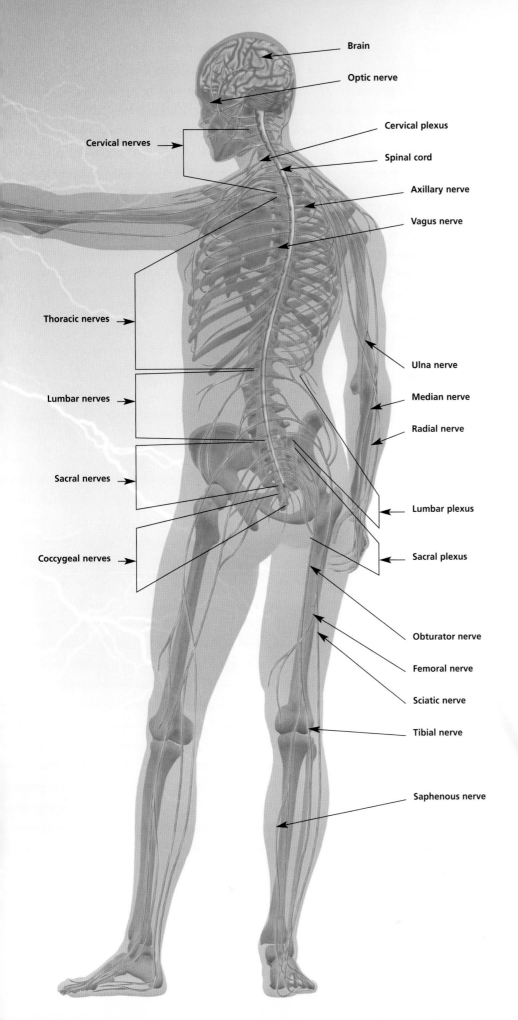

Brain

Optic nerve

Cervical plexus

Cervical nerves

Spinal cord

Axillary nerve

Vagus nerve

Thoracic nerves

Ulna nerve

Median nerve

Lumbar nerves

Radial nerve

Sacral nerves

Lumbar plexus

Coccygeal nerves

Sacral plexus

Obturator nerve

Femoral nerve

Sciatic nerve

Tibial nerve

Saphenous nerve

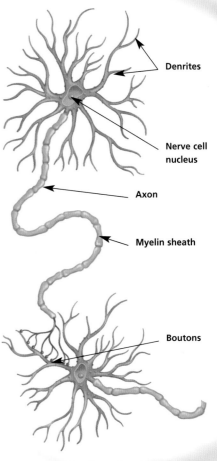

Denrites

Nerve cell nucleus

Axon

Myelin sheath

Boutons

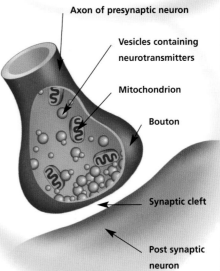

Axon of presynaptic neuron

Vesicles containing neurotransmitters

Mitochondrion

Bouton

Synaptic cleft

Post synaptic neuron

Synaptic clefts

These are the 'chasms' between each nerve cell, gaps between the spidery boutons (seen in detail above) and the body of the next cell across which chemical messengers jump. The synaptic cleft is less than one-millionth of an inch across.

Blood
the circulatory system

Blood is our principal transportation and communication system, carrying oxygen, nutrients, heat, immunity and hormones from the workshop organs of the torso to all parts of the body. Blood is a suspension of red cells (45 per cent) in a yellow plasma base (55 per cent). Red blood cells are purely a transportation system for oxygen (O_2), their whole structure allowing the maximum O_2 to be carried by the 280 million molecules of haemoglobin found in each red blood cell.

Each haemoglobin molecule has a protein chain, called a 'heme', with an iron-based pigment at its heart. Hemes are able to collect one oxygen molecule and transport it from the lungs to its destination. And about a quarter of the body's waste carbon dioxide is removed by blood haemoglobin on its return journey to the lungs, where it is breathed out.

A lack of haemoglobin leads to iron-deficiency anaemia, which is most commonly found in women (due to menstruation) as well as in children and the elderly in areas where iron – typically found in meat, shell-fish, nuts and beans – is not sufficiently represented in the diet.

PLANETARY PARALLELS
The interaction between oxygen and iron within the body is mirrored in the Earth's atmosphere and core. When the Earth was formed, more than 5 billion years ago, the iron sank to the centre of our new planet and the water and oxygen rose to the surface. This iron remains at the heart of the Earth, providing the centre of its magnetic field – not through its solidity, but by

virtue of the fluid circulation of the molten iron. The core itself comprises two layers of this iron-nickel magma, the innermost core being under such pressure that it is solid, even though its incredible temperatures would mean in other conditions it would be fluid. The outer core is also a molten alloy of iron and nickel, within which the churning convection of heat currents provides the electromagnetic environment of the whole planet. This outer core is tidal, in just the same way as the seas, air and crust of Earth respond to the Moon's gravitational pull. The pulse of the Earth – the heartbeat within its magma, crust, water and air – is governed by the rhythmic dance of the Moon.

About 66 per cent of the body's iron is held within the blood, the rest is found within the musculature, liver, spleen and enzymes. If this stored iron becomes excessive, it can increase the risk of cancer.

TRANSPORTATION AND PROTECTION
While the blood's transport role is primarily concerned with oxygen, it also conveys the chemical messengers that are hormones around the body, as well as digested nutrients from the digestive system, waste products of cells, and heat to where it needs to be.

Blood's universal presence throughout the body also allows it to perform its other key function: protection. Through the action of white blood cells, the whole body is defended from bacteria, oxidants, parasites, viruses, cancer cells and microbes. They dismember, poison or consume alien cells, working as complex teams with specialist cells for specialist jobs.

This specialism can help diagnostically when we need to know, for example, if an infection is caused by bacteria or a virus – neutrophils combat the former; lymphocytes the latter. Another protective role of blood is tissue repair and blood clotting. Adhesive cell fragments called platelets throng to the site of distress and patch up the injury as the first stage of repair.

HEART AND BLOOD VESSELS
Blood is pumped around the body by the heart, a fist-sized organ centrally positioned in the chest. The heart is a specialized engine with two cylinders: one pumping blood to the lungs to pick up oxygen; the other pumping newly oxygenated blood to the rest of the body. The rhythm of our heartbeat is initiated by a natural pacemaker system – a 'sinoatrial node'. This is a metronome of electrical pulses that provide the essential action of the heart, the rhythmic flow of blood that is heard when the pulse is taken.

Various medical traditions read the pulse in different ways, although most use the radial artery at the wrist for a primary reading. Western biomedical physicians read the rate, regularity and strength in assessing cardio-vascular health; practitioners of oriental medicine take readings corresponding to the health of the 12 internal organs, with Ayurvedic and Tibetan physicians employing similar procedures.

The various types of blood vessel have vastly different life cycles, some white blood cells living for years with platelets only having a five-day existence. During our foetal development, a whole network of organs work together in constructing the infra-structure of blood cells. After we are born, however, it is only in the red bone marrow of large bones that the process of blood cell replenishment takes place. Certain genetic disorders and cancers are treated by the transplanting of healthy red bone marrow into bones that have been cleared of the resident diseased marrow by radiotherapy.

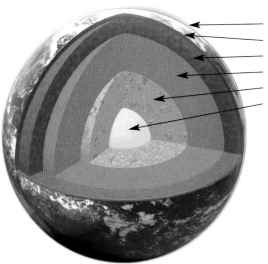

Atmosphere
Crust
Upper mantle
Lower mantle
Outer core
Pressurized inner core
80% iron
4% nickel
10% oxygen or sulphur
(percentages are approximate)

Planetary circulation
The flow of magnetism within the Earth depends on the currents of molten iron within the core.

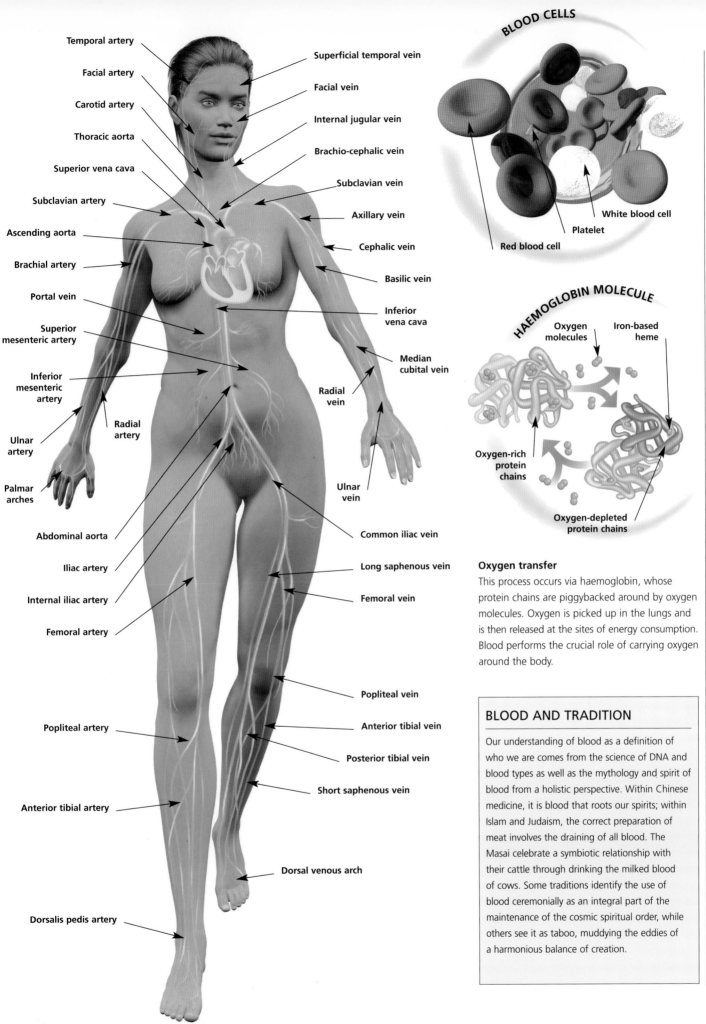

Temporal artery

Facial artery

Carotid artery

Thoracic aorta

Superior vena cava

Subclavian artery

Ascending aorta

Brachial artery

Portal vein

Superior
mesenteric
artery

Inferior
mesenteric
artery

Ulnar
artery

Radial
artery

Palmar
arches

Abdominal aorta

Iliac artery

Internal iliac artery

Femoral artery

Popliteal artery

Anterior tibial artery

Dorsalis pedis artery

Superficial temporal vein

Facial vein

Internal jugular vein

Brachio-cephalic vein

Subclavian vein

Axillary vein

Cephalic vein

Basilic vein

Inferior
vena cava

Median
cubital vein

Radial
vein

Ulnar
vein

Common iliac vein

Long saphenous vein

Femoral vein

Popliteal vein

Anterior tibial vein

Posterior tibial vein

Short saphenous vein

Dorsal venous arch

BLOOD CELLS

White blood cell

Platelet

Red blood cell

HAEMOGLOBIN MOLECULE

Oxygen
molecules

Iron-based
heme

Oxygen-rich
protein
chains

Oxygen-depleted
protein chains

Oxygen transfer

This process occurs via haemoglobin, whose
protein chains are piggybacked around by oxygen
molecules. Oxygen is picked up in the lungs and
is then released at the sites of energy consumption.
Blood performs the crucial role of carrying oxygen
around the body.

BLOOD AND TRADITION

Our understanding of blood as a definition of
who we are comes from the science of DNA and
blood types as well as the mythology and spirit of
blood from a holistic perspective. Within Chinese
medicine, it is blood that roots our spirits; within
Islam and Judaism, the correct preparation of
meat involves the draining of all blood. The
Masai celebrate a symbiotic relationship with
their cattle through drinking the milked blood
of cows. Some traditions identify the use of
blood ceremonially as an integral part of the
maintenance of the cosmic spiritual order, while
others see it as taboo, muddying the eddies of
a harmonious balance of creation.

Breath

our respiratory system

All cells in the body need oxygen to nourish and heal themselves, but the balance of oxygen in the air we breathe is key: too much, and its chemical by-products (superoxide free radicals) contribute to illness and ageing; too little, and we experience fatigue from the reduced capacity to process stored energy.

Such respiration is the whole process of getting and then using oxygen to unlock the stored energy in glucose. It includes breathing (external respiration); cellular respiration (internal respiration); and oxygen metabolism (unlocking stored energy in glucose).

THE PROCESS OF RESPIRATION

Breathing is the inhalation and exhalation of air by the lungs, within which oxygen (as well as other substances) passes from the air to the blood, and carbon dioxide (CO_2) from the blood to the air

The rhythm of breathing is spontaneous and consciously controlled. The basic movement is a reflex (enabling us to breathe when we are asleep). Inhalation is triggered by periodic nerve impulses travelling from the brain stem along the phrenic nerve to the diaphragm. The diaphragm then lowers within the abdomen, stretching the lungs like bellows and creating the suction needed for air to move into them. Exhalation is pre-dominantly automatic, as the lungs seek to bounce back to their naturally smaller size.

Once air has arrived in the alveolar sac, oxygen transfers itself to haemoglobin in the blood, which, at the same time, deposits waste CO_2. The background level of CO_2 in the blood is what determines the nervous system's messages to the respiratory centre in the brain.

Internal respiration occurs way beyond the sphere of the lungs and extends to every cell in the body. It is the exchange of oxygen between the blood and each cell by diffusion – a process in which oxygen molecules seep through the thin cell walls. CO_2 uses the return ticket to make its way back with the blood to the lungs and then out into the air.

Oxygen metabolism is the use of oxygen by cells to release energy stored in glucose.

BY-PRODUCTS OF RESPIRATION

Free radicals are natural by-products of cell respiration and are used in the body to fight infection and detoxify harmful chemicals. Superoxide free radicals are particularly aggressive because they are fond of bonding with and changing the nature of DNA. An excessive number can leave the body more prone to cancer and premature ageing.

The body has an antidote (antioxidants) for any negative effects of superoxide free radicals. Too many antioxidants, however, can lead to fatigue. It's important not to demonize free radicals, as they may have led to life on Earth through their capacity to mutate DNA.

Free radicals increase in the body on exposure to pollution, radiation (including sunlight, particularly at high altitudes), polyunsaturated fats and pesticides.

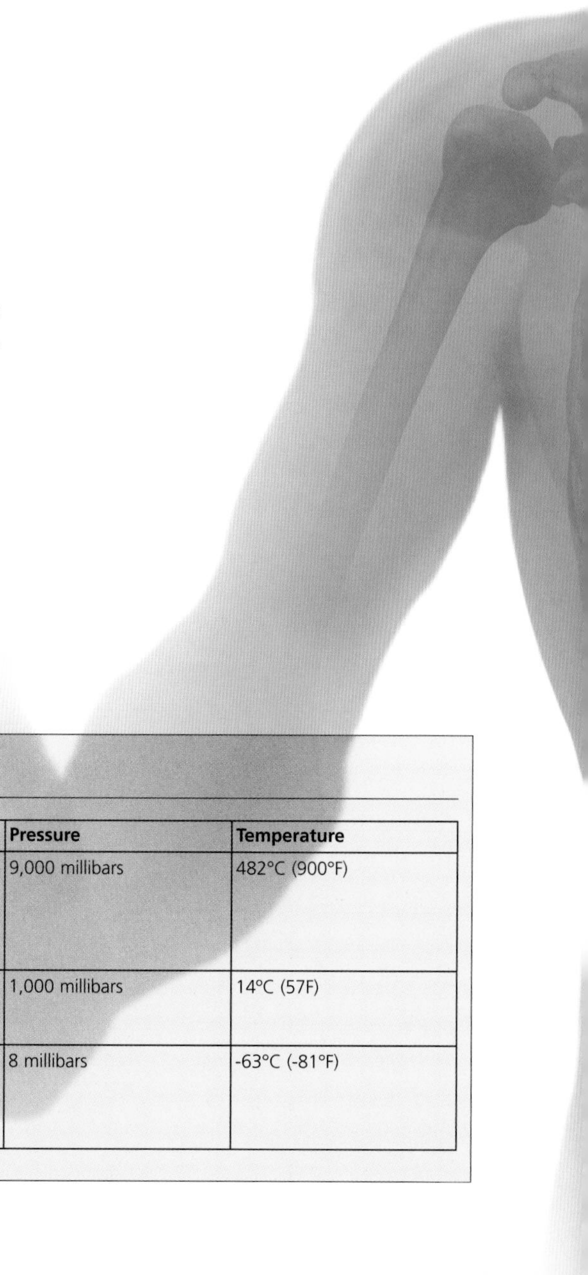

PLANETARY CONDITIONS

There is only a narrow range of oxygen concentrations that can sustain life, especially human life. In order for any atmosphere to be hospitable to human life, it needs a significant proportion of oxygen and to be within functional limits of atmospheric pressure and surface temperature. The atmospheres of our nearest neighbours illustrate the variability of planetary conditions; we don't know yet just how unique our planet actually is.

Planetary body	Atmosphere	Pressure	Temperature
Venus	95% carbon dioxide, with clouds containing sulphuric acid	9,000 millibars	482°C (900°F)
Earth	21% oxygen 78% nitrogen	1,000 millibars	14°C (57F)
Mars	95% carbon dioxide 2% nitrogen 0.13% oxygen	8 millibars	-63°C (-81°F)

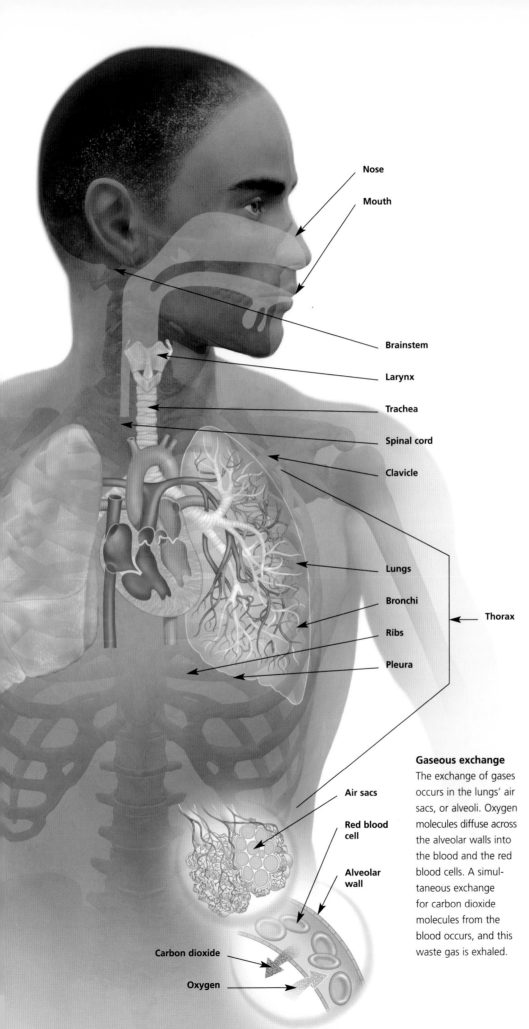

Nose

Mouth

Brainstem

Larynx

Trachea

Spinal cord

Clavicle

Lungs

Bronchi

Ribs

Pleura

Thorax

Air sacs

Red blood cell

Alveolar wall

Carbon dioxide

Oxygen

Gaseous exchange

The exchange of gases occurs in the lungs' air sacs, or alveoli. Oxygen molecules diffuse across the alveolar walls into the blood and the red blood cells. A simultaneous exchange for carbon dioxide molecules from the blood occurs, and this waste gas is exhaled.

THE CONSCIOUS BREATH

Breathing can be controlled through conscious movement of the diaphragm and ribs. Through concentrating on where we 'send' our breath, we can vary the shape in which our lungs expand. Sending our breath to the feet or perineum involves lowering the diaphragm as we breathe, while sending it to our fingertips involves the muscles between our ribs.

Both overbreathing and underbreathing reduce the lungs' efficiency and can cause health problems. Some therapeutic techniques directly address this. The Buteyko method, for example, is an anti-asthma treatment that guards against the overbreathing/hyperventilation that is seen to cause asthma. It seeks to train sufferers to control their breathing during attacks, rather than fighting for more breath.

Conscious breathing has been developed by various cultures to levels of sophistication that enable us substantially to control our metabolism and consciousness. Such sciences invariably use imagery to convey the way in which we develop advanced breathing practices. For example, to influence the efficiency of our metabolism, we might visualize the smooth and abundant potency of cosmic energy coming into the body on inhalation, and the thorough release of stale and spent energy leaving the body on exhalation.

The control of consciousness through breathing practices arises out of the structure of a particular tradition, but each uses the focus of intention to guide the breath and to shape the direction, rhythm and speed of breathing. Most traditions observe a relationship between the breath and spiritual experience as seen in the double meanings of words relating to breath and spirit. While cultural relativity can never equate concepts across traditions, there are enough correspondences here to suggest a shared human experience of the breath of life.

Practitioners of breathing sciences within traditions such as yoga, martial arts and meditation are also able to perform a wide range of seemingly supernatural feats. Many of these practitioners would say that they have merely taken the functions of the body to some of its natural potential. To others, however, the capacity to hold the breath for extended periods or to floor any number of attackers through a shout of power can seem extraordinary.

Hair
our surface senses

Hair is an often neglected part of our anatomy, commonly seen as merely an evolutionary remnant – the fur that never quite fell off. The most basic aspects of hair are in protection, sexual communication, heat regulation and the sense of touch. Each of these functions has dimensions that are as applicable to our energetic and spiritual bodies as they are to the more subtle and unseen functions of our physical selves.

PROTECTION
Eyebrows and eyelashes prevent objects from getting into our eyes, and nose and ear hair impedes the progress of dust and microbes into the nasal cavities and ear canals. Head hair protects the scalp from physical injury and from the harmful effects of the sun.

Body hair seems to serves little purpose in the way of protection. If you are exposed to cold or feel excited or fearful, your body hair 'stands on end'. In animals, such a response will 'puff out' the fur, causing the animal to look bigger (in the face of an aggressor) or trap more insulating air (in the case of feeling cold). Most people, however, simply get goosebumps as the arrector pili muscle at the base of each hair root causes our hair to stand erect.

ENVIRONMENTAL CHANGES
But even for us, body hair detects tiny changes in the surrounding environment, from air currents to the magnetic field of where we are. Such sensations are detected by the plexus of nerves surrounding the hair root. Our hair standing on end is often not backed up by our other senses, leaving us wondering what caused us to feel unnerved.

Such sensations are different from hair static, which is caused by a lack of moisture in the hair. Moist hair conducts electricity and forms part of our body's constant 'earthing' as mini lightning strikes transfer electrons from the Earth up to our body. Dry hair effectively operates as an electrical insulator, building up a static charge and causing it to 'float' above the head.

SEXUAL COMMUNICATION
Hair is also a strong aspect of our sexual communication. This happens in a very obvious way as the colour and style of our head hair advertises something about our biological nature and the qualities of our personality. We might, ourselves, feel more attracted to people with brown, black, red or blond hair and either a sparseness or an abundance of hair.

We have two types of the hair pigment melanin: brown pigment eurmelanin and red pigment phaeomelanin. The strength and combination of these pigments determine hair colour and is something inherited from our parents. Sexual preferences based on hair colour, style and amount vary between and within cultures. That they are based on biological impulses doesn't devalue or remove the mystery from them.

Hair is further involved in sexual communication, carrying the pheromones secreted at the base of the armpit and pubic hair (from apocrine glands) along the hair lengths so that they can be released into the atmosphere. Sex hormones are also involved in hair condition and function during pregnancy, when the hair thickens, and three months or so after childbirth when there is hair loss as the hormonal balance stabilizes.

RECORDING HISTORY
Hair is also our history. Growing at about 1cm (⅓in) a month, it records aspects of the mineral and chemical environment of our bodies, laying down a history in layers of cellular sediment. Laboratory analysis of hair is commonly used to identify the presence of certain metals and drugs for social, criminal and therapeutic purposes. Hair is routinely used to test for cocaine use – a drug that passes from urine in 72 hours, but remains in the hair of three months. Hair analysis is also used by some nutritionists to profile perceived deficiencies in trace elements that can then be remedied through the prescription of supplements. This practice is questioned by those who assert that there is as yet no appropriate baseline of normal mineral levels for the hair and that each of us may vary in our mineral profile through a number of environmental factors.

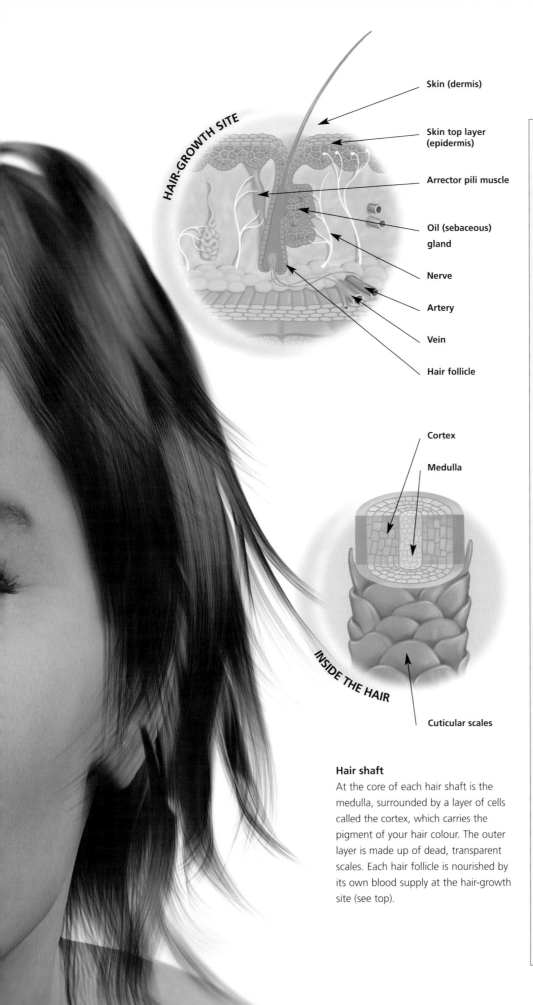

HAIR-GROWTH SITE

Skin (dermis)

Skin top layer
(epidermis)

Arrector pili muscle

Oil (sebaceous)
gland

Nerve

Artery

Vein

Hair follicle

Cortex

Medulla

INSIDE THE HAIR

Cuticular scales

Hair shaft

At the core of each hair shaft is the
medulla, surrounded by a layer of cells
called the cortex, which carries the
pigment of your hair colour. The outer
layer is made up of dead, transparent
scales. Each hair follicle is nourished by
its own blood supply at the hair-growth
site (see top).

THE SACREDNESS OF HAIR

Many traditions hold rituals surrounding hair and
its role in spiritual health. In Sikhism, a religion
that seeks to provide India, and the world, with
'saint-soldiers' in defence of multifaith religious
freedom, hair is not only a symbol of respect and
strength, it also protects the brain and mind from
harmful spiritual energies. The Sikh scholar Sarup
Singh Alag describes the top of the head as the
centre of solar energy in the body and the chin
as the centre of lunar energy. The hair covering
acts as an antenna that collects and downloads
such energy, insulating us from harmful energies
that could make us despondent, confused and
pessimistic. Women's lack of facial hair is due
to their stronger nervous systems and softer
dispositions, whereas for men their beauty, courage
and righteousness will depend on the strength
of the beard.

Many spiritual traditions adopt particular hair
styles to reflect part of their understanding of the
body's spiritual energetics, as well as being part
of the cultural life of that tradition. For example,
there are the shaved heads of Buddhist monks,
Christian monks' tonsures and the twisted hair
of native American medicine men.

Some traditions use hair as an archive of
knowledge and power in ceremonial items that
hold spiritual potency for either the individual
or the community. Such items are usually made
up of the shaman's own hair, but not all hair
ceremonial objects are derived from the human
variety. Concretized hair-balls from the stomachs
of animals have been used in traditional medicines
and magics for thousands of years. Collectively
known as 'bezoar' stones (from the Persian *pad*
meaning 'expelling' and *zahr* meaning 'poison'),
they were used as a heal-all and particularly as an
antidote for poisons. In India they were particularly
prized as providing an elixir of life. And while the
results of an oyster's stomach irritations led to
something that was both beautiful and precious,
bezoar stones had an equally precious but
stranger appearance.

Fluids
upon a water planet

Chalice Well
At Glastonbury, England, is one of the countless holy wells and springs across the world where life-giving water is honoured as a sacrament.

All known forms of life depend on water for their survival. Even rare plant seeds and bacteria that can survive desiccation return to life only once they have been rehydrated. Humans, however, cannot survive desiccation, and should we die of old age then our body's water content is likely to have fallen from something around 70 per cent to something nearer 50 per cent. At conception, it is 99 per cent. Our process through life is one of gradual dehydration.

Water is the foundation of all living cells. We exist in a moist internal environment held together by a waterproof skin and the infrastructure of each cell wall. Nutrients, chemical messages and wastes pass across cell walls and through rivers of blood, lymph and cell-cushioning fluid in a network of cohesion, communication and nourishment.

SUSPENSIONS AND DILUTIONS

Water is the foundation for all chemical processes in the human body. It is an almost universal solvent, able to take in molecules of other substances, to form both dilutions and suspensions. Suspensions occur when water molecules retain their integrity and carry other free-floating substances in their currents, releasing them when the flow stops. Dilutions are where molecules of a substance separate as they become more attracted to water molecules than they are to each other.

It is in this way that water-based fluids are able to transport chemical messages, nutrients and waste products throughout the body, picking them up and letting them go at the appropriate moment, releasing them from either suspension or dilution.

Waste products are removed from our body's fluids as blood passes through the kidneys, which retain the toxins and then return both water and a regulated level of hormones and minerals to the blood.

HYDRATION

Each type of cell in the body contains a different amount of water: muscles have a 75 per cent water component, for example, while blood plasma is around 92 per cent, with fat and bone being 50 per cent water. Digestion takes up significant quantities of water as food is broken down and diluted. Many digestive problems also arise when we are dehydrated, as the inner lining of the intestines loses its flushness and capacity to transfer nutrients efficiently.

We each need to drink about eight glasses of water a day in normal conditions. Dehydration should lead to thirst, but if we are chronically dehydrated, then our internal regulating mechanisms may accept the condition as normal and fail to give the appropriate thirst signals.

We can, equally, drink too much water, water toxicity occurring when body fluids become too dilute and cells bloated. This can, in extreme cases, lead to shock, coma and even death. Water toxicity can occur after severe dehydration, when fluids are reintroduced too quickly. Some dietary systems recommend no water is drunk, and that body fluids are replenished solely by the vegetables in the diet. This can be understood when we consider that 90 per cent of the water we use is to grow food.

WATER PURITY

The purity of water is determined by the absence of substances dissolved in it. Spring water is doubly valued as a health tonic by virtue of such purity and also the 'magnetism' that it gains as it rises to springs through layers of filtering and energizing rock. Many cultures venerate both springs and wells, as sources of spiritual energy where the life-giving energy of water is most vibrant.

Water is almost certain to become an increasingly scarce and valuable resource during the course of the 21st century, and the distribution of clean drinking water to all humans will be one of the key challenges to be faced.

THE BODY'S ACIDITY BALANCE

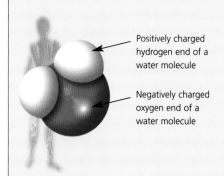

Positively charged hydrogen end of a water molecule

Negatively charged oxygen end of a water molecule

Body acidity is the balance of 'charged' molecules in the body as a result of water's activity in making new relationships through the processes of dilution. Any incoming substance to the body will make our internal environment more acidic if, in the process of its dilution, it leaves an excess of unattached positively charged molecules, and more alkaline if an excess of unattached negatively charged molecules.

Charged molecules are produced as incoming substances claim a greater bonding with water than they had with their neighbouring molecules. Salt

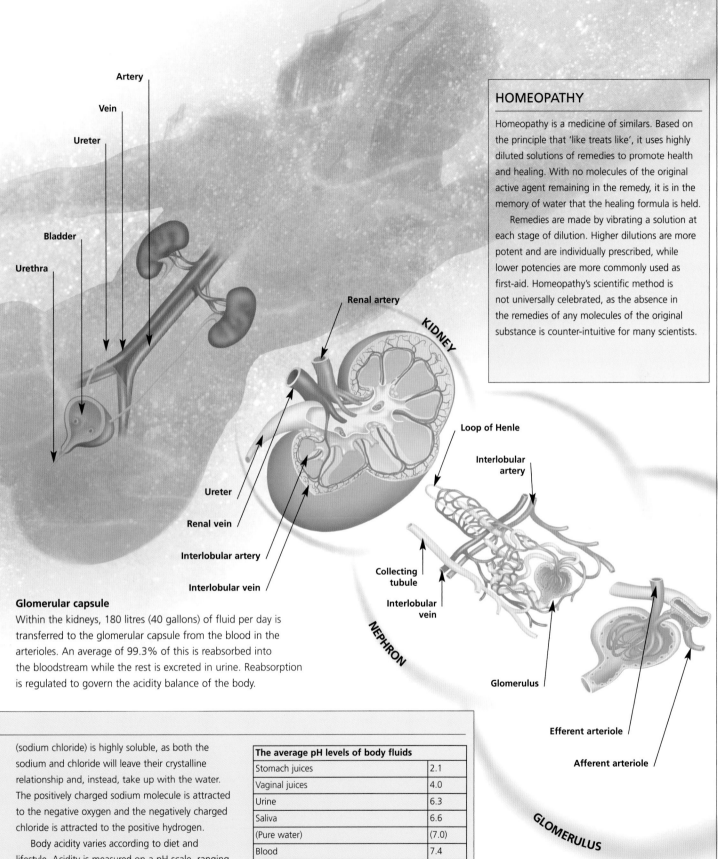

Artery

Vein

Ureter

Bladder

Urethra

Renal artery

KIDNEY

Loop of Henle

Interlobular artery

Ureter

Renal vein

Interlobular artery

Interlobular vein

Collecting tubule

Interlobular vein

NEPHRON

Glomerulus

Efferent arteriole

Afferent arteriole

GLOMERULUS

HOMEOPATHY

Homeopathy is a medicine of similars. Based on the principle that 'like treats like', it uses highly diluted solutions of remedies to promote health and healing. With no molecules of the original active agent remaining in the remedy, it is in the memory of water that the healing formula is held.

Remedies are made by vibrating a solution at each stage of dilution. Higher dilutions are more potent and are individually prescribed, while lower potencies are more commonly used as first-aid. Homeopathy's scientific method is not universally celebrated, as the absence in the remedies of any molecules of the original substance is counter-intuitive for many scientists.

Glomerular capsule

Within the kidneys, 180 litres (40 gallons) of fluid per day is transferred to the glomerular capsule from the blood in the arterioles. An average of 99.3% of this is reabsorbed into the bloodstream while the rest is excreted in urine. Reabsorption is regulated to govern the acidity balance of the body.

(sodium chloride) is highly soluble, as both the sodium and chloride will leave their crystalline relationship and, instead, take up with the water. The positively charged sodium molecule is attracted to the negative oxygen and the negatively charged chloride is attracted to the positive hydrogen.

Body acidity varies according to diet and lifestyle. Acidity is measured on a pH scale, ranging from 0 (very acidic) to 14 (very alkaline), with a reading of 7 being the balance of pure water.

The average pH levels of body fluids	
Stomach juices	2.1
Vaginal juices	4.0
Urine	6.3
Saliva	6.6
(Pure water)	(7.0)
Blood	7.4
Semen	7.4
Brain and spine fluid	7.4
Bile	8.1

Gender

the other half of life

Our differentiation into male and female is intricately linked with reproduction (see page 56) and sex (see page 74), but it also governs nearly every aspect of our lives. Gender is a fundamental polarity shared by most life forms on our planet. Above the level of bacteria, organisms do not generally swap genetic information from one cell to another. Instead, they develop specialized sex cells – gametes, such as egg and sperm – that take on the role of genetic exchange. For most species, including humans, the production of gametes is linked to the actual gender of the organism, with males generally producing only sperm and females only eggs.

The polarity of most species into male and female is determined by the combination of genetic material at conception. Each gamete has within it 46 pairs of chromosomes, which, as we are conceived, split down the middle to reconnect with those of our other parent.

SEXUAL CHARACTERISTICS

The development of secondary sexual characteristics arises from the influence of sex hormones on the body. These include our musculature, breast development, growth of body hair, voice pitch and bone structure.

While determination of gender happens at conception, its first signs are not apparent until a few weeks into our development. By our sixth week of life we have developed the origins of either testes or ovaries. This is activated by the presence of the male sex hormone dihydrotestosterone, which steers genital development in the direction of the male. Without its action, we are female.

CULTURAL ATTACHMENT AND BIOLOGICAL FUNCTION

Most cultures have strongly delineated roles for men and women. Taboos exist more around gender roles than any other aspect of human behaviour. Such roles can be seen as a very basic and biological compulsion that ensures the perpetuation of the species, yet we tend to remain attached to our cultural interpretation of biological imperatives. It is as if the cultural aspect is in some sense inferior to the biochemistry of our beings. There is often a presupposition that our biochemistry is unavailable to our conscious design, whereas it is perhaps more accurate

to consider a co-creation between the soft-wiring of our hormonal networks and the imagination of our cultural constructions of identity and sensation.

Confucian hierarchies of familial relationships is an example of the complexity of rules involved in how we relate to others, depending on age, gender and familial status. Such constructs are sometimes seen as recidivist in their adherence to prejudicial political structures. While this is undoubtedly true from one perspective, it can also fail to appreciate the cultural context and benefits of such traditions, and also the wider spiritual dimension to how we order our lives in relation to our understanding of the nature of the cosmos.

Some species of fish are hermaphroditic, functioning as a female for a few years before changing sex to operate as a male. DNA recombination also forms the basis for gender in fish species, but whereas hormones only prompt and regulate secondary sexual characteristics in humans, they can change the actual gender of some fish. This process seems to accelerate as levels of pollutants, such as detergents and hormone-based medications, increase in our waterways. In humans, such chemical pollution merely reduces the fertility of the male.

Most species also link gender to biological function, with the caring of young being the domain of the female. There are often practical reasons for this – for example, the female mammal's provision of milk. Equally, though, there are exceptions, such as the male sea horse, which becomes pregnant after being implanted with the female's eggs.

While the human species is increasingly managing the environment, we are also extending the variances of gender role and function. We are not solely choreographed by our gender, even though it remains a powerful determiner within some cultures, and the dialogue about the most effective and empowered expression of our procreation continues to rumble as we explore the scientific and ethical limits of our species.

A CONTINUUM OF GENDER

Society mandates the control of intersexual bodies because they both blur and bridge the great divide . . . in the long view the prize might be a society in which sexuality is something to be celebrated for its subtleties; and not something to be feared or ridiculed.

Anne Fausto-Sterling

While gender is often viewed as an off switch of either male or female, there are variances that have been viewed from different perspectives across history and culture. Mostly, any variance from the norm has been classified as deviation, and at times those of 'intersex' (who do not fit neatly into a polarized gender perspective) have been surgically operated on in order to emphasize either male or female development. Hermaphrodites, those possessing both sets of sexual glands and organs, have been known throughout history (usually having prescriptive laws applied to them), although they are only one expression of a number of genetic variancies of gender. On the continuum of gender, Anne Fausto-Sterling (Professor of Biology and Gender Studies, Brown University) has suggested that we would more usefully be served by recognizing three extra expressions of human gender:

- **Males** – genetically XY with testes and penis.
- **Females** – genetically XX with ovaries, uterus and vagina.
- **Herms (hermaphrodites)** – genetically both XY and XX with one testis, one ovary and both vagina and penis.
- **Merms (male pseudo-hermaphrodites)** genetically XY who have testes and some female genitalia.
- **Ferms (female pseudo-hermaphrodites)** genetically XX who have ovaries and some male genitalia.

There is wide variance in each of these groups (as we know within conventional patternings of male and female) that is expressed as secondary sexual characteristics and sexual behaviour and influenced by sex hormones.

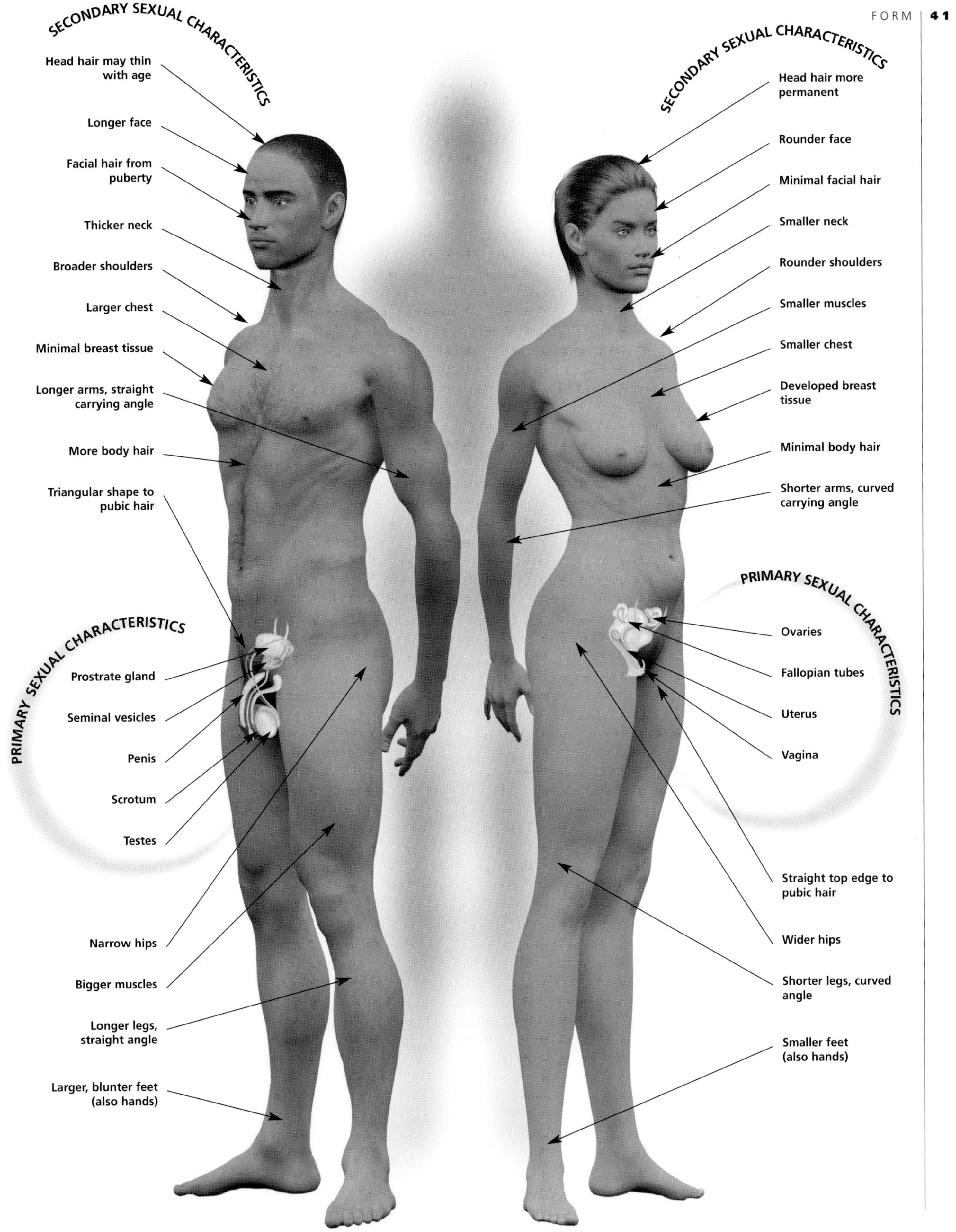

SECONDARY SEXUAL CHARACTERISTICS

SECONDARY SEXUAL CHARACTERISTICS

Head hair may thin with age

Longer face

Facial hair from puberty

Thicker neck

Broader shoulders

Larger chest

Minimal breast tissue

Longer arms, straight carrying angle

More body hair

Triangular shape to pubic hair

PRIMARY SEXUAL CHARACTERISTICS

Prostrate gland

Seminal vesicles

Penis

Scrotum

Testes

Narrow hips

Bigger muscles

Longer legs, straight angle

Larger, blunter feet (also hands)

Head hair more permanent

Rounder face

Minimal facial hair

Smaller neck

Rounder shoulders

Smaller muscles

Smaller chest

Developed breast tissue

Minimal body hair

Shorter arms, curved carrying angle

PRIMARY SEXUAL CHARACTERISTICS

Ovaries

Fallopian tubes

Uterus

Vagina

Straight top edge to pubic hair

Wider hips

Shorter legs, curved angle

Smaller feet (also hands)

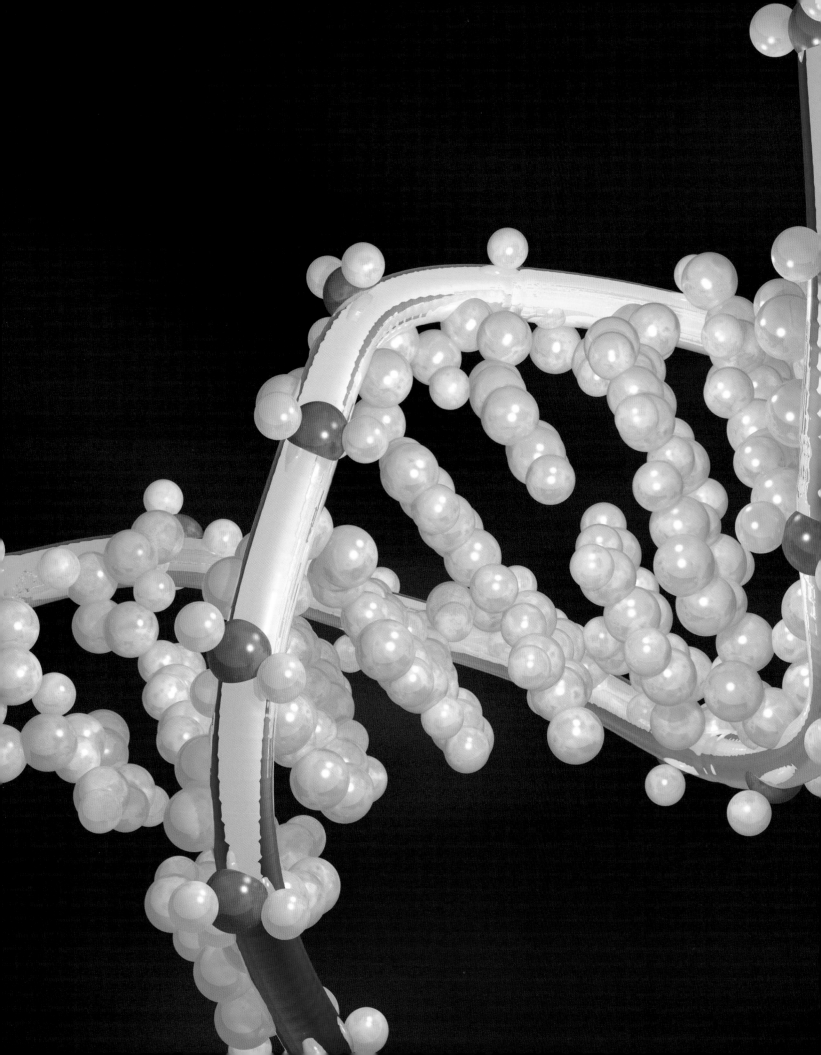

Function

The human maps of physiology

The movement and development of our bodies through time is the heart of the physiological processes. Who we are as individuals is mediated by intricate internal and external rhythms, body clocks and cosmic clocks that count time for us throughout the vast panorama of consciousness. It is here that we know birth and death, puberty and menopause, spring and autumn, dark and full moon, dawn and dusk.

Beneath the glare of these cosmic cycles the mêlée of the earth's teeming life has its own constancies of life, death, communication and development: our natural day would be 25.5 hours were the pineal gland left to its own regulation, but it adjusts itself to the planet's 24-hour cycle; our births are more common in the early dawn, during magnetic storms and during months of greater daylight.

And while the discipline of astrology captivates many and underwhelms an equal number, the effect of when we are born in relation to the intricate clockwork of the planets does seem to have some validity. The research of French psychologist (and astrological skeptic) Michel Gauquelin has shown there is a correlation of our future professions with the particular planet whose day is dawning on Earth's horizon as we are born: those born as Mars rises are more likely to become doctors or scientists; as Jupiter dawns, there is a higher probability of soldiers and politicians.

Our bodies, minds and spirits are constantly restored through the rhythmic ingestion and absorption of nutrients from our environment. This perpetual interchange between ourselves and the world around us is a highly sophisticated and complex regulation of nutrients and pathogens. We recognize and deal with such substances on many levels – from an automatic cellular level (digestion and immunity) to a conscious, cognitive level (food preparation and personal hygiene). Both, however, also give us meaning in terms of who we are as individuals and as a species.

The polarity of nutrients and pathogens pushes into the perspective of the human body as a sophisticated spaceship for bacteria as we invert the direction of life's evolution from one based on food to one based on transport. And while we often see the interaction of bacteria with 'higher' forms of life as conflict based, there are two fundamental interrelationships possible between the members of any ecosystem – entropy and syntropy.

Entropy is the dog-eat-dog dynamic of biological and social systems, where the food chain is one-directional and each member of the whole is scrabbling for their piece of the action. Syntropy is the tendency for members of a community to relate to each other in a way that is co-creative. Such a polarity of entropy and syntropy was initially conceived of by the Italian mathematician Luigi Fantappie at the beginning of the 12th century.

This chapter will track the choreography of our physiological rhythms. From the tidal flow of hormonal regulation to how we interface with the substance and sustenance of our planet, this is the unfolding of our blueprint across a backdrop of cosmic cycles. It is not merely the functioning of who we are, but the tracing of our unique signatures of being that are the basis of both consciousness and freedom.

the endocrine system

We as humans are composed of a kind of chemical messenger soup that is changing with each passing moment. While the body was once perceived to be a hierarchal mechanism largely controlled by the brain, it is now becoming clear that the body instead functions as an ever changing network of information with open lines of communication between all systems of the body, the brain and the processes of the mind.

Candace Pert

Our endocrine glands are the primary regulators of ourselves as an organism that is born, tracks its way throughout each day, month and age of our existence and dies. *Endocrine* means 'direct secretion into the bloodstream', with no mediating mechanism – as there is in the case of the nervous system. Nerve pathways are a combination of electrical impulses travelling down the nerves themselves and the chemical bridges between nerve cells that are then able to mediate and monitor the relays of lightning information around the body.

By contrast, the hormones (from the Greek *horman*, meaning 'to set in motion') of the endocrine system are a slower, but more precise way, of regulating the body's internal environment. The whole organization of the network is regulated by the on/off commands of various hormones. Some of our systems are set at a default position that is then amended by a specific hormone coming in with direct chemical commands (such as the 'stop eating!' hormone that limits our default position to 'eat!') Other systems have a seesaw regulation governed by two opposing mechanisms (such as the regulation of blood sugar levels by the presence of glucagon and insulin – illustrated by the Islets of Langerhans, see right).

OUR BEAUTIFUL CONFUSION

It is principally the endocrine system that gives us the capacity to feel emotion, which, together with the cognitive centres of the brain's cerebral cortex, combines to form the 'beautiful confusion' of the human condition.

Author Terry Pratchett's famous anthropomorphization of 'Death' is instructive regarding the nature of the glands of the endocrine system, in the reasoning as to why Death feels no emotion. His fictional daughter tells us: 'He never feels anything. I don't mean that nastily you understand. It's just that he's got nothing to feel with, no whatd'youcallits, no glands.' (We are told, however, that he does like rock music.) And while the influence of our glands is the basis of our emotional life, as can be seen during periods of hormonal change, such as puberty and menopause, the developing wisdom of how we feel emotion is increasingly pointing to an interactive field between the endocrine system and our nervous and immune systems.

The folk wisdom of 'mind over matter' is enjoying something of a revision and renaissance within contemporary research, particularly due to the work of the visionary neuroscientist Candace Pert, who has developed the notion of a psychoimmuno-endocrine system that is the basis for an interactive web for all our systems.

COMPOSITION AND FUNCTION

While the endocrine system is comprised of distinct and seemingly separate glands, they share similarities in their composition as well as their function. All of them, by definition, secrete hormones directly into the bloodstream, although some dwell within the bodies of major organs, such as the intestines, heart, placenta and kidneys. in order to fine tune our internal equilibrium.

At the other end of the scale, the endocrine system is capable of managing emergency responses for short periods of time – the hypothalamus/pituitary diverting resources away from maintenance systems to route emergency supplies of glucose and oxygen to the brain, heart and skeletal (running) muscles whenever we should need them. Such a state is not capable of being maintained, however, and immunity is one of the first systems to suffer in its effectiveness, demonstrating once more the link between our various systems. Such attrition can, in extreme circumstances, cause death, as the prolonged stress of hormonal imbalance fails to support our biochemical balance.

SEVEN RAYS AND ROERICH'S SHAMBALA

***Path of Shambhala* by Nicholas Roerich**

For much of the 20th century, the Hindu system of mapping the energy body with chakras reinitiated many Western esoteric traditions. Both the Rosicrucian revival (MacGregor Mathers *et al*) and the Theosophical movement (Madame Helena Blavatsky *et al*) at the end of the 19th century blended the then growing understanding of the endocrine system with Hinduism's teachings of chakras. Here, each of the glands corresponds with one of the seven chakras and, in particular, to a 'cosmic ray' (Shambhala).

Blavatsky was responsible for the dissemination of much occult knowledge throughout the West. This Russian medium created a synthesis of magic and mysticism that took the work of Theosophy to Germany, France, Britain and America.

Of particular note were C W Leadbeater, Rudolph Steiner and Alice Bailey, from whose writing many of the mysteries of the rays come to us, and Nicholas Roerich, the painter who managed to convey some of the immediate mystery of Shambhala through his work.

While there is a resonance and a validity in such alignments, it needs to be approached with caution in case we slip into the tendency to conflate systems and give fuel to our quest for one over-arching truth at the cost of historical discipline and the essential diversity of holistic bodies of knowledge. As long as we hold in parallel such systems, any correspondences can helpfully illuminate both bodies of knowledge.

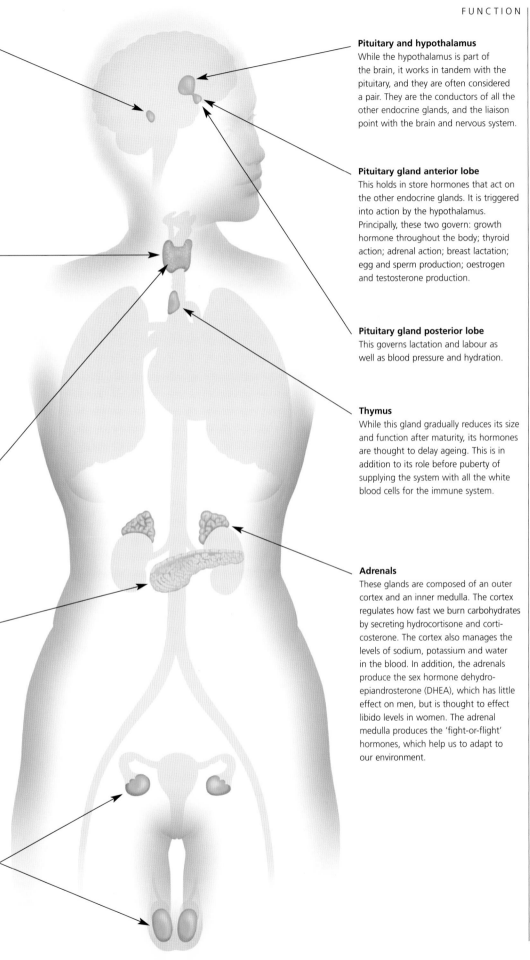

Pineal

This gland sits at the heart of the brain, between the cerebrum, brain stem and the limbic system. It is about the size of a redcurrant, and through the secretion of melatonin it is understood to conduct our rhythms of day and night, as well as holding in check the development of our primary sexual characteristics until puberty.

Thyroid

The thyroid releases thyroxine (T3) and triiodothyronine (T4). Thyroxine is involved with tissue building, nervous-system development and metabolism. If, during pregnancy and infancy, there is a deficiency, brain and nerve development is impeded. A lack of thyroid hormones in adulthood can lead to lethargy, coldness and depression; an excess to hyperactivity and a higher body temperature.

Parathyroids

The parathyroids make sure that blood calcium levels maintain an equilibrium. It monitors how much calcium is absorbed from our food intake by the small intestine, how much is absorbed in the kidneys, and, under conditions of calcium scarcity, how much is reclaimed from bone mass.

Islets of Langerhans

Clusters of these glands populate the pancreas and principally secrete glucagon and insulin, regulating the amount of sugar in the blood. If blood sugar levels fall, glucagon will release sugar stores in the liver. Insulin, however, is mobilized if we have higher levels of sugar than is necessary, and so will stimulate the general absorption of glucose by cell membranes. Diabetes occurs when there is a disruption in the equilibrium of sugars within the body.

Ovaries and testes

The ovaries and testes, in addition to producing eggs and sperm, also produce the sex hormones that govern sexual maturity and the development of secondary sex characteristics at puberty.

Pituitary and hypothalamus

While the hypothalamus is part of the brain, it works in tandem with the pituitary, and they are often considered a pair. They are the conductors of all the other endocrine glands, and the liaison point with the brain and nervous system.

Pituitary gland anterior lobe

This holds in store hormones that act on the other endocrine glands. It is triggered into action by the hypothalamus. Principally, these two govern: growth hormone throughout the body; thyroid action; adrenal action; breast lactation; egg and sperm production; oestrogen and testosterone production.

Pituitary gland posterior lobe

This governs lactation and labour as well as blood pressure and hydration.

Thymus

While this gland gradually reduces its size and function after maturity, its hormones are thought to delay ageing. This is in addition to its role before puberty of supplying the system with all the white blood cells for the immune system.

Adrenals

These glands are composed of an outer cortex and an inner medulla. The cortex regulates how fast we burn carbohydrates by secreting hydrocortisone and corticosterone. The cortex also manages the levels of sodium, potassium and water in the blood. In addition, the adrenals produce the sex hormone dehydro-epiandrosterone (DHEA), which has little effect on men, but is thought to effect libido levels in women. The adrenal medulla produces the 'fight-or-flight' hormones, which help us to adapt to our environment.

Immunity
defence or dialogue

Man had earned his immunity, his right to survive among this planet's infinite organisms.
War of the Worlds, H G Wells

Immunity is the innate skill of the body's systems to recognize and resist invading pathogens. We each have strategies for developing our immunity that centre around the scouting function of antibodies and the destructive function of macrophages.

This cellular-based immunity is a search-and-destroy quest for virus-infected cells, fungi, cancers, bacteria and protozoans. Killer cells perform their function by the action of antibodies that have 'marked' invading pathogens for expulsion. Our memory of what is alien is the biological database of inherited and acquired immunity. Inherited immunity comes from our parents, while acquired immunity is gathered as we come into contact with pathogens as we grow.

Inoculations are based on this basic understanding. Small amounts of weakened pathogens are injected into the bloodstream in order to 'prime' the immune database. Immunization is almost globally accepted as a valid healthcare intervention, though some voices highlight the timing of the benefits ascribed to mass immunizations with increased public healthcare generally. Some perspectives from Chinese medicine have also questioned the exposure to pathogens at the blood level, where the route of infection for many conditions is via the air.

VIRUSES AND BACTERIA

The literal meaning of *virus* comes from the Latin for 'poison', and generally refers to an organic but non-living particle. It is organic by virtue of its composition from chemical compounds that include carbon. The origin of viruses is as yet unknown, though theories suggest they emerged alongside their host organisms as part of the evolution of life.

As for bacteria, the other main culprit in human ill-health, their main difference from larger life-forms is that their genetic material is relatively free floating within their cells; in larger life-forms, it is bundled within each cell's nucleus.

The economic infrastructure of most Western healthcare is based on a mechanistic model of health where pathogens such as viruses and bacteria are to be exterminated rather than helping us learn to live within a continuum of health in which we manage the systems of life more effectively, either within our own bodies or between us and the environment.

Within modern medicine complications arise from our advances, with, for example, radiotherapy and chemotherapy leaving us more prone to immunodeficiency diseases, where we either fail to recognize the 'self' of our own tissues or become less active in rebutting the invasion of pathogens. Multiple sclerosis thus arises from the misplaced attrition of antibodies on the myelin sheath around nerves, and rheumatoid arthritis from the immune system inappropriately targeting joints. The immune system can, however, become excessively responsive in the case of allergic reactions, where we are unable to tolerate substances and conditions that are usually harmless.

The continuum of our 'cellular self', mediated by the immune system, has been further challenged by the advent of organ transplants. In order for transplants to work, the highest chance of success is through transplanting from an identical twin. Siblings and other family members also offer a good chance of success, but the probabilities drop to one in 150,000 when extended to unrelated members of the general population.

Whether we perceive the universe as co-operative or predatory affects our approach to hygiene and health. As the 20th century closed, children raised with little exposure to either viruses or bacteria were seen to have weaker immune systems. It began to seem that the workout provided by sporadic engagement with pathogens was beneficial to the immune system. The miraculous discovery of antibiotics in the mid 20th century gave way some decades later to a realization that they were helping bacteria adapt more quickly and effectively. As a result, a reversion has begun to the folk-wisdom that a little bit of dirt is good for you.

THE GIFT OF VIRUSES

Viruses are essentially not alive, since they do not have distinct and replicable genetic material, as do bacteria. Viruses are nature's hijackers, needing to invade and take over the genetic material of cellular life in order to replicate themselves. Nor do viruses exist as distinct cells, but rather as strands of DNA with a protein sheath around them. Our knowledge of their value and role is still limited, despite our expansion into microbiology and genetics, and it may be that they actually perform a 'postal' role between all DNA-based life, updating us on the more recent adventures of our ecosystem.

Any serious rebranding of viruses in this way is unlikely due to the intense personal distress that can arise from the illnesses they cause and because our perspective is usually one of our local world rather than a genetic planetary ecosystem. Furthermore, their invasive and parasitical characteristics do not lend them to any kind of appreciation. Such attributes have led them to being used as 'splicer' cells in genetic engineering – exploiting their natural capacities to invade other cells in order to alter DNA sequencing (mostly of tomatoes so far).

The debate over this level of engineering prowess has only just started in relation to nano-technology – the extremely miniaturized generation of tiny, self-replicating devices, which, it has been suggested, may be able to assist us in managing our planetary environment.

For as many voices that celebrate such a nanotechnological dawn, at least an equal number fear the consequences of a self-replicating class of entities that has no natural predator or life-span, and could, theoretically, clog up the arteries of our planet's ecosystem. It may, rather, be that we assign our energies to decoding further the intricacies of how we manage both our internal and external environments, not through the technology of Armageddon, but by a greater insight into our own complexities of genetic defence and dialogue.

Fungus
In some ways, fungi are similar to protozoa in their function of breaking down material in the food chain. This they do outside of their cell walls, taking in the nutrients after digestion.

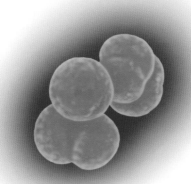

Bacteria
Staphylococcus is a family of bacteria commonly found on the skin and in the nasal passages of humans, and can lead to a wide variety of bacterial infections, including MRSA.

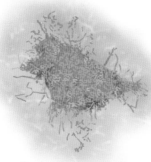

HIV
HIV (Human Immuno-deficiency Virus) attacks the mother ships of the immune system, latching on to and invading the white blood cells that co-ordinate immune response.

Protozoa
This class of organism abound in water and soil and are essential in the food chain, breaking down biomatter and acting as a predator for bacteria.

Carcinoma in the brain
About 25% of metastatic cancers spread to the brain. Many benign brain tumours can lie low for years without being detected.

First contact
Macrophage latching on to a microbe.

Macrophage
These are the battlestars of the immune system – large, slow but deadly effective. It is the macro-phage that actually 'eats' the bacteria and alerts the rest of the immune system that there is an invasion under way.

Processing
Macrophage then digests microbe while loading new microbe antigens onto its surface.

Blueprints
DNA and the human code-breakers

Within nearly all of our cells there is the basic blueprint of who we are; within each cell nucleus there are 23 pairs of chromosomes, each one a tightly packed strand of DNA – the fundamental language of life on Earth. And since it is found in the cell nucleus, DNA is called a nucleic acid.

All organisms, from bacteria and amoeba to whales and redwoods, are designed from the blueprints held within the DNA of their chromosomes. Yet there seems little to account for the number of chromosomes in the cellular nucleus of each species: a moth has 62, for example, a crab 6, a mouse 48, a tomato 24 and barley 14.

DISTINGUISHING CHARACTERISTICS
What distinguishes the DNA in cellular organisms such as bacteria or baboons from that in viruses is that cellular organisms can reproduce. Viruses survive and reproduce by hacking into other cells and hitching a ride on their reproductive processes. Cellular organisms reproduce by unwinding their DNA and having the separate strands generate new partners. The blueprint in DNA (the designer molecules) is translated by RNA (translator molecules), assisted by enzymes (worker molecules). Each type of cell makes only the proteins that its part of the body needs. As these cells reproduce, they make very occasional mistakes, so giving rise to mutations. It is the evolutionary value of random mutations achieving dominance through natural selection that is at the basis of Darwinism. And yet the dialogue of how we came to be here, and exactly how we came to be as we are, continues.

In addition to natural mutation we have the gene-splicing activities of viruses as well as the chaos of combining two different sets of chromosomes from each of our parents. As our parents' genetic material combines, certain hereditary traits manifest as dominant (freckles, say), while others are recessive (such as baldness). The intricacy of inheritance arises from complex interactions of dominant and recessive genes as well as the effect of other genes and the environment. This can range from unimportant variances such as the colour of hair to crucial differences that determine survival or threaten our lives.

OUR GENETIC FUTURE
Genetic medicine is the quest to use the library of our biological blueprints to decode the challenges that arise from genetic traits. Gene therapy already exists for conditions such as cystic fibrosis, where viruses are used to splice missing genes into affected chromosomes. Research is currently exploding as we search for new possibilities in what can be achieved by inducing random mutations in DNA and seeing what we get.

As this quest continues, we are presented with many ethical challenges. There are equally graphic dreams and nightmares that could arise for us as a result of the gene pool being unlocked. The dreams invite us to a world where we are able to eradicate disease and suffering and where we can choose the characteristics of our children. The nightmares feature an unzipping of the DNA helix in ways that mean we might not be able to put it back together again, leading to a cascading genetic chaos that could result in a melt-down for DNA-based life.

Just as there are two spiralling strands to DNA, so there seem to be two themes to its exploration. On the surface, it appears as though we are choosing to dissect our genetic blueprints so that they can be manipulated through modification. Such an approach can tend to mechanize medicine and isolate each person within his or her own distinct ecosystem. But alongside there is an equally explorative strand to genetic research that is less inclined to unpick the component blocks of life, but as it maps them, it seeks how to manage, optimize and blend with the natural processes of evolution. Some the questions asked within this strand involve understanding how certain genes are activated by environmental factors, how conscious choices regarding lifestyle and education can co-create with the natural development of genetic evolution. It is clear that at a basic level, genetic material is merely a predisposition to either disease processes or traits of genius, and that our developmental environment provides the activation of that potential.

JUNK DNA AND DARWIN'S RADIO

Just as the Human Genome Project has mapped the sequencing of our DNA, other scientists have been hunting around the 'junkyard', seeing if anything can be made of the rest of the code.

While not all of the sequences in any DNA strand might be meaningful, it may be that the junk DNA largely discarded by the momentum of genetic medicine does have some role. Some suspect it of containing sequences that modify the actions of other genes. It may be the scars of viral battles fought and won (or lost). The human viruses have been shown to be associated with the transfer of genetic material from animals (smallpox from cattle or flu from pigs or, more recently, birds). But it may be that viruses are not just bringers of death and ill-health, but also trade genetic information between their hosts.

Novelist Greg Bear has suggested that the dynamic between DNA and viruses is the evolutionary operation of 'Darwin's Radio' itself – where junk DNA is 'woken up' by viruses that may cause disease and malformation, but also, crucially, may also cause spontaneous and vast jumps in the genetic coding of human beings. And there is a seeming infinity of perspectives on this interrelationship between us and our world.

Shamanic traditions almost universally engage with the spirits of the environment, including those of plants and animals. Jeremy Narby suggests it may be that these alliances with DNA's wider family enable an activation of some areas of our own junk DNA, yielding not only abilities beyond the usual range of activated DNA within humans, but also a more deeply activated emotional connection with other forms of life. If DNA had any intelligence at all, surely it would look something like this.

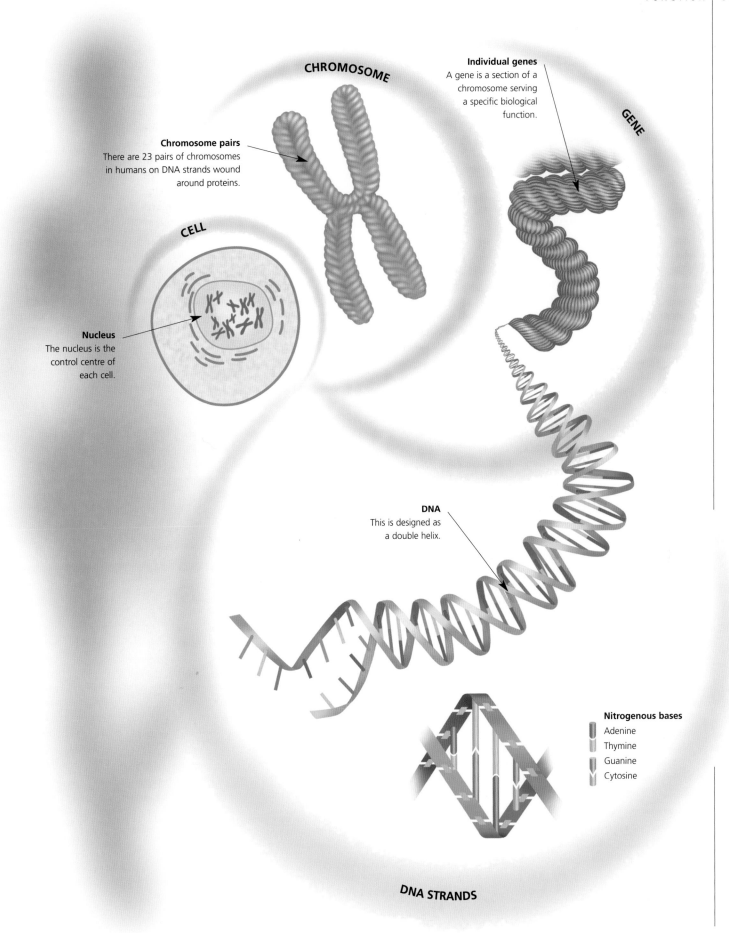

CHROMOSOME

Individual genes
A gene is a section of a chromosome serving a specific biological function.

GENE

Chromosome pairs
There are 23 pairs of chromosomes in humans on DNA strands wound around proteins.

CELL

Nucleus
The nucleus is the control centre of each cell.

DNA
This is designed as a double helix.

Nitrogenous bases
Adenine
Thymine
Guanine
Cytosine

DNA STRANDS

Nutrients
the vitality of food

Nutrients follow a complex process of identification, ingestion and absorption as they make their way into our internal environment. The first stage is the dynamic of taste and cognition that should provide us with the nutrients we need. There is, however, a world of difference between choosing our diet prompted by a sense of nutritional need and choosing it from, say, a sugar craving.

GENETIC MEMORY
We are designed to be browsers, sampling a wide range of foods to minimize exposure to any one toxin, and maximize the harvesting of as many nutrients as possible. The scarcity and nutritional benefits of sugar, salt and fat within our young species' environment meant they were rich prizes, and so highly valued by our taste mechanisms. Equally, the aversion of most children to green vegetables is likely to arise from that time of early childhood from when the bitterness of toxic plants is still retained in our evolutionary memory.

The question of whether we now succumb to such evolutionary biddings is unfolded in part by our cognitive skills. So, nutritional analysis of foods together with knowledge of any toxins added during the food's production or preservation contributes to our judgement as to whether or not to eat it.

When we look at the electrochemical functioning of the brain, our habits of behaviour, thought and appetite create their own 'grooves' within the brain – the more we do something, the more we get used to doing it and recognize it as part of who we are. Some grooves are so overpowering that they are able to exert a greater influence over our cognitive centres regardless of whether they are beneficial for us or not.

FOOD GROUPS
Despite the complex and perhaps confused mechanisms of our appetites, the human body has certain basic requirements for its optimal maintenance. We need, for example, enough minerals and vitamins to moderate our biochemical processes and the energy (as calories) to fuel us. Calories can be had from a wide range of foods, and the diversity of cultural preferences and corresponding levels of health are helping us decode the myth of an 'ideal' diet.

Certain constants apply to us all, however, as we need sufficient protein to repair and build tissue, carbohydrates for energy, fibre to ease the digestive process and vitamins and minerals for biochemical reactions. Fats are needed only in small quantities, offering a concentrated form of energy, while simple sugars are not actually necessary.

Globally, health problems arise from nutrition either due to deficiency or excess in any one major food group. Obesity, for example, occurs when there is an energy input/output imbalance, where too many calories are ingested for what is needed.

There is an added question in nutrition: are seemingly identical molecules of various nutrients truly identical in their effect according to their origin? Is it true, for instance, that a synthetically produced and intensively farmed vitamin ingested via an artificial supplement has the same nutritional value as one that was ingested via an organically grown vegetable?

Qualifications as to the benefits of our food from this perspective do not just stray into the toxicology analysis of nutrients, but involve an ecological awareness of how the harvesting of that nutrient affected the wider ecosystem. As such, each meal that we eat has a wider impact on the planet ranging from the relative harmony of farming methods to the human impact of the fairness of trade. The context of a product's cultivation, harvesting and trade forms a profile within the overall energetic network of the planet, and every act of consumption is reinforcing that profile, so that eating becomes both a spiritual and political act.

KINESIOLOGY

Kinesiology is literally all about the practical knowledge of movement. Aristotle and Leonardo da Vinci were past masters of the mechanics of human movement, our physical logistics. But the scope of this field of study substantially expanded with the work of American Chiropractor George Goodheart in the 1960s.

Dr Goodheart combined his observations of patients' muscle weaknesses with a wide range of possible causes of disease and developed a diagnostic system of 'muscle testing' that essentially asks questions of the body.

What is now known as 'kinesiology' – and there are many schools of thought and practice – is essentially a form of body dowsing. Dowsing is a 'way of finding out' that has been used for centuries to discern the courses of underground streams, the trackways of ley lines as well as the relative strength or otherwise of the body's subtle energies. Many water dowsers have traditionally used forked sticks to focus a perception of their own body's sensitivity. One of the most common contemporary methods is a pendulum (usually made from crystal or wood), the speed and direction of rotation of which will indicate the layout of the energetic field being researched.

More recent developments in kinesiology use just the practitioner's fingers to determine the course and/or rightness of a particular energy signature. One of its principal benefits is determining food allergies beyond the biochemical and exclusion-diet route of identifying problematic food combinations. In this way, the relative appropriateness of a particular food substance can be tested alongside the array of energetic and nutritional needs we might have, and in this way help narrow down specific substances that could cause problems without needing to cut out whole classes of foods. While kinesiology is a modern formulation of theory and practice, its essential skill is shared in other traditions, with some chi kung masters able to point their finger at a particular food or drink to determine its suitability for their system at that particular time.

KREB'S CYCLE

This is the end-point of all energy transfers within the body. It is the meeting of breath and food – key components of our day-to-day sustenance. In Chinese medicine, these are classified together as 'post-heavenly chi', distinguishing it from the finite amount of 'pre-heavenly chi' that we inherit from our parents in the form of our basic constitution. This bio-chemical meeting-point of breath and food takes place within each and every cell, as oxygen helps liberate the energy stored in ATP (adenosine triphosphate), the final refinement of our food's power.

Fats, proteins and carbohydrates all take their own route through our digestive processes. Carbo-hydrates (complex sugars) are broken down into simple sugars, and then to enzymes (protein catalysers). Fats also reduce to enzymes, while proteins are broken down into their constituent amino acids and then cleaned up by the liver before entering Kreb's cycle. Kreb's cycle is the final chemical adjustment of both amino acids and enzymes so that they might yield ATP.

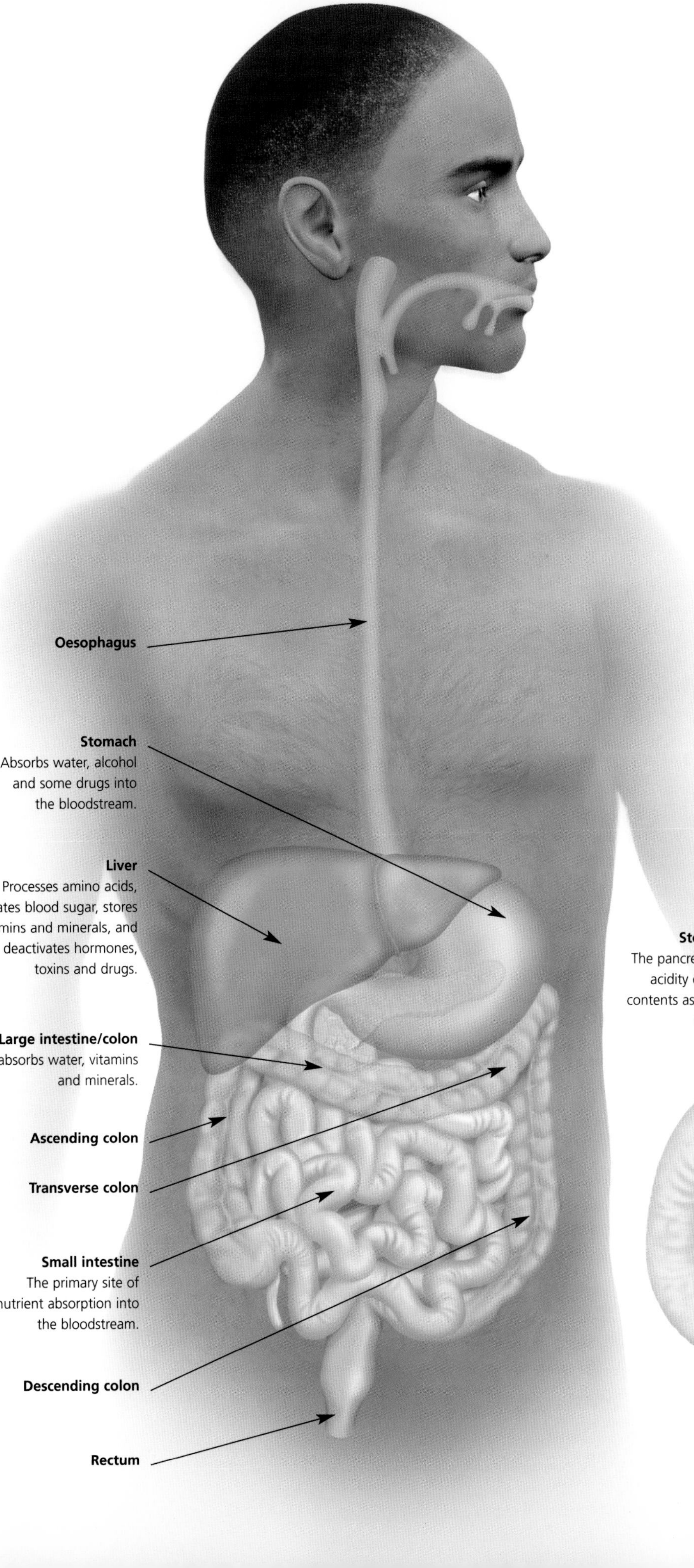

Oesophagus

Stomach
Absorbs water, alcohol and some drugs into the bloodstream.

Liver
Processes amino acids, regulates blood sugar, stores vitamins and minerals, and deactivates hormones, toxins and drugs.

Large intestine/colon
Reabsorbs water, vitamins and minerals.

Ascending colon

Transverse colon

Small intestine
The primary site of nutrient absorption into the bloodstream.

Descending colon

Rectum

Stomach acidity
The pancreas reduces the acidity of the stomach contents as they enter the small intestine.

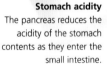

PANCREAS

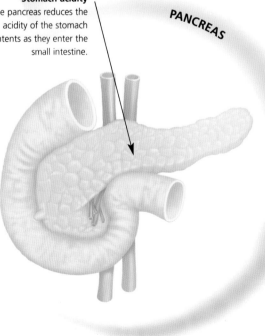

Drugs
our biochemical balance

Just as soon as we began to refine our choice of the foods that fed us, so, too, did we develop an understanding of which foods were able to heal us. Throughout the ancient world, trade routes exchanged Egyptian, Greek, Arabian and Chinese cures. As much as this wisdom was shared, the vast wealth of herbal medicine remained local, with the benefits of a particular root or leaf remaining within the ecosystem within which it grew. But not all drugs are derivatives of plants; others are micro-organisms, such as penicillin, and biological spies, such as vaccines.

ANTIBIOTICS AND VACCINES

The use of antibiotics came from the folk knowledge that mouldy bread keeps cuts clean. While Louis Pasteur in the 1870s and Alexander Fleming in the 1920s contributed to its development, penicillin (the first antibiotic) was not widely used until the 1940s when Howard Florey was able to produce and test it in time to treat wounded soldiers during World War II. Penicillin was then able to counter a range of bacteria, including pneumonia, anthrax, tetanus and syphilis.

Vaccines came online about a decade later, during the 1950s, with polio vaccine being the first to be used. Debate raged then about whether 'live' or 'dead' vaccine should be used to prime the body for a future viral attack, and while the range of vaccines has dramatically increased since their inception, debate still continues about their potentially harmful side-effects.

MODERN MEDICINE AND DRUG USAGE

The systematic development of medicines and drugs didn't begin in earnest until the beginning of the 20th century, when chemical compounds were able to be synthesized and their reproducible quality relied on. The practical wisdom of herbalists who prepared their own remedies was generally replaced by the requirements of mass production. Chemical analysis and marketing became key components of the new medicine chest, pushing aside the concerns of folk medicine, such as the relationship with the patient.

Having been through a period of development when the magic pill was the holy grail of medicine, we are now entering a new phase of asking how these pills might be best used and applied to optimize our functioning as part of the wider context of what makes us well. Just as the willow tree gave us aspirin and allowed us to reduce fever, we are now asking when it is best to use it, or when fever is helpful and healthy and when it is dangerous.

The evolutionist physicians Randolph Nesse and George Williams have suggested that our responses to the symptoms of illness might be analysed by asking whether those symptoms serve the host or the invading pathogen. In the common cold, a slightly raised fever is beneficial in making our internal environment less comfortable for the attacking virus, while profuse sneezing only serves to further circulate the virus.

Medications today are classified in many ways. From a social and legal perspective, we might consider which are prescribed by licenced physicians, those on which there are no legal controls and those that are traded illegally.

Just as drugs are able to heal and harm, they have enraptured us with their powerful emotional effects. Drug addiction is a global problem, ranging from sugar and caffeine cravings to the chemical bondage of opiates and alcohol. American researcher and writer Ralph Metzner has noted that 'it is vital to distinguish between the consciousness-contracting, anti-social nature of addictive drugs and the consciousness-expanding, psychotherapeutic nature of psychedelics and hallucinogens'.

What users of psychedelics often forget is that our folk wisdom of hallucinogens includes the strict diets and ceremonial disciplines that enable us to ride the biochemical revolution such plants offer. As we continue to develop our awareness of the internal biochemical environment, perhaps we will begin to include in our prescriptions the subtle but essential information of how to take drugs and medicines, and how we can optimize their use by conscious choices of lifestyle and intention.

THE COSMIC SERPENT

Ayahuasca Vine

While many herbalists and ethno-botanists explore the diverse benefits of plants on both health and consciousness, the Canadian-Swiss anthropologist Jeremy Narby took his immersion into the plant world one stage further.

Living in the Peruvian Amazon in the 1980s, Narby encountered the psychotropic vine called ayahuasca, a sacrament of the Ashaninca Indians. Psychotropic plants have long been known to both challenge and expand the consciousness of those taking them. What was groundbreaking in Narby's journey, however, was the realization that the visions (what the Ashaninca called 'forest television') were a means by which the vine (and the Earth) could communicate with us.

In his visions, Narby came face to face with the huge snakes of the spirit of ayahuasca (which he equated with the global 'cosmic serpent' known by other civilizations) and began to realize that there is a relationship between these beings, the spirit of the Earth and the DNA of all life.

His previous questions regarding how the Ashanincas had come to realize which medicinal plants were appropriate for which conditions were cast in a new light as he considered the possibility that the plant itself possessed a consciousness that was communicating to them.

Antidepressants
Generally work by raising the level of
excitatory neurotransmitters.

Antipsychotics
Recalibrate the brain's receptivity
to itself.

Bronchodilators
Forcibly relax the musculature inside
the lungs in order to widen the airways
during asthma.

Anticancer drugs
Seek to interrupt the growth of cancerous
cells by damaging their nuclei, blocking
their source of nutrients, or controlling the
hormones stimulating their growth.

Beta blockers
Cancel out some of the action of the 'fight-
or-flight' impulse generated by the adrenal
glands, sometimes helpful in angina and
high blood pressure.

Antacids
Help neutralize stomach acids.

Diuretics
Adjust the reabsorption of sodium and
water into the blood as it flows through
the kidneys, increasing urine production
and lowering blood pressure.

Antibiotics
Attack bacteria colonies
that cause disease.

Hormones
Used to remedy the deficiency or excess
of the endocrine system's regulation
of essential body functions.

Fertility drugs
Stimulate the pituitary gland in its
production of follicle stimulating
hormone, which will encourage
ovulation or sperm production.

Antihistamines
Suppress the body's natural sensitivity
to allergens, preventing the inflammation
of the sensitive area.

Antivirals
Used to combat persistent viruses
by invading the cell of the virus and
stopping it reproducing.

Anticonvulsants
Slow down the electrical cascades that
happen during fits and seizures.

Vaccines
Prime the immune system to promote its
own defenses in the form of antibodies
to combat viruses.

Digitalis
Slows down the electrical impulses flowing
through the heart when its beat is irregular
or too fast.

Muscle relaxants
Suppress the brain's instructions to
muscles to contract.

NSAIDs
(Non-steroidal Anti-inflammatory Drugs)
Block instinctive promotion of inflammation
at site of injury.

Immunosuppressants
Dampen the immune system when it
is attacking normal body tissue.

Corticosteroids
Block instinctive promotion of
inflammation at site of injury and
suppress white blood cells.

Vasodilators
Relax the muscles within the walls of
blood vessels, allowing more blood to
flow through.

Analgesics
Pain killers that generally work through
reducing pain at the site of inflammation.

Metabolism
gearshifts of body regulation

Most life on the planet is dependent on the sun for energy. Plants derive this from sunlight through photosynthesis, during which chlorophyll uses sunlight to transform carbon dioxide and water into more complex molecular structures. Humans, however, lack the capacity to photosynthesize. Instead, we harvest the sun's energy through eating the already synthesized molecules in plants and, for some, animals.

Metabolism is the process of chemical change within who we are, overseeing both the intake and release of solar energy. It is the construction of new chemicals and tissues to maintain the body and their corresponding destruction so that their components may be recycled. Metabolism is the rate of our decanting or the laying down of these complex internal chemistries.

The building phase of chemical change within us is called anabolism. This is the synthesis of larger, more complex molecules – for example, the making of proteins by joining amino acids and then, in turn, combining those proteins to make muscle and bone. Catabolism, however, involves the breaking down of larger molecules derived from food so that the energy in them can be released in the body at the site of need.

Once food has been broken down into its various nutrients, these energy sources can be used immediately to build new tissues or stored as ATP. Carbohydrates, fats and proteins each have their own pathways of conversion, but its fundamental nature, while still holding some surprises, is the basis of our relationship with food.

BODY WEIGHT
While our intake of food and water will vary from day to day, our body weight tends not to respond immediately. Regulation of body weight is not well understood and our best efforts at this involve a cocktail of probable factors. The most obvious and direct links are with our levels of energy intake and expenditure, principally as food consumption and exercise. These processes are different for us all and this is the variance that we often call our metabolism, referring to the kind of gearbox that we have and the efficiency with which we burn fuel. Correspondingly, those who do not put on weight while eating

heartily are often referred to as having a fast metabolism, while those who do, even if they eat moderately, a slow metabolism.

THE EATING IMPULSE
We are not in a position to decode the exact processes by which we feel hunger and decide to eat. Principally, the hypothalamus at the core of the brain is our regulator of hunger. Part of the hypothalamus is constantly primed to urge us to eat (see opposite). This abates only when overridden by the 'satiety centre' in the ventromedial hypothalamic nuclei.

In mediating between this perpetual neurological hunger and the times of respite, the hypothalamus is informed by receptors monitoring odours, tastes, chemicals and the elasticity of the stomach and intestines (how 'full' they are), as well as receptors related to light (the time of day).

In terms of our external environment, warmer conditions tend to inhibit hunger while cold ones stimulate food intake. This is because if it is cold, the body generally needs to consume more energy in heating itself, and this it will do most effectively through food consumption.

Regulation of body temperature is also achieved by part of the hypothalamus – the Pre-optic area, our internal thermostat that triggers appropriate responses. In particular, the hypothalamus triggers the adrenal medulla to release adrenaline, which increases the rate at which our cells burn energy. Body heat rising above our normal range is a fever, which is usually beneficial for short periods as it assists our immune system to destroy invading pathogens. Prolonged or excessive fever can be just as dangerous as prolonged cold (hypothermia).

Metabolic rate is the rate of our energy consumption. It is recorded in relation to our height and weight, being proportional to the size of the body in terms of how much fuel is required to maintain a certain size of body. Metabolic rate varies according to age and gender, though should it stray beyond certain tolerances, warning bells may ring in terms of the health of our thyroid gland.

HUMAN PHOTOSYNTHESIS?

Sunrise and sunset – key times for holding 'greeting the sun' ceremonies

Many cultures have practised sun-gazing for millennia. In addition to the practical effects of the sun on life on the planet, we have also courted its rays to promote health and raise consciousness. While regular and moderate exposure to the sun builds a level of resistance in lighter-skinned humans, purposeful 'sunbathing' is increasingly causing skin damage.

Gazing at the sun causes eye damage, so sun-gazers have tended to use the few minutes immediately after sunrise and before sunset to look on the sun directly. In some Native American traditions, the ceremony of 'greeting the sun' uses the hands to frame the sun in one's own energy. For Taoists, there is often the guidance to wait until the sun has fully crested the horizon before beginning one's meditation. Sun-gazing as a meditation practice has been taught for more than 2,000 years by the Jains, an Indian spiritual tradition that emerged in the 6th century BCE. Essentially, Jainism is a non-violent and ascetic tradition that seeks to liberate us from the cycles of karma through non-violence, charity, retreat and fasting. Its wisdom concerning surya (sun) yoga includes facing the sun and standing on the earth in bare feet as it rises.

Hira Ratan Manek, an Indian engineer living in the US, not only practices sun-gazing, but also connects its benefits to prolonged periods of fasting. He speaks of 'human photosynthesis', relying on sunlight and water alone for energy.

Whether the rest of us could adopt the methods of such sun-gazers, the principles remain true – a more conscious absorption of sunlight and oxygen can and does affect health and, in particular, our individual metabolism.

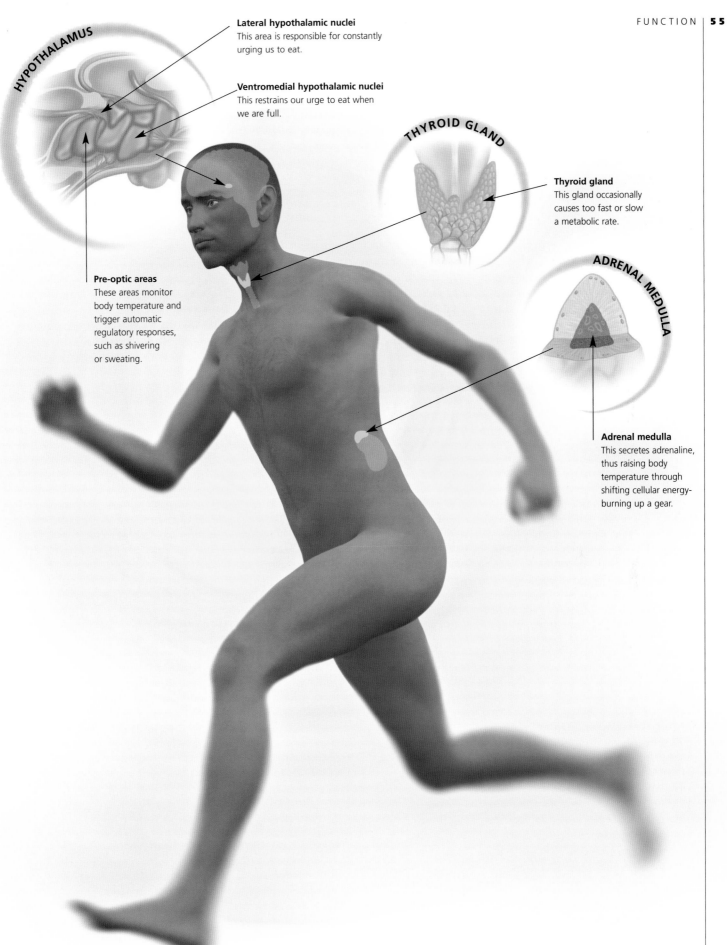

HYPOTHALAMUS

Lateral hypothalamic nuclei
This area is responsible for constantly urging us to eat.

Ventromedial hypothalamic nuclei
This restrains our urge to eat when we are full.

THYROID GLAND

Thyroid gland
This gland occasionally causes too fast or slow a metabolic rate.

Pre-optic areas
These areas monitor body temperature and trigger automatic regulatory responses, such as shivering or sweating.

ADRENAL MEDULLA

Adrenal medulla
This secretes adrenaline, thus raising body temperature through shifting cellular energy-burning up a gear.

Reproduction

perpetuation of the species

The delicately balanced ecosystem of our planet can be viewed from any number of perspectives, placing at the centre of the equation any one species or life-cycle. In this way, bacteria may be viewed as the initial origin of life that humans now have to manage as we find our way through the edges of our solar system. Equally, humans may be viewed as complex but nevertheless manageable hosts for the needs of bacteria.

As all lifeforms adapt and develop within this environment, their interactions can be seen as much as a biological arms race as they can a co-creative exchange of genetic information, DNA's own dialogue with itself. Sexual reproduction is the primary means of this dialogue, as it yields offspring that are genetically different from their parents. Most importantly, however, it does this with a random creativity.

ASPECTS OF REPRODUCTION

Apart from rare, perhaps even mythological, exceptions such as parthenogenesis (virgin births), the process of human reproduction is achieved through sexual intercourse. The relative success of reproduction depends on a number of factors, including the overall health of the parents, the vibrancy of the gametes (egg and sperm) themselves and the success of the sperm in finding its way to the uterus and avoiding the spermicidal secretions of the vagina.

It is a strange aspect of our reproduction that committed partners can be less likely to conceive than spontaneous sexual meetings due to the natural spermicidal aspects of vaginal secretions, which become accustomed to a particular partner's sperm while having fewer defences against a new variety.

Such aspects of our reproductive processes can be uncomfortable from a social and interpersonal perspective, and in this way many of our customs to do with repro-duction seem to be heavy-handed attempts to manage the biological urges to create new life as well as mediate between the varying psychological needs of men and women as they bring up children.

All species that use sexual reproduction vary in the timing of their sexual maturity and their number of offspring. Such equations of evolution reflect the basic environment of a species and the cusp of any evolutionary challenges. For humans, the size of the infant's head at birth and the aperture of the mother's pelvic girdle reflect the limits of our current evolutionary status quo.

ETHICAL CONCERNS

Just as insights into reproductive health are helping us understand more about how we can manage menstrual cycles, pregnancy and childbirth, as well as sexually transmitted diseases, so, too, are we wrestling with the ethical boundaries of our science. The advent of cloning animals, while still fraught with problems, is inviting some to consider what implications asexual reproduction might have for humans. The selection of fertilized eggs for those who will come to full term is beginning to be used to select for gender, with other 'traits' not far behind.

Where we go from here is uncertain. There might seem an inevitability to such exploration, but the extent to which research meets the needs of the population of the planet as a whole is questionable. Some commentators suggest that our declining fertility is not only due to increased chemical toxins in the environment, but is also a natural regulatory function of the planetary ecosystem as a whole.

Globally, we still debate the meaning of decadence and freedom, repression and right living. Such a multitude of perspectives will continue to be heard, while we get on with the job of perpetuating our species, asking questions of ourselves about how best to do this, how best to cultivate our young.

A DIALOGUE OF SOULS

How to manage reproduction has challenged most cultures, with complex and stringent rules being developed for who is allowed to mate with who. From the inter-tribal rivalry of Shakespeare's insightful *Romeo and Juliet* to the common injunction not to marry beyond your race, such cohesive social forces are often overridden by life's desire for diversification.

At one level, the whole area of reproduction, from love and sex to courtship and parenting, could be seen as an elaborate drama to cultivate the best environment for offspring. Perhaps our so dearly held views about child-rearing are nothing more than genetic impulses.

For many cultures there has always been the perspective that children were a gift rather than a right, and while such feelings may have little currency in our current culture, perhaps the wildcard nature of the goddess's gift echoes the essential randomness of reproduction. For those parents who do invite rather than command, such a conscious moulding of the family will affect both them and the child, and in the event of the grief of not having children, leave the potency of life's mystery intact.

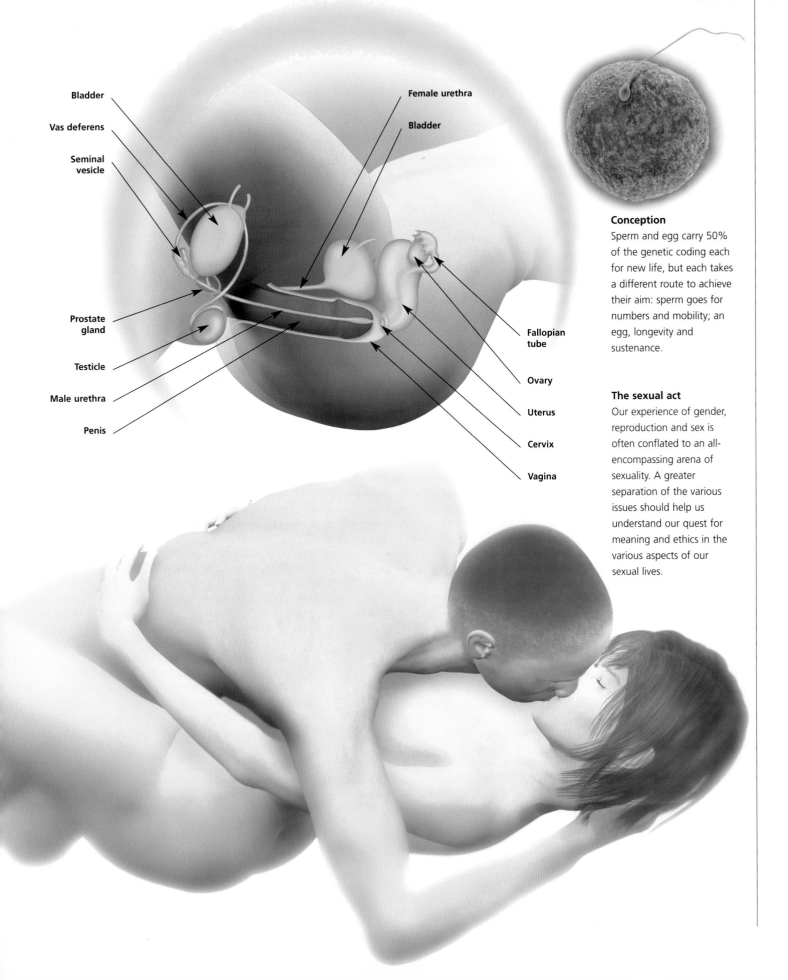

Bladder

Vas deferens

Seminal vesicle

Prostate gland

Testicle

Male urethra

Penis

Female urethra

Bladder

Fallopian tube

Ovary

Uterus

Cervix

Vagina

Conception

Sperm and egg carry 50% of the genetic coding each for new life, but each takes a different route to achieve their aim: sperm goes for numbers and mobility; an egg, longevity and sustenance.

The sexual act

Our experience of gender, reproduction and sex is often conflated to an all-encompassing arena of sexuality. A greater separation of the various issues should help us understand our quest for meaning and ethics in the various aspects of our sexual lives.

Death
turning out the lights

In time's desert I feel your presence.
In the rock's silence I hear your footstep.
Emotion overcomes me.
Then, like a sudden downpour
Fear of death startles me.
Abd Al-Sabour

Death exists only in relation to life, denoting a state of being for entities that once were alive and whose integrity as distinct organisms has passed away and cannot be reformed. And yet even in relation to life we make the distinctions of consciousness and 'non-sentient' beings, as if they have no identifiable way of perceiving the world, no power of action upon the world, no chemical potency.

Life is also distinguished in relationship to the distinct organism that held the virtue of life, so even though the bacteria in our intestines might live on in the ground and our genepool might live on in our offspring, 'we' are generally considered to be dead once our body has ceased walking and talking for good. And while we once placed the boundary of death at the door of breath and heartbeat, medical technology has now moved our final countdown to the presence of electrical activity in the brain.

RITUALS AND MYSTERIES

Just as we have developed a vast array of rituals that oversee our transition into death, so we have many understandings of what happens in that process. It is only relatively recently in our histories that we considered death to be an end and there to be no continued existence beyond memories of us in the world. Most people have an expectation of some type of after-life, where the selfhood of the person, the soul, finds a continued existence. Such realms usually involve a supramaterial reality, such as the heaven and hell of Christianity, or a recycling of the soul in the reincarnation of Hinduism. Most cultures also have specific bodies of wisdom relating to how we die, from the Egyptian and Tibetan *Book of the Dead* to the *Ars Moriendi* (*Art of Dying*) of 15th-century Christian Europe. Of concern are not only our processes and customs this side of the curtain of bodily death, but also,

often, a roadmap for the soul as it attempts to navigate a post-bodily existence.

Biological organisms at all levels of complexity, from amoebas to human beings, engage in photon-exchange within a sea of light that enables them not only to regulate their own wavelength integrity, but also to communicate with others. It has been suggested that this is how schools of fish are able to move in synchrony as well as being the basis for human intelligence.

As we will later (see pages 82–95), multi-dimensional lightwaves may prove to be the basis for both consciousness and life, carrying data and vitality, reflections of each other within the electro-chemical bedrock of our bodies. In her 2001 book *The Field*, Lynne McTaggart presents a synthesis of cutting-edge quantum science from researchers such as Fritz-Albert Popp, who have: 'developed a way to identify carcinogens through their property of scrambling the frequency of UV light as it was passed through them. This discovery prompted him to analyse the light emissions that all living organisms give off and to identify that most of our light is both stored and shone by our DNA.'

So perhaps we have come full circle. If we consider the possibility that the wavefields once held within the structure of the body continue to flow and grow within a wider fabric of consciousness (including the connections that an organism has made within its lifespan to surrounding fellow wavefields), then perhaps it might be true that the memories of us held by the world are a factor within our new body. Certainly for Egyptian pharaohs, the perpetuation of their names through prolific architectural monuments was believed to add fuel to the journeys of their spirit.

LIVING AFTER DEATH

Certain shamanic traditions describe the intended progression of consciousness through life as a series of deaths. These are life experiences where bodily death does not occur, but the personality and consciousness goes through such a powerful upheaval that it feels as though part of the self has died.

These 'deaths' can involve either great suffering or great enjoyment. What is significant is that they transform the sense of self to such a degree that we are fundamentally changed by the experience. They can include marriage, divorce, childbirth, bereavement and redundancy as much as they can witnessing a sunset, an eclipse, a waterfall. What matters is that we are changed.

Such a process fundamentally teaches us how to adapt to changing circumstance, and to form within ourselves an identity that is characterized by our patterns of response to external stimuli, rather than any perceived attachment to those stimuli themselves. Each death releases us from the limitations of who we previously thought we were, strips away the assumptions and refines the patterns at the core of our self. Perhaps it is within the sustained continuity of such patterns and dimensions that we discover the mysteries of life and death, and the interregnum world of consciousness.

THE IMMORTAL *Where do all the waves go?*

Notwithstanding all the alchemical and shamanic techniques people attempt in order to navigate the gateway of death when it actually comes, at least an equal number of people strive after immortality. From the philosopher's stone of Western alchemy to the ambrosial elixirs of the Orient, each culture has identified the transformative power of miraculous objects, elixirs and meditative disciplines. Such dreams are perhaps equally viewed as symbolic and actual paths of development, although at some point the on-going research into holography may yet guide the art of dying, just as alchemical traditions may provide a few keys for the revelation of how we process, store and live within our sea of consciousness.

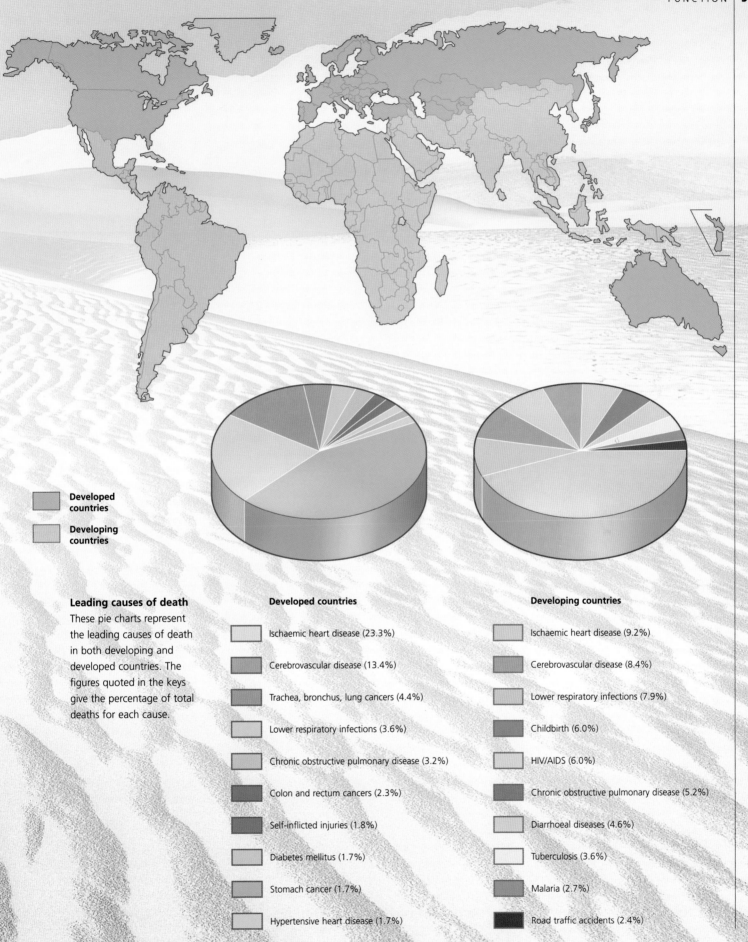

Developed countries

Developing countries

Leading causes of death
These pie charts represent the leading causes of death in both developing and developed countries. The figures quoted in the keys give the percentage of total deaths for each cause.

Developed countries

Ischaemic heart disease (23.3%)

Cerebrovascular disease (13.4%)

Trachea, bronchus, lung cancers (4.4%)

Lower respiratory infections (3.6%)

Chronic obstructive pulmonary disease (3.2%)

Colon and rectum cancers (2.3%)

Self-inflicted injuries (1.8%)

Diabetes mellitus (1.7%)

Stomach cancer (1.7%)

Hypertensive heart disease (1.7%)

Developing countries

Ischaemic heart disease (9.2%)

Cerebrovascular disease (8.4%)

Lower respiratory infections (7.9%)

Childbirth (6.0%)

HIV/AIDS (6.0%)

Chronic obstructive pulmonary disease (5.2%)

Diarrhoeal diseases (4.6%)

Tuberculosis (3.6%)

Malaria (2.7%)

Road traffic accidents (2.4%)

Freedom

Senses and consciousness

*Mankind is the only creature for whom
it is natural to be un-natural.*
Mike Fuller

As our lives take place within the context of extensions in space (our bodies) and time (their rhythms), so, too, do they exist in the present of the immediate moment, the eternal 'now' that is our consciousness of who we are, the 'I' that swims throughout these great currents of life.

In our contemporary world of analytical science, it is the discipline of psychology that devotes itself to exploring further this notion of identity and individual consciousness. But this is not merely a contemporary phenomenon or quest; the question of who 'I' am in relation to my experience and world has always tested us.

Each civilization has approached the quest in its own unique way, shaped by its geography, science and religion. For us as a species, however, there have been many focal moments of discovery that have shifted the direction of our reflections and changed the tenor of our experience. Events such as seeing images of the Earth from space, the atomic explosions of Hiroshima and Nagasaki, the great flood, the ice ages, the use of fire, all have moulded our lives in ways from which we have not looked back. As such leaps take place, many of our old certainties fall away and throughout history we have managed such shifts through stories about what such changes might mean. So we will tell each other tales of the beginning and the end of the world, of the creation and of the apocalypse, or of the great ages of time, aeons of the world's own transitions held by both myth and prophesy, history and hope.

One of the central questions of such stories has always been our relationship as a species with the creation and end of space and time itself, whether we are part of some great universal plan orchestrated by a supreme being or whether the miracle of our existence is the result of an endless, cosmic (probably comic) accident.

The question of the existence of any such supreme being or intelligence in the universe often polarizes us into 'Does he?/ Doesn't he?' perspectives, and for those of us who say 'Yes', then the argument is about who he or she is and what his or her pronouncements are for human life. But to approach such stories with a perspective of space, time and constructive doubt can cast us into the realm of co-creation, where we begin to see our questions as part of an ongoing adventure. And every sacred belief we might hold of who we are, where we have come from and where we are going is cast into the hall of mirrors that enclose our world. The mirrors are then turned outwards, to illuminate what we can of the worlds that we never thought possible.

This process happens as we turn our god, our atheism, our questions as well as our answers back into ourselves as part of the story we have at this time, and begin to see the shape that we make within the world, defined by this very dialogue. By negation, by looking at the questions that are then not asked, the strange and non-sensical worlds of impossibility and ridiculous imagination, we can take more active responsibility for what we know of the world and ourselves. Such a double vision need not mar the passion and depth with which we hold our positions, our dance with faith and belief. It may, rather, cast these deep perspectives of who we are into more of a continuum, a continuous dialogue between ourselves and the universe as to what on earth is going on.

Brain

our electrochemical hub

We are an intelligent species and the use of our intelligence quite properly gives us pleasure. In this respect the brain is like a muscle. When we think, we feel good. Understanding is a kind of ecstasy.
Carl Sagan

The brain accounts for 2 per cent of our body weight and floats in a cushioning bath of cerebrospinal fluid inside the skull. Inside this bony shell, it is further protected by the three meninges – sleeves made from collagen-based connective tissue. The brain itself is mostly nerves and the blood vessels that supply them.

OUR CEREBRAL LANDSCAPE

It is the nerve cell bodies (heads) of the brain, rather than the elongated fibres (tails), that reach down the spinal column and on to the rest of the body. These cell bodies are the 'little grey cells' making up the outer shell of the brain. This is the cerebrum, and is the arena of much of our consciousness and processing power, responsible for perception and action, reflection and creativity.

The lower down the brain we go, into the brain stem and spinal cord, the less conscious is the relay of neurological input and output. Many biofeedback techniques seek to increase conscious control over these regions, so extending the limits of what we can influence of our consciousness and biochemistry.

The brainstem comprises the midbrain, the pons and the medulla oblongata, which then merges with the spinal cord. Collectively, they are the relay station between left and right hemispheres, and between the brain and the spinal cord.

Between the cerebrum and brainstem lies the diencephalon, housing the interface of our electrical and chemical selves. Here, we have the control centre of the endocrine system; the hypothalamus, which, together with the pituitary and pineal glands, choreographs the seemingly indecipherable vortex of electrical and chemical signals regulating our consciousness and physiology.

An interruption of blood to the brain for even two minutes can cause brain damage. Because there is limited storage of carbohydrate in the brain, blood supply is crucial in supplying glucose to nourish the nerves as well as oxygen to help in the release of energy. Such supply is made more complicated by the intricacy of the blood–brain barrier. This is the result of the higher level of protection the brain receives, where the walls of the blood vessels supplying the brain have thinner filters and tighter junctions to remove large, potentially toxic molecules.

We are finding that the linear progress of information from nerve to nerve is not the whole story of consciousness. More and more neurotransmitters are being discovered that cascade through the crevices between

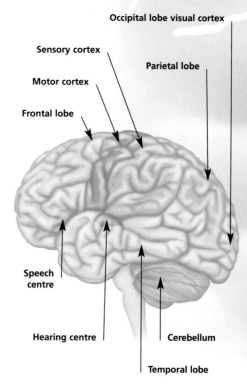

Occipital lobe visual cortex
Sensory cortex
Parietal lobe
Motor cortex
Frontal lobe
Speech centre
Hearing centre
Cerebellum
Temporal lobe

each cell throughout the body, finding the organs and systems where receptor cells eagerly take up their call to arms. Such discoveries are suggesting that we are soft-wired, that our emotions, regulated by the endocrine system and the rich cocktails of hormones that constantly stream through our systems, are actually responsive to conscious thought. We can literally decide how we are feeling.

That such a suggestion seems counter-intuitive is testament to the lack of volition we generally feel and a distinct immaturity with regard to our technologies of consciousness. Many forms of meditation are still viewed by science as mere superstition. We could, rather, choose to consider them as sophisticated methods of regulating the human organism that could dovetail with neuro-physiological research to yield positive results. This is happening in isolated islets of special interest, but it is not a strong current in how we choose to apportion our research funding and healthcare budgets.

ON HAVING NO HEAD OR ONLY A HEAD

The location of identity is something we explore overleaf, when we examine the notion of self, but the criteria for such an association can be cast between the opposing perspectives represented by Douglas Harding and Chet Fleming.

Douglas Harding is a British mystical teacher whose teachings most closely resemble those of Zen Buddhism. His 1961 book, *On Having No Head: Zen and the Rediscovery of the Obvious*, describes the paradoxical experience of living inside our own heads and not being able to perceive them, as they are in fact the agents of our perception. To reason subsequently for the existence of our head is to leave the potency of our perception of the immediate moment.

At the other end of the scale are the speculations of Chet Fleming, who, in 1989, patented the logistics of keeping a severed head alive. Motivated by ethical doubts regarding cryogenic research, he wanted to stall the development of any devices that might be able to achieve successful freezing of a head by imposing a legal hoop developers would need to jump through. However, many researchers now consider that it is merely a question of time before such devices come into production, and we encounter a very particular formulation of where we consider our consciousness to reside.

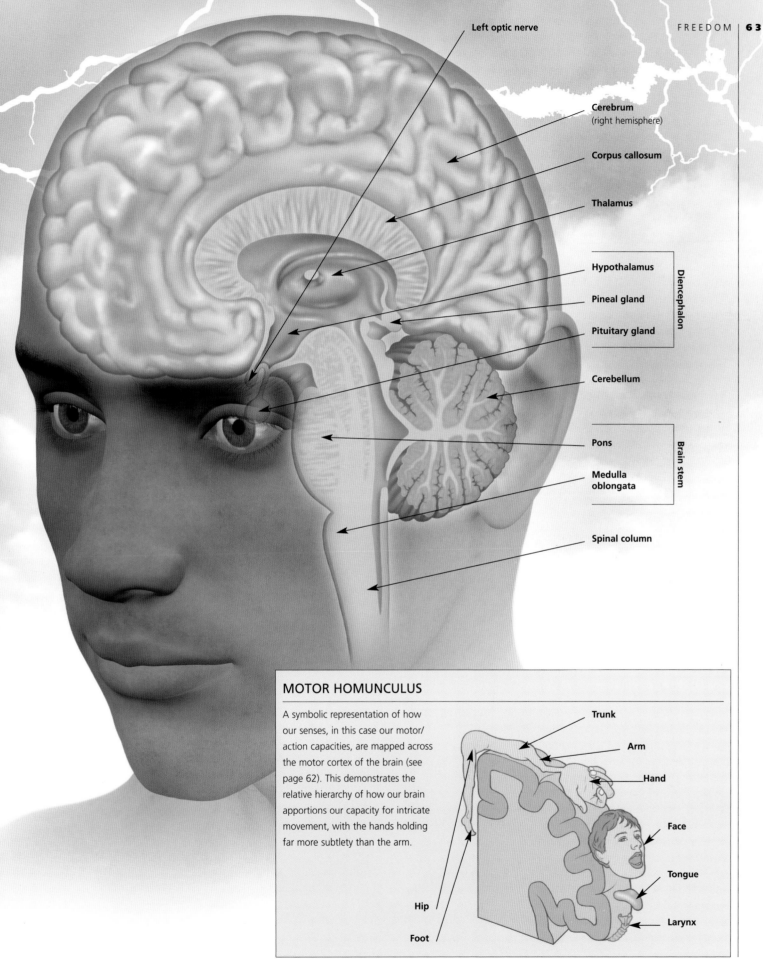

Left optic nerve

Cerebrum
(right hemisphere)

Corpus callosum

Thalamus

Hypothalamus

Pineal gland

Pituitary gland

Diencephalon

Cerebellum

Pons

Medulla
oblongata

Brain stem

Spinal column

MOTOR HOMUNCULUS

A symbolic representation of how
our senses, in this case our motor/
action capacities, are mapped across
the motor cortex of the brain (see
page 62). This demonstrates the
relative hierarchy of how our brain
apportions our capacity for intricate
movement, with the hands holding
far more subtlety than the arm.

Trunk

Arm

Hand

Face

Tongue

Larynx

Hip

Foot

Self

the location of identity

I have a body closely bound up with myself; but at the same time I have, on the one hand, a clear and distinct idea of myself taken simply as a conscious, not an extended, being; and, on the other hand, a distinct idea of body, taken simply as an extended, not a conscious, being; so it is certain that I am really distinct from my body, and could exist without it.

René Descartes

As civilizations and individuals develop, there is usually a point where we achieve a sense of self. This is the dawn of an independent consciousness separate from the stream of sensory data we experience. Along with the apex of this process is usually a deep bonding with a type of signifier that marks us out as separate. It might be symbolic (the totemic identity of the bear clan) or it might be linguistic (the conceptual notion of our individual name). Should there be a purely neurological basis for this sense of self, or whether it is immaterial and beyond physical existence, is a question that has concerned us for millennia.

Our ancestors have seen the self in a variety of guises: as part of an immaterial soul and independent from the body (Descartes said the bridge was the pineal gland, while Malebranche said the bridge was god); belonging to the physical body and having no other basis than the brain; belonging to an interregnum world that encompasses both what we know of as the physical body and the non-physical aspects of the soul.

WHERE AM I?

As we will see in the following chapters, there are various suggested 'locations' in the body that we might consider a 'dock' for the soul, spirit, or personal identity should we choose to cleave it from the body. Many tribal peoples consider the soul immanent within physical form, but might we fundamentally exist as an evolving pattern within the swirling chaos of creation rather than a distinct subject with substance?

A SENSE OF SELF

Varying world traditions have located aspects of the self within rather than beyond the body, generally holding the realms of spirit and matter as immanent. Given the cultural context of science, however, it is important to detail briefly the notion of self as it might apply to the physiology of the brain.

For some of us, our unique sense of self is marred by conditions such as personality disorders, autism, schizophrenia or substance abuse. Here, we might lack a recognition of a distinct self and a working insight into the effects that our uniqueness can have. Our contemporary wisdom suggests that such conditions are a varying mix of nature and nurture with, probably, other salient factors that we have hardly even guessed at. What such experience does show us, however, is that the self is something that can be crafted and cared for, that it develops rather than just pops into existence, but that it also has the raw material of memories and its own unique blueprint of being.

In psychological-attachment theory, children are understood to have much more of a permanent sense of self if they have bonded and attached strongly in early childhood. At an emotional level, this means a close relationship with a primary carer, preferably a nursing mother, and, as we then grow, being able to transfer such attachment to other definitions of 'our' world.

Given the dominance of our olfactory senses at this stage of development, attachment inevitably involves the limbic system, which mediates mood and, particularly, odour. Equally, though, perhaps the defining mode of consciousness that distinguishes our sense of self is that of perspective – being able to compare and contrast differing views we may take of our world and make decisions as to how we are going to interact with it. But perhaps the main cerebral factor in the construction of self is the frontal cortex. This part of the brain is most highly developed in humans compared with other animals, and governs a wide range of higher cognitive functions, but primarily a sense of the self in relationship to our environment.

These possibilities increase the more we consider that neurotransmitters, which are the messengers of consciousness, are not just limited to the functions of our brain but have an effect on the whole of the body. Each cell has a memory, an emotional state, and a blueprint of our basic coding as unique beings. Given such immanence of biochemical information, it is reasonable to assume that consciousness exists and permeates throughout the whole of the body, even though it is undeniable that the principal command post of consciousness is the brain.

DESCARTES

The distinction between mind and body, brain and self that still pervades much of Western culture in many ways evolves from René Descartes. But while Descartes' perception of the body and mind as distinct was a development of earlier Greek and Christian thinkers, it came at a time during the great materialist dawn of the 17th century when we began to see images of machines everywhere, even in the human body.

René Descartes recognized the importance of the pineal gland

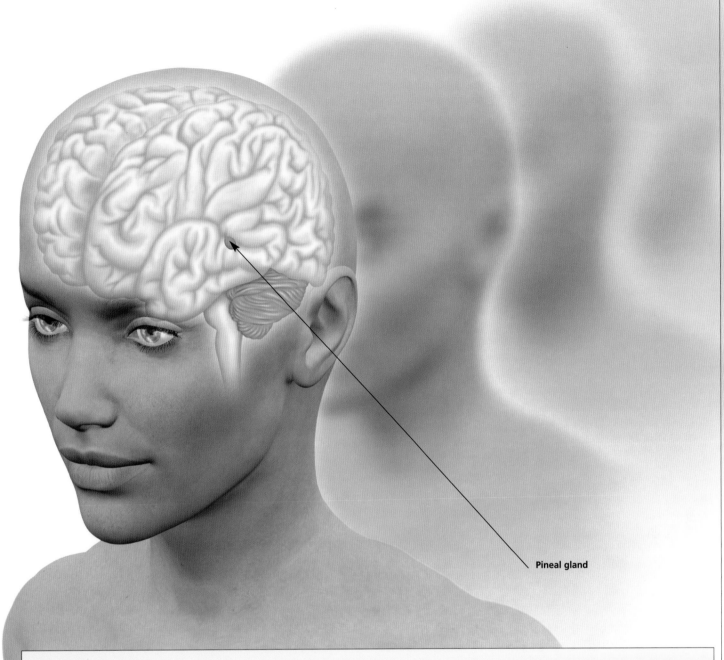

Pineal gland

WHO AM I?

Once people have asked the Flowering Tree questions for a period of time: who am I, where am I from, where am I going, what is my path with heart, they come to a place where the glamour of the answers begins to fade. Gone are the fabulous names of distant star systems; gone are the reincarnated avatars or wronged witches; gone too are the destinies of saving the Earth and single-handedly bringing about the redemption of the people. Once this place of normality has arrived, we are open to being taught, and to hearing how we truly are noble born of Earth and Star.

Arwyn DreamWalker

There is a range of responses to a question such as 'Who am I?' Depending on our culture, we use different symbols and markers to help other people 'locate' us and also to help ourselves remember who we are. Most spiritual traditions aim at stripping away these markers so that the pure awareness of consciousness, beyond even thought and perception, can find a home within us and we can include infinity within such an answer.

This is the potency of being that the Existentialist movement of the mid 20th century struggled with in its paucity of symbols and reference points. The practical goal of surfing such 'nothingness' in

relation to who we are is to wear such labels with a lightness, remembering this paradox of identity and the dangers of certainty.

To anchor any sense of self in opposition to the infinity of possible experience that greets us when we look beyond our own heads is to invite a closing down of possibility and wonder.

Mind
maps of thought

No, I don't believe in God, I know God.
Carl Jung

Descartes' separation of mind and body continued a tradition of dissociating the core of our consciousness from our physical form. The challenges, then, of how the two find an interface is a perpetual problem. But whether or not the nature of mind is in the end found to reduce to the patterns of neurological sequence dancing, or whether we do indeed find an ephemeral realm of mind is a question ultimately for ideological dualists.

We have been mapping the mind ever since we began to reflect on our varying natures. For some cultures, our own natures are inseparable from the outside world – are we Horse, Eagle or Bear clan? We use the symbology of our stories, environments and day-to-day life to map our natures and to try to understand them.

Increasingly over the last few centuries, however, there has been an attempt to classify more formally the structure of our minds and the varying ways in which we use them, while realizing that the Hindu, the Maya and Taoist have done just that for thousands of years.

FOUNDING FATHERS
In 1905, Freud was the first to coin the term 'psychoanalysis', and he is the father of much of what we know today as Western psychology. One of Freud's great gifts was being able to share the blessings of Jewish culture's emphasis on talking with each other with a 20th-century Western world that had almost forgotten how to do this. He certainly formalized his observations in a richly sophisticated way, but also remained held within his time.

The other great innovator of mind at the beginning of the 20th century was Carl Jung, who not only developed Freud's ideas, but also integrated some of the wisdom and insights of other world traditions. Jung was the first to use the term 'archetype' and also took our knowledge of the collective unconscious to a more holistic and positive level.

Today, psychoanalysis typically allows far more intervention than psychotherapy, and both tend to emerge from the work of Freud and Jung. Counselling is much more widely applied and as a profession demands less training and is more neutral in its interventions. Each enjoys the fertility of sustained and head-on battles between different schools, but this sphere of human interaction and knowledge still comes down to people talking to each other.

PSYCHOLOGICAL TYPES
One of Carl Jung's principal contributions to modern psychology was the classification of how we each process information and interact with the world around us. The four sets of polarities Jung initiated in the 1970s were formulated into the Myers-Briggs Type Indicator personality test in the 1980s.

• Extroverts relate to the objective world of what is happening around them; introverts relate to the subjective world of their own thoughts and feelings.
• Sensors see things as they appear and prefer the concrete realities of things; intuitives see things for their potential and prefer the abstract realities of historical waves.
• Thinkers enjoy the structure and patterns of the world's interactions; feelers enjoy the immediacy of emotions.
• Perceivers are motivated by the changing patterns of the world; judgers are motivated by their perspective on the changing world.

Each classification is combined with a polarity with one of the others yielding a potential 16 possible psychological types. We might, for example, be a Extrovert-Intuitive-Feeling-Perceiver. Jung's observation was that no matter we operate within any of these polarities, its opposite will usually characterize our unconscious functioning and provide the occasional flip-side to how we present ourselves to the world.

TRANSACTIONAL ANALYSIS (TA)
TA was developed in the 1950s by Eric Berne. Following on from the researches of Dr Wilder Penfield, Berne sought to 'analyse' the 'transactions' that happen between us every day. He suggested three core inner states of the subconscious that interact with each other and also with the inner states of others.

First, the inner parent is our template of authority and empowerment, it is our received, external wisdom. Next, the inner adult is our template of self-determination, our reasoned, independent and mediating wisdom. Finally, the inner child is our template of immediate and uncensored reaction to the world, our emotional and sensory wisdom.

In analysing transactions, Berne identified that our relationships with others comes under strain if our 'transactions' become 'crossed'. Psychological therapy based on TA examines the states that we operate from, both in relating to ourselves and other people, in order to release our own insights regarding how we are operating and trigger new, more helpful patternings.

MASLOW'S HIERARCHY OF NEEDS

In the 1940s, American psychologist Abraham Maslow began to bridge a gap in Western thinking between biological promptings to behaviour and psychological motives. His now famous 'hierarchy of needs' identifies the sequential capacity of humans to focus their attention.

This model is as applicable for a teacher, psychologist or parent as it is for each of us in developing our awareness of how we can best understand and choreograph our reactions to the world. For example, a teacher attending to the temperature in a classroom so that students can concentrate on learning is wise to the fact that the physiological needs of temperature regulation underpin any 'higher' needs for learning.

While other 'hierarchies' of needs have been proposed since Maslow's initial conception, and debate flourishes as to the accuracy of his model, it remains the benchmark around which we have our discussions about human needs.

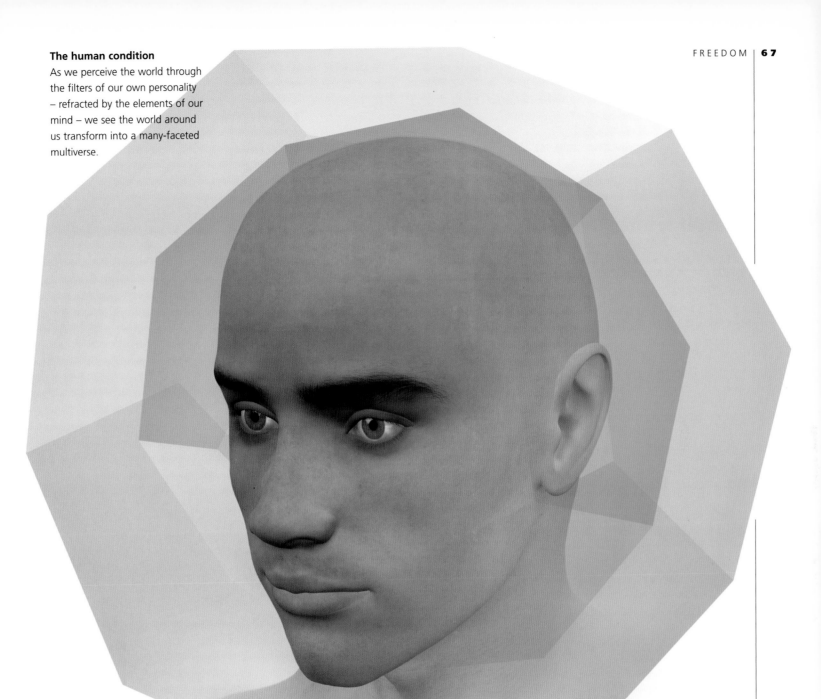

The human condition
As we perceive the world through the filters of our own personality – refracted by the elements of our mind – we see the world around us transform into a many-faceted multiverse.

PSYCHOLOGICAL ADAPTATIONS

In 2002 Vann Joines and Ian Stewart, two leading writers and practitioners of TA, published *Personality Adaptations*, a milestone that identifies some of the key ways in which personalities adapt to our unique upbringings. Another practitioner of TA, Paul Ware, took this work further, combining these descriptions with the pathological labels drawn from traditional psychiatry. Their success at such a formulation and synthesis perhaps inevitably meant that some of the pathological themes in Freud's work were incorporated. In this way, some of the language describing each adaptation echoes the pathology model of mind rather than describing the 'home' territory for each of us. That this was a bridge, however, between psychiatry and psychology ensured the work's importance and impact. The translation of some of the terminology of Western psychiatry into phrases that make sense to most of us also contributed to a reclamation of our internal states from the loaded language of pathology.

Terminology translated	
Histrionic	The enthusiastic over-reactor
Obsessive-compulsive	The responsible workaholic
Passive-aggressive	The playful resister
Schizoid	The creative daydreamer
Antisocial	The charming manipulator
Paranoid	The brilliant sceptic

Sight
the vision of lightbodies

I have not seen what you have seen, and I do
not know what you know.
Peter Chelsom and Adrian Dunbar
(from 'Hear My Song')

Sight is the last of our senses to develop.
Our eyes do not open inside the womb
until after the sixth month, long after the
other senses have had a running start. This
allows the retinas to develop fully, but once
they have and the eyes open, the foetus can
distinguish sunlight – indeed, many babies
will turn towards it. Twins, once their eyes
are open, will typically touch each other's
faces and hold hands. Immediately on birth,
our vision is fuzzy and we can generally see
only 30cm (12in) – enough to see whoever is
holding us. Depth perception gets under way
at four months and while colour perception
is present from birth, the subtle distinction of
colours does not fully engage until six months.

DYNAMICS OF VISION

Vision has a double meaning: the capacity to
experience light-based sensory stimuli and
the capacity to project forward in time to see
conceptually what paths we might follow.
This metaphorical capacity is intertwined
with our developing understanding of vision,
as we struggle to decipher the exact process
involved in translating the raw data of lightwaves into the shapes we see and the
meanings we derive from them.

The history of philosophy is littered with
attempts to track these complex dynamics
and how we navigate those experiences

where our understanding of vision might
falter. Simply put, the common understanding
of how we see things involves the progress of
light from an object through the aperture
of the pupil and onto the retina at the back of
the eyeball, both focused and inverted by
the lens. The light-sensitive cells of the retina
then translate the image of the object into
nerve impulses.

While the brain's visual cortex is responsible for receiving and processing such
information, tracking the changing shapes
and movements of incoming data, it is the
involvement of the parietal and temporal
lobes that enable us to recognize the image
and make sense of it. Intrinsic to such recognition is the comparison of the raw data of
light-based sensory stimuli with the images
we have stored in our memory. The processing
and reorganization of our visual databases is
part of the role of dreaming and the bedrock
for us being able to manage a constantly
changing environment.

MANAGING VISUAL DATA

The notion that we do not see what we do
not want to see is an aspect of human
perception. We need a certain level of continuity in recognizing visual stimuli in order
manage the environment we live in – to
assume a level of similarity between objects
that we see rather than constantly assessing
each vision anew. Our tendency to become
too fixed in what we recognize is the currency
of stage magicians as they count on us to
see what we expect to rather than what they
show us. At the other end of the scale,

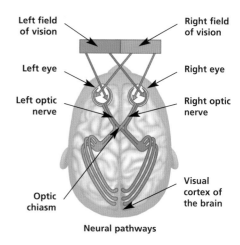

Left field of vision

Right field of vision

Left eye

Right eye

Left optic nerve

Right optic nerve

Optic chiasm

Visual cortex of the brain

Neural pathways

should we become too flexible in our
capacity to recognize the data stream of
images we are presented with, our psychological stability can come under pressure
and even fall away into hallucinations where
the incoming data, our resident maps and
resulting interpretations begin to fragment.
Such descents into psychosis are managed
in many ways by different cultures and, for
some, can form the basis of elevated status.

While the loosening of the bounds of
everyday reality is fraught with danger and
uncomfortable in the extreme, it is also
an essential function of survival for us
personally and as a species. To be able to
surf the interface of external stimuli and
internal filters with as panoramic vision as
possible, while holding a place in society,
is the essential role of the shaman.

Today, such appellations might apply
to physicists or science fiction writers. It is
often a hard path to tip the weight of the
collective consciousness towards more of a
balance within both its external and internal
environment. This is the skill of expanded
perception, where we can trust ourselves
enough to see both the terror and beauty
of our world, the grief of the holocaust, the
wonder of chi, always with the factor of
mystery that this is our perception at our
time, secure in the fluidity of uncertainty,
surfing the chaos that is at the heart of
perception and vision.

CAN YOU SEE THE SHIPS?

Erik Erikson was many things beyond the skilled
and insightful therapist and philosopher of Freudian
theory. Immersed, too, in the anthropological
complexity of human development, he attended
with great care to the stages of growth we each
experience in life, extending Freud's fivefold pattern
to an eightfold map that, crucially, included the
time of the elder. His studies among the Lakota
Sioux helped expand both his theoretical and
experiential understanding of human development,
an expansion he passed on later during his life.

When visited by students, he would show them
his model ships and ask them what they could see
while taking them into an expansion of their own
boundaries of perception. While many have sought
such expansions through the devices of hallucinogens and meditation, it is often the mere presence
of an expanded human that can trigger for us
more fluidity in our perception of the world.

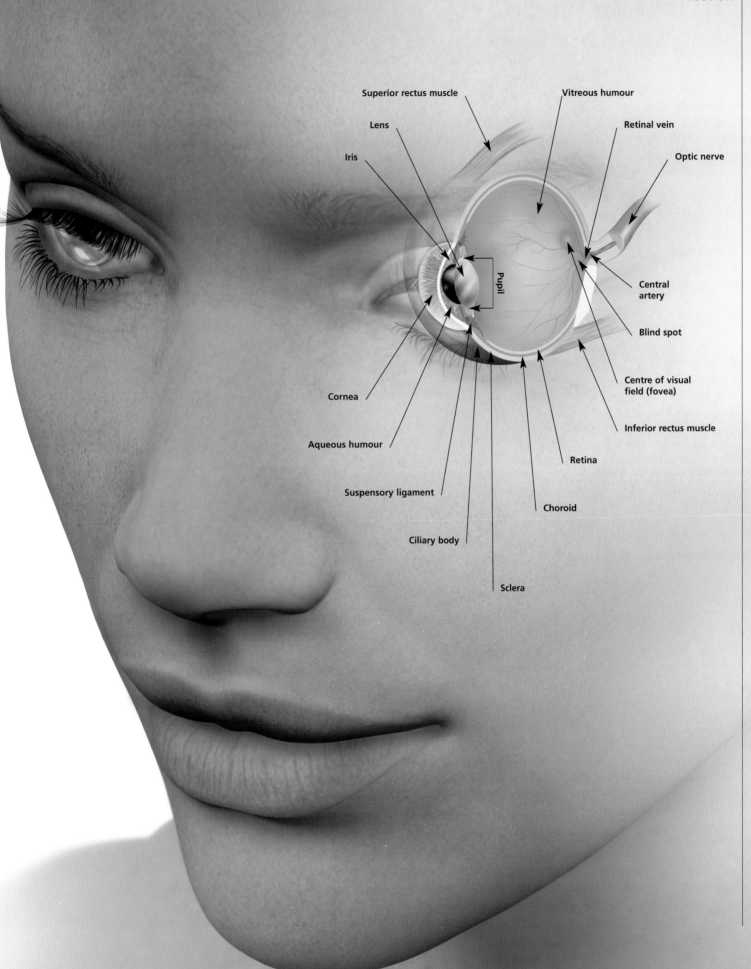

Superior rectus muscle

Vitreous humour

Lens

Retinal vein

Iris

Optic nerve

Pupil

Central artery

Blind spot

Cornea

Centre of visual field (fovea)

Aqueous humour

Inferior rectus muscle

Retina

Suspensory ligament

Choroid

Ciliary body

Sclera

Smell and taste
navigating our world

*We have long lost the more subtle of the physical
senses, have not even the proper terms to express an
animal's intercommunication with his surroundings,
living or otherwise, and have only the word 'smell' to
include the whole range of delicate thrills which
murmur in the nose night and day, summoning,
warning, inciting, repelling.*

A S Byatt

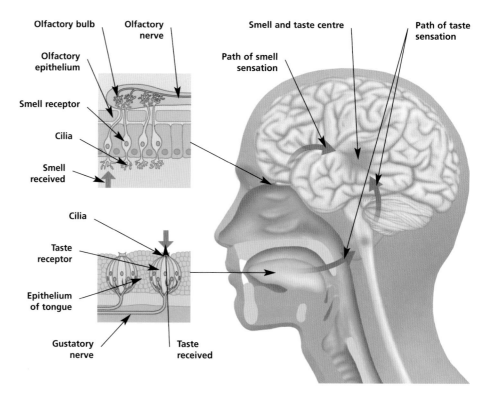

Smell and taste are two of the most closely allied of our senses. Taste is a subset of smell, as the four principal tastes that we identify from the tongue (sweet, sour, salt, bitter), even in their 24 permutations, in no way encompass our subjective experience of taste. It is up to the olfactory bulb within the bridge of the nose, constantly detecting odours, to expand our repertoire.

Smell is a process of chemical recognition (identifying molecules in the atmosphere), and it performs a number of functions – assessing the freshness of food, recognition of family/tribe, courting, navigating our environment among others.

The process of smell is reasonably simple as molecules from the atmosphere dock with receptor cells on the surface of the olfactory bulb. This triggers neurological switches that find their way to the limbic system in the middle of the brain governing emotions, behaviour and memory, as well as the cortex, where conscious thought occurs. As we process and identify smells we may find that they evoke memories and emotions that can surprise us. As such, smell is one of our least conscious, developed and articulated senses.

OLFACTORY ABILITIES

Compared with some animals and insects, we are incredibly limited in our olfactory capacities. Silkworm moths can detect chemicals at a molecular concentration of 1:1,017 up to a distance of 11 km (7 miles), while dogs use smell as the principal way of mapping their environment. For people, however, it is only perfumiers and vintners who develop their sense of smell to levels of artistic and scientific expertise.

While this skill does diminish with age, it is the sense most able to regenerate, with nerve fibres regrowing specific smell receptors. The only exception to our

downward trend in relation to smell is the experience of pregnant women, who respond strongly to either pleasant or unpleasant smells that are very much linked to food cravings. These cravings are not completely understood, but it is likely that they are the body's chemistry laboratory, which, having identified the immediate need of both mother and baby, sends out its orders.

This skill, of being able to determine our own biochemical requirements, is obviously latent in all humans and has the capacity to be cultivated. There are exceptions to this innate body sense and wisdom, especially when we come to addictions.

The olfactory reading of our body's needs, however, can be developed in other contexts. Physicians routinely utilized odour to make basic distinctions regarding certain disease conditions – gangrene smells of apples, liver problems of almonds, typhoid like whole-wheat bread. Traditional forms of medicine tend to use odour more intrinsically, in the way that 5-element acupuncture will use odour diagnosis in order to contribute to the overall picture of a person's health.

Such skills can also operate as a warning system in navigating our environment. This is often developed by tribal peoples in

relation to warfare and protection of their environment, as invading troops will often send ahead of them very strong olfactory advertisements.

This use of odour in relation to territory is echoed in the construction of perfumes, which rely on primal instincts, such as marking of territory, in order to attract buyers. When such a cacophony of odours occurs, as it often does on public transport, for example, it is enough to send the whole olfactory system into meltdown.

Pheromones are closely related to sex and in how we choose our mates. We tend to be attracted to those with different genetic immunity profiles than our own, thus maximizing the diversity of our immunity as a species. And it is pheromones that are the primary regulators of menstrual cycles of women living in close proximity to each other. At a basic level, each individual sperm has an olfactory receptor – its own periscope in navigating its onward journey as a separate biological organism.

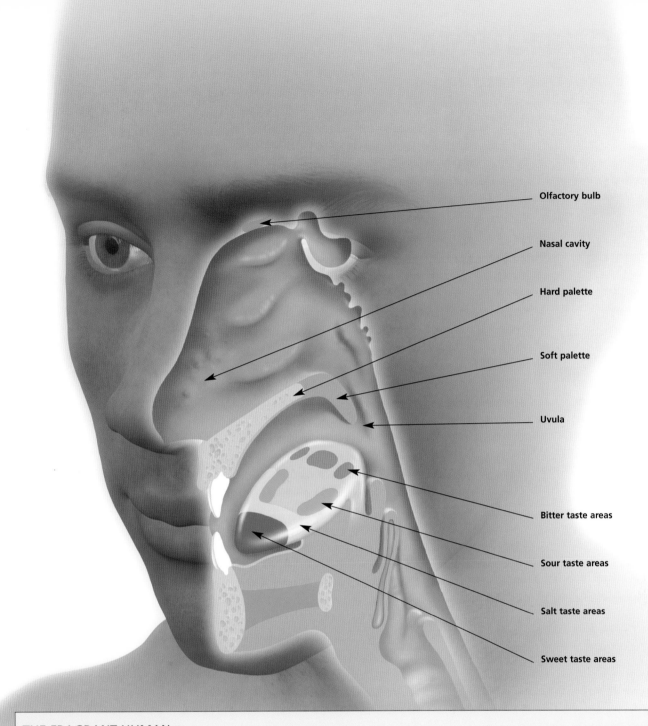

Olfactory bulb

Nasal cavity

Hard palette

Soft palette

Uvula

Bitter taste areas

Sour taste areas

Salt taste areas

Sweet taste areas

THE FRAGRANT HUMAN

The more we rely on tools to experience our world, the more we allow our senses to fall away through disuse, losing some of the refinement and potency that is our hallmark as humans. While our sense of smell is central to many physiological functions, our unconsciousness in relation to it threatens to allow a sidelining and amnesia of our biochemical basis, a further digitalization of experience.

The fact that we have a complex and intricate chemical analysis lab within us could, rather, be an opportunity for extending our skills as humans, rather than closing such areas down in favour of the consistency of mechanical tools.

Aromatherapy is the medicine of mood – affecting the human organism through the stimulation of various odours. This is more than a glorified massage, or the simplicity of the smell of lavender promoting calmness or of lime making us feel clean. It is the science of emotion and the links between how we feel and our overall health.

It has been shown that those who suffer from schizophrenia are less responsive to olfactory stimuli and the mediation of mood that odour offers is essentially our capacity to moderate and communicate our feelings, either consciously, through scents and perfumes, or in the immediacy

of our pheromones. Whether we choose to develop these skills as our own natural perfumier is unlikely given the current momentum of our global culture, but perhaps occasionally, some of us, somewhere, might experiment with extending the limits of our sense of odour, and reprogram our olfactory software so that our awareness of and intention within the olfactory world just might meet and take the human experience off for a spin in a new and different direction.

Sound and touch
on hearing the world

The new sound-sphere is global. It ripples at great speed across languages, ideologies, frontiers and races. The economics of this musical esperanto is staggering. The politics of Eden come loud.

George Steiner

Sound and touch are intimately related as senses that help us to detect changes in the texture and quality of our environment. In the same way that those people who have restricted hearing ability via their ears and yet are still able to 'hear' sound through the vibrations passing through their feet, so, too, do we all exist within a constantly changing chamber of sound and vibration.

THE NATURE OF SOUND

Sound is fundamentally the transport of a wave through an intervening medium, such as air or water. The 1979 film *Alien* based its headline 'In space, no one can hear you scream' on the fact that sound cannot travel through a vacuum.

Each medium is different in the way that it transmits sound. We, for example, hear better in air than we do in water because we are designed to detect and decode air-borne frequencies (it's different for whales). In this way, we hear our own voices differently than others do, as we hear them through the medium of our own skull rather than the less resonant medium of air.

So, too, does the way in which we receive sound waves affect the nature of the sound itself, responding to the architecture of the outer ear as that structure moulds the incoming waves for the most advantageous reception and transmission towards the eardrum. This factor determines acoustic architecture, just as the shape and density of any building affects dramatically the nature of the sound both produced and heard. And the shape of acoustic musical instruments, such as strings, woodwind and drums, is the basis of the sound they produce.

THE RECEPTION OF SOUND

The resonance of drums is exactly the beginning of our own process of hearing, as the eardrum is finely formed enough to receive the range of frequencies that we hear. The vibration of the eardrum is a response that is gradually transferred into increasingly subtle movements. A precise system of gears refines the movements so that when they reach the hairs within the cochlea they become the impulses within the auditory nerve itself that transport the input to the hearing centre situated in the temporal lobe of the brain, where interpretation of such raw data can take place.

The organs of auditory perception of each species determine the range of sounds it is able to hear. Dogs are famously able to hear more highly pitched sounds than can humans, and elephants are able to emit and hear very low (infra) sounds that, at night, can communicate with others of their kind up to 100 km (60 miles) away.

BEYOND OUR RANGE

Just as we underestimate extent and nature of animals' auditory abilities, we ignore the potential benefit and danger of such different hearing ranges. It has long been thought that sonar is damaging to whales' navigational systems, causing mass disorientation and beachings. Equally, however, the infrasonic hearing skills of elephants during the 2004 earthquake in the Indonesian Sea that led them to safety were benefited from only by those humans 'primitive' enough to observe the elephants' behaviour, and to listen to it.

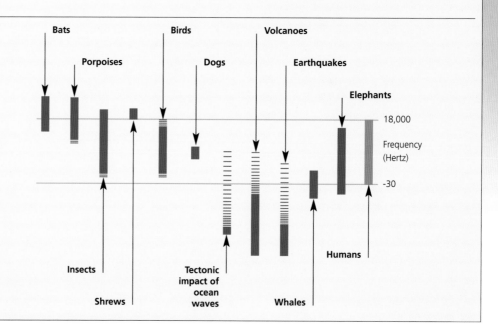

Bats
Porpoises
Birds
Volcanoes
Dogs
Earthquakes
Elephants

18,000
Frequency (Hertz)
-30

Insects
Shrews
Tectonic impact of ocean waves
Whales
Humans

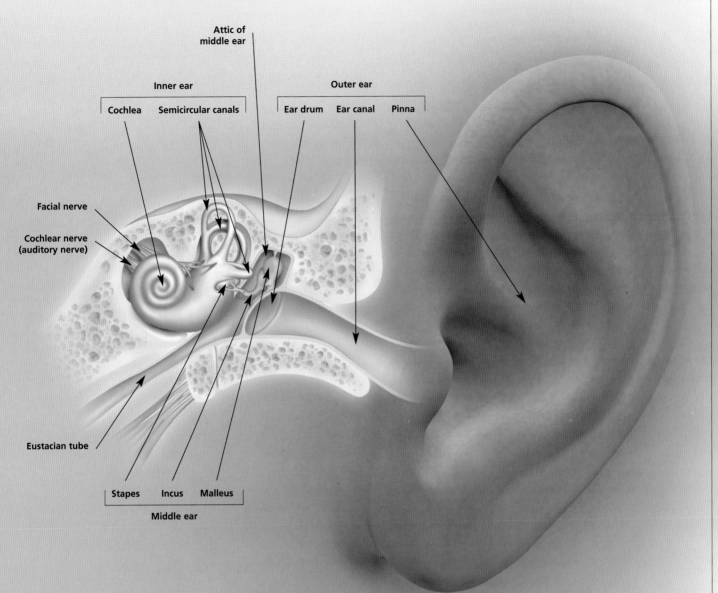

Attic of
middle ear

Inner ear

Cochlea   Semicircular canals

Outer ear

Ear drum   Ear canal   Pinna

Facial nerve

Cochlear nerve
(auditory nerve)

Eustacian tube

Stapes   Incus   Malleus

Middle ear

THE MEANING OF SOUND

It is in this context of communication and
relationships with each other that we often
judge harshly depending on the sound of
a person's voice – for example, interpreting
them as immature if the voice is highly
pitched, or as dull if it lacks a certain degree
of rhythm and modulation.

Tonal fashions can also be vigorously
adhered to in terms of subcultures, as in
the tonal differences between different
gangs in many of our large cities, and
between national cultures (our 'anthems').

Sound has an effect on the whole body
that can be both pleasant and healing or
disturbing and harmful. These negative
effects range from that acutely annoying
tune that becomes lodged in your mind
(a *wurmohr* in German – meaning an 'ear
worm') or the alienating effects of a music
or sound that disorientates. In the late 1980s,

for example, special troops of the
United States Army, known as Psyops,
ringed the Vatican Embassy compound in
Panama, where General Manuel Noriega
had taken refuge, with loudspeakers and
played loud rock music 24 hours a day until
the general could stand it no longer and
surrendered.

Sound has also been purposefully
developed as distinct weapons, such as the
acoustic cannon. Such weapons have their
basis in nature as some whales have been
known to stun their prey with sound. As
John Cody writes: '. . . called "gunshots",
whales focus these powerful blasts at large
squid and other fish to paralyse and catch
them. In some instances, they have been
known to burst their prey apart by tonal
projection alone.'

Experienced in small doses, infrasound
can be stimulating to humans, but beyond

tolerable limits, it can cause ill-health, low
mood, disorientation or even death. Thankfully, we retain the power of song and
speech and, inspired by songbirds, still find
a place for cultivating sounds that are not
only healing and sacred, but also offer us a
reflection of our own tribe, a sonic home
and refuge. This is more than the 'wallpaper'
sounds that attempt to lull us into a false
sense of refuge in stores and shopping malls;
it is the authentic rhythms and melodies
that bring both people and planet together.
It may yet be that our research into the
potency of sound begins to veer as much
into medicine and consciousness as it
already does into armaments.

Sex
reunion and renewal

How wonderful sex can be, when men keep it powerful and sacred, and it fills the world, like sunshine through and through one!
D H Lawrence

In the explosion of orgasm we can know the dissolution of the self, the bliss of divinity, the tenderness of opening our hearts to another. For sex – as distinct from gender and reproduction – is a wide-ranging area of our experience. A narrow definition might restrict sex to the reproductive activities arising from our polarity of gender, while a wider understanding might allow the sensory and spiritual experience of our energetic interaction with the rest of the world.

As the history of sexuality shows, sex is not just about sexual intercourse or courtship; it involves complex dynamics of empowerment, individuality and pleasure. For the number of civilizations that have repressed and hidden sexuality, at least an equal number have celebrated and normalized it. Whether or not we are now at a global cultural crossroads in our understanding of sex, or are tying ourselves up in yet more knotty argument and confusion, remains to be seen.

AROUSAL
Within relationships, sexual stimulation is most often induced by the engagement of our imagination and emotions, followed only then by direct physical stimulation, particularly to body areas such as the genitals, ears and nipples. Sexual arousal will often arise from a specific set of stimuli. In relation to other people, these will classify us as being attracted to members of the same sex, the opposite sex or a mixture of both.

We are all unique and satisfactory sexual relationships often involve a mutual sharing of those aspects of a relationship or those parts of the body which, on stimulation, bring most pleasure. Even more varied are the range of non-physical sensory cues for stimulation – such as sights, sounds, smells and tastes.

While there are certain gender tendencies, such as men being more visual and women being more textural, the variety of ways in which we become stimulated diversifies even more when we consider emotional and psychological cues. Again, there are cultural, historical and hormonal trends where the sexual behaviour of men is generally expected to be dominant and that of women to be responsive. But the behavioural and sensory content of these preferences is infinitely variable – whether we are male or female, we may be aroused by gentle music or floral scents, strong or weak characters, blue skies or dark evenings. Each trigger will have been soft-wired into us as we grew up – linking periods of intense pleasure to the hormonal circuitry of our bodies.

SEXUAL ETHICS
Ethics of consent, choice and respect are beginning to find a critical mass across the globe. At the same time, any taint of shame from our experience of sex takes time to be released as we find an equilibrium between freedom and responsibility. Many of the sexual yogas concern themselves with such an alliance of sexual and heart energies, a uniting of sex and love.

As we cultivate the ethics of consent, choice and respect in our experience of sex, its historical development intertwines with that of love and spirituality, with religious and cultural movements contributing to our working out of what love, sex and spirit mean to us. Here, there is a continuum of whether or not sex, in and of itself, can ever be considered sacred. At one end of such a continuum is the notion that sexual energy can be a path to enlightenment; at the other, that it is intrinsically tainted with the realm of matter and so alien from the spiritual life. Mythologist Joseph Campbell distinguishes between the various manifestations of love in Western history, identifying:

- Eros – the biological sexual passion (impersonal).
- Agape – the love of opening one's heart to another (spiritual and impersonal).
- Amor – the romantic love of another (personal and can be spiritual).

The journey of Amor since its championing by 12th-century European troubadours has undergone tumultuous fortunes. Each culture and religion has played its part in our global dialogue. Campbell reminds us, though, that the virtues of the knight who sought above all the 'realization of love that is nature's noblest work' also had as one of his virtues the ethic of courtesy, 'respect for the society in which you are living'. Global acceptance of our diversity as sexual beings is slowly allowing us to question what might be a set of ethics we develop together as a growing species with a maturity to its biology and destiny.

TAOIST SEXUAL YOGA AND LONGEVITY

The human organism is designed by DNA to maintain an optimum of strength and health to sexual maturity – and just a few years beyond. Once it has presumably done its procreative duty, 'tis kissed off, abandoned to steadily deteriorate. What Alobar and Kudra did was to keep their sexual fires so hotly stoked that DNA was fooled into believin' that they were just entering into sexual maturity.
Tom Robbins

Each of our civilizations has held vastly different attitudes towards sex, some seeing it as a necessary evil, others as a path to enlightenment. The *Kama Sutra* is one of the most famous and celebrated guides to sexual practice, closely followed by the Chinese classic the *Art of the Bedchamber*. The intricacies, ethics, positions and guidance regarding sex are largely shared by both texts, and they both have a bold approach that is neither abashed nor self-conscious.

Each also links sexuality to spiritual practice and even the development of longevity through the refinement of orgasm and the purposeful development of intention and body awareness. It is mainly through sex, sport and meditation that we can extend our insight into the body, and blend all three with great style.

Sleep

the bodyclock of consciousness

Sleep is that period of relaxation essential to all lifeforms when our physiological processes and responsiveness to external stimuli drastically reduces. For humans, sleep allows a restoration of our biochemistry that crucially includes the equilibrium of our immune system (the manufacture of white blood cells) and the constant update of our brain's neural network as it assimilates new experiences and reformulates our personality. Essentially, sleep is the main anabolic (building) stage of our metabolism as we get ready for a new burst of waking activity.

READING THE BRAIN

Sleep is generally classified in six stages that cycle between the poles of wakefulness and rapid eye movement (REM) sleep. Each stage of sleep is characterized by corresponding brain wave activity, usually measured by an EEG (electroencephalogram), which tracks the frequency of the brain's constant electrical activity (see right) through electrodes attached to the scalp.

EEG readings identify four basic types of brain waves: alpha, beta, theta and delta. These correspond not only to the sleep cycle, but also to various states of waking consciousness. Beta waves are the fastest, with between 15 and 40 cycles per second. They are our most alert state of consciousness and typify engaged conversation. Alpha waves, with between 9 and 14 cycles per second, typify a relaxed, meditative state. Theta waves, with between 5 and 8 cycles per second, characterize a mental disengagement from what we are doing where we enter a creative and dreamlike state where we can almost lose our sense of time and place. Delta waves occupy the realm of fewer than 4 cycles per second when we are asleep. A reading of zero would indicate brain death, but above that is a deep, dreamless sleep or the restorative trancelike states of deep meditation.

FUNCTION OF SLEEP

As we progress through the stages of sleep we are increasingly restored. During the first stages when the eyes close, our muscles begin to relax and we might experience strange images or thoughts as our conscious mind begins to let go. As we drop deeper, heart rate slows and there is a decrease in body temperature. Deep sleep comes when the prefrontal cortex at the front of the brain switches off and we temporarily lose our sense of self.

Once deep sleep has sufficiently restored us, our brain waves change again and enter into REM (rapid eye movement) sleep. This is characterized by a rise in heart and respiratory rate and an increase in cerebral activity, experienced as dreams. In order for us not to act out our dreams while asleep, we also experience a level of muscular paralysis.

Our natural circadian rhythm would be around 25 hours, but we receive a timecheck from sunlight via the optic nerve that regulates our sleep–wake cycle. Our rhythms of sleep and dreaming are not just governed by the time of day, as both physical and mental exercise will precipitate a greater need for sleep, while stress and a more tightly charged central nervous system can falter our descent into deep sleep. As we leave adulthood and continue to age, we enter REM sleep more quickly and stay there longer. Other physiological effects of sleep are an increase in our production of proteins (needed by neurons in the constant construction of new knowledge networks), a reduction in the breakdown of proteins and a drop in the amount of growth hormone.

The respite of sleep is essential as we learn any new skill, our ability to assimilate and demonstrate our new proficiencies does not take place until we have slept and assimilated the information.

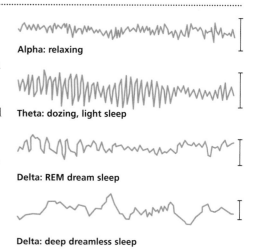

Alpha: relaxing

Theta: dozing, light sleep

Delta: REM dream sleep

Delta: deep dreamless sleep

States of sleep

The EEG (electroencephalogram) brain traces above show unique characteristics depending on the state of sleep, or relaxation, the subject is experiencing.

THE HEART OF DREAMING

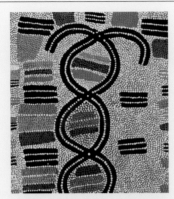

Aboriginal dreamtime serpent, the embodiment of creation within the landscape

Lucid dreaming is a relatively modern Western approach to dreaming. The term was coined by Dutch psychiatrist Frederik van Eeden in the early 20th century, and has gradually grown in acceptance since then, especially as psychology began to exploit technology in assessing brain waves.

Tibetan yogis and Sufi mystics have equally expounded techniques regarding the integration of our dreams within our conscious selves, a theme expounded by both Freud and Jung. Jung, however, had also visited Mexico and the American southwest and in his commentaries cited the distinction made by tribal peoples of 'little dreams' and 'big dreams'.

'Little dreams' are those that we all experience, of assimilating and sorting our daily experience, whereas 'big dreams' are more typically experienced by medicine men and women who are able to access, interpret and even affect the rhythm of our collective consciousness. Such an emphasis has less to do with personal mind-control techniques and sleep therapy and more to do with the shamanic experience of dreaming that permeates both sleep and waking, and is at heart a connection of consciousness within the dreamtime.

The term 'dreamtime' is often used to describe not only the Earth's origin, but also her continued spiritual realm from the perspective of the Australian Aborigines. In this way, the dreamtime involves a wider definition of consciousness, one that includes the experiences of animals, plants, ancestors, mountains and stars as part of an interconnected spiritual community.

Just as any EEG will record the dominant set of brain waves rather than the number of different rhythms that constantly exist for us alongside each other, dreaming traditions teach an extension of consciousness where it does become possible to multi-task our consciousness to extreme levels, experiencing consecutive and parallel states of being.

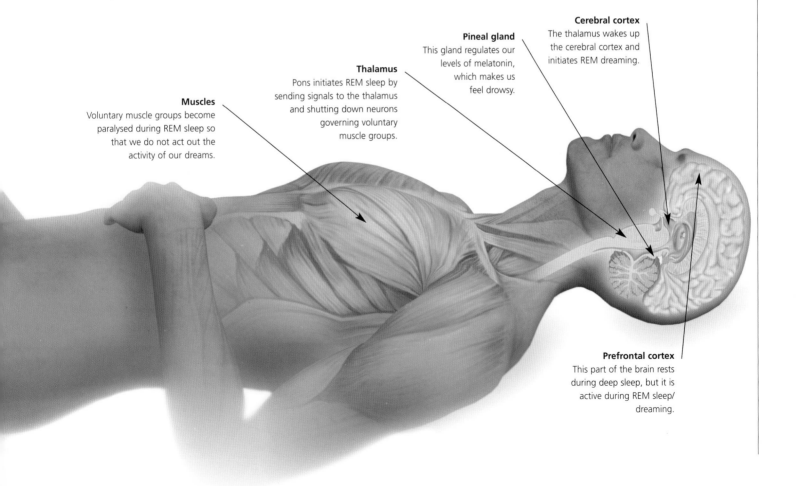

Muscles
Voluntary muscle groups become paralysed during REM sleep so that we do not act out the activity of our dreams.

Thalamus
Pons initiates REM sleep by sending signals to the thalamus and shutting down neurons governing voluntary muscle groups.

Pineal gland
This gland regulates our levels of melatonin, which makes us feel drowsy.

Cerebral cortex
The thalamus wakes up the cerebral cortex and initiates REM dreaming.

Prefrontal cortex
This part of the brain rests during deep sleep, but it is active during REM sleep/dreaming.

Myth
the metaphorical human

Mythology is the study of whatever religious or heroic legends are so foreign to a student's experience that he cannot believe them to be true.

Robert Graves

Mythology is the story we tell of ourselves, either as an individual or as a people; it is the 'dressed-up' version of history that allows us to navigate our world and experience. Shared stories are what unite a group of people – family, tribe, nation, planet – rather than any set of definitions that attempt to describe or govern. But as the great enlightenment project of Western rationalism wavered during the 20th century, mythology became less of an unsavoury subject and, at times, it even lost its association with superstition and primitivism.

The scholarship and passion of thinkers such as Robert Graves and James Hillman brought mythology to a far wider audience. The gradual retreat of imperialist politics and the relegation of native peoples to a romanticized naturalism also began to equalize our collective human experience of the world. It began to be acceptable for non-Western cultures to have sciences, as well as for Western cultures to have mythologies.

RITUAL AND MYTH

This shift has been facilitated by a growing insight into the relativity of cultural symbols and the many faces of divinity within our global human experience. In this way, I become you and you become me, neither diluted nor assimilated by our connection, but with a greater insight into who we are – expanding our reference points for those symbols that we are born to and those that we choose.

Mythology traces the great initiations of life and most myths are intricately wound up within the heart of rituals. Transitions of birth, death, adventure, marriage, childbirth, childhood, parenthood, foolishness, wisdom, fortune and disaster all become decked in the sacred paraphernalia of our stories about them, the wisdom of the ancestors told in those stories. Each age recycles these eternal tales, and they underwrite the efforts of both psychology and science. Indeed, for physics to be able to share its insights with a wide

audience it needs a constant translation into images that evoke immediate and emotional responses, whether or not the intricacy of the analysis is understood. In this way we have the 'worm holes' of interdimensional travel, the 'big bang' at the start of the universe and the 'primordial soup' of life's first stirrings.

Among others, feng shui master Harrison Kyng has spoken of how we should choose carefully the mythological roles for ourselves to play out. While the psyche will often hold its own wisdom and way through the trials of the human journey, the trackways of some stories can at times be challenging – even fatal if there is a lack of individuation within our association with the story. In this way, as we engage with our inner king, be mindful of the sacrificial and succession myths within those of kingship, and so loosen our own identification with the images and narratives.

It is in a similar way that certain schools of psychotherapy teach of returning to the story and images of a difficult dream in order to remodel the experience. Here, we effectively negotiate our own destiny and inner world. Such skills might involve a mythological double vision – allowing ourselves to be within the entirety of our experience while recognizing its relativity and perspective. In the familiarization with the great beings that are the source of much of our mystery, the aim is not to normalize but to lay claim to a double vision that liberates us from our own entrapment in relation to our inner world, opening a new vista of mythology in whose creation we share.

Mythology continues to be an essential part of our discovery of our world. Shared stories and rituals will shape us as a people far more than the legislation of our leaders. Mythological beings, landscapes and images provide the rich references from which our scientific horizon expands. And, as individuals, heroes and villains will continue to people our inner world. Mythology is a mêlée of deep human experience that the universe's rhythms play themselves out on. To relegate it to a level of being 'only' a story disempowers our capacity to navigate our way through it and to choose our own endings.

A 20TH-CENTURY HERMES

Joseph Campbell

He [Joseph Campbell] was a man with a thousand stories, this was one of his favourites. In Japan for an international conference on religion, Campbell overheard another American delegate, a social philosopher from New York, say to a Shinto priest, 'We've been now to a good many ceremonies and have seen quite a few of your shrines. But I don't get your ideology. I don't get your theology.' The Japanese paused as though in deep thought and then slowly shook his head. 'I think we don't have ideology,' he said. 'We don't have theology. We dance.' And so did Joseph Campbell – to the music of the spheres.

Bill Moyers

Joseph Campbell was an American scholar whose fascination with mythology helped a generation at the end of the 20th century make the transition towards a more global sense of unity. His meetings with mystic Krishanamurti, rock musicians The Grateful Dead and journalist Bill Moyers all catalysed a far wider acceptance of the role of mythology in all our lives. Campbell held the view that ritual and myth were intimately related and that as the wisdom of our native rituals fall away and we deny the truth that we are ceremonial beings, the vacuum that is left is not a creative expression of rationalism, but a spiritual poverty that fails to guide its young. His books – *The Hero with a Thousand Faces* and *The Masks of God* – developed his scholarship and bequeathed a rich heritage of ways out of the labyrinth.

Extraordinary senses
within, beyond and between

Miracles do not happen in contradiction to nature, but only in contradiction to that which is known to us in nature.
St Augustine

There are usually limits we ascribe to our senses beyond which we consider them extraordinary. These limits set the boundaries of sensation, perception and recognition and so include finely tuned sensory organs, good cognitive processing and analysis of sensory data and an exceptional memory of previous sensory impressions.

At the edge of our normal sensory limits are those of us who have highly developed senses – the vintner or perfumier or the musician with perfect pitch. But beyond these limits there are those who experience extraordinary forms of sense perception that lie beyond the collective experience.

BEYOND THE BOUNDARIES

Such perception is often called 'extrasensory perception' (ESP) or 'clairsentience', even though both descriptions fail to describe the phenomenon. Essentially, the sounds (often voices) that are heard, the visions that are seen and the cognition that arises have no identifiable trail of causality. The stimulus so essential for most of us when we perceive something is not apparent. This is why the term 'extrasensory perception' hampers our science – there is an in-built assumption that there is *no* sensory stimulus, rather than there being none of which we are aware. More accurately, we would be better referring to 'extraordinary senses'.

Mentalism is being able to discern what somebody else is thinking by observing subtle cues. These include the subvocalization of words and sounds through the movement of the jaw and throat and tiny deviations in the eyes as the brain searches for memories. In the same way, we can cue other people to think, feel and act in a certain way, using the knowledge of how the brain takes cues from one sphere of sensory input and outputs them in the simplest way possible. The phrase 'leading one up the garden path' is an accurate description of this type of step-by-step manipulation of another person using the basic laws of psychology and cognition.

This behaviour has ethical implications and it is rarely employed to benefit others – except in healing contexts, where it can be intrinsic to the process. While Western medicine predominantly identifies this as 'bedside manner', other traditions have developed sophisticated ways to map and develop skills to prompt the inner power of patients without affecting their volition. Indeed, the banner of much 'alternative medicine' during the late 20th century was predicated on stimulating our own innate healing capabilities.

There are many hypotheses for the mechanisms of extraordinary senses. Rupert Sheldrakes 'morphic fields' are one such basis for non-linear experience and lean to the 'collective consciousness' suggested by Carl Jung. These terms still reside at the borders of mainstream biological science, but it will not be until we dive fully into the chaos of our experience that we might yet find more answers. Somewhere, this necessitates the return journey from our entry into mechanistic life – when we first made fire and picked up a tool – to realize that consciousness itself is the most advanced tool we will ever possess.

We may decide to loosen our attachment to a smooth and uniform truth, and reclaim the scientific quest to include human experience. Should we do this, we then might see the polarities of the unknown components of our physiology and the unknown wonder of our experience, and in the seeing of them, they may begin to converge. That as we begin to identify the patterns rather than the laws of the universe, so, too, we identify more of how we co-create those patterns.

We now launch ourselves into the chapters of this book that seek to honour and describe some of the visions we have had of the body's spiritual and experiential landscape, hopefully surfing this interface between. And so we may also find our own patterns, our own insights, both into ourselves as individuals and the nature of what it means to be human.

PURPLE HAZE

Synaesthesia – genetic predisposition or neurological development?

Jimi Hendrix described the E7#9 guitar chord as 'purple', and its use in his song *Purple Haze* corresponds each time to his singing of that word. Synaesthesia is this crossing of sensory input and reception, where we see sounds and hear colours.

The cause of this is not fully understood, but our best guess involves a combination of genetic predisposition and neurological development – as the neurological pathways governing perception form (all babies are synaesthetes), the wiring somehow 'crosses'. Whether such a condition can be cited as an illness is debatable – as eight times more artists experience it compared with the general population. It is certainly a state that allows more flexibility in terms of perceiving and, therefore, interpreting phenomena and experience – the flexibility sought by meditation techniques, where the walls of the senses are asked to fall in on themselves so that we may see behind the boundaries of our universe.

This is a triangulation of awareness. Triangulation is a navigational tool that is able to discover the location of an unknown third point by plotting two reliable existing points. Synaesthetes, as well as those artists able to immerse themselves in metaphor, are able to plot their experience in ways outside the collective consciousness. When combined with their own crazy vision, this can yield a third point that reflects back to us the nature of perception.

Mirrors

Holograms of form

To see a world in a grain of sand,
And a Heaven in a wild flower,
Hold infinity in the palm of your hand,
And eternity in an hour.
William Blake

Blake's vision of interconnectedness is the mystic's capacity to utilize a distinct and seemingly insignificant part of creation to perceive its totality (a basic virtue of holism). This capacity has, until recently, been a spurious fantasy for mainstream science, and the fact that principles of holism have been applied to disciplines such as iridology and auriculotherapy have been equally dismissed. But microcosmic gateways of accessing and influencing the whole of the body (or of the world) are now finding an arena of explanation within holography – a discipline that perhaps leads us into the realms of the fantastic more than any other field of science before it.

Holograms are forms of light, cinematic projections of (at least) three dimensions. These images are initially recorded by shining different laser beams at the object and capturing the different reflections that the object then bounces back. Together, these reflections are recorded as an interference pattern, which can then be used to create a projected image of that object in free space.

On these foundations more fantastic aspects of holography have opened a door into the world of quantum theory. For if a photographic plate holding the record of a hologram's interference pattern is shattered, each and every part of that plate will hold an imprint of the full recording. This is holographic multi-imaging, something that goes against our current intuitive understanding of the world. It occurs because of the way that lightwaves store information, which is neither linear nor finite, but rather omnipresent and infinite.

Experiments in the 1980s led by Alain Aspect demonstrated the (non-locality) property of sub-atomic particles to share information at speeds seemingly faster than that of light. For Einstein's relativity theory, this is impossible, but the late London-based physicist David Bohm has suggested a solution: his idea was that there is neither any travel nor transmission of information involved because there is no separation between the two particles – there is no 'locality' between them as they are two perspectives of one fundamental reality. Lightwaves share a realm of no distance, a nullpoint that is beyond space and time.

This chapter profiles some of the disciplines that employ holographic maps. These arise from the capacity of holograms to envision the whole through one of its parts. While many disciplines predate by vast periods of time the emergence of holographic science, the general principles of holography are embedded within their holistic systems. Each holistic mirror will have its own history and associated therapeutic applications, but depending on which part of the body is used as the mirror, there will also be a unique perspective arising from the specific function of that part.

Iridology
drums of light

We are light beings. We are nourished by light, and operate by the 'drums of light'. The study of cellular 'vision' may be the door to our next quantum leap in the development of medicine. Obviously we need to learn the language of cells if we want to carry medicine to this advanced level.
Guenter Albrecht-Buehler

Iridology is a diagnostic technique that uses the eyes, specifically the irises, as a holistic mirror for the whole Body/Mind/Spirit. This diagnostic technique has systematically mapped the eyes allowing us to identify subtle variances of constitution, physiological functioning and psychological wellbeing.

WINDOWS OF THE SOUL

What we see in another's eyes is often not consciously processed, even though there is a wealth of information. Commonly this is at the level of social protocols and how we communicate intentions of status and respect, love and intimacy. Here, we share similar behavioural characteristics as pack animals, establishing social rank through the length and intensity of our gaze. This instinctive ability to read the nature and intention of another through their eyes is part of why they are known as the 'windows of the soul' and within Chinese medicine how they indicate our shenming 'radiance of the spirits'.

THE IRIS

The coloured portion of the eye – the iris – emerges from its role as the regulator of light levels reaching our retina. The fibres are as unique as fingerprints and invaluable to modern security system. To the iridologist, however, the irises are 'drums of light' yielding a vast dimension of light-based information.

The origins of reading the eyes reach back to China, Native America, Babylon and Egypt. When the tomb of Tutankhamen was opened in the 1920s, silver plates were found depicting iris records in great detail. While Phillipus Meyens published a commentary on iris diagnosis in his *Chiromatic Medica* in the 1670s, the father of modern iridology was Hungarian doctor Ignatz von Peczely.

Professional iridologists now usually combine diagnostic skills with a therapeutic discipline, such as herbalism, nutrition or homeopathy, as well as lifestyle advice. One unique aspect of iridology is the capacity to predict when certain systems are likely to come under particular pressure. This arises from a combination of charting the basic constitution shown by the 'weave' of the iris fibres and the particular areas of stress indicated by marks on the irises themselves.

Practitioners use the diagnosis to identify toxins in the body and nutritional deficiencies, and there is a range of emphases on body, mind or spirit according to the preference of the practitioner. Typically, the structure of the iris will give basic information about our constitutional make-up from the weave of the fibres:

- **Silk iris** Tightly woven fibres indicate an active constitution that is productive, but can over-wind and crash.
- **Linen iris** This is the most common, with an even weave, indicating less nervous energy but also a less rigid personality.
- **Hessian iris** The loose weave indicates somebody who is more able to relax.
- **Net iris** Resembles a spider's web and indicates a weaker constitution that is best served by health maintenance.

The results of research studies on its validity have been conflicting, with double-blind trials showing little success. However, real-time studies of practitioners show a high relevance with regard to constitutional patterns and predispositions.

A problem that remains for iridology centres around the dozen or more systems mapping features of the iris to various parts of the body. This causes scientists to pass iridology over as pseudoscience. However, Italian doctor Vincenzo Di Spazio has suggested that not only does the iris reflect the state of the body (and so act as a holographic mirror), but it is also a receptor, and that particular lights can positively affect those internal balances of both function and chronology. In this way, the mirror of the eyes becomes the interface as well as the expression of the relationship of light, consciousness and the body.

THE LANGUAGE OF LIGHT

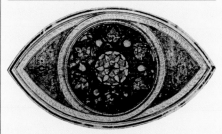

Arabic amuletic eye

The cutting edge of iridology research involves the suggested links of light between the iris and the rest of the body, where the internal organs are directly affected by the quality, intensity and colour of light coming into the eye. This may, at some point, show one of the ways in which the Body/Mind/Spirit is affected by looking at images such as yantras, mandalas, calligraphy, symbols, icons or fractals, and how they can affect both health and consciousness. It is the direct effect of this type of imagery on the energy body, by-passing the restrictive and interpretive filter of the mind, that is used by spiritual traditions – however ornate or simple those images are. This is the intentional use of visual stimuli to bring about a change of consciousness.

Visual catalysts of this nature are experienced as activating and opening the various levels of consciousness that exist within the energy body, enabling the achievements developed on a spiritual path to be anchored, and opening new gateways to the next realms of expansion. Just as holograms in general will open more of their secrets as we engage the technology of consciousness that synchronicity provides, so too will the holistic mirror of the eyes be reflected as we realize the whole of the body receives and reacts to the information and dimensions within the wide spectrum of light. That nearly all tissues of the body contain flavin molecules (our human photoreceptors that make up the retina) would correspond to the full body engagement of the traditional use of yantras.

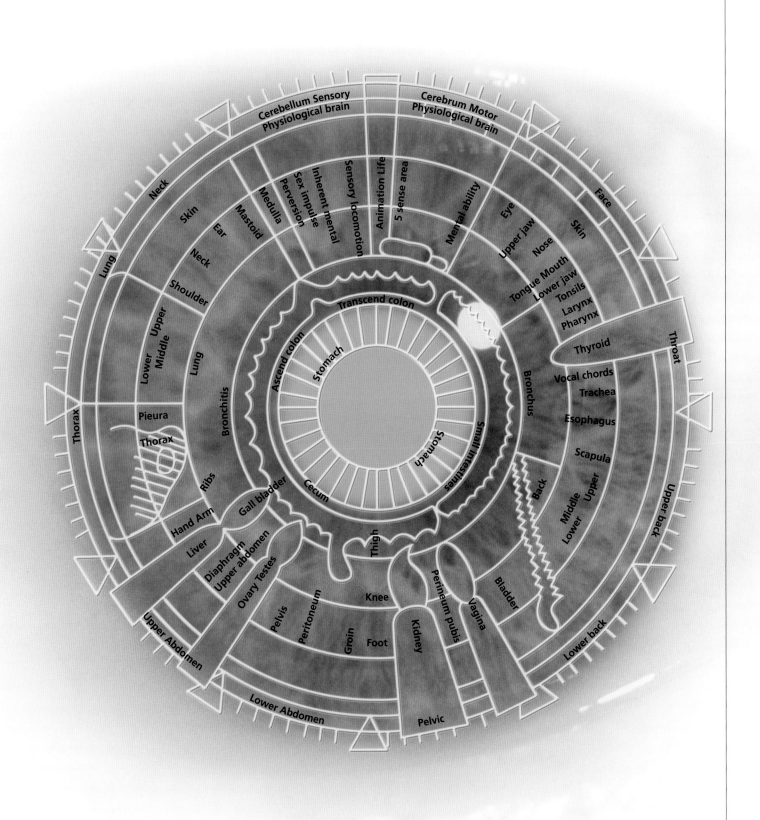

Cerebellum Sensory
Physiological brain

Cerebrum Motor
Physiological brain

Neck

Skin

Ear

Neck

Shoulder

Lower Upper Middle

Lung

Medulla

Mastoid

Sex impulse
Perversion

Inherent mental

Sensory locomotion

Animation Life

5 sense area

Mental ability

Eye

Upper jaw

Nose

Tongue Mouth

Lower jaw

Tonsils

Larynx

Pharynx

Face

Skin

Lung

Thorax

Thorax

Pieura

Thorax

Bronchitis

Ascend colon

Transcend colon

Stomach

Stomach

Small intestines

Bronchus

Thyroid

Vocal chords

Trachea

Esophagus

Scapula

Throat

Middle Lower Upper

Upper back

Ribs

Hand Arm

Liver

Diaphragm
Upper abdomen

Gall bladder

Cecum

Thigh

Back

Bladder

Ovary Testes

Pelvis

Peritoneum

Knee

Groin

Foot

Kidney

Perineum pubis

Vagina

Lower back

Upper Abdomen

Lower Abdomen

Pelvic

Reflexology
holistic mirror of the feet

It was no longer possible to pick my way between the boulders that covered the ground; night had completely overtaken me; and yet to my amazement I jumped from boulder to boulder without slipping or missing a foothold, in spite of wearing only a pair of flimsy sandals on my bare feet. I had become a lung-gom-pa, a trance walker, who, oblivious of all obstacles and fatigue, moves on towards his contemplated aim, hardly touching the ground, merely skimming the surface of the earth.
Lama Govinda

Reflexology is a complementary therapy that uses foot massage to bring healing to the rest of the body. Through the holistic mirror of the feet, reflecting the whole of the Body/Mind/Spirit, the reflexologist identifies and clears blockages throughout the system.

THE ORIGINS OF REFLEXOLOGY
The development of reflexology as a distinct healing discipline only occurred in the 20th century, but its origins are far older than this. It is likely that we have been massaging our feet ever since we began walking on them, as foot massage is both an instinctive and a comforting act.

The Chinese practice of rwo shur arises from such ancient lineages, but it differs from Western expressions of reflexology. It applies pressure from stone or wooden sticks to various pressure points, often using stronger stimulation and different massage movements (including sliding thumb motions) than found in reflexology.

CULTURAL TRADITIONS
In many cultures around the world the feet have both strong sacred and sexual connotations. Customs and practices range from those in the Middle East of anointing of feet with oil, the oriental kissing the feet of gurus, masters and elders, the ancient Greek taboo against seeing a maiden's feet to the Hindu and Muslim tradition of removing shoes when on hallowed ground.

The dual sacred and sexual aspect of the feet may arise neurologically due to the proximity of the areas that correspond to the feet and sexual organs in the brain's sensory cortex (see page 64). The symbolism, sacredness and eroticism of the feet have found expression at various times in human history that ranges from the expressive to the repressive.

In China between the 10th and 19th centuries, high-caste women's feet were broken and reset so that they were small and resembled a 'golden lotus'. High-heeled footwear has been at the height of fashion, for both men and women, during different periods of history. In the late 20th century, the use of synthetic materials in footwear tended to prevent the feet from breathing as they need to, a trend that both increased foot odour as well as insulated the body from the energy of the earth. In addition, this practice certainly prevented any trance walking of ley lines, as displayed by shamans across the world.

Such fashions and practices have an effect on the health of not only the feet, but also of the whole of the Body/Mind/Spirit, to the extent that the 'sole' of how we interact energetically with the earth is either supported and cultivated or restricted and insulated. It is in this way that sandals are highly symbolic across many cultures worldwide, allowing the contours and energies of the earth to be felt by the feet as well as providing both ceremonial and practical protection.

Few of us when buying shoes will consider the archetypal and energetic implications of our preferred footwear, and the way in which they shape how we walk on the planet.

ANKMAHOR'S MEDICINE

This 5,000-year-old Egyptian pictograph from Saqqara (just south of Giza) shows foot massage taking place with an excellent example of professional ethics. The caption to the carving has the patient asking the practitioner not to hurt him, to which the practitioner replies: 'I will act so that you praise me.' That this was not just an idle illustration and was rather something indicating a medical process is made clear by the fact that the pictograph was found in the tomb of Ankmahor, an esteemed physician of the time.

Foot healers of the Nile Delta

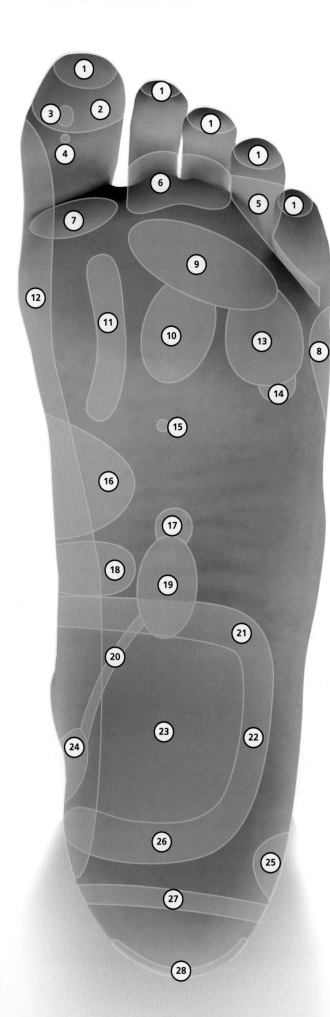

LEFT FOOT

1 Sinuses
2 Brain
3 Pituitary gland
4 Pineal gland
5 Ears
6 Eyes
7 Parathyroid gland/neck
 and throat
8 Shoulders
9 Lungs and bronchi
10 Thymus
11 Thyroid gland
12 Spine
13 Heart, arteries
 and veins
14 Spleen
15 Solar plexus
16 Stomach
17 Adrenal glands
18 Pancreas
19 Kidneys
21 Ureter tubes
22 Transverse colon
23 Small intestine
24 Bladder
25 Hips
26 Sigmoid colon
27 Sciatic nerve
28 Haemorrhoids

THE MODERN ANCESTORS OF REFLEXOLOGY

Reflexology is very much rooted in the self-help folk-medicine tradition of massaging the feet. It eventually combined with the zone therapy research that had been bubbling in Europe since the 16th century to evolve into the practice of reflexology we know today. This increasingly systematic exploration of the neurological intricacies of links between the surface of the skin and the internal organs involved an international cast of researchers:

• In the 1870s in Russia, Ivan Pavlov developed the work of other Russian psychologists on conditioned responses.

• In the 1890s in London, England, Henry Head linked hypersensitive areas of the skin to diseased organs.

• In the 1890s in Germany, Alfons Cornelius developed the growing discipline of reflex massage and focused on prolonged massage on tender areas.

• In 1917 in Vienna, William Fitzgerald published his book *Zone Therapy*, which detailed the ten equal longitudinal zones of the body.

• In 1919 in America, Joseph Riley published *Zone Therapy Simplified*, which included detailed diagrams showing the reflex zones of the feet and their correspondences.

• In the 1930s in America, Eunice Ingham formulated the practice of Reflexology, using foot massage in the context of the zones of the body.

Reflexology has since developed as a distinct complementary therapy and has integrated within its approach many of the meridian structures of oriental medicine.

Sooji Chim

korean hand acupuncture

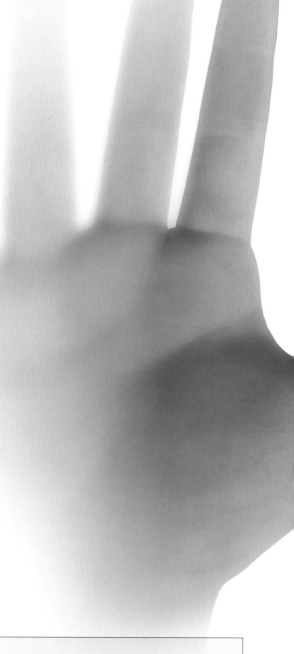

Other parts of the body assist the speaker, but the hands speak for themselves. By them we ask, promise, invoke, dismiss, threaten, entreat, deprecate. By them we express fear, joy, grief, our doubts, assent or penitence, we show moderation or profusion, and mark time and numbers.

Marcus Fabius Quintilianus

(1st-century Roman orator)

Sooji Chim, or Korean hand acupuncture, is one of the most detailed and elaborate landscapes of the hand. Even though oriental medicine's map of the meridians has been developing for millennia, it is only during the last 50 years or so that both ear and hand acupuncture have emerged as distinct systems of diagnosis and treatment.

As the mapping of meridians expanded across the centuries, the hands were not classically isolated as holographic maps, even though they have been integral to almost half of the body's meridians. It is also at the hands and feet that the polarity of the meridians changes from yin to yang, and vice versa. As each meridian reaches the tip of a finger or toe, it becomes more distinctly one polarity (for example, yin on the front of the body), and then switches to the opposite polarity as its journey begins up the other side of the hand or foot. This is why traditional acupuncture points needled on the hands and feet are usually more painful than those on the arms, legs or torso. Even so, Korean hand acupuncture is known to be less painful than most other forms of acupuncture.

MAPPING AND TREATMENT

The holographic correspondence of the hands with the body in Korean hand acupuncture employs both physical and energetic mapping. In this way, the middle finger provides a mapping of the centre of the torso, the neck and the head, as well as holding full representations of the kidney, stomach and conception vessel meridians. More intuitively, the front of the hand corresponds to the front of the body, with the back of the hand corresponding to the back of the body.

The system itself was discovered and developed in the 1970s by a Korean doctor, Woo Tae Yoo. It has grown to such an extent that the therapy is used as a home-based treatment throughout South Korea; patients attend sessions with trained acupuncturists for more sophisticated diagnosis, treatment and subsequent home prescriptions. The home-treatment aspect to therapy is partly enabled by the use of mini-pellets taped to the skin to provide ongoing balancing without the need for needling.

There are many treatment protocols shared with more traditional systems of acupuncture and simply transferred to the landscape of the hand. 'Surrounding the Dragon' is a classical approach that has found particular pertinence within Sooji Chim. This is where the acupuncture points surrounding a distressed part of the body are all stimulated.

While Sooji Chim might provide the most extensive map of the hand, it is certainly not the oldest tradition using the hands to focus and change the body's energy. Sign language can be seen as both the formal systems used predominantly by deaf people, as well as the colloquial hand signs developed on the streets across the world. But these are primarily a means of communication, whereas there are traditions that teach hand signs to control, change and channel one's own energy. This is principally seen in martial arts, such as wing chun, where there is a great emphasis on the fluidity of speed and form of the hands, and in Hindu and Buddhist meditation where the hands channel the energies of the body in order to change and regulate consciousness. This is the hand as both talisman and weapon (see below).

THE HAND AS TALISMAN

Mudras (see also page 100) purposefully shape the energetics of the hands, moulding the focus of our consciousness. Each formulation will harness the energies of individual fingers, as well as aspects of the palm, wrist and the back of the hand. Within each tradition, each area of the hand carries the connotations of usage: the palms to hold, the knuckles to strike, the index finger to point. Beyond these universal themes, the hands are also resident to maps of the elements and individual meridians, as well as to the complete map of this form of acupuncture known as Sooji Chim. It is the shaping of the hands that then choreographs these energies in specific ways, and that can form a template for us during meditation, guiding our consciousness into trackways of development.

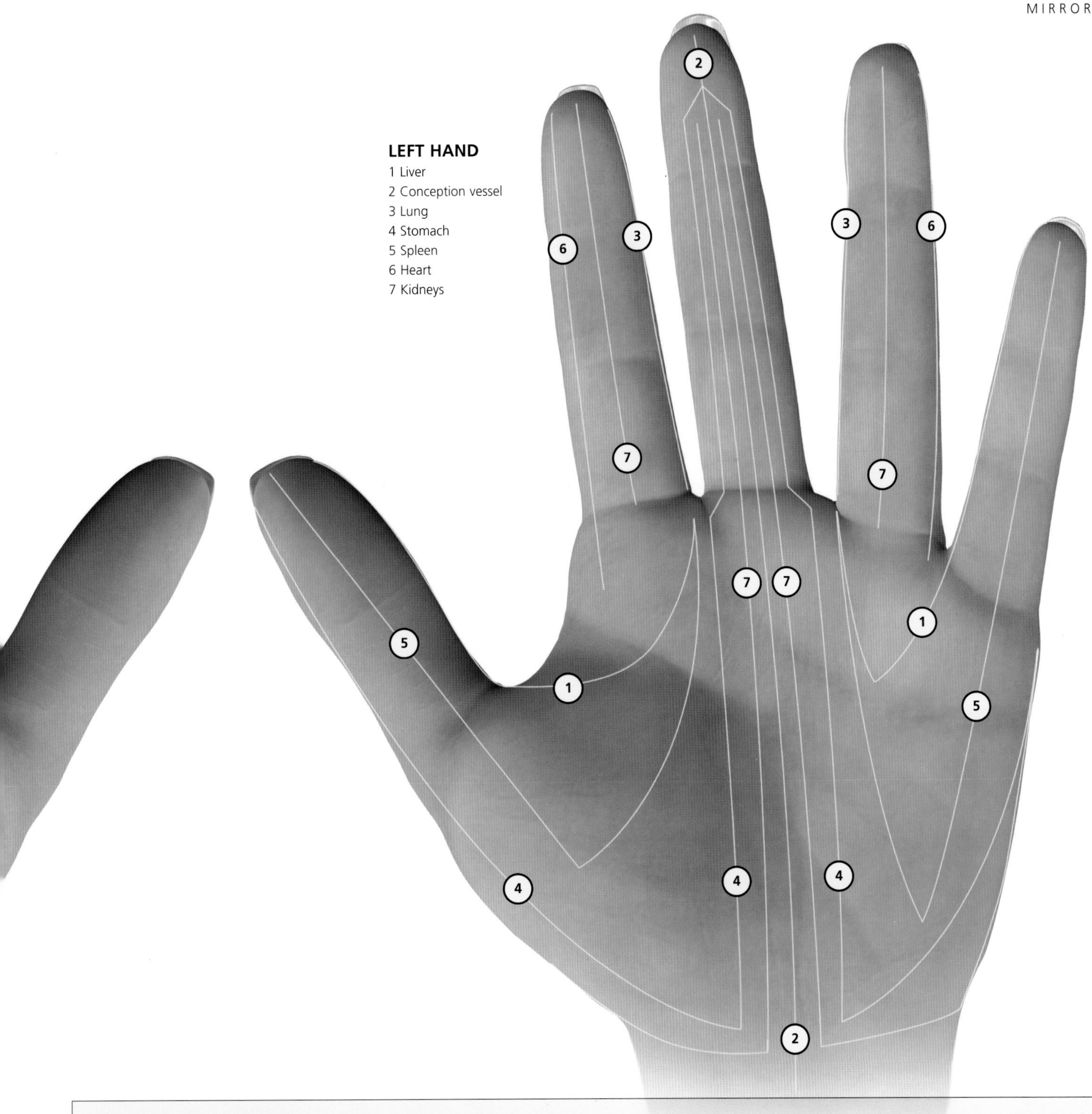

LEFT HAND

1 Liver
2 Conception vessel
3 Lung
4 Stomach
5 Spleen
6 Heart
7 Kidneys

THE HAND AS WEAPON

Just as palmistry has been a staple of folk wisdom across the world, so the hand has held many reflections within the spheres of healing, meditation and martial arts. As the hand forms different poses, it can shape the energy of our intention in very specific ways in order to direct, transform and protect our consciousness.

Fist strike

Knife hand

Crane strike

Palm heel strike

Spear hand

Tiger claw hand

Face reading
countenance and perspective

The profile reveals the karma to those who know about such things. If you look carefully at any face, you will see in the profile the story of past lifetimes. Your task now is to consider the profile, and determine what connection this bears to love. Consider, for example, why the Egyptians would paint the eyes in frontal appearance, even when they showed the face in profile. Consider also the Uraeus snake, which reveals its pent-up energies of striking only when viewed from the side. The true man is seen from many places, and none is ever the same.

David Ovason

The face we present to the world is both a conundrum and a cocktail of the various layers and truths as to who we are. For some cultures, truth tends towards the mono-dimensional, with legal and value systems designed to reflect such singularity. Other cultures, however, take pride in the wealth of terminology within their languages for lies, so signifying the varying intentions and consequences of such 'tall tales'.

PHYSIOGNOMY

The modern Western history of face reading (physiognomy) developed out of phrenology, or head reading (see pages 94–5). In the 1930s, a Los Angeles judge, Edward Vincent Jones, began to log his perception that he could 'read' the likely character and behaviour of the miscreants who appeared before him by their facial features. Some research was supposedly done on his findings but this has not survived. Fully developed methodologies principally emerged out of India and China, sharing many of their themes in much the same way that ayurvedic maps and meridians share much in their development and practice.

Indian face reading is called Samudrika Lakshana and is linked with Vedic astrology, assessing the face from the perspective of the zodiac. Chinese face reading, Siang Mein, claims a 3,000-year history and its practices permeate the disciplines of astrology, shamanism and Eastern medicine. Strongly anchored in the five elements, the shape of the face belongs to wood (long face), fire (triangular), earth (thick), metal (square) and water (round), with each area of the face displaying the vibrancy and balance of each of the internal organs, as shown opposite.

DECODING MEANING

From the perspective of neuro-psychology we have been able to identify the neural processes involved in understanding sarcasm and rhetorical humour. While the left hemisphere language cortex of the brain processes literal meaning, the frontal lobe and right hemisphere read emotional cues, body language and social context. These inputs are then compared with our memory bank of similar situations in order to determine the true meaning of what is being said.

Such social cognition also extends into the arena of interpersonal skills and includes the mythical gift of truthsaying. Deception is an evolutionary aspect of the relationship between all organisms, from microbes to mammals, as it fundamentally enables us to adapt to changing environments and choreograph our physical and emotional reactions to events.

Interviewers and interrogators, as well as stage magicians and mentalists, employ standard techniques for decoding facial expressions, the most telling of which are the identification of 'probing points' where a person's facial expression and what they are saying are at odds. From an evolutionary perspective, our facial expressions arise from the varying responses we have to our environment. In this way, experiences of pleasure open up our face and sensory organs, while those of displeasure close both the face and senses down.

This polarity between expressions of attraction and those of aversion mirrors our polarities of trust and deception. Our ability to perceive and convey trust is just as crucial as the necessities of the occasional 'poker face'. A sophistication in sculpting emotions and thoughts becomes important in the realm of cultivating synchronicities, the means and substance of navigating a holographic universe. If we are able to raise ourselves out of a perspective of real or not real we again engage in a process of empowering our choices rather than our constrictions.

Rearranging our faces
KARMIC PROFILES AND REVELATION

Kathakali dance mask

While 'rearranging faces' is gangster slang for inflicting facial injury, it also denotes the depth of healing that can be achieved when the patterns of pain locked into the muscles, meridians and dimensions of the face are released to allow our deeper natures to emerge. That there is a correlation between the radiance of our inner life and our outward appearance is an intuitive truth that we also, quite naturally, seek to contradict.

Whether we employ the contemporary developments of cosmetic surgery and botox or the devices of make-up, we do generally seek to mask, enhance and change the face that we present to ourselves and the world.

While certain traditions approach this from the perspective of divining one's karmic history, the most prevalent dynamics of energy within the face are the display of our inner radiance. It is in this way that the toxins within our skin, the vibrancy of our circulation and the health of our hair all contribute to our appearance, but cannot participate in the expression of who we are. We are generally able to intuit the emotions behind someone's facial expression and know the difference between a textbook beauty with no charisma and the seemingly plain wallflower with the smile of a sunrise. And as the infrastructures offered by face-reading systems such as Siang Mein might be passed over by some scientists, they do provide an unequalled depth of analysis to chart the karmic rearrangement of our faces.

FACE

1 Kidney
2 Gall bladder
3 Bladder
4 Liver
5 Stomach
6 Three heater,
  liver, kidney
7 Stomach, kidney,
  liver meridians
8 Kidney
9 Heart
10 Colon
11 Lungs
12 Spleen
13 Stomach
14 Colon
15 Stomach
16 Intestine
17 Kidney, bladder

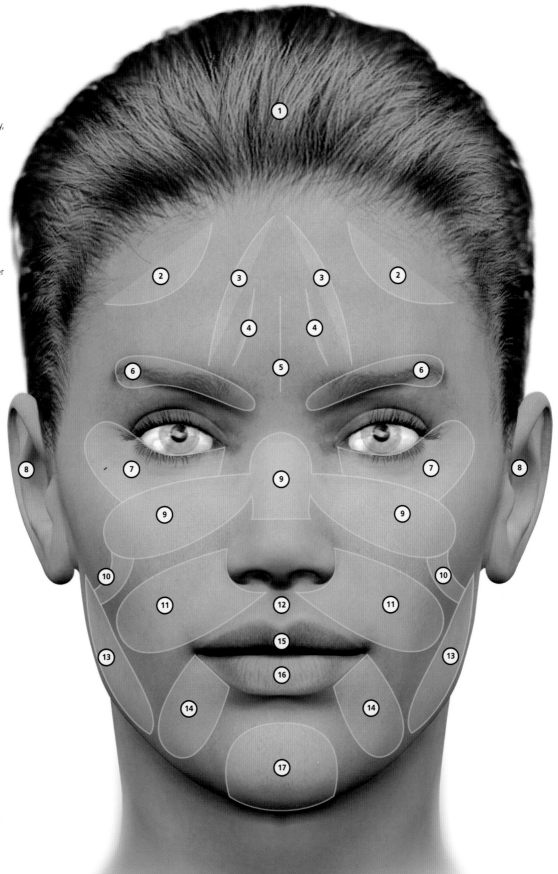

Auriculotherapy
detot from the ears

For you bring certain strange things to our ears.
We want to know therefore what these things mean.
Acts 17:20

Just as traditional acupuncture has mapped the hands with meridians, so, too, have points on the ears been equally present throughout acupuncture's 3,000-year history. But ear acupuncture's deployment across the world began only in the 1950s, and since then it has become one of the most effective protocols for dealing with addiction.

ORIGINS AND DEVELOPMENT
Auriculotherapy's central insight of the holographic map of the whole human within the ear was made by French physician Paul Nogier in the 1950s. From observing scars on the ears of patients who had been successfully treated for sciatica by traditional acupuncturists, Nogier theorized that the whole human organism could be mapped on the ear by envisaging an inverted foetus cradled within its shape.

His theories were published and a year later China's Nanking Army conducted extensive research, which verified Nogier's findings. Such confirmation combined with the therapeutic accessibility of the ear and a relatively simple methodology led to ear acupuncture being included in the armoury of Mao Tse-tung's 'barefoot doctors'. These were primary-care practitioners who were taught a comprehensive set of first-aid techniques to make medicine accessible to the vast Chinese population. Such widespread and free application was to be echoed in its later adoption by those attempting to turn the tide of addiction among America's poor neighbourhoods (see right).

Extensive research has been carried out into the mechanisms of ear acupuncture and how each point correlates to a different part of the body. The potential freedom of ear acupuncture from traditional theories has made it popular with medical explorers uneasy with what have been seen as superstitious, rather than scientific theories. Research has examined the 'somatotopic' performance of ear acupuncture points (from the Greek: *soma* – body; *topos* – a place). This refers to the anatomy of our neural pathways and the linkages we make between receptors in the skin and areas of the brain. While such research does not defer to the holographic map underpinning auriculotherapy, it may yet come to dovetail with its vision.

USE WITH ADDICTIONS
Despite trends to sanitize auriculotherapy from its traditional roots, it has found success in both clinical effectiveness and ease of provision as a simple and direct way of combating addictions. While it remains an integral part of acupuncture's traditions of diagnosis and treatment, it has come to be widely known for its detoxification protocols.

The primary birthing ground of ear acupuncture detox (acudetox) was the Lincoln Memorial Hospital in the South Bronx, New York (see right), where the five-point detox protocol was developed. This built on the work of neurosurgeon Dr Wen, who had observed that electrical stimulation applied to the ear acupuncture point associated with the lungs reduced opiate withdrawal symptoms.

Michael Smith developed Wen's work, initially by adding shen men (Gate of the Spirits) – an ear acupuncture point that promotes feelings of calm and peace, and then later the points for the sympathetic nervous system, kidneys and liver. This protocol is often termed the NADA protocol after the organization Smith founded – the National Association of Detoxification Acupuncturists.

It is a formula treatment to nourish the yin of the body, our fundamental stillness and capacity to be at peace. It is this stillness that is widely deficient in the side-effects of withdrawal. The five points stimulated during acudetox are associated with the yin organs of the body.

Most detox programmes also teach some form of meditation or chi kung in order to help patients develop skills for cultivating such stillness once they have left a treatment programme. This association of yin tonification and the ear is present within traditional acupuncture theory in the association of the ears with the kidney meridian and network (see pages 158–9), and their further association with wisdom and longevity.

South Bronx pioneers
THE LINCOLN MEMORIAL HOSPITAL

Frontier medicine has always been the application of our healing skills to those environments and diseases that we discover anew as we expand the limits of what we know of as civilization. This has involved the unique challenges posed by war (shell shock, shrapnel injuries, radiation poisoning) just as much as it has those posed by expansion into space (weightlessness, immunity reduction, loss of bone mass). But our frontiers also include the often forgotten backwaters of civilization where we encounter poverty diseases of both spirit and resources. Addiction is one of these backwaters, often heavily disguised within economic and social interests.

In 1969, the radical black American party known as the Black Panthers occupied the Lincoln Memorial Hospital in the South Bronx and took over its drug detox programme. Campaigning against drug trafficking and distribution throughout the city, the Panthers' programmes used tai chi and acupuncture as primary drug detox techniques.

Although they were driven out of the hospital in 1977, Michael Smith (the future pioneer of the NADA five-point detox protocol) stayed on to provide continuity, and the programme continued to hold strong community links and pioneer free and alternative treatment for addicts.

It was well placed to provide a level of relief during the crack-cocaine epidemic of the 1980s, and today the NADA protocol has been rolled out across the world and similar programmes are also proliferating in prisons. Its target audience is among those people wanting low-cost, effective treatment programmes who either can't or choose not to purchase mainstream healthcare.

EAR

1 External genitalia	32 Stomach
2 Lower blood pressure	33 Liver
3 Haemorrhoids	34 Elbow
4 Urethra	35 Appendix
5 Uterus	36 Shoulder
6 Heel	37 Thorax
7 Ankle	38 Mammary glands
8 Sciatic nerve	39 Lateral lung
9 Hepatitis	40 Oesophagus
10 Knee joint	41 Heart
11 Fingers	42 Thirst
12 Lesser occipital nerve	43 Mouth
13 Liver yang	44 Heart
14 Hip joint	45 Spleen
15 Knee	46 Lateral lung
16 Lower abdomen	47 Lower lung
17 Liver yang	48 Upper abdomen
18 External genitalia	49 Thyroid
19 Prostate	50 Neurasthenia
20 Urethra	51 Lower palette
21 Anus	52 Forehead
22 Bladder	53 Brain stem
23 Large intestine	54 Throat and teeth
24 Kidney	55 Neck
25 Pancreas/gall bladder	56 Clavicle
26 Abdomen	57 Nephritis
27 Lumbar vertebrae	58 Mandible
28 Duodenum	59 Tongue
29 Appendix	60 Eye
30 External ear	61 Inner ear
31 Diaphragm	62 Tonsil

Ear acupuncture points

The points identified here are a selection of those points used within the numerous schools of auriculotherapy.

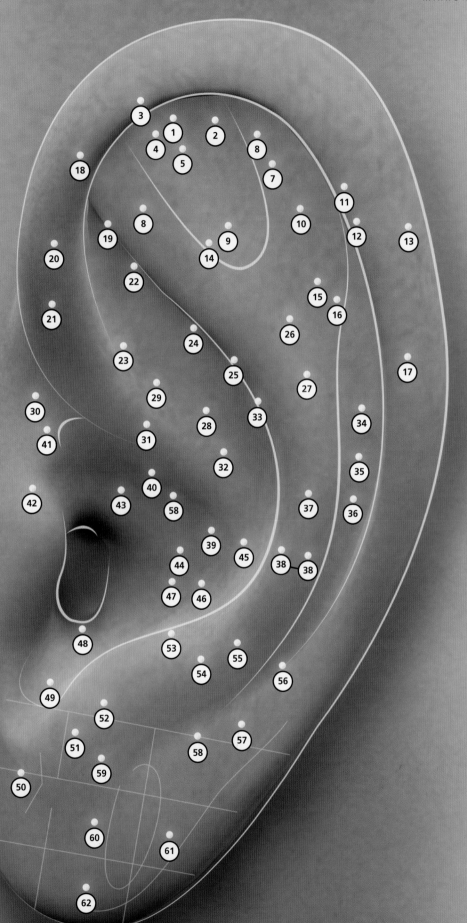

Phrenology
discarded wisdom of the scalp

A Fox entered the house of an actor and, rummaging through all his properties, came upon a Mask, an admirable imitation of a human head. He placed his paws on it and said, 'What a beautiful head! Yet it is of no value, as it entirely lacks brains.'

Aesop's Fables, 'The Fox and the Mask'

Theories about our heads and skulls have yielded as much ridicule as they have opened doors of discovery. Phrenology itself laid the ground for the identification of areas of the brain to be associated with specific functions of cognition. But in its most remembered form, it concentrated on the interpretation of the shape and other idiosyncrasies of the skull so that character and personality could be determined.

ORIGINS

As a distinct discipline it had its heyday in the 19th century; by the 20th it was largely discredited, nothing more than a fairground attraction, with the Fowler Heads (china heads showing the phrenology maps of the skull) reduced to curios in antique shops.

Phrenology suffered a distorted appropriation during the 20th century as racist ideologies, such as Nazism, brought some of phrenology's notions of head shape into their perspectives of diversity. Such tension was also present in Napoleon's earlier dismissal of phrenology because it had been developed by a German, Franz Joseph Gall. These racial tensions thankfully evolved into the realms of the fantastical with the notion of head modification.

HEAD MODIFICATION

This is the purposeful alteration of some aspects of the head for cosmetic or cognitive purposes. The most common technique employed by some South American tribes and one shared with some Tibetan groups is trepanning – boring a small hole in the base of the skull to relieve intra-cerebral pressure and induce higher states of consciousness. Even though trepanning was prescribed by Hippocrates, and was briefly celebrated in the 1960s, it remains an illegal procedure across much of the world.

Other traditions of head modification include sculpting infants' heads by strapping wooden boards to the skull. While some cultures consider this abusive, one native perception is that it enables an expansion of consciousness through channelling the focus of the person's head. The Malakula tribe of the Pacific favour a cone shape; a Colombian tribe a flattened, plate-like skull; and a South American tribe opts for a pyramid shape.

This practice might seem fantastic and abusive if viewed from a singular cultural perspective, but it also raises the question of how we as humans adapt to our environment through the use of tools, affecting not only our physical experience, but also our cognitive and spiritual experience.

PHRENOLOGY AND OSTEOPATHY

While phrenology split into cognitive neurophysiology on the one hand and fairground tricks on the other, its wisdom resurfaced within cranio-sacral therapy – an offshoot of osteopathy. It developed out of the osteopathic discipline of working with the rhythm of the cerebrospinal fluid that cushions the brain and spinal cord.

In the early 1900s, osteopath William Sutherland theorized that the cranial bones were not 'set' as had been thought, but rather moved against each other. This observation was picked up in the 1970s by another osteopath, John Upledger, who merged it with his observations during surgery of a 'pulse' or 'tide' moving in the craniosacral fluid. The cranial bones, while they are solid and interlocked, still 'breathe' and experience their own balance, which can be affected by stress and muscular tension.

Craniosacral work is a strong component of much osteopathy today, and has developed as a therapy in its own right. By using the anchor and fulcrum of the therapist's hands for the skull to sink into, the cranial bones reorganize themselves within the rhythms of the cerebrospinal fluid. The therapist listens for the 'tides' present within these rhythms, and allows them more space and presence within the patient's overall energy field.

CRYSTAL SKULLS

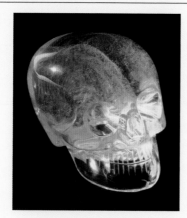

Phenomenon and odyssey of crystal skulls

Just as each holographic mirror in this chapter rests to some degree on holography as a way of understanding the whole through the portal of one of its parts, the crystal skulls also embrace the infinite nature of holography's data storage. The teachings of the crystal skulls are an intrinsic part of the traditions of Turtle Island. These teachings centre around a circle of 13 quartz crystal skulls, the size and shape of a human skull, that challenge the consensus that extraterrestrials are a fiction. They tell of the arrival of the antecedents of modern humans, who brought the skulls as a gift, a symbol of all their advanced technology and wisdom.

The prophesies of the crystal skulls reach back both to lost civilizations and forwards to future transitions of humanity. Their structure suggests a correlation with the holographic nature of consciousness. Quartz crystal regulates and amplifies energy, whether electrical currents or auras. Because of the regularity of its molecular structure, we know exactly how quartz will react to an electrical current or a wave of light.

Quartz orders information. A block of quartz the shape and size of a skull is going to have a significant effect on our energy field, both by virtue of the regulating nature of its quartz composition, and also the resonating impact of the symbolism of a skull's shape – the silent language to each of our cells – death as transformation or death as oblivion.

Mapping the brain
In the 19th century, china heads such as these, made by LN Fowler & Co, were considered as serious aids in mapping the different areas of the brain and assigning different cognitive functions to specific areas.

Chakras

Yoga's map of the energy centres

The practice of Yoga induces a primary sense of measure and proportion. Reduced to our own body, our first instrument, we learn to play it, drawing from it maximum resonance and harmony. With unflagging patience we refine and animate every cell, unlocking and liberating. Each unfulfilled area of tissue and nerve, brain or lung, is a challenge to our will and integrity, or otherwise a source of frustration and death.
Yehudi Menuhin

Chakras are the lotus-petalled wheels of energy in the subtle body that underlie and give rise to our physical form. Typically numbered as seven, they offer a template for the development of cosmic consciousness and, as such, bear the hallmarks of states of being, rather than concrete physical structures. As the originating civilization is Hindu, so their manifestation involves the deities and symbols of the Hindu culture.

Hindu literally means 'of the Indus', the great river that runs from the Tibetan Himalayas through Kashmir and along the length of modern-day Pakistan. Highly sophisticated civilization has been developing here for millennia, the history of the Hindu people reaching over 5,000 years and blending at least three different racial groups.

Originally native to the region were Dravidians, whose descendants now predominantly populate Sri Lanka and southern India, and the Munda-speaking tribes, who share links with the peoples of Australasia. Into this rich ground of totemic culture came the Aryans from what is now Iran, bringing their own cosmic pantheon as well as the complex social structure that was to evolve into India's caste system. The richness and diversity of India's culture over the centuries has allowed it to both adapt and retain continuity through periods of great change.

It is within such richness that one of the world's greatest sciences of consciousness evolved. It has given rise to variants and off-shoots, and many Buddhist and Sufi versions of the chakras almost certainly stem from the main Hindu branch, with even Westernized versions emerging in the 20th century.

The chakras described here seek to honour the disciplines of Indian yoga, rather than their latter-day interpretations. It is because of this that the astral body is not referred to, such terminology coming to us from the Latin notion of the stellar quality of our energy body and belonging more authentically perhaps within the realms of Kabbalah and Western magic. And while the chakras are not to be found within the physical body, their expressions as nerve plexuses and endocrine glands reflect often the potency of any one particular chakra as it governs both form and consciousness.

Within yogic lore, it is the activation of kundalini (the serpent power of divine energy) in the base chakra that gives rise to the development of the charkas in sequential order along the route they trace up the spine of the subtle body. In so doing, they open us up to increasingly depersonalized levels of consciousness. But the knots and glitches in the body of the aspirant can take some clearing and it requires a level of discipline not to become distracted with the psychic phenomena and ego temptations that can arise as each chakra is opened.

Muladhara
chakra wheel of root-support and cohesion

मूलाधार

In this lotus is the square of Earth, surrounded by eight shining spears. It is a shining yellow and beautiful like lightning, as the seed-sound Lam which is within.

Sat Cakra Nirupana

The word Muladhara is Sanskrit for 'root' or 'support'. It is the first of the chakras and lies within the subtle body at the base of the spine. As its name suggests, it is the basis of our existence and the anchor of physical knowledge and survival. The consciousness that surrounds us in this place is exactly that of existence, whether the 'to be or not to be' of self-doubt or the environmental battle to stay alive. Such physicality is held by the corresponding element of earth that reigns here, seen within the subtle realms as the yellow square at the heart of the lotus and borne by the tethered physicality of the grey elephant. This level of grounding and manifestation continues to impose its relevance as the spine rises through the back as the physical reflection of the rise of the chakras within the subtle body.

Lotuses rise most successfully from rich mud and the chakras rise from the very root and convergence of all the subtle energy channels that span the body. These *nadis* carry vital force through each of their channels in a similar way to the flow of chi through the meridians. They have been numbered to as many as 72,000 or even 350,000, but most commentators cite 14 principal pathways, of which three play a key role in the path of the chakras.

MAJOR PATHWAYS

The central channel, the sushumna channel, holds the roadmap for our ascent up the chakras, while the attendant ida and pingala nadis track the rhythmic helix of sun and moon currents. Our awareness that travels up sushumna is kundalini, the coiled serpent power of divine consciousness achieved through yoga practice. In yoga, we 'yoke' the consciousness in order to focus it inwardly and expand the sphere of our awareness beyond that proscribed by the earth element.

For most of us, however, kundalini lies dormant. For at this first chakra, Shiva is stopped, Shakti slumbers. This is the knot of Brahma, the three main nadis clasped tight to each other in the potency of illusion that this knot carries. In order for the kundalini to rise, this knot needs to be dissolved. To do this and liberate both god and goddess, the attention of the senses and our object of desire must become focused not on external experience, but on an inner awakening of consciousness. Each of the chakras is commonly inverted, and as the kundalini passes over them, they become more upright, activated and holding the awareness of that chakra's insights. In those who do not explore the nature of experience beyond the material realm, and for whom the subtle body is not awakened, the chakras are understood to hang with their heads facing downwards.

While Brahma presides here, Ganesha, the elephant-headed god, is often identified with this chakra, partly due to the emanation of the seed mantra, *Lam*, from the elephant guardian of this sphere, but also because Ganesha was crafted from the dew that the great goddess Parvati collected from her own body. Ganesha is the guardian of her dwelling, and came by his elephant head through challenging the right of Shiva to enter (at which point Shiva beheaded him and cursed him to take the head of the first animal that he saw). Ganesha is, thus, the master of all beginnings, and is invoked at the start of Hindu ceremonies as lord of obstacles with the strength, power and wisdom to surmount them. That he should appear here at Muladhara is hardly surprising.

THE THREE BODIES OF INCARNATION

In yogic traditions, we are said to possess three bodies (sariras) that then correlate with the sheathes (kosas) that further form the links between our chakras and the totality of who we are.

The gross body (sthula sarira) is expressed by the five elements and enclosed by the annamaya kosa (food-formed sheath) and the pranayama kosa (sheath of vital energy).

Influencing and manifesting into this gross body is the subtle body (suksma sarira) within which the chakras reside. This manifests via the sixth chakra and comprises manomaya and vijnanamaya kosas, the mind and intelligence sheaths.

Finally, the causal body (karana sarira) is of itself the anandamaya kosa 'bliss sheath' and the karmic vehicle for our soul, or jiva.

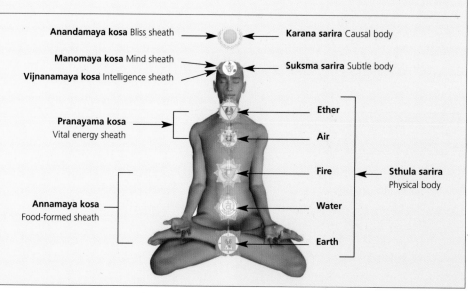

Anandamaya kosa Bliss sheath — **Karana sarira** Causal body

Manomaya kosa Mind sheath
Vijnanamaya kosa Intelligence sheath — **Suksma sarira** Subtle body

Pranayama kosa
Vital energy sheath

Annamaya kosa
Food-formed sheath

Ether

Air

Fire — **Sthula sarira** Physical body

Water

Earth

The elephant
This is the sheer power that underpins Muladhara.

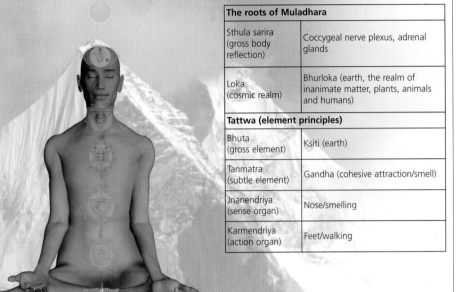

The roots of Muladhara	
Sthula sarira (gross body reflection)	Coccygeal nerve plexus, adrenal glands
Loka (cosmic realm)	Bhurloka (earth, the realm of inanimate matter, plants, animals and humans)
Tattwa (element principles)	
Bhuta (gross element)	Ksiti (earth)
Tanmatra (subtle element)	Gandha (cohesive attraction/smell)
Jnanendriya (sense organ)	Nose/smelling
Karmendriya (action organ)	Feet/walking

Presiding god energy
Brahma, creator lord of the physical realm, who rules all directions.

Presiding goddess energy
Dakini, doorkeeper of the physical realm, whose name means beholder.

Bija-mantra
Seed syllable *Lam*, when sounded creates a block against our energy descending beneath our foundations, and encourages concentration.

The first chakra
Muladhara is the foundation of the vedic energy body arising from the meeting point of the nadis – subtle energy channels that network the whole of our being. Sculpted from the clay of the earth, this is the grounding of our being and can either provide us with stability, support and momentum or act as an excessive anchor, weighing us down with tethered physicality.

Svayambhu lingum
Residence of the knot of Brahma, which must be dissolved if we are to emerge from the illusion of binding to the world of matter and see Earth as a gateway rather than a prison.

Animal guardian
The elephant is the carrier-vehicle of the sound mantra. It is the power of life going the distance, to harness our power to dwell fully in physical existence and find the momentum for inner transformation.

Svadhisthana
chakra wheel of self and sweetness

स्वाधिष्ठान

Within Svadhisthana is the white, shining, watery region of the shape of a half moon, stainless and white as the autumnal moon. He who meditates upon this stainless Lotus is freed immediately from all his enemies (Kama – lust, Krodha – anger, Lobha – greed, Moha – delusion, Matsaryya – envy).
Sat Cakra Nirupana

Svadhisthana, the second chakra, comes from the Sanskrit *sva*, meaning one's own, and it is here that our self-identity is moulded from the establishment of our own tides and rhythms. From within the suksma sarira (the subtle body), Svadhisthana influences the lower abdomen and is particularly manifest within the functioning of the sacral nerve plexus, testes, ovaries, and the urogenital system. The governance of water and the influence over the bladder involves the chakra in the refreshment and cleansing of the Body/Mind/Spirit.

These aspects reflect the development from the fight-and-flight sphere of Muladhara chakra. Here, the concern is for rhythms rather than for survival, and from within the sphere of rhythms arise the questions of regularity and harmony.

BRAHMACHARYA
The 'yoking' of this level is expressed in the virtue (charya) of Brahmacharya (continence). The essence of water within this chakra, the upturned crescent moon mirrors the bowl of the pelvic cradle as a symbolic retainer of fluids and a vessel that marks out our own containment within the cosmos.

Incontinence can manifest in various ways and Brahmacharya is one of the five virtues that together form the first spoke of the eight-spoked wheel of yoga itself. Continence is essentially an ability 'not to leak', which can involve celibacy, but is essentially a sculpting of one's mind and appetites in order to form a vessel from which the expansion of consciousness can progress. In a tantric context, this would involve a constant devotion to the awakening of divinity; in a classical Vedic context, a devotion to a study of scripture and the capacity to see the lord

Brahman in every aspect of creation. Here, the presiding deity is Vishnu the preserver, capable through the retention and reflection of the waters to be able to see the emanations of Brahman. The virtue of Brahmacharya literally holds the meaning of 'grazing', in the way a cow would continuously graze throughout the day. It is constancy and practice that is indicated here, the constancy of one's focus throughout life on the creative divinity within everything.

This, then, provides a containment and vessel from which we can turn the rhythms of our own concerns and appetites to a focus on how we might further manifest the awakening of kundalini. It is the filtering of our desires, and the decisions as to which appetites we cultivate, it is the sphere of self-expression and creativity within such decisions. In this way, too, our rhythms of sleep, food and sex all contribute to the integrity of this chakra.

THE HINDU TRIAD
As the presiding deity of Svadhisthana chakra, Vishnu began as one of the principal cosmic forces of Vedic India (1500–300 BCE). Subsequent development saw him evolve as the second god of the Hindu triad, together with Brahma the creator and Shiva the destroyer. His in-breath and out-breath are the rhythmic flow of the cosmos, he embodies not only the great sea from which all life emerges, but also the rhythms of that life and essentially its divine purpose.

Vishnu had ten incarnations (avatars), but his avatars number far more and include the Buddha (although this is in part an attempted assimilation of Buddhist doctrine into Hindu lore). It was Vishnu who came as Matsya in the form of a fish to save humanity from the great flood; as Varahavatara the wild boar to rescue the Earth from the demons. And he came as the divine lover Krishna, whose gentle eroticism invites humanity into a relationship with the ground of all being, and to realize our sacred origin and potential. This is the orientation of our rhythms towards a devotion to the divine.

Mudras
DIVINE GESTURE

Hand-set mudra for concentration

Mudra is the ritualised body-language of both offering and surrender. The body is depersonalised and the deity is invited to enter its pure dwelling space.
Ajit Mookerjee

Each of the chakras find embodiment through organs of sensation and action. For Svadhisthana, the associated sense is that of taste, our capacity to experience the sweetness of the world. The action here comes through the hands, which are able to shape the world and ourselves, and in the sacred context this is most apparent through the teachings of mudras.

Mudras translates as 'symbols', and they are the symbolic gestures that accompany ritual and ceremony, especially through the hands. Classically, each of the chakra deities will express one or more of the mudras with their hands (and as they often have more than one pair of arms, they do so while holding ritual implements).

Mudras are seen in the hands of deities, sages, aspirants and, most prolifically, in the disciplines of Indian dance. Each mudra conveys a blessing or energy and this is how saints and sages transmit much of their knowledge. Within the very particular aspects of tantric yoga, each one of the deities of the chakras is detailed according to body colour, shape, the number of arms and the mudras they express.

Vishnu
Lord Vishnu is the eternal preserver of the universe.

The roots of Svadhisthana	
Sthula sarira (gross body reflection)	Sacral nerve plexus, ovaries/testes, kidneys
Loka (cosmic realm)	Bhuvarloka (sky, the space between the earth and the sun)
Prana (vital breath)	Vyana, rose coloured and responsible for the circulation of blood
Tattwa (element principles)	
Bhuta (gross element)	Ap (water)
Tanmatra (subtle element)	Rasa (viscous attraction/taste)
Jnanendriya (sense organ)	Tongue/taste
Karmendriya (action organ)	Genitals/sexual action

Presiding god energy
Vishnu, preserver lord who balances the creation of Brahma and the destruction of Shiva.

Presiding goddess energy
Rakini shakti, celestial and exalted as she drinks the nectar from the seventh chakra.

The second chakra
Svadhisthana is the creative fluidity of self-expression as our energy rises from its inception at the first chakra to a level of aspiration and imagination. When successfully engaged and activated, this chakra enables a rhythmic flow and contained integrity to our passions and desires that aims them along the path of development provided by the chakras.

Bija-mantra
Seed syllable *Vam*, which, upon sounding, nourishes and purifies body fluids and brings alignment with the waters.

Animal guardian
The makara crocodile is the vahana (carrier-vehicle) of the sound mantra of this chakra. This is the playful cunning of our desires, mostly unseen beneath the waters.

Manipura
chakra wheel of the city of jewels

At the root of the navel is the shining lotus of ten petals, of the colour of heavily laden rainclouds. Meditate there on the region of Fire, triangular in form and shining like the rising sun. Outside of it are three Svastika marks, and within, the seed-mantra Ram. By meditating in this manner upon the navel lotus the power to create and destroy the world is acquired.

Sat Cakra Nirupana

Manipura literally translates as 'city of jewels', and is so called because of its lustrous, gem-like radiance. This is the chakra of tejas, the fire principle, symbolized by a brilliant red triangle whose sides are edged with the T-shaped Svastika symbol of auspicious blessing.

This is the centre of man and the pivot of the first five chakras, which hold the five tattvas, or elements. Theosophical interpretations of the chakras throughout the 19th and 20th centuries took the associations of the sun and solar plexus to this chakra rather literally in placing it at the level of the solar plexus on the abdomen, rather than on the navel, where it lies in the subtle body and whose name it bears as nabhi sthana (navel region).

THE SPIRITUAL AND THE PHYSICAL

The kundalini accomplishment of this chakra awakens a mastery over the element of fire. These gifts are described by Swami Sivananda as 'even if he is thrown into the burning fire, he remains alive without fear of death'. Such mastery is one of the key elements that author Mercia Eliade identified as marking any tradition as shamanic. In this way, both fire and light reveal themselves as emblematic of spiritual power.

The physical aspects of the body into which Manipura manifests reflect the consuming qualities of fire, and include the nervous, immune and digestive systems as well as the solar nerve plexus and the pancreas. These are regulatory functions of the body that enable us to retain a balance on the web of life. It is the great database, the bejewelled chakra that is able to map the universe whose creation we have witnessed at Muladhara, contained at Svadhisthana and now networked at Manipura. One of the later Upanishads, India's oldest philosophical and religious texts, the *Dhyanabindu*, speaks of the divine associations of breath control as 'Brahma is said to be inhalation, Vishnu suspension of breath, Rudra exhalation'. For in the physical body, as the nervous system links the extension of sensory messages, the immune system provides the references for who and what is family in the world, with the digestion consuming and absorbing all that we ingest. This is the city of life to which all roads lead, the hilltop beacon that shines both warning and guidance, and it is here in the subtle body that we develop and archive this wisdom, finding the refining qualities of fire as it strips away and cleanses our subtle body as well as fires it.

The blue petals that surround Manipura are the blue flickers we see at the centre of a flame, the subtle and enigmatic balance of fire in its generative and destructive aspects. This complexity is mirrored by the Rudra, the presiding deity of Manipura, He is an aspect of Shiva, here at Manipura in his form of the great chariot rider of the sun whose arrows cause death and disease. He is a more ancient aspect of Shiva, arising from the Vedic lore as god of storms as well as lord of animals. Rudra represents the sphere of the mind, the cataloguing organizer of experience, who with this fire 'burns' both our food and experience, providing the motive force for digestion and cogitation as we purify our experience.

Ayurveda THE SCIENCE OF LIFE

Ayurvedic forehead oil-flow treatment

Ayurveda is the traditional medicine of India, and aspects of its science date back more than 7,000 years. Today, ayurveda is finding its feet amid a rapidly changing world. In India, questions arise as to whether one can practise ayurvedic medicine without knowing the ancient texts.

Outside India, ayurveda is sometimes thought of only as Indian herbalism or a particular type of massage therapy. It is certainly true that the complexity and sophistication of ayurveda's massage techniques are almost unparalleled, with an intricate choice of pressure points, oils and techniques interwoven within the diagnosis. The breadth of traditional ayurveda, however, is huge. Its practice involves the identification of the primary dosha (humour) a patient is suffering from and then using an in-depth knowledge of the polarities within nature (such as smooth/rough, slow/quick) to restore and adjust the patient's constitutional response.

Some of the challenges practitioners now face reach back to the occupation of India by the British and a refusal to acknowledge ayurveda as medicine. In classical times, ayurveda had eight branches: internal medicine; surgery; ear, eye, nose and throat medicine; paediatrics; psychology/demonology; toxicology; fertility; and rejuvenation. Skills needed included horticulture and cooking as much as they did pharmacology and operations, and in some ways ayurveda was the original holistic medicine.

The roots of Manipura	
Sthula sarira (gross body reflection)	Solar nerve plexus, pancreas and the digestive, immune and nervous systems
Loka (cosmic realm)	Svarloka (heaven, the space between the sun and the Polestar)
Prana (vital breath)	Samana, green and responsible for digestion.
Tattwa (element principles)	
Bhuta (gross element)	Tejas (fire)
Tanmatra (subtle element)	Rupa (light and form/sight)
Jnanendriya (sense organ)	Eyes/sight
Karmendriya (action organ)	Bowels/excretion

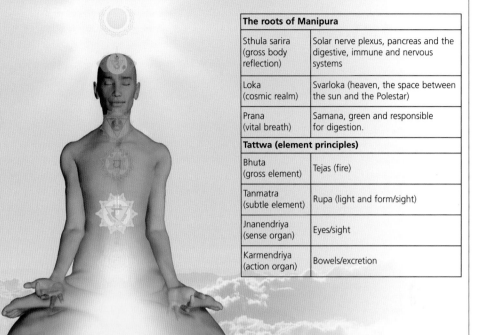

Lakini Shakti

The presiding goddess of this chakra is an expression of Parvati, whose presence tames all wild animals.

Presiding goddess energy
Lakini shakti, who holds focus and aspiration, being the compassionate form of Kali, goddess of destruction.

Presiding god energy
Lord God Rudra, a more ancient aspect of Shiva the destroyer.

The third chakra

Manipura is our centre of gravity and gravitas, enabling a balanced development of our own personal power and potency, while opening to right action and charity in the world. It is here that we might address the repeated patterns of our karma and invite the stored and precious jewels of our dharma.

Bija-mantra
Seed syllable *Ram*, which, upon sounding, assists longevity and the rising of kundalini.

Animal guardian
The ram is the vahana (carrier-vehicle) of the sound mantra of this chakra. This is the strength and courage of who we are in the world.

Anahata
chakra wheel of golden lightning

अनाहत

In the heart is the charming lotus of the colour of the Bandhuka flower. It is like Kalpa-taru, the celestial wishing tree, bestowing even more than desire. It is beautified by the Sun (Hamsa), which is like unto the steady tapering flame of a lamp in a windless place.
Sat Cakra Nirupana

Anahata chakra is so named because the sound of the universe is heard here by the sages – 'the sound which comes without the striking of any two things together'. It is the cosmic pulse of life. This is heard by the subtle body and becomes manifest as Anahata expresses itself in the physical realm as the rhythms of heart and lungs, the cardiac plexus and the thymus glands. This is our own pulse that keeps the beat of our lives but also marks out our constant tread back and forth between what we know of ourselves and the world of experience.

ISVARA
As kundalini arrives at Anahata she has traversed the territory of Brahma, Vishnu and Rudra (Shiva) and the almost unlikely deity found here at the fourth chakra is Isvara. *Isvara* means 'lord' or 'master' and he shares an equally ancient lineage as his brother-in-law Shiva, the Lord God Rudra. Where Isvara differs is in the paucity of myths told of him, and his tendency to inhabit a more mystical sphere than the all-singing, all-dancing magical realm of the Hindu triad.

Another sense of Isvara is his expression of the diversity of the many ways in which space and time are revealed. It is this diversity and union held by Isvara that follows through into the miraculous powers (siddhis) of this chakra. These arise from the mastery of air and space, and can involve not only levitation, but also flying through the air in the manner of birds.

These fantastical notions certainly challenge the collective consensus of what is and what is not possible, but that is not the primary concern here, as the virtue of Anahata is the expansion of mind and an appreciation of the many ways of looking at reality. For such flexibility and lightness

is symbolized by the guardian of this chakra, the antelope, whose fleetness of foot embodies the elevated sense of the mastery of air. Such universality echoes constantly in an acknowledgement of other ways of being as well as other paths of travelling.

GRANTHI
This is where the second of the granthis (locks) are found – bundles of bound energy, closed gates to the uninitiated that hold the challenges of incarnation (the three locks are to be found at Muladhara, Anahata and Ajna chakras). These are the unopened doors of divine unity – places within the subtle body where the grip of maya (illusion) is strong.

Awakened kundalini swathes through each of these locks, liberating their power and dissolving the illusions that each one holds. The locks themselves are the divided parts of divinity manifest as linga (the cosmic penis, modelled as a rounded pillar) and trikona (yoni, the cosmic vagina, modelled as an inverted triangle) in a static equilibrium that perpetuates the sleep of separation. The first of these locks dwells within Muladhara chakra, and is the kundalini herself wrapped around the lingum. Once the kundalini fire is released into the slipstream of sushumna (the central channel), it moves reasonably unimpeded until it arrives here at Anahata, the heart centre. The challenge of Anahata is the Vishnu knot of the Bana Linga.

Just as the sequence of the Hindu triad Brahma, Vishnu and Rudra (Shiva) walks us through the first three chakras, so, too, do they accompany us as we attempt to dissolve the illusions of the knots at the first, fourth and sixth. It is the blessing and insight of Brahma that liberates Muladhara and the blessing and insight of Vishnu that dissolve the blocks of our heart. This is the place where we must acknowledge that there is, in truth, no separation between us and all that we see and experience around us.

Yoga **A POISE OF THE SOUL**

Yoga means the disciplining of the intellect, the mind, the emotions, the will; it means a poise of the soul which enables one to look at life in all its aspects evenly.
Mahadev Desai

Yoga has become a common and well-used term throughout the world, commonly signifying the postural and breathing exercises that are but a small part of the vast wealth of India's sacred traditions. The word *yoga* comes from the Sanskrit for 'to yoke' or 'to harness' and 'union', and it is in this sense that it is applied to all of those practices, both physical and mystical, that orientate human beings towards a sacred life, and cultivate their union with the divine. But the postures (asanas) with which yoga is often initially identified belong to just one branch of the wheel of yoga, identified by the sage Patanjali in the 2nd century BCE:

1 Yama (ethics)
2 Niyama (conduct)
3 Asana (posture)
4 Pranayama (breath control)
5 Pratyahara (sense control)
6 Dharana (concentration)
7 Dhyana (meditation)
8 Samadhi (awakening)

Traditionally, schools of yoga have been identified according to the focus of their work, such as raja yoga (royal yoga), kundalini yoga (awakening the coiled goddess energy) and karma yoga (liberation through service). As yoga traditions expanded globally during the 20th century, schools tended to take on the names of their pioneers and yielding, for example, the Iyengar Yoga of B K S Iyengar and the Bikram Yoga of Bikram Choudhury.

The roots of Anahata

Sthula sarira (gross body reflection)	Cardiac nerve plexus, respiratory and cardiac systems, thymus gland
Loka (cosmic realm)	Maharloka (the middle region, abode of the siddhas/saints)
Prana (vital breath)	Prana, yellow and responsible for respiration

Tattwa (element principles)

Bhuta (gross element)	Marut (air)
Tanmatra (subtle element)	Sparsa (impact/touch)
Jnanendriya (sense organ)	Skin/touch
Karmendriya (action organ)	Hands/holding

Krishna

As one of the avatar incarnations of Vishnu the preserver, Krishna is the great inspiration of the heart's opening to love.

Presiding god energy
Lord God Isvara is an aspect of the cosmic Shiva, and whose absorption of passions helps us to remove any separation between us and the world.

Presiding goddess energy
Kakini shakti is the great and beautiful benefactor of devotion who synchronises the beat of our heart with the beat of the cosmos.

Bija-mantra
Seed syllable *Yam*, which, upon sounding, gives us control over the breath and the dawn of true knowledge.

Bana lingum
Residence of the granthi of Vishnu, which must be dissolved if we are to emerge from the illusion of separation between us and all that there is.

The fourth chakra

Anahata is our opening to compassion and the expression of heart in everything we do. Here is the expansion of our sense of self into the devotion of spiritual love, where, through identification with all forms of life, we find a connection to the greater family of the universe. This is the song of Krishna carried both by the winds and upon our breath.

Animal guardian
The antelope is the carrier-vehicle of this sound mantra. This is the joy of our participation in life, restless passion of sights, smells and songs.

Vishuddha
chakra wheel of golden lightning

In the throat is the Lotus called Visshudha, which is pure. This is the gateway of great liberation for him who desires the wealth of Yoga and whose senses are pure and controlled. He sees past, present and future ad becomes the benefactor of all, free from disease and sorrow and long-lived.

Sat Cakra Nirupana

Vishuddha chakra is the final chakra that holds any resonance with the elements that shape our lives. It is the staging post between these sculptors of form and the realms of vision and consciousness. Such a transitionary phase is marked by the guardian of this chakra, Airavata, the celestial elephant with six trunks and no retaining band that was worn by the grey elephant of Muladhara. Airavata is the god-king of all elephants and the leader of those celestial elephants that are the mounts of the gods. His other name, Ardh-Matanga, means elephant of the clouds, and the celestial elephants are said to still hold power in that realm.

This realm of ether (akasha) can be seen and translated as 'space', for it is that notion of extension into the great beyond that is achieved here. And this is how the chakra came to be named Vishuddha – meaning 'pure' – by virtue of its capacity to perceive and become flooded with the rays of the cosmic sun, Hamsa.

RULING DEITIES

Such a halfway house is further indicated by the divine presence of Shiva and Shakti in their progress down the road of kundalini's awakening, here as a hermaphroditic compilation of each other. The deity's left side is in the form of a golden Shakti; the right side, in the form of a white Shiva. They are still distinct but are now joined, not yet melded into each other but experimenting with the absolute balance that is the apex of elemental form. Such an apex is also found in Vishuddha's function as the gateway of the individual soul both at night and during the death process.

Vishuddha chakra engages with the physical body through the cervical plexus and the thyroid glands. This is echoed in the pace of our breath and anticipates the meeting of the nadi currents as they bank around the throat and neck prior to meeting at the top of the nostrils, and, should they become clear, uniting at Ajna chakra.

It is this clearing of the channels and the synchronization of life's rhythms that allow us to move beyond our needs for outward expression. While our voice empowers and guides us, enabling communication and clarification, it is also transcended as kundalini makes its final ascent.

STAGES OF HARMONIZATION

As we heard the 'unstuck' pulse of life at Anahata, Vishuddha is the centre from which the myriad sounds of the universe may be heard. It is the pathway along which each seed syllable of the chakras guides the yogi to dissolving the accretions within the subtle body and consciousness. This assists the chakras' harmonization, rather than them lurching from one aspect of illusion to the next.

One of yoga's most important texts, *Hatha-yoga-pradipika*, by Yoga Swami Svatmarama, speaks of the four stages of development along this path as the granthi knots at the first, fourth and sixth chakras are released. This begins with the dissolving of the first knot on which one hears the 'sweet tinkling sound of ornaments heard in the ethereal void in the heart', followed by the dissolution of the second knot where 'sounds are heard like those of a kettle drum'. The third stage is the release of the knot at Ajna chakra, where a 'drum-like sound' is heard. The final stage is where vibration reaches the seventh chakra and the sounds become subtle and lead the aspirant into soundlessness.

Mantra POWER AS SOUND

Six-syllable mantra (*Om mane padme hum*) that liberates sentient beings, near Thimphu, India

At its simplest level, mantras are syllables and sounds chanted to activate and develop each aspect of the human form. All music has a resonant effect on our gross and subtle physiology, but mantras are particularly designed to activate and awaken specific layers of consciousness.

Just as the first six chakras hold the 50 letters of the Sanskrit alphabet, so, too, do they reflect such a totality of creation, and it is not until we reach the sixth chakra that we achieve the unifying vibration of *AUM*. Here at Vishuddha we have the capacity through the power of breath to launch ourselves towards the transcendence of such a state of being.

The stimulating power of sound and music has such deep effects on us that each religion, spiritual discipline and cultural movement utilizes it to some degree. In yoga, it is less the seed syllables of each chakra that are chanted, but rather specific chants and mantras focused on deities and festivals. It is particularly common within some forms of yoga for gurus to give to their disciples a unique mantra solely for their personal use, designed to awaken the disciple's energy field in very particular ways.

The roots of Vishuddha	
Sthula sarira (gross body reflection)	Laryngeal nerve plexus, vocal cords, trachea and oesophagus, thyroid and parathyroid glands
Loka (cosmic realm)	Janaloka (realm of Brahma's sons – Sanaka, Sananda, Sanatkunara)
Prana (vital breath)	Udana, violet blue and responsible for swallowing, transporting the Jiva/soul to Brahman in sleep, and separating the gross and subtle bodies at death

Tattwa (element principles)	
Bhuta (gross element)	Vyoman (ether)
Tanmatra (subtle element)	Sabda (vibration/sound)
Jnanendriya (sense organ)	Ears/hearing
Karmendriya (action organ)	Mouth/speaking

Ardhvanarisvara

The androgynous Sadasiva, half male, half female, signifies that here, at the throat, we find a first blending of male and female cosmic principles.

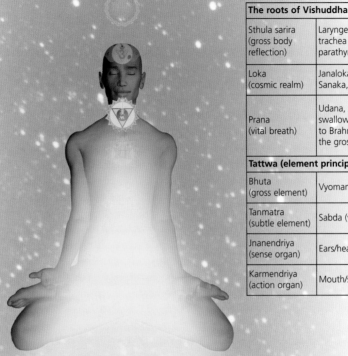

Presiding god energy
Ardhvanarisvara's five heads represent mastery over and union within the five elements.

Presiding goddess energy
Sakini shakti also bears the five heads of elemental mastery, and in particular, sensory sophistication and extra-sensory perception.

The fifth chakra

Vishuddha is our capacity to hear the sounds of the universe and give expression to the sounds of our own hearts as we speak our truth within the world. And yet this is the place of aether (akasha), of void (shunya) as we have blended each of the four elements, and now begin to find the expression of the universe beyond its sounds, and beyond our words to describe it.

Bija-mantra
Seed syllable *Ham*, which, upon sounding, vibrates and energizes the brain and throat, bringing sweetness and harmony to the voice.

Animal guardian
The white elephant is the carrier-vehicle of the sound mantra of this chakra. This is the elephant now bringing grace and harmony with the natural world, balanced within each of the elements.

Ajna
chakra wheel of self-command

आज्ञा

Ajna is like the moon, beautifully white. It shines with the glory of meditation. Within this lotus dwells the subtle mind. When the yogi . . . becomes dissolved in this place, which is the abode of uninterrupted bliss, he then sees sparks of fire distinctly shining.

Sat Cakra Nirupana

Ajna chakra is the centre of command or order known as our third eye. Here we move beyond the elemental realms held by each of the first five chakras and move into a deeper seeing of consciousness. Even though the throat chakra was in some ways a blending of the elements, at Ajna chakra we find a consciousness that moves beyond mere conceptions of reunion, as there is no division to be found.

THE SACRED THREE

It is such a state of non-duality against which we test ourselves within Ajna chakra, for here is the third and final granthi (knot) that meets the ascent of kundalini. This is the Rudra knot of the Itara lingum that radiates the brilliant white lightning as it holds the compacted illusion (maya) of self and other. Here is the challenge to move beyond duality, most clearly represented within our universe as male and female, Shiva and Shakti, and to penetrate the vision of the third eye that sees everything as it is, infinite and holy.

Ajna chakra rejoins the light and darkness of the world to the place of neutrality that is neither the hermaphroditic aspect of duality conjoined that we see at Vishuddha (where the deity is half male and half female), nor the place of no form that is beyond incarnation in Sahasrara chakra. This is the blended unity of oneness that is a third gender in and of itself. It is here that the sacred syllable AUM arises as the conveyer of such achievement.

THE GURU

It is to the Ajna chakra that the yogi, at death, raises his vital energy, so as to re-enter the realms beyond incarnation, for the awakening here of the kundalini during life serves to erase all karma and elevate the yogi to a place of holding all the magical powers. But it is not through the knowledge of the elements that such an awakening occurs, for Ajna chakra is the place that we receive the teachings and wisdom from our guru rather than the proscribed cleverness of the world of separation and duality.

The syllable *gu* means 'darkness; *ru* 'light'. Thus, a guru dispels darkness with enlightenment and, in the words of BKS Iyengar: 'The conception of a Guru is deep and significant . . . He transmits knowledge of the Spirit.' Such relationships do not sit well with many today. Too often, the notion of a guru is misinterpreted as an autocratic misuse of power, which, at times, it can be. But so, too, do we come across 'upagurus', those who, regardless of where, when and how, teach us something from beyond the realm of the everyday. It is from Ajna chakra that receptivity to these teachings arises.

BEYOND EVERYDAY EXPERIENCE

The aspects of the physical body into which Ajna chakra manifests are our sensory faculties and cognitive processes. For Ajna chakra is closely associated with the mind and our abilities to form abstractions, to conceptualize that which is beyond everyday experience. When Ajna chakra is activated by the rise of kundalini and we have dissolved the knot of the Itara lingum, we are able to see beyond the gross physical realm.

The achievement of Ajna chakra is the expansion into an activation and awareness of the subtle body. The sixth chakra governs the two sheaths that together form the whole of the subtle body (suksma sarira). These sheaths (see page 98) are manomaya kosa (mind sheath) and vijnanamaya kosa (intelligence sheath). It is within this subtle body that the mystical physiology of the chakras reside, intimately influencing and being influenced by aspects of the gross physical body, but in and of itself a far wider vista of perception and consciousness. The shining brow of Ajna chakra allows us to find the path to the true self and see beyond the illusions of duality present in our normal lives. It is this path that opens us to the possibility of ourselves as guru, the dispeller of darkness.

Mandala

The four guardians of space and the vedic demons

Mandalas and yantras are symbols and drawings that operate in many dimensions. At their first level they form a virtual temple space within which disciples travel, meeting guardians and signposts in the journey towards an expanded insight. In the same way that mantras are a manifestation of energy in the form of sound, so yantras and mandalas are facets of that same energy appearing as crafted symbols, letters, shapes and colours.

Within yogic traditions, yanras will comprise the visual form of the seed syllables in the way in which the calligraphy for the bija-mantra AUM is as much used as a focus for meditation as is the chanted or spoken mantra. Mandalas and yantras can operate as triggers to awaken kundalini, contributing to the dissolution of blocks in the subtle body. Such devices are used across cultures and traditions, being particularly developed within Native American art and Tibetan Buddhism.

The roots of Ajna	
Sthula sarira (gross body reflection)	Pituitary gland
Loka (cosmic realm)	Tapaloka (the mansion of the blessed)
Presiding deity	Paramasiva, the inseparable Shiva-Shakti, appearing as the sun
Animal guardian	The black antelope or gazelle, vehicle of Vayu, the god of winds
Tattwa (element principles)	
Ajna is beyond the five kanchukas (veilings) and tattwas (elements)	

Shiva
The lord god of destruction and divine cosmic dancer – the deities of each chakra have now stepped back as the feminine power of the kundalini in the form of Hakini Shakti presides.

Presiding goddess energy
Hakini shakti's six heads bear each of the aspects of perfect meditation: enlightenment, thought control, attention, concentration, meditation and super-conscious concentration.

Bija-mantra
Seed syllable *AUM*, which, upon sounding, connects us to the primal cosmic sound itself, and is a combination of sun (A), moon (U), and fire (M).

Itara lingum
Residence of the granthi of Rudra, which must be dissolved if we are to sustain the insights that have so far been achieved through the rise of kundalini.

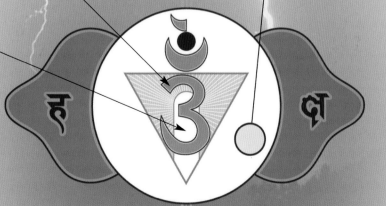

The sixth chakra
Ajna is our third eye that sees through duality into the all-pervading unity of the eternal syllable, *AUM*. It is here that our inner eye opens to the deeper reality of both the universe and the self as it begins to dissolve in a restoration of its divine nature.

सहस्रार

The lotus of the thousand petals, lustrous and whiter than the full moon, has its head turned downward. It charms. It sheds its rays in profusion and is moist and cool like nectar. That most excellent of men who has controlled his mind and known this place is never again born the Wandering, as there is nothing in the three worlds which binds him.

Sat Cakra Nirupana

Sahasrara chakra is located four finger widths above the top of the head, and is the lotus of 1,000 petals. For the first time since kundalini has risen and turned each of the chakra lotuses to face upward, we now find a chakra lotus facing downward. For it is here that the yogi becomes free of the tasks of evolution and experiences the divine rain that drips down from each of those petals.

DIVINE BOUNTY AND HARMONY

One of the stories of the river Ganges tells of its descent to Earth. The drop of such a great volume of water was about to destroy the Earth and sweep it away, until Shiva intervened, stepping in to allow the falling torrent to land first upon his head, and through its entanglement with his hair to run into many tributaries and, in so doing, become sanctified. The rain of the Ganges as it sweeps through Shiva's hair echoes the cool, moist nectar of Sahasrara's cosmic rays.

The nectar of heaven is a theme that echoes across many traditions, including the Hebrew manna and the ambrosia of the Greeks. Each of the chakras will at some level hold its own nectar, being lotuses, but here at Sahasrara the nectar does not merely dwell within the petals, but it rains down throughout the whole of the body.

In terms of the journey of Shiva and Shakti, this nectar is the liquid fruits of their union, and there is no accident to the frequent and abundant sexual imagery with which it is depicted.

In total, 50 is the number of the first six chakras' petals; here, Sahasrara's 1,000 petals denote the 50 letters of the Sanskrit alphabet multiplied by their 20 permutations, so symbolizing all the various permutations of existence. It is with such all-encompassing embrace of the 1,000 permutations of the alphabet that Sahasrara chakra is able to coordinate the other chakras, ensuring harmony.

Here, again, is the place of meditation on our gurus as they serve their role as our projected passport of ascension. For both they and us might now inhabit the infinity of the 1,000-petalled lotus and fulfil the absolute aspect of all teachings, beyond the relativities of time and space.

ASPECTS OF INCARNATION

Sahasrara chakra is not part of the classical listing of the body's six chakras, for not only does it lie beyond the bounds of body, it takes no part in either the gross or subtle bodies. Sahasrara comprises the fifth kosa of the human form (see page 98), the anandamaya kosa (bliss sheath) that is the karana sarira (causal body). This aspect of consciousness clothes the soul with the attachments of life that attend us from incarnation to incarnation. It is a two-way path – we both bring and receive patterns into and out of each of our lives and, as such, this is the karmic vehicle for our soul.

Once we achieve a level of liberation from such a causal body we then inhabit at some level one of the three higher cosmic worlds (lokas). The particular association of Sahasrara is Satyaloko, the 'abode of truth' and liberation from the wheel of life and rebirth. This is the last accomplishment of the yogi and the final freedom from the cycles of seven that are the chakras and the worlds.

At the centre of sahasrara beneath the rainbow cascade of the 1,000 petals of infinity is a smaller trikona triangle at the centre of which rests the radiant bindu (point) that is the void. This bindu within the centre of Sahasrara is a doorway to the absolute reflection of infinity – the one – held within its relative abundance – the many (see pages 112–13).

Samadhi ENLIGHTENMENT AND BLISS

Samadhi is the state of 'beingness', 'absorption' or 'concentration' and, as part of the terminology of transcendence, varies depending on whether it is used in a Buddhist or Hindu context.

From a Buddhist perspective, it echoes the state of nirvana, where differentiations fall away and a state of pure concentration or beingness resides. Here, it forms part of Buddha's threefold teachings of conduct, concentration and wisdom. From a Hindu perspective, its association with the teachings of Krishna in the Bhagavad Gita portray a more devotional element, and the themes of immersion in adoration and worship (bhakti yoga) allow ascension to Samadhi. It is also the eighth branch of Patanjali's classification of yoga in the 2nd century BCE, following the development of both meditation and concentration.

The Sanskrit term itself conveys the sense of the Buddhist and Hindu meanings of 'beingness' and 'absorption'. It is also used to denote a tomb, as well as the conscious ascension from life of a yogi.

As we are seeing with the progress of consciousness at these higher levels of the human landscape, there are stages of such ascension, and Samadhi is given many layers within yogic schools, but is usually identified as having two aspects. The first is savikalpa samadhi, where we experience momentary glimpses of absorption but remain attached to worldly phenomena. The second is nirvikalpa samadhi, which is the state where our identification shifts to the state of being itself, and allows the final dissolution of karma and the purification of all the sariras – the physical, etheric and causal bodies – where there is a nourishing stream of divine love cascading through every level of being. This state might presage a conscious death or a return to everyday awareness (of course, forever changed).

The roots of Sahasrara	
Sthula sarira (gross body reflection)	Pineal gland
Loka (cosmic realm)	Satyaloka (the abode of truth)
Presiding deity	This is Brahma-randhra, the transcendent meeting of Shiva and Shakti
Shakti (goddess energy)	
Bija-mantra (seed syllable)	All sounds, all syllables
Tattwa (element principles)	
Beyond space and time	

Between Shiva and Shakti

This chakra is the realm where the divisions between Shiva and Shakti are at one level, resolved, for this is the goal of the journey of Dakini goddess from her dormancy at the first chakra to her awakening here at the seventh.

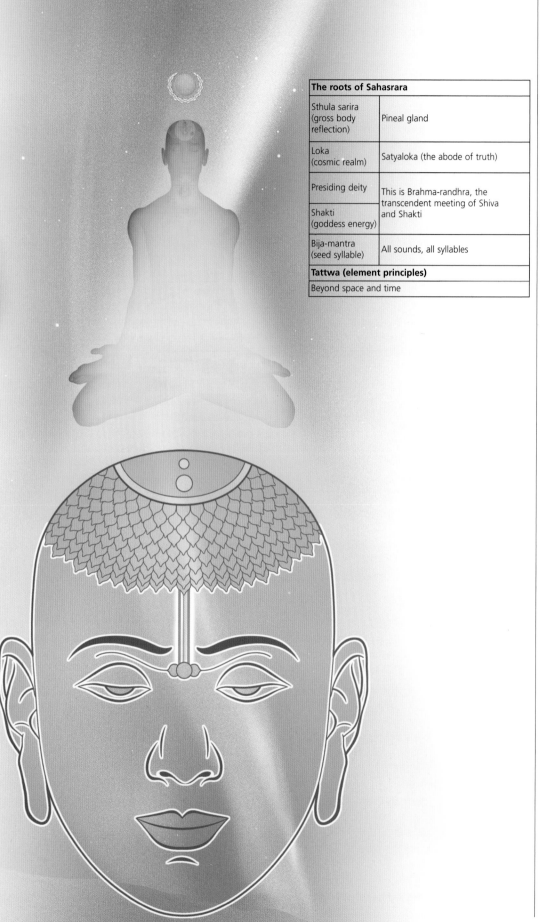

The seventh chakra

Sahasrara is the 1,000-petalled lotus of our cosmic freedom. This is the place of freedom from incarnation, from the elements and from the divisions of gender. But, in the words of Mercia Eliade, 'Everything depends on what is meant by freedom,' and here at Sahasrara there is the final illusion of freedom itself, restored into the mystery of pure consciousness.

Mahabindu
realms beyond the infinite

Within Sahasrara is the full moon resplendent as in a clear sky. Inside it, constantly shining like lightning, is the triangle and inside this again shines the great void which is served in secret by all the devas. Well concealed and attainable only by great effort, is that subtle bindu which is the chief root of liberation.

Sat Cakra Nirupana

Mahabindu is the absolute void beyond many manifestations of chakra wheels, kundalini or nadi channels. While Sahasrara describes the universe in all its infinity, at its very centre resides mahabindu, the great one point where all relativities return to a oneness. In some respects, this is in no way separate from the multiple infinity of Sahasrara, except to express it as a singular infinity. This is yet another expression of the many and the one that permeates our perennial attempts to describe the limits of consciousness with both paradox and allusion. It is for this reason that many different ways are used to track and locate the development of those spheres beyond human incarnation where we are no longer in possession of a causal body to guide us, where existence itself operates within a blended infinity.

FROM RELATIVE TO ABSOLUTE

These realms are beyond the relativity of our consciousness and within the absolute realms of pure freedom. Some teachings track their development as taking place between Ajna and Sahasrara chakras in order to locate it within our conceptual sphere. However, within the historical and cultural variations of the chakras, there are many variations and deviations of the body's subtle physiology, minor chakras identifying sub-routines of our consciousness.

In most of the art there is representing the chakras, and within the virtual guides into the virtual landscape of our developing consciousness, it is both within and beyond Sahasrara that the journey from relative to absolute infinity takes place, from bindu, the Sanskrit word for 'point' or 'seed', to mahabindu, 'absolute void'.

The bindu is a perennial yogic symbol for unity, and throughout each of the chakras two tend to appear side by side, symbolizing

the distinct aspects with which Shiva and Shakti appear at any of these stages. So we have a black bindu for Shakti and a white one for Shiva, in a similar way that within the Chinese traditions we have the cocreation of yin and yang within the symbol of the great ultimate. It is within these bindi that we can envisage each of the deities attending the chakras.

Within certain tantric schools it is the exact identification with the iconographic form of the deity that takes the aspirant into the correct state of being. It is this guidance that allows us to transcend the challenges experienced at that chakra. For such schools, the iconography is not mere visualization, but a distinct activation of the subtle body through a specific symbolic visual language.

It is within this scheme that we find the symbolism of tantra's sacred geometry. The bindu (seed or point) is both zero and infinity. The straight line signifies development. The triangle is a sacred enclosure and the delineation of creation itself. The circle is the essence of all cycles – and, in particular, their reflection as having no beginning or end, is commonly seen as the vehicle of time. The square carries the notion of space and

bounded reality, held and protected by the four directions, elements and guardians. The lotus symbolizes the developing consciousness, attracted by light and transforming its home of darkness. Within Kashmir Shaivism philosophical tradition, the levels of development from the relative to the absolute pass through ten stages that are demarcated from the ground of such sacred symbolism.

At the heart of the yogic mysteries are the constant transcendence of the everyday reality of our senses and attachments and, at the same time, an equally constant immersion of divine love within them. Just as the great history of the Hindu epic text the Mahabharata (see below) spans aeons and yet is concerned with the smallest of ordinary, everyday human detail, so, too, do the chakras chart a development of consciousness that cares for the ultimate cosmic destiny of each seed (bindu) of who we are.

Mahabharata THE GREAT HISTORY OF MANKIND

Together with the Ramayana ('story of Rama'), the Mahabharata is the great classic of Indian literature. It had come into being by the 3rd century BCE and existed for centuries, primarily as an oral and dramatic tradition of stories and plays, until it was written down in Sanskrit by the 4th century CE. It is the world's second longest epic poem (after the Tibetan classic the *Epic of King Gesar*).

The title *Mahabharata* can be translated as 'great India' or 'Great Epic of the Bharata Dynasty'. As with many cultures, there was a general identification with all peoples and nations, and its translation has been justifiably extended to translate as 'Great History of all Mankind'.

Within the work are often extracted segments for their religious import. Thus, the Bhagavad Gita is the sermon that Krishna delivers to Arjuna on the battlefield when Arjuna's resolve falters and he questions the right action to take amid the illusions presented by the world. Another extract takes the

form of the Vishnu Sahasranama, a devotional hymn to Vishnu describing each of his 1,000 names. But as well as containing detailed and elaborate aspects of divinity and yoga, the Mahabharata is also great literature and superb drama, and continues to hold fascination today across India. During the 1980s, life in India (including government cabinet meetings) was scheduled around a long-running television version of the classic, and internationally there have been stage and film productions of the epic.

At one point, the hero Yudhisthira is in exile. He engages with a voice in a lake and in his dialogue demonstrates the perennial relevance of paradox within our everyday lives, and that the presence of the absolute permeates our existence.

In the centre of Sahasrara's effulgence lies a tiny and fascinating beautiful light, the blue pearl. The blue pearl is subtler than the subtlest, it contains the entire cosmos. As you meditate and meditate, one day the blue pearl will explode and its light will fill the universe.

Swami Muktananda

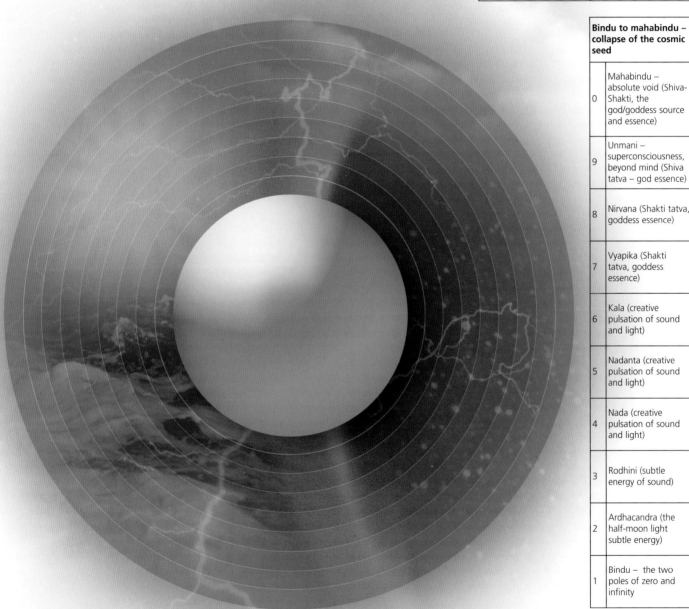

Brahma randhra – the hole of Brahma	
Sthula sarira (gross body reflection)	Anterior fontanelle

Bindu to mahabindu – collapse of the cosmic seed	
0	Mahabindu – absolute void (Shiva-Shakti, the god/goddess source and essence)
9	Unmani – superconsciousness, beyond mind (Shiva tatva – god essence)
8	Nirvana (Shakti tatva, goddess essence)
7	Vyapika (Shakti tatva, goddess essence)
6	Kala (creative pulsation of sound and light)
5	Nadanta (creative pulsation of sound and light)
4	Nada (creative pulsation of sound and light)
3	Rodhini (subtle energy of sound)
2	Ardhacandra (the half-moon light subtle energy)
1	Bindu – the two poles of zero and infinity

The blue pearl

The bindu is both the cosmic dot on which the universe rests and the Hindu pilgrim's mark of blessing and protection on the forehead. This progression is from a singular infinity to an absolute one and is tracked in ten stages as we count down towards the centre of the universe, taking in: 1 bindu (the outer ring); 2 ardhacandra; 3 rodhini; 4 nada; 5 nadanta; 6 kala; 7 vyapika; 8 nirvana; 9 unmani; and finishing with 0 mahabindu (the blue pearl) at the centre.

Kundalini

courting the serpent power of awakening

She is beautiful like a chain of lightning and fine like a lotus fibre, and shines in the minds of the sages. She is extremely subtle; the awakener of pure knowledge; the embodiment of all bliss, whose true nature is pure consciousness. Shining in her mouth is the Brahma-dvara (Kundalini's entrance and exit in her path to and from Shiva). This place in the entrance to the region is sprinkled by ambrosia.

Sat Cakra Nirupana

The chakras themselves are more properly the domain of kundalini yoga rather than any of the other tributaries of the vastness of Indian science. It is only within the context of the awakening of the kundalini energy that the chakras come into their true potential.

Kundalini, meaning 'coiled up', is the potential of divine awakening dormant within every human. It resides as the Brahma knot within the heart of the Muladhara chakra at the base of the spine, and, indeed, within every aspect of creation. For the polarities of male and female, god and goddess, are understood to be immanent throughout all things, within which arise these poles of light and dark, stillness and movement, energy and consciousness. For the human being, rising kundalini is the activation of every aspect of their energy (represented by Shakti) in union with every aspect of their consciousness (represented by Shiva).

TANTRA

As yoga has spread across the world in the 19th and 20th centuries, kundalini yoga and tantric yoga have sometimes come to be associated only with specific branches of its original expression – the teachings of worship that include ritualized sex. Not surprisingly, little of the depth of this part of kundalini yoga comes across, as in translation it tends to remain within the realm of voyeuristic fantasy rather than engaging the power and sacredness of what is more properly called the left-hand path of tantra.

Tantra translates as 'technique' and has a wide range of relevance throughout yogic history and practice. Each of its practitioners are concerned with the awakening of kundalini and the union of energy and consciousness, goddess and god. But there are two main manifestations of techniques –

dakshina marga and vama marga – the right-hand path and the left-hand path. The key difference is that practitioners of vama marga (left-hand path) practise the pancha-makara rites, in which the five 'm's – madya (wine), mamsa (meat), matsya (fish), mudra (cereal) and maithuna (sex) – are enjoyed as sacraments rather than shunned as spiritual pollutants, as they are in the right-hand path.

But the key to the awakening of kundalini is not which route one takes, the left- or the right-hand path. It is more whether the chosen path is one of awakening. Within each there are obstacles, within each are the knots at Muladhara, Anahata and Ajna chakras. It is more the guidance of the guru and the weight of one's spiritual community, including the sacred writings, the deities, and the messages left at each of the ascending realms, that will ultimately help the aspirant more than a doctrinal debate about the rightness or wrongness of a particular path.

In the history of yoga, the rise of tantra between the 3rd and 6th centuries CE was as much a backlash against the vedic austerity as it was a new branch of Hindu lore. Indeed, the movement found much application within Buddhism and the power of kundalini echoes throughout expressions of Indian spirituality, as the cobra's cowl is equally shown as a symbol of Buddha and of Vishnu.

From a historical point of view, we could say that it was a reinstatement of the role of the goddess within the Indo-Asian spiritual world. Such a reinstatement inevitably saw lineages rise up where the Divine Mother was worshipped in very particular ways that continue to this day and modern Indian saints, such as Mother Meera and Amma, hold the blessings of the goddess. Indeed, it is usually only within the tantric tradition that we find female gurus. But ultimately tantra is about balance, the consensual dance between Shiva and Shakti within us, whether or not we are male or female and follow the left- or right-hand path.

Khajuraho Temple
HOMAGE TO SACRED UNION

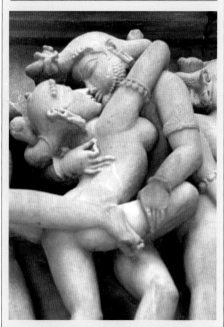

One of the many statues at Khajuraho temple celebrating sacred eroticism

The temples at Khajuraho in northern India were built during the 10th century by the kings of the Chandella dynasty. They depict a wide variety of scenes, but are most famous for their depictions of sexual union. While it is not unusual for temples throughout India to show such images and sculptures, those at Khajuraho are perhaps the most extensive.

Amid the many great expressions of left-hand tantra are the collective rituals the like of which were celebrated at the great yogini temple at Ranipur-Jharial, at the centre of which was a statue of Shiva and in the 64 niches around the walls were statues of yoginis in various poses.

The kundalini, in the form of latency, is coiled like a serpent. One who impels this goddess to move will attain liberation.
Hathayoga Pradpika

Energy of awakening
The rise of the kundalini energy of awakening is symbolized by the snake, and in particular the king cobra. His spreading hood is protective, evocative of the increased dangers of power and illusion the more that we become 'awake' and are able to find our way through the distractions that call us away from the sheer power of cosmic consciousness.

Sephiroth

Cosmic spheres of the Kabbalah's Tree of Life

A 16th-century woodcut of the Tree of Life

Sephiroth are spheres of energy within the body and aura and function on many levels. Taken together, all ten of the Sephiroth form the *Ets Chayim*, or Tree of Life, a conceptual and literal map of the universe, human beings, and the cycles of all energy processes. This map is central to the Kabbalah, a Jewish mystical school that emerged in the Levantine Nile Delta more than 2,000 years ago. The earliest explorations concern the Maaseh Merkabah, 'workings of the chariot', that Ezekiel saw in his great vision, the intricate and transcendental machinery of heaven and earth. The Sephiroth as presented here are an expression of Hermetic Kabbalah, an aspect of the Hebraic lineages as they arose within European mysticism, sharing a wide range of confluences with Greek panentheism and numerology, Christianity, Gnosticism and Egyptian magic.

Sephira (plural: *sephiroth*) is Hebrew for 'emanation'. Each sephira represents stages of the divine spark of creation that cascades from the universe's emergence from the 'big bang'. Described as a lightning flash of creative force, it is infinity's attempt to find a reflection of itself in manifest form.

As a map of human form and consciousness, the Tree of Life is a blueprint for the divine human. This blueprint provides a pathway for the return journey along the lightning flash, back up the Tree of Life in a quest to regain a conscious and persistent sense of the original source from which we came. The return journey is the 'path of the serpent'. This name reflects not only the fear and danger associated with knowledge and awareness, but also the power and energy. A third way of traversing the tree is the 'path of the arrow', the ascent directly up the middle pillar of equilibrium. Archangels, Hebrew letters and Egyptian deities all hold the wisdom of the spheres.

The Sephiroth themselves resemble spheres of light, each of which appears within our aura to the extent that it is embodied and manifest within our consciousness. It is coloured and textured according to which part of creation it arises from and which correspondences are associated with it. These associations with planets, herbs, scents and divinities all shape a sephira's manifestation within our bodies.

The Tree of Life is more conceptual than some other world views mapping the spirit within the body. It offers a vision of life in relationship with the infinity of its ultimate source. Such a vision offers us understanding and progress along the path of restoration, a renewal of the divine spark within each of us.

Malkuth

sphere of the kingdom and the elements

*Man has no Body distinct from his Soul
for that call'd Body is a portion of the Soul
discern'd by the five Senses,
the chief inlets of Soul in this age.*
William Blake

Malkuth is the substance of our sensory experience, the interface of our bodies with the external world. Every sight, sound, taste and texture we experience through our body is the world of the kingdom of heaven, most strongly felt through our feet. This is neither subjective perception nor objective reality, but the intersubjective realm of life's experience of itself enabled by the senses.

Malkuth is the sphere of the manifest world and the elements. It is the phase of creation where matter is the gateway for all other realms of consciousness. Just as the crown sphere Kether holds the divine blueprint of the whole universe, so Malkuth holds the manifestation of its realms. Along the lightning flash of creation, it is the last of the spheres; along the serpent's path of return, it is the first. One of the central axioms of Kabbalah is 'Kether is Malkuth, Malkuth is Kether'. Kether is the first (or last) sephira at the top of the tree – the Tree of Life has no spiritual hierarchy, for it is said that 'Heaven is the Earth, the Earth is Heaven'.

VISION AND ENGAGEMENT

The guiding vision of Malkuth is that of our holy guardian angel residing in Tiphareth, the sphere of balance at the heart. Here, the higher self is our mediator between heaven and earth, spirit and matter, reminding us that they are each but one expression of a core reality of who we and the universe truly are. With this, the spiritual challenge of Malkuth is that of a deep inertia, a stasis that arises from an ambivalence about fully engaging with life, with the terrible and graceful abundance of the sensory world. This lack of engagement follows through becoming a fear of death, either of the great transformation of our physical passing or of the little everyday deaths of letting go of our attachments within the sensory world.

The physical manifestation of these challenges often leads to conditions of the whole body as well as mental states arising from an ambivalence about life. Within the human form, Malkuth is the sphere at our feet as well as the expression of the whole of our body and our senses.

The primary trap of Malkuth is to divide our experience horizontally, as represented by heaven and earth, spirit and matter, rather than to employ our discernment in every experience, at whatever level of consciousness. The virtue of Malkuth is this capacity to make distinctions that serve our blended knowing of heaven and earth rather than separate our world into the sacred and the profane. Sandalphon and Geb stand as guardians of this wisdom, embodiments of the signature of Malkuth's blessing of life.

GODS AND GUARDIANS OF THE SEPHIROTH

Most traditions describe, at some level, the beings that populate the various realms of the universe. 'Angels' are an awareness of such people from a particularly Judaeo-Islamic-Christian lineage that owes much to the Sumerian civilization that flourished in the Tigris-Euphrates basin more than 5,000 years ago. This desert culture knew the spirits of heaven as *igigi* and described them as 'sons' or 'messengers' of the gods.

Opinion is divided as to the nature of such angelic and divine dimensions, with some commentators knowing them as aspects of the human imagination and others knowing them as beings in their own right that interact with and assist us in our journeys. In both Sumerian angel lore and the Egyptian divine pantheon, such realms are peopled and guarded by specific beings. And as the Kabbalah developed over the centuries, each of the Sephiroth were associated with angels and gods who embodied the essence of that aspect of creation, and who held a beacon for an evolving humanity.

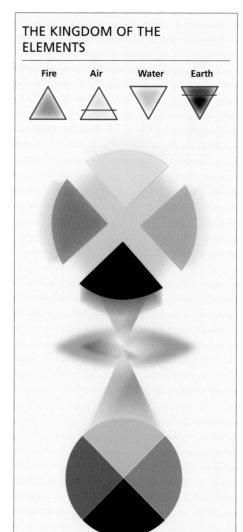

THE KINGDOM OF THE ELEMENTS

Fire Air Water Earth

The Kabbalah's elements are those of Western civilization, including Greek, Egyptian and Christian traditions. In the Hermetic Kabbalah (the branch that blended with Western magical traditions), they are symbolized both as primary colours (for example, fire a bright red) and also their form having passed through the spectrum of the rainbow (again, fire, now a deep russet). This transformation emphasizes that they are not separate, but they are facets of a wider whole. The elements of the kingdom are not those of building blocks waiting to be assembled; rather they are those of the awakened celebration of life and form.

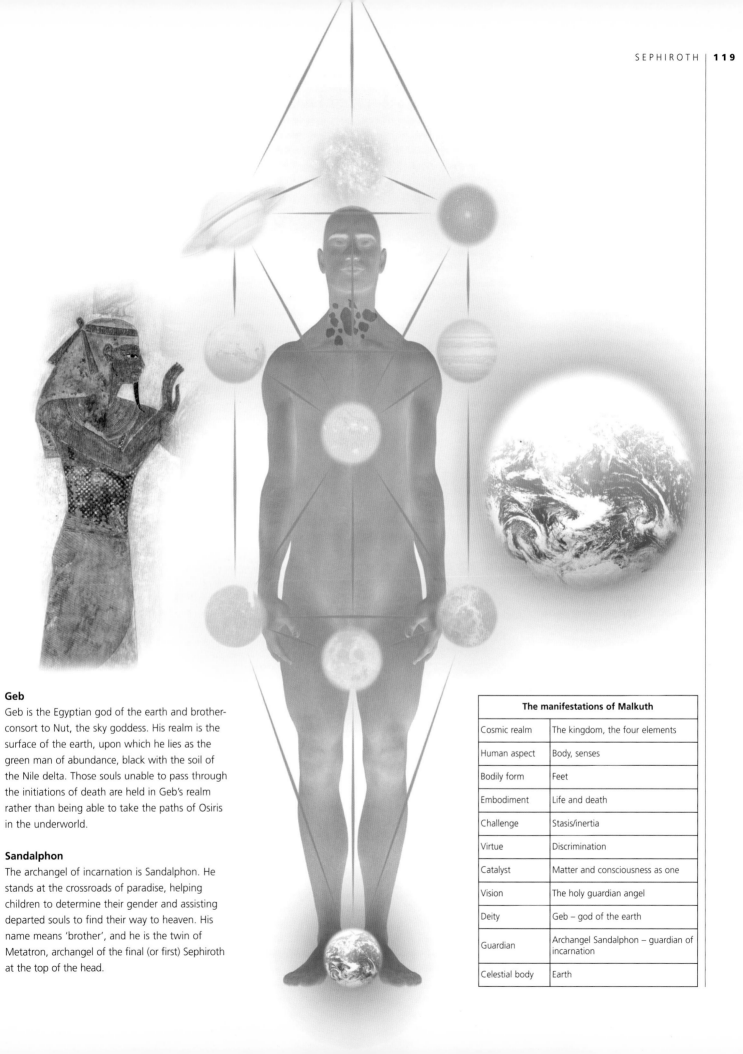

Geb

Geb is the Egyptian god of the earth and brother-consort to Nut, the sky goddess. His realm is the surface of the earth, upon which he lies as the green man of abundance, black with the soil of the Nile delta. Those souls unable to pass through the initiations of death are held in Geb's realm rather than being able to take the paths of Osiris in the underworld.

Sandalphon

The archangel of incarnation is Sandalphon. He stands at the crossroads of paradise, helping children to determine their gender and assisting departed souls to find their way to heaven. His name means 'brother', and he is the twin of Metatron, archangel of the final (or first) Sephiroth at the top of the head.

The manifestations of Malkuth	
Cosmic realm	The kingdom, the four elements
Human aspect	Body, senses
Bodily form	Feet
Embodiment	Life and death
Challenge	Stasis/inertia
Virtue	Discrimination
Catalyst	Matter and consciousness as one
Vision	The holy guardian angel
Deity	Geb – god of the earth
Guardian	Archangel Sandalphon – guardian of incarnation
Celestial body	Earth

Yesod

sphere of foundation and instinct

Healing is to enter into with mercy and awareness that which has been withdrawn from in pain and hatred.

Steven Levine

Yesod is the sphere of our rich and vivid subconscious, the centre of personality and powerhouse of our instinctual drives. It is the penultimate phase before the final manifestation of creation in the world. It is the mirror of mists where incarnations, patterns, blessings, motives and currents swirl within the moonlight of our lives. This is the astral light that is pregnant with the potential of all that is possible.

Yesod is the lunar plasma of potentiality, the bridge between matter and consciousness, the astral light known as Akasha. This is the foundation of magical practice that finds its other pole in Daath, bridging the middle of the tree as conducting rod of heaven and earth as they manifest in Malkuth and Kether. And as the rod is planted in the foundation of both consciousness and reality, so too does it divide and know the polarity of the two pillars, wings of the heart and columns of holding that can find balance and discord within their polarity. Yesod is the hidden balance of life itself. And the greatest polarity

of what it means to be human is held within our own gender, and it is here at Yesod that the archetypes of male and female energy find a fantastic collision in reunion and bonding. Sexuality and sexual activity are aspects of this cosmic quest for unity. The immediacy of a thunderstorm's 'equalizing' of electrical forces between the atmosphere and the ground is an example of this cosmic reunion of opposite energies.

PHYSICAL AND SPIRITUAL CHALLENGE

The spiritual challenge of Yesod is idleness. Our instincts can lie dormant in a tired unwillingness to engage with the chaos of the world, or we can project our unacknowledged self onto other situations and people. Yesod is overseen by the moon, and the dual blessing of this tidal magnet and midnight mirror is reflected in Yesod's role as the centre of our personality.

The physical manifestation of these challenges often concern the reproductive system and the extent to which we allow the passions of sexuality to ride through us. This can be expressed as much in gardening as in sexual activity, but it is often our moon cycles (menstrual for women, more hidden for men) that reflect the vitality of our foundation.

For each of us there will always be some aspects of our shadow that drives us in unseen ways. The path of Yesod is to reveal to ourselves as much as possible the

dynamics of these impulses so that they do not hijack us in ways that do not serve our life path. This is not about repression – if that happens, the psychic generator of our being is quashed and we lose energy and form as we twist and suppress our essential nature. It is, rather, about allowing enough of a gentleness with our own internal world to be able to free up those lost sparks of consciousness trapped within the memories of disappointment, grief, oppression, abuse.

So the virtue of Yesod is independence, and the discipline is always to remember that our strong reactions to people or places often hold a charge because of our own unconscious patterns and symbols. The work of Yesod is to observe the left-field impulses and to acknowledge their role. The more they are acknowledged, the more power we have to steer through the tidal rhythms of our lives that are governed by the moon, and respond to these currents with grace. Gabriel and Bast assist with this perpetual balance of guiding our passions and instincts and find the centre of who we are within the vast currents of the collective.

THE LESSER BANISHING RITUAL OF THE PENTAGRAM

Resist the desire to gossip and speak bad about others! Kabbalistically, the sin of murder is not limited to physical death; it includes character assassination. Terminating a conversation or changing the subject, is therefore the equivalent of saving someone's life.

Yehuda Berg

The spiritual discipline arising from Yesod is that of not projecting our own unconscious prejudices onto others. One of the precepts taken by Buddhist monks and nuns is that of abstaining from false speech. This is almost universal in spiritual traditions, for how we speak of others is the foundation of our quest to reclaim the light of our soul.

This level of internal guardianship is also to be found in Western magic's 'Lesser Banishing Ritual of the Pentagram'. This form of the ceremony was developed within MacGregor Mathers' Order of the Golden Dawn at the end of the 19th century. This is a complex body of teaching and ritual magic practice, but this part derives almost entirely from a Kabbalistic classic, the Sefer Yetzirah, which concerns itself with the symbolism of numbers and letters of the Hebrew alphabet.

The Lesser Banishing Ritual of the Pentagram is similar to many rituals of other traditions that demarcate sacred space and energetically and spiritually cleanse an area before embarking on a period of prayer or ceremony. Each tradition will

employ methods in keeping with their spiritual landscape, but at the heart of these practices is the clearing of unwanted unconscious influences, both on the astral radio frequencies and, particularly, within oneself. The pentagram itself holds the near universal blessing of the outstretched human standing between heaven and earth.

Tarot paths of wisdom

XXI Universe teaches that our horizon is not the limit of our consciousness, and that, through journeying within ourselves, we can achieve a knowledge of the universality of life.

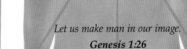

Let us make man in our image.
Genesis 1:26

God of the moon

Bast is the Egyptian god of the moon, inhabiting the region between the sky and earth. Once goddess of the sun, in her later role she is the patron of childhood and child-rearing, passion and secrets.

Herald of incarnation

The archangel Gabriel is the herald of incarnation. Sometimes seen as the only female archangel, she was herald to the births of Samson, Mary, John and Jesus. She is understood to be the teacher of wisdom to children within the womb, aided by her association with the moon.

XXI UNIVERSE

The foundation of Yesod	
Cosmic realm	Foundation
Human aspect	The etheric body, sexuality, subconscious
Bodily form	Sexual organs/reproductive system
Embodiment	Stability in change
Challenge	Idleness
Virtue	Independence
Catalyst	Quest for union
Vision	Machinery of the universe
Tarot guide	XXI universe
Deity	Bast – goddess of passion
Guardian	Archangel Gabriel – herald of incarnation
Celestial body	Moon

Hod

sphere of splendour and thought

*The answer that uproots the question from
its ground is truly inspired.*
Sufi saying

Hod is the content and nature of our mental lives; our thoughts and ideas, philosophies and beliefs, doubts and lies. It is here that we decide how to engage with the vastness of the universe, and whether we employ our minds to illuminate or imprison our perceptions. For Hod is the realm of splendour where the wonder of life's harmony is revealed. It is an intellectual appreciation of the intricacy of the universe as well as the beauty of each human intellect.

VISION AND CHALLENGE

The guiding vision of Hod is splendour – the radiance of the harmonious universe. This is a mental appreciation of the vastness of infinity's design that prompts the awe and wonder of the eureka moment. The history of science is abundant with these moments of great insight, where the dynamics of the world's working is appreciated in its beauty and complexity. This is where the rightness of a vision or a theory resonates within the mind of the researcher and the available evidence slots into place for that moment in time, waiting for the next expansion of insight and understanding. Such vision applies as much within mathematical mysticism and numerology as it does within astronomy and quantum physics, and it is this vision that is the core of magical traditions as they seek to find the associations within consciousness that will allow an intellect to flow along the pathways of the universe's own patterning.

The great library founded by Pharaoh Ptolemy II at Alexandria in Egypt symbolizes the human quest for knowledge that is embodied within Hod. It especially held the ethics of multi-cultural and multi-disciplinary approaches to wisdom, as all the scrolls that entered the city were copied and then returned to their owners. The library is said to have been founded with Aristotle's personal papers handed down to his close disciples.

The splendour of Hod is apparent in the appreciation of beauty shown by philosophies that arise from the natural rhythms of the universe – the music of the spheres that describe astronomy's great synchronicities and patterns, the mathematical precision of a nautilus shell, and the sheer diversity of snowflakes' forms. Such visions are, however, countered by the employment of the intellect to dominate and oppress, whether politically within totalitarian regimes, or environmentally where the landscape is mutilated rather than honoured.

And so the spiritual challenge of Hod is that of untruth and domination, ranging from outright lies to the spin and subtle interpretations of our experience in the service of a tidy mind. Most often this will manifest as a rigidity in our belief systems and a sureness of our intrinsic rightness. This is not the certainty of our knowledge of god or the inner knowing of our soul's path, but a rigidity in attaching ourselves to the exact form of the signposts themselves, and gives rise to fundamentalism and extremism.

The physical manifestation of these challenges is the right side of our bodies, especially the right kidney, leg, arm and hand. This is our 'best foot forward' that steps out into the world with intention, boldness and vision. Along the path of the serpent rising up the Tree of Life, Hod is the first sphere to share a level of consciousness with another – that of Netzach (feeling). Their influence comes together in the solar plexus and belly, forming the power of our gut instincts. When out of balance, the rigidity of Hod can be reflected in an overall physical stiffness, particularly in the joints, or in the compulsive desire for order. The appreciation of splendour can also become unhooked from the rest of the tree to the extent that the associations it provides reel off into a dissociated world of meaningless fantasy and mental constructs devoid of passion, relevance or beauty.

THE IMPLICATE ORDER AND THE 72 NAMES OF GOD

In giving us the capacity to conceive the whole of creation, Hod necessarily takes us out of our own limitations of mind. Poetry, paradox and nonsense have typically been central to such an intellectual discipline, but within both mysticism and science there are also threads of revelation that enable us to employ our minds in ways that account for their limitations and introduce the disciplines of thinking with infinity.

In the *Or HaSeichal* (The Light of the Intellect), the 13th-century Sicilian Kabbalist Abraham Abulafia developed the vision described in Exodus 14 of the 72 names of god. He elaborated them as a meditational guide to facilitate the presence of light within our lives. Each name is a three-letter sequence in Hebrew that is not intended to make sense to the conscious mind but rather impact on the whole of our energy field, triggering a response, a blessing and an illumination within the whole mind. This is a spiritual technology of the body-mind where the infinite is invited to have a place within the everyday challenges of our lives.

This vision of infinity's presence within life finds a contemporary echo in the vision of the late David Bohm, an American quantum physicist and author of *Wholeness and the Implicate Order*. Bohm explained that within the universe everything is connected to everything else, an 'ultra-holistic cosmic view'. Essentially, Bohm said, there are no boundaries or borders within the universe, and no particle, plant or personality that is separate from its world. Bohm developed his theories in response to the activities of sub-atomic particles that acted in tandem across vast distances with no perceivable ways of communicating with each other, apart from an intrinsic 'implicate' connection. He extended this into saying that every particle has infinite knowledge and connection to every other particle in all dimensions.

Fundamentally, the particle is only an abstraction that is manifest to our senses. 'What is', is always a totality of ensembles which intermingle and interpenetrate each other throughout the whole of space.
David Bohm

Tarot paths of wisdom
XX Judgement teaches of the divine patterns
present within our everyday experience, and
the rhythms that enlighten and expand
rather than those that punish and
imprison. XIX Sun brings the blessings of
the unconscious to light, shining into the
darkness of the unknown and releasing the
mysteries of the moon into the realm of thought.

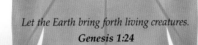

Let the Earth bring forth living creatures.
Genesis 1:24

XIX SUN

XX JUDGEMENT

God of the soul's journey
Anubis is the Egyptian god of the soul's journey
in both life and death. He is the gatekeeper of
the Halls of the Underworld. He is the overseer
of the weighing of a deceased's soul against
the feather of truth belonging to Ma'at, goddess
of truth.

Scales of justice
The archangel Michael holds aloft the flaming
sword of his strength in the battle between light
and darkness. Original slayer of the dragon, his
form has been claimed for many sides in the
'good fight' and the 'holy war'. He stands with
the scales of justice in preparation for the last
judgement when he will weigh all deeds and
serve as the great balancer of time.

The splendour of Hod	
Cosmic realm	Splendour
Human aspect	Thought
Bodily form	Right hip, kidney, leg
Embodiment	An expanded and anchored mind
Challenge	Dishonesty
Virtue	Truthfulness
Catalyst	Holism of truth
Vision	Splendour
Tarot guides	XX Judgement, XIX Sun
Deity	Anubis – god of the soul's journey
Guardian	Archangel Michael – viceroy of heaven
Celestial body	Mercury

Netzach

sphere of victory and feeling

*Our feelings are our most genuine
path to knowledge*
Audre Lorde

Netzach is the flow and form of emotions; of our joy and sorrow, hopes and fears, peace and anger, celebration and despair. It is here that the shape of our emotional life rises from cultural and family history as well as our own individual flows of feeling. This is typically the level where we can experience imbalance and favour one side of the Tree or the other.

Hod (thoughts) and Netzach (feeling) are these primary polarities of the personality and within each we can tend to favour either the bright or shadow side; acknowledging the range of our thoughts and feelings allows us a roundness and lends authenticity to these Sephiroth. Venus, the planet that embodies the celestial vision of Netzach, is both the morning and evening star, guiding the dawn and the dusk of our days.

For Netzach is the sphere of victory as creation's lightning flash finds first manifestation in the realm of the personal consciousness. Here it is that the beauty of the universe is responded to with a passion and expressed by artistic endeavour, in balanced and creative opposition to the intellectual beauty of Hod's philosophies and thoughts.

VISION AND CHALLENGE

The guiding vision of Netzach is that of 'triumphant beauty'. This is the full openness of a vibrant emotional relationship with the world around us, either in ecstasy and celebration or in the witness of our terrors and disappointments. Hathor, the Egyptian goddess of this sphere, had more festivals dedicated to her than any of her peers. She oversaw the ecstatic celebration of life and the fertility of both humans and the earth.

The spiritual challenge of Netzach is the retreat into lust. This could be a closed door to emotions that then become distorted and whose energy finds a warped expression in thoughts, physicality or the unconscious. Or emotions separate themselves off from the rest of the Tree and, having no context, relationship or ritual to guide the torrent of our emotional world, become unbridled.

The physical manifestations of these challenges are a lack of integrity and holding together of form. Where Hod imbalances are likely to tend towards rigidity, Netzach going into imbalance gives rise to a looseness, of muscles, bowels, body fluids. Joints are likely to become weak rather than stiff and the adrenal balance of the kidneys will lack the stimulating rhythm of adrenaline. Most perceptibly, though, will be imbalances of emotion as their relationship with the rest of the Tree allows a latitude and lack of cohesion. Such polarities are more common than we might think, as emotional fluency has been undervalued in a world that often places rationalism as the mark of intelligence.

This is exacerbated by a tendency not to take responsibility for our feelings, but rather to blame others for the way we feel. There is a vast difference between saying to someone 'You make me angry' and 'When you do that I feel angry'. Such a discipline of communication lies at the heart of much mediation and conflict-resolution work and, in particular, the 'non-violent communication' system developed by Marshall Rosenberg.

The common experience that the sharing of feelings provides is taken further within Netzach as the sphere of bondings. It is here that the cohesion of the universe shows itself as our attractions to each other become powerful forces within family and social structures. This is the realm of a love that calls to the altruistic tendencies within us all.

Whereas Hod can be a relatively solitary realm of thought, emotions are far more collective beings that are nurtured in group ceremony and celebration. In this way, it is emotion that can power us up to take the leap from the sphere of the personality in the first four spheres to the realm of soul at Tiphareth (see pages 126–7). Hanael and Hathor offer us the wisdom held within Netzach of the balance between context and expression and the gifts of emotional intelligence.

APPLICATION OF THE TREE OF LIFE IN EVERYDAY LIFE

Businesses, political structures, national identities and personal relationships can all be mapped onto the Tree in order to identify which aspect of the creative cycle is out of balance. This perspective can help to mitigate the damaging oppression of unrestrained emotional archetypes, such as fear, anger, rapture and despair. When any part of a whole becomes overtly strong or weak, the resulting imbalance can distort the health and viability of the collective.

Apply the following questions (see right) to any chosen situation and then write down your first spontaneous answers. The areas that you struggle with or leave blank may be as instructive as those that you complete. The 'X' question is for the no-sphere of Daath (see pages 132–3), and so has no number.

As you answer these questions, allow your awareness to trace up and down the questions to discover where the imbalances are. Try not to solve any riddles; just be aware and trust yourself to discover the keys of rebalancing.

10 What is actually, factually happening?

9 What habits might be shaping the situation?

8 What ideas or beliefs are around?

7 What feelings are there?

6 How is this situation serving your soul's vision?

5 How is divine protection showing itself?

4 Where does an unconditional love arise?

X What gem of knowledge is hidden from you?

3 How did it all begin?

2 What was the original plan?

1 What is your inspiration?

Tarot paths of wisdom

XVIII Moon is the subtle stream of our emotional responses to the beauty of the world. XVII Star guides the glistening ecstasy within our shadow into the stardust of our potential. XVI Tower is the discipline of surrender as we allow the rhythms of our emotions and our fallibility of mind to unleash the splendour and victory of both.

Let the waters swarm with living creatures.
Genesis 1:20

XVI TOWER

XVII STARS

XVIII MOON

God of fertility

Hathor is Netzach's deity, the Egyptian cow-horned goddess of fertility. She is the patron of singing, dancing, love, art and women, and the irrepressible fertility of the plant world. Mistress of jubilation and queen of the dance, she preserves through nurturing and was one of the most popular of old Egypt's deities, with more festivals dedicated to her than to any of her fellow gods.

Seeds of happiness

Hanael (glory of the grace of god) stands as the archangel of friendship and beauty, bringing love and harmony to humankind. Equally manifesting as a beautiful woman or a handsome man, Hanael transforms sadness and anxiety and helps us find the seeds of happiness within ourselves.

The victory of Netzach	
Cosmic realm	Victory
Human aspect	Feelings, both welcome and unwelcome
Bodily form	Right kidney and leg
Embodiment	Emotional intelligence
Challenge	Lust
Virtue	Selflessness
Catalyst	Altruism of community and celebration
Vision	Triumphant beauty
Tarot guides	XVI Tower, XVII Star, XVIII Moon
Deity	Hathor – goddess of fertility
Guardian	Archangel Hanael
Celestial body	Venus

Tiphareth
sphere of harmony and resurrection

The Sixth Path is called the Mediating Intelligence, because in it are multiplied the influxes of the Emanations; for it causes that influence to flow into all the reservoirs of the blessings with which they themselves are united.

Sepher Yetzirah

Tiphareth is the meeting point of the 'as above' and the 'so below' and centre point of the whole structure of the Tree of Life. Its mediating intelligence bridges the world of spirit and matter through the medium of soul. This balance of worlds is symbolized in the interlocking equilateral triangles of the seal of Solomon. The central pillar of the Tree of Life can be seen as an answer to the question 'Who am I?' How we associate ourselves with the vast infinity of spirit (Kether), the foundations of our unconsciousness (Yesod) and the presence of the physical world (Malkuth) is a process that comes together in Tippareth at the very centre of our circle of soul. It is here that an awareness of previous incarnations unfolds as we locate the soul at the centre of our lives rather than the rhythms of the personality.

The reflection of Tippareth in the human form is within the chest, including the heart, lungs and solar plexus, and in particular the breastbone and thymus gland. This is the *Sacré Coeur* of the eternal soul, the risen Christ. Here, all sun gods reign as a symbol of the perfected soul walking; Amoun Ra, Mithra, Krishna, Osiris. Tiphareth holds the planetary resonance of the sun at the centre of the solar system and carries with it all the characteristics of our cosmic nourishment, the energy, the healing, the upliftment and the light of our own planetary star.

Within Christian expressions of the Kabbalah, this is the sphere of the Christos, the sacrificed god who is initially seen as the totality of the godhead, but reveals himself as the radiance of the solar sun. His ultimate task is that of both inspiring devotion and showing the way of sacrifice, making sacred our lives by releasing the investments of our personality so we come into the essence of service. This is the devotional ecstasy that helps us ascend into the place of soul, initially called by the solar personification of divinity, be it the Christos, Osiris or Mithra, and then met by our own soul and shown the next stage of the journey as our soul and sun cast their gaze across the abyss towards Kether, crown of the great source, and centre of the Milky Way.

SPIRITUAL AND PHYSICAL CHALLENGE

The spiritual challenge of Tiphareth is pride – the temptation to harness the soul's gifts and insights gathered so far on the journey to employ them in service of the personality. It is here that the issue arises of to what do we dedicate our lives. It is through the mediation and embodiment of Tiphareth that all gifts and skills the adept acquires remain aligned with the Tree itself, in service to the collective unfolding of the life, choreographing the work of the personality.

Physically, these challenges will manifest in the respiratory and circulatory systems. The rhythms of our heartbeat and breath provide a basic focus and centring. When we are off-centre, the cadence of our lives is lopsided, and lung and heart problems deliver distress signals of congestion, weakness or deficiency. There is a stillness and surrender required by the soul that is empowered by the silent running of our principal life-support systems.

The virtue of Tiphareth is devotion to the 'great work'; part of all wisdom traditions is the teaching that the personality is required to pass over its demands and whims to an often unseen and unknown higher good. In accepting the harmony of a life centred on one's soul, our perspective changes to one where we can see equally the vastness of the cosmos and the abundance of the natural world. This consciousness is our saviour that counters the illusions of redemption being found outside of ourselves, and the full realization that one's own inner world is the gateway of service, a gateway held by the transformative presence of Osiris and Raphael, masters of healing and service.

ISAAC BEN SOLOMON LURIA (1534–72)

Of the many scholars and mystics who moulded the Kabbalah, perhaps one of the most charismatic and influential was Isaac ben Solomon Luria. Born in Jerusalem of German parents, he studied the Zohar – the classic of Jewish mysticism – in depth, and became a devoted Kabbalist while running his family's spice-trading business on the banks of the Nile. Influenced strongly by his contemporary Moses Cordevo, he moved with his family to Safed in Palestine to join the Kabbalistic community there. He taught in the oral tradition and his teachings were written down only after his death in 1572 during the epidemic that swept Palestine.

Luria was known for his fantastic spiritual insights and skills. Some stories about him inform us that he believed himself to be the messiah. Among his amazing gifts was the ability to see the nature of people's transgressions simply by looking at their foreheads, and he taught disciples his methods of dialogue with the souls of *tazddikim*, or the righteous.

In addition to this, Luria taught disciples about the application of Kabbalah in everyday life and specifically the responsibility to make clear the light and consciousness of god within the world in a practical way.

The Ari was expert in the language of trees, the language of birds, and the speech of angels. He knew the mysteries of gilgul (reincarnation), who had been born previously, and who was here for the first time. He could look at a person and tell him how he was connected to higher spiritual levels, and his original root in Adam. By a person's scent he was able to know all that he had done. All this we saw with our own eyes.

Rabbi Chaim Vital

Tarot paths of wisdom

XV Devil is the playful capacity to be our own Devil's advocate, liberating us from rigidity or negativity in our thinking. XIV Art is the liberated crafting of our unconscious and sexual natures in harmony with the rest of creation. XIII Death challenges the notion that in raising the frequency of our body of light we will lose what is most dear to our core essence.

XV DEVIL XIV ART XIII DEATH

Let there be luminaries in the firmament.
Genesis 1:14

Lord of resurrection

Osiris, lord of resurrection, guides humanity through the mysteries and trials of death and initiation. Osiris was murdered by Set, his son, who cast his dismembered body across the span of Egypt. But each part was reassembled and his life restored by his other son, Horus, so giving him sovereignty over death.

Serpent archangel

Raphael is 'the shining one who heals', the serpent archangel guardian of our ascent up the Tree of Life. He is our companion as we seek healing for all that ails us, for his sacred task is that of healing both humanity and the earth.

The balance of Tiphareth	
Cosmic realm	Cosmic balance
Human aspect	Solar self, soul, eternal self
Bodily form	Heart, thymus, lungs, breastbone
Embodiment	The circle of soul
Challenge	Pride
Virtue	Devotion to the great work
Catalyst	Saviour of self
Vision	Harmony
Tarot Guides	XIV Art, XV Devil, XIII Death
Deity	Hathor – goddess of fertility
Guardian	Archangel Raphael
Celestial body	Sun

Geburah
sphere of will and strength

גבורה

The Fifth Path is called the Radical Intelligence because it resembles Unity, uniting itself to Binah, understanding, which emanates from the primordial depths of Chokmah, Wisdom.

Sepher Yetzirah

Geburah is the power of our will, the refinement of Hod's philosophies into the realm of the soul. Geburah and Chesed (see pages 130–1) share this middle level of the Tree with Tiphareth, and can be seen as the wings of Tiphareth's realm of the soul. It is at Geburah that we bring forward the mighty warrior within ourselves to stand in defence of the integrity of our sacred truth.

Geburah governs the right shoulder and arm, and it is in this arm that we see the flaming sword of the archangel Khamael, guardian of this sphere. This both lights our way as a beacon and stands as a warning, banishing vindictive forces who would do us harm or seek to usurp the power of our soul.

The question that arises in all traditions asks whether what is seen and known as evil is intrinsically so. The shadow of Geburah would say yes, and attempt to annihilate it. The strength of Geburah, however, would use the power of the sword to discern the misplacement of energy that gave rise to vindictive harm. As the noted psychiatrist, occultist and author Dion Fortune (1890–1946) wrote: '… we recognise that good and evil are not things in themselves, but conditions. Evil is simply misplaced force; misplaced in time, if it is out of date … Misplaced in space, if it turns up in the wrong place …'

STRENGTH AND WEAKNESS

The enemy of Geburah is the lassitude of our appeasement of evil, of not standing witness to that which threatens the integrity of the Tree of Life and the sacred laws of the universe. Here we are again laden with paradox, as Geburah itself is perhaps the most maligned of the Sephiroth, and can be judged warlike and violent. And yet by definition, construction and original nature each of the Sephiroth share equally the burden of the shadow of the Tree, the shells present

behind each of the spheres. And so just as Geburah can be identified as bearing more of the unwelcome aspects of the warrior, so, too, does this Sephiroth stand forward in defence of the Tree.

Here is the brilliance of Mars, the value of conflict, the necessary definitiveness of what supports the momentum of awakening and what perpetuates suffering and addiction. So this can be an uncomfortable place as the unrestrained warrior is neither the divinely inspired berserker nor the intentful assassin – the shadow shell of this sphere is the petty cruelty of power abused in the oppression of the weak. Such a breakdown of the chivalric code of honour is the distortion of the guardian and so the essence of fascism.

Geburah's true warrior is far more likely to be the wandering knight than the worldly general, as it is heaven's laws of balance and consequence that this sphere holds witness to rather than the transient human laws of regimes and so-called 'holy wars'. It is the eternal protection of the children and earth, the witness to laws of cycle and return rather than the protection of dogma and influence.

Violence is a distraction in this place. Ghandi can be seen to have had a strong embodiment of Geburah as he championed non-violent direct action. It is the direct action that is key here, rather than the non-violence. Choice enables us to create the boundaries and containment for our energy. Ambivalence and regret lead to leaky vessels and weak trees. With a sharp and decisive pruning knife we are able to promote better and more useful growth within ourselves. It is the mercy of a swift kill, a clean stroke with a sharp blade free from inflection or doubt. So, too, do we become guardians of the cruel inside of us where we make the sacrifice of choice, of making something sacred by the power of one's will, of dedicating energy in the cause of our soul, never at the expense of another, but rather by the positive application of our own energy, the celebration of our own inner warrior.

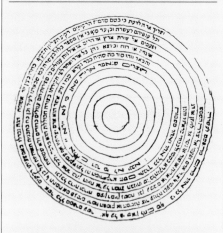

A 16th-century printing of the Sefer Yetzirah

SEFER YETZIRAH: THE BOOK OF FORMATION

The Sefer Yetzirah emerged before the 10th century CE from Jewish and Gnostic communities, and blended elements of Greek and Egyptian philosophy to generate the earliest Kabbalistic text. It is a brief codex primarily concerned with the mystical symbolism of Hebrew letters and numbers and the mystical aspects of astrology. There is a number of versions of the Sefer Yezirah and rabbis such as Moses Cordevo produced their own commentaries. Controversy surrounds the various versions, although recent scholarship is revealing more of the text's origins and influences.

The book is structured according to an analysis of numbers and letters that total the Kabbalah's 32 'paths', and are explored in their embodiment of aspects of creation itself. These paths arise from the three 'mother' letters ascribed to fire, water and air, the seven double letters associated with the planets and the 12 single letters of the signs of the zodiac. The ten numbers (associated with the Sephiroth and the emanations of creation) complete the 32 paths.

The Sefer Yetzirah elaborates the intricacies of number mysticism and is often cited as the manual used by creators of the Golem (see page 141) in its description of the eternal formation of the universe.

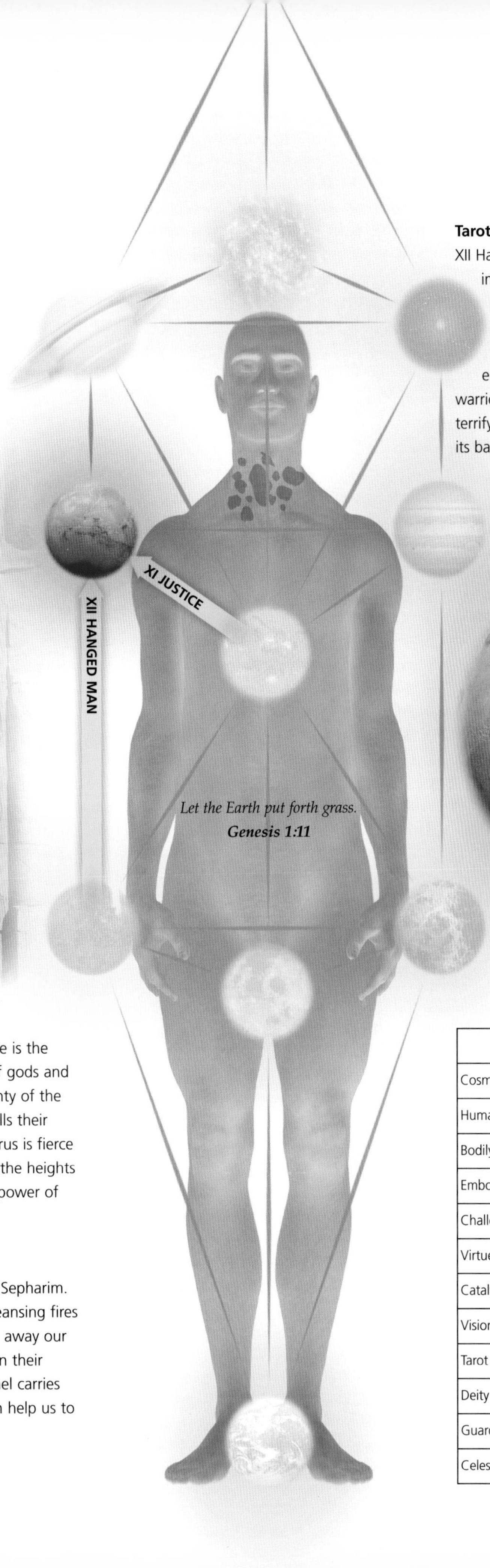

Tarot paths of wisdom

XII Hanged Man is the gambolling loss of self-importance that allows the severity of the left-hand pillar to serve soul rather than personality, holding witness to myriad opponents within ourselves. XI Justice enables us to emerge into the guardian warrior of our archetypal self, the strength so terrifying that it is only the heart that tempers its balance.

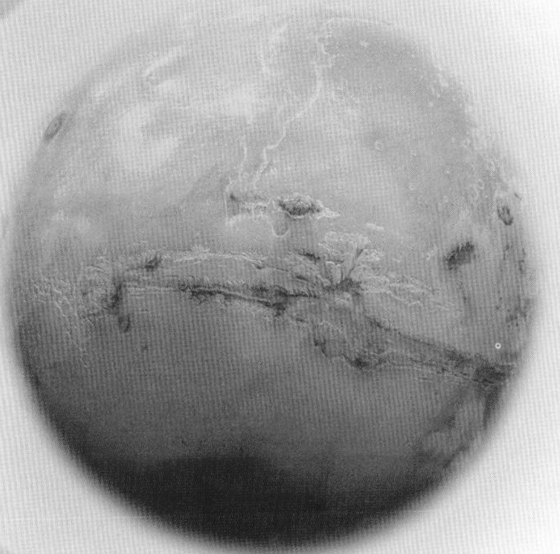

XII HANGED MAN

XI JUSTICE

Let the Earth put forth grass.
Genesis 1:11

God of might

Horus is the Egyptian god of might. He is the hawk-headed avenger of the family of gods and the warrior who restores the sovereignty of the realm after his usurping brother Set kills their father Osiris and takes the throne. Horus is fierce in his determination, far-sighted from the heights of heaven, and carries the archetypal power of the winged disc.

He who sees god

Khamael (he who sees god) leads the Sepharim. These fiery serpent angels hold the cleansing fires of god's protection that not only burn away our impurities, but also temper our souls in their preparation to cross the abyss. Khamael carries the skills, prowess and power that can help us to carry through the visions of our will.

The strength of Geburah	
Cosmic realm	Strength
Human aspect	Will, courage, spiritual discipline
Bodily form	Right shoulder and arm
Embodiment	Discipline of restraint
Challenge	Cruelty
Virtue	Courage
Catalyst	Internal arena of battle
Vision	Power
Tarot Guides	XI Justice, XII Hanged Man
Deity	Horus – god of might
Guardian	Archangel Khamael
Celestial body	Mars

Chesed
sphere of love and grace

חסד

The Fourth Path is called the Cohesive or Receptive Intelligence; and it is so called because it contains all the holy powers, and from it emanate all the spiritual virtues with the most exalted essences; they emanate one from the other by the power of the Primordial Emanation, the Highest Crown, Kether.

Sepher Yetzirah

Chesed is our awareness of love – the universal extension of our being towards all other forms of life. Along the lightning flash of creation, Chesed is our first Sephiroth below the supernal triad and abyss, it is the matrix of love that holds the universe together, the generosity of mercy that allows the universe's diversity to pull together in cohesion amid its infinite difference.

Chesed governs the left arm and shoulder. While Geburah holds a flaming sword, the arms of Chesed hold the orb and sceptre of kingship. This is not the sovereignty at the heart of Malkuth, but the patterning of divine law held by the soul. Chesed is the king of love, the peace chief whose domain holds infinite compassion for each individual within the realm.

This expansiveness of heart is equally echoed in an expansiveness of mind, as the capacity to cascade one thought after another in an unlimited creativity fuels Chesed's gift of abundance. The embodiment of Jupiter's vast generosity and magnetic force as the planetary ally is another aspect of unfolding and connectivity. Our mental scope and scale are determined by the extent to which we can adopt the imagination, synthesis and freedom of Chesed's adventure

The aspect of Chesed that is expansive of heart in forgiveness and mind in imagination is equally so at the level of the soul. Here, Chesed affords us the capacity to see the images and phenomena that play themselves out in the drama of our own dreamtime as the surface appearance of deeper currents of an archetypal nature. Failure to have the humility to perceive the archetypal aspects of who we are leads to an over-identification with the images of the collective soul as they swarm through us and map the territory and

path of our soul. The challenge here is in the glamour of Chesed as the expansive wonder of god's manifestation is held as something personal. When we are touched by dreams of angels, when we enjoy business success, when we fall in love, in all the great narratives of our lives we are part of a wider tapestry of human manifestation of divine forces. Should we consider ourselves to be the angel, to be the essence of love, then we can become entranced with such images and close off for a while any further unfolding of the Tree within us.

And we should be careful which archetypes and guides we accept, which roles we step into within the collective myth, as each has a scripted ending and consequences that have inevitable repercussions. Should we find such a place of awareness and choice within such a cacophony of archetypes, we touch the potential of dialogue with the masters of this sphere, that we might co-create such avenues of exploration and manifestation for our soul.

CHALLENGES AND BLESSINGS

In the midst of such expansion at the levels of mind, heart and soul, the challenge of Chesed becomes the alignment along which the expansion unfolds. Given the infinity of trackways we can explore, Chesed holds the discipline of alignment so that there is a trajectory of development rather than an indiscriminate overflowing.

Both Geburah and Chesed share the middle level of the Tree with Tiphareth, and as such are the wings of the soul in the middle sephira. Their mutual challenges are their strength and potency in use in the service of the personality. Their mutual blessings are the guidance and strength of the masters and teachers that inhabit these realms, guiding us, as we learn the fullness of the seven spheres below the abyss, protecting us from the harsher realities of the shadow, and encouraging us in our preparation to cross the abyss, should we choose to do so, and whichever way we go.

SEFER HA-ZOHAR: THE BOOK OF SPLENDOUR

Zohar Harakah – explanation of the Zohar by the Ari

The Zohar emerged from the wisdom of Spanish Kabbalists during the 13th century and was written by Moses de Leon, a rabbi influenced by Maimonedes' great philosophical work of the 12th century, *Guide to the Perplexed*, but who unfolded a more mystical appreciation of the universe. The Zohar concerns itself with the 'raiment of the soul' and the levels at which the soul is in communion with its divine source. The intimate dance of male and female throughout all of creation is one of its central themes, returning again and again to the love of men and women, of god and the universe. It is in this context that the Sephiroth of the Tree of Life are expounded, aspects and emanations, 'precious vessels' of the divine light.

The Zohar came to hold a place of reverence in some Jewish circles that almost equalled the status given to the Torah. Its mystical expression of the Sephiroth has also retained for it a central place within any body of knowledge regarding the Kabbalah. Its rich paradox and deep references to Kabbalist cosmology do not prevent the images from having a direct effect on the imagination, whether we are aware of the references or not. As renowned scholar and author Gershom Scholem says in the introduction to his translation of the Zohar: 'The final conclusion which has since earliest times been drawn in the recognition of a sacred text, namely, that the effect upon the soul of such a work is in the end not at all dependent upon its being understood.'

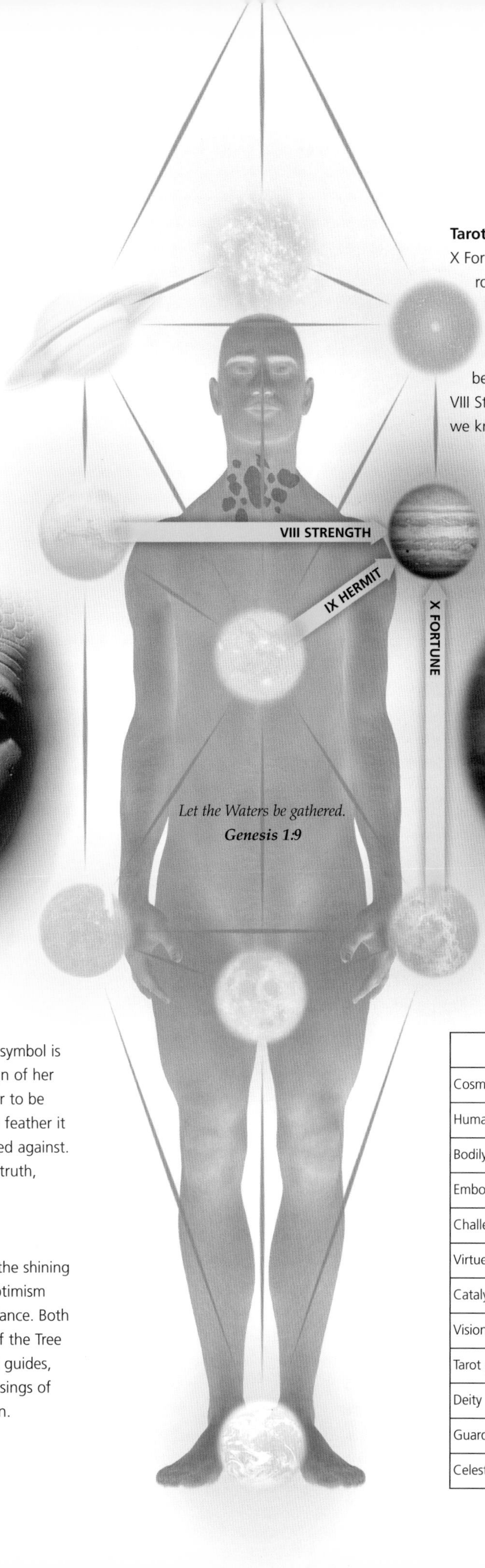

Tarot paths of wisdom

X Fortune is the flamboyant abundance of our rollercoaster ride into the realm of soul, aware of the cyclical return to places of home.

IX Hermit is the witness of our internal solitude, the intimacy of our own signature before we expand into the universal.

VIII Strength is the place of self-dominion where we know the defining discipline of the warrior.

VIII STRENGTH

IX HERMIT

X FORTUNE

Let the Waters be gathered.
Genesis 1:9

Lady of judgement

Maat stands attendant to Chesed. Her symbol is the ever-straight ostrich feather, the sign of her ethical greatness, an aspect that led her to be the lady of judgement at death, whose feather it is that the deceased's heart was weighed against. She is the expansive benefactor of our truth, guardian of our light.

The righteousness of god

Tzadkiel leads the Chashmalim angels, the shining ones who hold for us the beacon of optimism that is a reflection of the world's abundance. Both Geburah and Chesed form the realm of the Tree of Life associated with beneficent spirit guides, and Chesed, particularly, holds the blessings of those beings who support our evolution.

The abundance of Chesed	
Cosmic realm	Mercy
Human aspect	Love, compassion, expansiveness
Bodily form	Left shoulder and arm
Embodiment	Joy of freedom
Challenge	Favour and bigotry
Virtue	Alignment
Catalyst	Unity of love
Vision	Love
Tarot guides	IX Hermit, X Fortune, VIII Strength
Deity	Maat – goddess of righteousness
Guardian	Archangel Tzadkiel
Celestial body	Jupiter

Daath

the no-sphere of knowledge

Such a person must confront his own real fear of God and his own real love of God. And then he must consciously broaden his awareness to let the presence of God into his mind and heart, permit himself to stand in the Presence of God – person to Person, presence to Presence. At the outer limits of this mode of Kavanna (raising consciousness), the praying rabbinic Jew must, in his own awareness, be ready to die, in that moment. He must be ready to immediately cast himself into the abyss.

David Blumenthal

Daath is not a sphere. It is both a barrier and a gateway. It inhabits the realm of the abyss – the no-man's-land that separates the seven lower spheres from the 'supernal triad' of divinity: Binah, Chokmah and Kether.

These upper Sephiroth were commonly made inaccessible to humans when we were banished from the Garden of Eden. Daath is the rabbit hole through which we tumbled, it is the 'apple' of the knowledge of good and evil of which we were not meant to partake, but which we did, and so 'fell' from familial harmony with god. Whether this was a tragedy or an essential part of the process of the universe coming to know itself is a matter we each face at this point on the Tree. The knowledge of good and evil can appear as a poisoned chalice or as an essential initiation into the maturity of questioning how we co-create our universe.

INTERPRETING DAATH

There are many stories and interpretations of Daath, its cosmic nature and its reflection in the evolution of human consciousness. For medieval commentators, Daath was the gateway to the realms of hell, guarded by Chronozon, the arch demon. There is little help here for the initiate, no guarding deity or archangel, no paths of insight from the Tarot, merely the intense gaze of our own shadows and demons warning us never to stray beyond the perceived limits of our humanity. The archetypal Grail knight – Perceval – has his journey centre around the issue of whether he has the courage to claim his humanity and ask his sick uncle, the Grail king, what ails him, to ask what gives rise to the wasteland around them. Perceval fails to do this at first, instead following the advice of his elders not to ask too many questions. This is the archetypal injunction against the immature human – of innocence and obedience – that is transgressed by Adam and Eve as they eat of the Tree of Knowledge, of good and evil. For the apple that is eaten then sticks in Adam's throat and becomes Daath, Adam's apple itself.

For each of us, the relationship with unknown knowledge will be different, marked largely by the flavour and construction of our ascent up the Tree of Life, of the unique blend of personality and soul that we are. Whichever perspective of this cosmic region we take – of avoidance, reckless abandon or surrendered passivity – we will be the architects of our own bridge over the chasm and our quests to find its treasures. For Daath is also a direct gateway to the dark side of the Sephiroth, sometimes called 'Qlippoth'.

All forms of radiance and light will cast their own shadow – each sephira has its shadow. There is always a continuum of experience for each of us in every facet of who we are: the illuminated mind of Hod can spin its own version of truth, the feelings of Netzach can themselves become berserk. The evolutionary paths of the Sephiroth are of coming to know our own continuum within them, our own light and dark sides.

This happens naturally as we shine the light of our attention onto ourselves and begin the serpent's path of awakening, the return journey up the Tree in search of reunion with our divinity and a restoration of the fall. The trap is the glamour and temptation to elevate our current awareness as a false godhead or to avoid the shadow of who we are. Some Western magical traditions, such as the work of Abra-Melim, specifically seek to conjure demons in order to barter with them for dominion over one's shadow, to control and seek to regain dominion over such realms of hell.

RECONCILING PARADOX

Daath, in essence, is the master gateway to our shadow, to the reverse of each of our sephira, where we are asked to bring the shadows that our own radiance casts and bring them firmly beneath our feet – neither separate from who we are nor projected onto any other person, being or phenomenon. It is the accepted abyss of what we do not know of ourselves and the universe.

For the abyss annihilates all aspects of personality, soul and collective consciousness in the mystery of the I and the Thou, where any individual identity, even that of the circle of our soul, with all its memories and wisdom of incarnations and cosmic spheres, is obliterated as our speck of consciousness prepares to rejoin the great sea of Binah.

This challenge of annihilation is the temptation of allowing the personality to form an unholy alliance with those parts of our shadow or the collective, our individual or collective demons, and to remain stuck in the abyss, anchored through addiction into the unnatural power of compulsion that is unwilling to surrender to the cleansing annihilation of our own shadow and pass through to the light of divinity.

It is in this way that Daath forms an alliance with Yesod that is the axis of magical work. Daath is the no-sphere of knowledge that is not to be spoken, the forbidden apple. Yesod is the realm of our unconscious and the powerhouse of energy within us and the world. Together, they form a lightning rod of initiation as we unnaturally bridge that which we do not know, either from the depths of our personality (Yesod) or the depths of the universe (Daath) and seek to form an alliance of revelation – activating the allure of the hidden, not in an attempt to usurp the godhead, but to manage our own limitations of knowledge, the paradox of our primal desire as humans to know the unknowable and to reconcile our stellar and earthly natures.

And as this realm of strangeness is absorbed into the energy body of the initiate, we enter the realm of the initiated artist – those writers, painters and musicians who have seen the expanse of forbidden knowledge in the depths of the abyss and returned to tell the tale. Daath is the realm where humans become makers and learn how to shape consciousness, to create realms of dream and possibility.

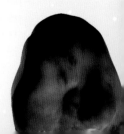

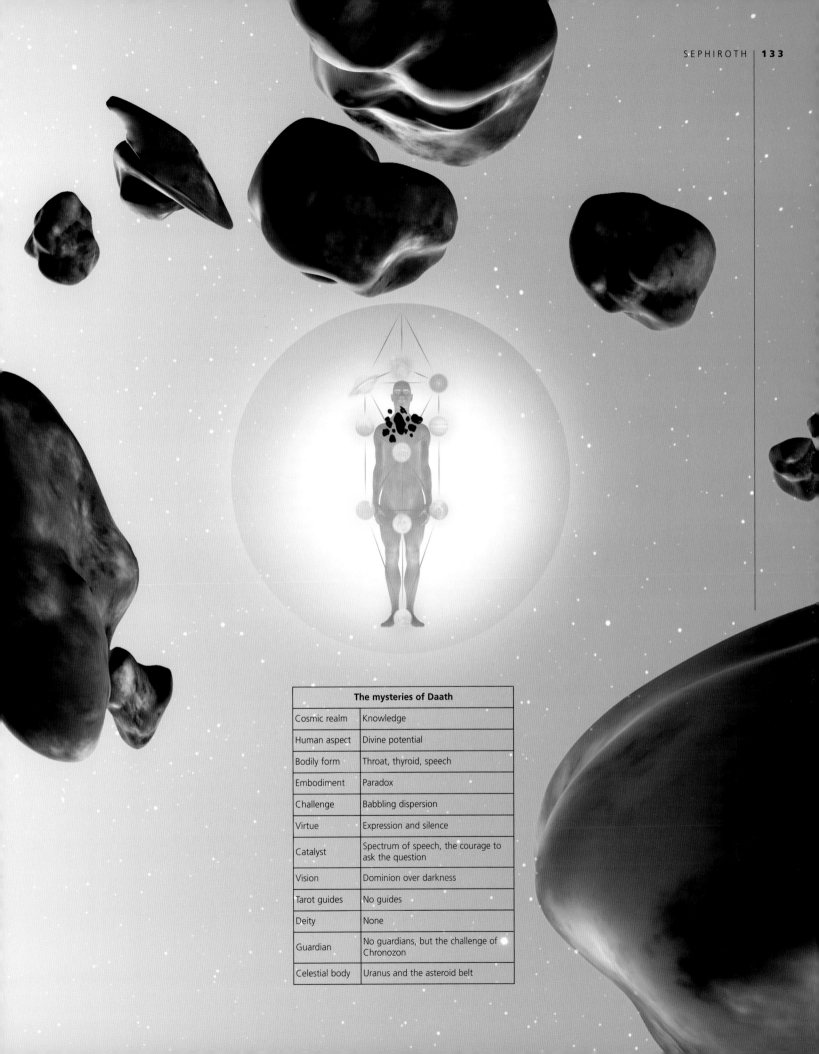

The mysteries of Daath	
Cosmic realm	Knowledge
Human aspect	Divine potential
Bodily form	Throat, thyroid, speech
Embodiment	Paradox
Challenge	Babbling dispersion
Virtue	Expression and silence
Catalyst	Spectrum of speech, the courage to ask the question
Vision	Dominion over darkness
Tarot guides	No guides
Deity	None
Guardian	No guardians, but the challenge of Chronozon
Celestial body	Uranus and the asteroid belt

Binah

sphere of manifestation and understanding

The third path is the Sanctifying Intelligence, and it is the foundation of Primordial Wisdom, which is called the Creator of Faith, and its roots are AMeN; and it is the parent of Faith, from which doth Faith emanate.

Sepher Yetzirah

Binah is the ascension of consciousness to a place of blending with the great sea of matter. For Binah is both beyond form, as it sits above the abyss, and yet is the great sea from which all form arises. Where Malkuth is the sphere of form, Binah is the sphere from which it arises, it is our return to the embrace of the heavenly mother, from whose darkness we were clothed before we embarked on phenomenal existence. Binah is the machinery of the universe, the stuff of its making after it has been created in the flash of Kether and the expanded grand design of Chokmah. In the lore of the alchemists we return to Binah once we have left all attachments behind us and achieved the crossing of the Abyss. We then come to the 'City of the Pyramids', where the remains of each successful adept are interred as they continue on up the path of the serpent. It is at this level that the imagery associated with the evolving adept begins to fall away and the grandeur and glamour of the adventure are released.

DUAL ASPECTS

The guiding vision of Binah has two aspects: wonder and sorrow. Binah's wonder is the expanse of our arrival at the supernal sphere above the abyss, beyond duality, where creation is perpetually unfolding and being made. Such wonder is the huge expanse of the eternal womb of creation.

The sorrow that arises is the dismay at incarnation itself, putting on the robe of mortality, form and substance in order to experience the treasures of the rest of the Tree of Life below the abyss and complete the equation of the soul's coming to know itself. It is only this spiralling mutuality of immersion between spirit, soul and matter through which the wonder of the universe is revealed.

But as we embody the sphere of Binah, there is opportunity for an integration of intuition within us, held as the beacon of our feminine natures, navigating with understanding the mysteries of form, neither neglected nor smothered by who we are as our own cosmic mother. Such a dance is, on occasion, a challenge, as the shadow aspects of Isis can stall our embrace with her. As the eternal womb of creation, exactly those attributes that enable manifestation can appear oppressive. It is here that the nature of Saturn, Binah's planetary guide, is revealed, often viewed as a malefic force – limiting and constricting. Such a perspective can indeed be true when viewed from below, by the entreaty of a child or aspiring adept for whom the limitation and constriction of the great mother can appear ungenerous. And yet when this level is achieved and its insights embodied, the force of restriction is revealed as the true agent of achievement.

As Binah is the receptive principle, so its virtue is silence, the quietude that hears the wave of creation and allows it form. Within such labour the challenges that arise are those of greed or avarice, where the accumulating force of matter finds no balance of generosity and so continues to stack up its treasures without feeding its children. This perpetual dance with form is the gift of Isis, where limitation is finally understood as liberation, and the womb of creation the gateway of awakening.

THE MYSTERY OF POLARITIES

The three pillars of the Tree of Life represent the two polarities of life and their resolution in the centre. The two pillars are those of severity (the left hand, female pillar) and of mercy (the right hand, male pillar). They form the fabled entrance to the temple of Solomon and are commonly reproduced in the temples of Freemasonry and other Western magical lodges. As we ourselves stand between them, we become the pillar of equilibrium in the centre, regardless of our gender, where we are the resolution of opposites and the middle path of ascent.

The association of the virtues of the left pillar with feminine virtues might at first seem counter-intuitive once we drop below the level of the abyss. Within the supernal triad, it is more straightforward to associate Binah's great sea with the feminine and Chokmah's grand design with the masculine. The feminine pillar, however, continues with Geburah and Hod, realms of the warrior and the philosopher – attributes traditionally associated with men. Equally, the masculine pillar continues with Chesed and Netzach, realms of the lover and the feeler, attributes traditionally associated with women.

Nothing in this alchemy is either unintentional or inaccurate, and there are many layers to uncovering such mysteries. At the most immediate level, it is indeed the female principle that restricts growth through the dynamics of severity, with the male providing the path of mercy and expansion. Such insights are widespread throughout most mystery traditions. But there are other layers of this truth, as the polarity of the pillars does indeed switch as it crosses the Abyss. Initially, there is a diagonal echo between the two pillars, but more centrally Daath governs the neurological nexus, where the sensory nerves of the left side of the body cross over to register in the right side of the brain. This crossover is utilized and reflected by various traditions in different ways. Within Kabbalah, it may be the origin of the prayer practices of some Hassidic Jews, where the vowels within prayers, when 'mentioning the Holy names' are accompanied by very specific movements of the head and neck.

Tarot paths of wisdom

VII Chariot is the speed and wildness of the
journey across the abyss, the discipline to be
able to go the distance without distraction.
VI Lovers is the vision of unity that the
heart carries, bridging the spheres of
matter and spirit.

Let there be a firmament.
Genesis 1:6

The greatest goddess

Isis is arguably the greatest of Egyptian goddesses,
whose temples abounded in the Mediterranean
region throughout middle antiquity, and who,
in many guises, is honoured as a goddess across
the world. Apuleius' 2nd-century Roman classic
The Golden Ass is an adventure of magic, mysticism
and comedy that culminates in an initiation into
the mysteries of Isis (and lesser realized, those of
Osiris too). She is the great mystery of life itself,
and gateway to the earth's dreams.

Builder of thrones

Tzaphkiel is the archangel known as the builder
of thrones and it is at this phase of our ascent up
the Tree that we review the ways in which we
have resourced the manifesting power of Binah
to build a vehicle for ourselves within life.

The manifestation of Binah	
Cosmic realm	Understanding
Human aspect	Will, courage, spiritual discipline
Bodily form	Right temple
Embodiment	Balanced intuition
Challenge	Greed
Virtue	Silence
Catalyst	Liberation of form
Vision	Wonder and sorrow
Tarot guides	VII Chariot, VI Lovers
Deity	Isis – the great mother goddess
Guardian	Archangel Tzaphkiel – the 'beholder', or 'eye', of god
Celestial body	Saturn

Chokmah

sphere of illumination and design

The Second Path is called the Illuminating Intelligence. It is the crown of creation, the Splendour of Unity, equalling it. It is exalted above every head, and is named by Qabalists the second glory.

Sepher Yetzirah

Chokmah is the naked energy of raw force and primal power. It is our meeting with the unfettered vastness of our heavenly father who perpetually pours forth all the energy and dynamism of creation. Chokmah is the design and blueprint of the universe, the wisdom beyond knowledge that holds within it the eternal presence of all creation.

Some Kabbalist traditions speak of this level as the vision of seeing god face to face, and essentially involving the death of physical form, unable to stand in the face of such light and radiation. But still there is the reflection that Adam Kadmon – the primordial man, the first man of the Kabbalah – holds at our left temple governing the right side of the body, and other Kabbalists work closely with this sphere and how we can approach its presence within us. For it is the collective holding of the right way for us as a people, our choice of good over evil, of positive action. This is not the negation of the feminine, receptive principle, but rather an embrace of Chokmah's own alignment within itself, the power of the universe that is served by design and consciousness, rather than its own mirror of unpatterned chaos.

Chokmah's naked explosion of raw energy maps the expanse of space that we know of as the zodiac of 12 constellations. Israel Regardie, 20th-century occultist and author, sees our zodiac as the 'ever expanding genesis of the universe', what the Zohar describes as: 'acting as guardians over this world are all the stars of the firmament, with each individual object of the world having a specially designed star to care for it.'

Such interconnectedness of life and its choreography, according to the great plan of the universe, is Chokmah's wisdom, for here is the blueprint of life itself. Here, the god Thoth (and in his other shapes – Hermes, Merlin, Solomon) is known as the scribe of the divine pantheon whose skill with words, mathematics, proportion and foundation, movement and season, enables the impossible clockwork of the universe to function.

This outflowing of design is the apex of the masculine principle in the universe, the essence of movement not divorced from stillness but immersed and existent within and because of it. At this level of the three supernal Sephiroth beyond the abyss we are dealing with realms intrinsically paradoxical. This is the strength and vision of the cosmic phallus. Just as Binah is the great womb of the universe, from whose darkness all manifestation emerges, so Chokmah is the lingam from whose seed gushes the cosmic fertility of the male principle, rather than the local fertility of manifest beings and tribal gods.

GAZING ON THE DIVINE

The challenges of Binah, should we gaze upon her face, are also those of Chokmah. For here we need to clear from our consciousness those terrors of the patriarch and the power of the masculine. Both Binah and Chokmah are the grandmother and grandfather who have moved beyond gender and are able to hold a place for both men and women. This is an ancient tribal knowing of balance, unavailable to many in the modern world, at the heart of wisdom traditions. And in the midst of Kether's platinum white light and Binah's dark velvet blackness, Chokmah holds the starlight of the heavens.

The ultimate path of Chokmah is the vision of the self, in preparation for our soul union in Kether, here our seeing of both ourselves and the divine. This is the dance of every stage of the journey being a disciplined release of all aspects of personality. This is the culmination of every time we step aside from ourselves to let the holy ones speak through us, allowing more and more of the divine light to take up its place within our being until, eventually, we realize that we are the holy ones, and that as we gaze upon the face of the divine, we gaze upon ourselves, the vast countenance of Kether.

GIOVANNI PICO DELLA MIRANDOLA

17th-engraving of Pico Della Mirandola

Pico was one of the brilliant innovators of the European Renaissance. Born in Italy in 1463, he was a devout student of philosophy and theology, having an in-depth classical training in Greek, Latin, Chaldee, Arabic and Hebrew. A devout Christian, he was introduced to the Kabbalah by his Hebrew teachers and Pico eagerly embraced its mysticism. Pico was one of the first Kabbalists to explore the Kabbalah in relation to the revelations of mystical Christianity (apart from early Gnostic schools). He further expanded his Kabbalistic studies into the divine revelation that Renaissance science was unfolding at the time. He skirted controversy with the Church and many subsequent Kabbalists did not thank him for applying the wisdom of the Kabbalah to Christianity, but he remains a bright beacon of the Florentine Renaissance, whose writing holds the essential rhythms of the Tree of Life, both in its lightning flash of creation and the serpentine path of return:

We shall fly up with winged feet
To the embraces of our blessed Mother,
And enjoy that wished-for peace,
Of one accord in the friendship
Through which all rational souls
Shall, in some ineffable way, become altogether one.
Let us wish this peace for our friends, for our century.

Pico Della Mirandola

Tarot paths of wisdom

V Hierophant is the sacred light of our inner priest
tracking the development of compassion as
we emerge into the love and wisdom of
the elder, the ever-young grandfather.
IV Emperor is the centredness with which
we might behold the great plan. III Empress
is the deep knowing that every nut, stone
and leaf is an expression of the divine plan.

III EMPRESS

IV EMPEROR

V HIEROPHANT

Let there be light.
Genesis 1:3

Divine scribe

Thoth is the guardian of Chokmah, the speaker
of the secrets of the universe whose words, both
spoken and written, are the invisible codex of
creation. Divine scribe and herald, it is his wisdom
that holds the infrastructure of the vast and
complex design of all that there is. He holds the
keys of sound and sigil that are the perpetual
ways of creation and its continued invitation
to the people to join the quest.

Guardian and teacher

Raziel is the archangel guide of Chokmah,
guardian of the golden spheres, teacher of the
secrets, and master of the holy Kabbalah's
transmission to humanity.

The design of Chokmah	
Cosmic realm	Wisdom
Human aspect	Love of life
Bodily form	Left temple
Embodiment	The eternal presence of power
Challenge	Illusion
Virtue	Purpose
Catalyst	Vision of the holy ones
Vision	Of self
Tarot guides	V Hierophant, IV Emperor, III Empress
Deity	Thoth – scribe of wisdom
Guardian	Archangel Raziel – the herald and secret of god
Celestial body	The zodiac of constellations (and Neptune)

Kether

sphere of crown and source

During the war in heaven between God and Satan, between good and evil, some angelic hosts sided with Satan and some with God. The Grail was brought down through the middle by the neutral angels. It represents that spiritual path that is between pairs of opposites, between fear and desire, between good and evil . . . The Grail represents the fulfilment of the highest spiritual potentialities of the human consciousness.

Joseph Campbell

Kether – crown – is the first of the Sephiroth, the horizon of eternity from which our universe springs. It is the 'source' of all that is, the first point of emanation that shines as a blinding, platinum-white brilliance that is both divine union and a gateway to realms of infinity. Within the divine human, it is both the energy field and consciousness, appearing as the crown at the very top of the head, an aura, a halo. Within the structure of the Tree of Life, it is the highest of the high, beyond duality.

Kether as source is in many ways indescribable – beyond the expanse of the universe mapped out by the constellations of the zodiac – the perimeter of all that is held by Chokmah. The planetary intelligence that Kether emerges from is the axis around which the universe moves and from which it arose. This axis is variously understood as the entwined serpents of the Earth's axis,

the constellation of Draco or the Milky Way. Here is the arrival of the serpent at the apex of the Tree of Life, having completed its journey of awakening and healing. This is the place wherein the restoration of the spheres that Luria the Ari called for is complete, aligned again with their cosmic source, plugged into the divine radiance from which they first came.

Alongside the aspect of Kether as cosmic axis and point of emergence, is our own alignment at energetic and physical levels. This becomes the basis and extent of our evolution, for what do we allow to be the axis of our lives, what is the core that we will revolve around? The increasing alignment of the Sephiroth in all their expression within us has a direct effect on the efficiency of our energy field. Should all aspects of our being agree to work to the same rhythm and call the same melody, then the resulting harmony from such internal teamwork can cause a cascade of energy and enlightenment that echoes a unity with the divine at the heart of Kether.

UNION BETWEEN ALL THINGS

And so as we come under the radiance of Kether, in whatever guise, the question arises as to what extent do we allow this full brilliance of our light to shine, how do we allow the echoes of such brilliance to find their own equilibrium and truth? The overbearing influence of brilliance can lead us to dictatorship at political, spiritual and psychological levels. It is the wisdom of Kether

to know the retreating cycle of creation, the unobtrusive radiance, so that the true flourishing of life may be known. This retreat is not a dissociation, nor a transcendental seclusion, but rather a resting in myriad complexities of the universe's expression in the affairs of everyday life. Part of this discipline is not alienating ourselves from the emanations of the divine because of any feelings of unworthiness.

This deeper truth of Kether is that here there is indeed a union between all things. Kether is the place where the universe becomes 'something' rather than 'nothing'. It is the place of pure being, undifferentiated and undivided, the root of all existence, and, for this reason, it holds the silver thread of every individual being in our ultimate potentiality and cosmic light.

Such balance and ultimacy hold dangers of absolutism should we be tempted to fixate any aspect of our mutual source and origin. Whereas Daath is guarded by all and every demon, Kether holds the more terrifying spectre of the righteous, the part of who we are that knows the right way, not just for ourselves, but for all beings. Such surety is held in check by the neutral angels who hold the Grail of all traditions, the balancing heal-all that is the essence of the all and the everything.

EHEIEH AND SHEKHINAH

For man was yet imperfect,
for only when Eve was made perfect,
was he then made perfect too.
Sefer ha-Zohar

The Tree of Life is an eternal dance of the reconciliation of polarities, of heaven and earth, male and female, light and dark. At Kether (crown), we not only have the reconciliation of left and right pillars, we also have the realm of the supernal triad, the upper three Sephiroth within whom there exists no polarity. Here is the ultimate reconciliation,

the beginning and the end of creation. This is the place where the union of Kether and Malkuth is reflected in the form of the male and female aspects of the godhead, of Eheieh and Shekhinah. Shekhinah is variously identified with an ancient Canaanite goddess, the spirit of Israel herself, the sphere of Malkuth as consort to the higher nine spheres or as the moon reflecting the glory of the sun. Essentially, Shekhinah is the feminine aspect of the godhead whose name means 'dwelling in the divine presence'. This is the quietened phase of creation, where the lightning flash is then seen for

what it is, a phase no less crucial than the outgoing impulse. And it is within her presence that we come to the symbolic representation of her kingdom, the realm of the holy apple trees. This is not the forbidden fruit of Daath, but the deeper reflection of the Grail quest, the place of the beloved to whom the Song of Songs reach out in divine courtship.

I MAGICIAN

0 FOOL

II PRIESTESS

Tarot paths of wisdom

II Priestess holds our devotion of heart to the source of all things. I Magician is our willingness to engage with the brilliant chaos of the universe and bring an exquisitely balanced mastery of the vast darkness of the Mother's realm. 0 Fool holds the wisdom of having seen and known the great plan, a controlled folly of abandonment to the design of the universe.

In the beginning God created the Heaven and the Earth.
Genesis 1:1

God of creation

The Book of the Dead describes Ptah as the 'master architect and framer of the universe' who created heaven and earth by the words of his tongue and the thoughts of his heart. This power of speech and thought Ptah bestows in both life and death, overseeing the reincarnation of souls.

Overseer of the books of life

Metatron is the king of the angelic host and angel of the covenant. Once the prophet Enoch, he is the knower of secrets and the transmitter of mysteries between angels and humanity, overseer and keeper of the akashic records, the books of life of all beings.

The source of Kether	
Cosmic realm	Crown, source
Human aspect	The ultimate self, the spark of divinity
Bodily form	Consciousness, the whole aura
Embodiment	Paradox of creation
Challenge	Separation
Virtue	Atonement
Catalyst	Equilibrium of brilliance
Vision	Union
Tarot guides	0 Fool, I Magician, II Priestess
Deity	Ptah – the creator
Guardian	Archangel Metatron – the 'sent forth of god'
Celestial body	The Milky Way (and Pluto)

Ain

Nothing

אין

Ain Soph

Infinity

אין סוף

Ain Soph Aur

Absolute limitless light

אין סוף אור

Within the most hidden recess a dark flame issued from the mystery of the Infinite, like a fog forming in the unformed – enclosed in the ring of that sphere, neither white nor black, neither red nor green, of no colour whatever. Only after this flame began to assume size and dimension, did it produce radiant colours. From the innermost centre of the flame sprang forth a well out of which colours issued and spread upon everything beneath, hidden in the mysterious hiddenness of the Infinite.

Sefer ha-Zohar The Book of Splendour (13th century)

Ain Soph is the place beyond, within and between this and all universes. Whereas the Sephiroth are akin to mirrors that reflect, channel and emanate the brightness of divine cosmic light into the manifest world, Ain Soph holds the realm beyond existence, time, space and dimension. Within Jewish Kabbalah, it is the place where there is no separation between creator and creation.

And so how even to begin to speak of this place. It goes beyond the forbidden knowledge of the Tree of good and evil, beyond the terrors of the abyss. This is a place inaccessible to us by virtue of the limitation that we are created beings.

And yet there are those traditions within Jewish and Hermetic Kabbalah that do seek to go beyond the boundaries proscribed for us as children of god. There are many facets to this heretical quest, and the mythology of the Golem is one of the most esoteric and fantastical aspects of Kabbalistic lore. In our mythology, a Golem is an artificial being constructed of clay and animated by the lore of a rabbi, typically by inscribing the name of god on its forehead. As a story it prefaces Frankenstein, the Sorcerer's Apprentice and the many androids found in contemporary science fiction.

Central to these stories is the concern of limiting and controlling the superhuman strength of created beings. Deeper still is the (particularly Christian) cultural taboo of not reaching too high in one's aspirations, of not imitating god, of not breaking the seals of the greatest mystery of this universe – the creation of life. For Kabbalists, however, such a quest was one of the highest mysteries of their ancient lore, and less the search for a servant but more the call of co-creation with the divine.

At the height of the Tree we are beyond existence, irradiated with the intensity of a light beyond space and time. Here we have undergone the surrender that necessitates such a blending, and our navigation is more one of following the trackways already set for us – of stepping aside for the holy ones so that we get out of our own way, only to realize that we are, ourselves, the holy ones.

This place of the infinite is commonly seen with Kabbalistic lore as threefold, and described as the three negative veils. Each aspect of the Tree of Life holds the alchemy of the three, from the three pillars of severity, mercy and equilibrium to the supernal triad itself. In the place of the infinite, the spatial notion of three separate veils might seem nonsensical, but there is a cascade and hierarchy to their unfolding.

As we step backwards into infinity from the crown of Kether, we first find Ain Soph Aur, the 'absolute limitless light' that the Sephiroth have both obscured and reflected. Here the light is blinding should we hold within ourselves any limitation. This is the first barrier of this universe, the wall of brilliance that has no end and no beginning, no colour or dimension, containing within it all hues and intensities.

Beyond this wall of light is the expanse of dimension itself, Ain Soph, the infinite. Unbounded, it is the 'something' that arose from the 'nothing' of Ain, the final stage of infinity. For Ain is nothingness itself – the primordial state of all absence of space, light, time, dimension, the furthest reach into the absence of being. Here, in Null, it can only be the maturity of our philosophies that are able to springboard us beyond limitations of form and cultivate a deeper sense of consciousness, that place in ourselves where we can be within the embrace of nothingness, touch the blessings of self-annihilation.

These are the veils that mask the threefold nature of infinity. Veils that echo across many traditions with a longing to describe the nature of that which is beyond our conscious reach. And yet it is humanity's nature that as our vocabularies expand and, as more of a critical mass of humanity is able to absorb the impossibilities of infinity within who we are at this conscious level, then perhaps the taboos of co-creation might recede to allow a deeper participation in the continued unveiling of the universe.

It is possible to conceive that
that which it is impossible to conceive
is nevertheless possible.
Mike Fuller

AWEN: THREE PURE RAYS

Pharaoh Akhenaton receiving the sun's rays

The threefold nature of the infinite holds echoes in many traditions: the Christian trinity of Father, Son and Spirit; the Persian triad of Ormzad, Mithra and Ahriman; Taoism's Three Pure Ones. Equally, the radiance of divine energies emerging from within the unknowable mists of infinity appear within an equally varied number of paths, including early Kabbalistic texts and Egyptian codices. For as Hermetic Kabbalah claimed the Egyptian mysteries as part of its lineage, so, too, did an aspect of radiance find an expression in the hieroglyphic art of the dynasties, typically as representations of the blessings bestowed by the sun god Aten, who in another aspect is Ra (pronounced 'ray').

Madame Blavatsky's school of Theosophy, which blended Western and Eastern mystical traditions, unfolded the heart of their philosophy around the radiance of the rays. The three rays of the Druidic Awen is, in one of its forms, an aspect of the British Druidic revival of the 17th century (and means 'inspiration' or 'flowing spirit' in middle Welsh). But it holds within it the essence both of Egypt's radiance and Kabbalah's triple infinity. Within the perennial philosophy (the insight that all traditions reflect a facet of universal truth) it is sometimes suggested that each nation-soul shares a realm of collective unconscious with other nation-souls, revealing deeper truths of the human family tree.

Meridians

The energy lines of oriental medicine

Anatomy of the meridians and acupuncture points

Above, examine the outlines of the Milky Way.
Below, the progressive contours of the Earth.
Between them, explore the human heart,
And combine these three talents together as one.
Can Tong Qi (Akinness of the Three)
(Taoist alchemical classic, 3rd century CE)

Meridians are channels of energy, rivers that flow mostly over the surface of the human body. Each meridian has powerful connections to: the organs, tissues, structures and functions within the body; the cosmic origins, spiritual experience and destiny of the totality of our being; and the elements, spirits, vibrancy and consciousness of our environment.

What flows in these rivers is called 'chi', which is typically translated as 'energy' or 'breaths'. Chi is the life force within us and manifests in various ways – from the densely physical to the incredibly subtle and commonly unobservable. It is the common goal of oriental medical and meditation practices to balance and refine the flow of chi.

The discovery of meridians gradually came about through the sophisticated practices of healers, meditators and adepts of Taoist sexual practices more than 3,000 years ago. The accuracy of the meridians' locations is largely unchanged and science is just beginning to have the imagination and technology to observe their mapping as well as their therapeutic value.

Each of the points along a meridian is characterized by its position on the body, its links with other meridians and internal organs, as well as its role within the great cosmology of the human form from an oriental perspective – including designations according to yin yang and the five elements (see page 152). All the points, in fact, have their own names and their specific attributes, but because of the available space only the most significant are highlighted on the following pages.

Chi kung, acupuncture and tui na (see pages 145, 147 and 155) are some of the traditions from which practitioners can decode the mysteries of these meridians and balance their dynamics. Within some traditions, practitioners know that each of us will experience one of the meridians as particularly relevant – holding our constitutional weaknesses and potential for brilliance. We often have a sense of which is our meridian of change and destiny, and it may be that some of the meridians in the following pages sound as if they are central characters within your personal energy field.

The LUNG Meridian

fei **acceptance**

The lungs hold the office of Minister and Chancellor. The regulation of the life-giving network stems from it.
The Yellow Emperor's Classic of Internal Medicine

The lung meridian flows from a position at the front of the shoulder, down the inside of the arm and right to the edge of the thumb. It's 11 points trace the lungs' journey of receiving the first breath of life, and it is for this reason that it is usually cited as the first meridian in the cycle. The principal function of the lungs is the rhythmic flow of air into and out of the body – hence the lungs play a central role in determining the amount of energy we have available to us throughout our lives.

CAPACITY AND INCAPACITY

Our capacity to breathe well and efficiently will often determine how much 'puff' we can muster. But breathing also involves most of the other meridians of the body – especially the kidneys, since they have the effect of 'rooting' the sometimes flighty energy of the lungs and grounding it in the body.

The power of the lungs manifests itself in our voices, and people who have weak lung energy can often be heard to lose power to their voices as their sentences trail off, to the point where they can sound as though they are weeping. Weak lung energy can be further reflected in not being able to manifest all of who we are, not only through our speech, but in the deeper expression of our lives.

On a physical level, skin problems, colds and sore throats are all typical expressions of a lung imbalance. But the lungs also manifest in the body hair, in our fine 'outer covering' that corresponds with the skin as the third lung, and in the function of lung energy for providing the energetic protection of our energy field. Wei chi (which means 'protective chi') is governed by the lungs, and ensures that we have protection from a wide range of potentially invasive factors within our environment. These include

viruses, emotions, winds, bacteria, damp, radiation and thoughts. The lungs are, therefore, central to the proper functioning of our immune system.

The lungs master incarnation, as the first breath we each take is the pivotal moment of our full engagement with life. The subsequent rhythm of our breathing is the constant renewal of this engagement and presence, and weak lung energy can betray ambivalence with fully incarnating. We can appear absent, as if not fully 'here'. Meditation exercises that focus on observing the breath typically aim to correct this by promoting a sense of 'presence'. Not being present energetically can arise because somewhere in our being there is a perceived perfection of heavenly chi, and an unwillingness to bring such perfection into the realm of everyday life means that one remains addicted to the grief of unachievable beauty. Consequently, it is the capacity to engage fully with one's own incarnation, one's own being, that in the end transforms the challenges of the lungs, and embraces the blessings of our 'acceptance' of life.

FISH REGION

Lung 10 holds the essence of fire within the lung meridian. Each meridian belongs to one of the five elements, which, themselves, correspond to the seasons. The lungs (and large intestine) belong to the metal element and the season of autumn. But as a fire point, Fish Region brings warmth and the essence of summer to the lungs. People with a weak lung meridian may tend to become abstracted, sharp and brittle. Fish Region softens the sharpness in the same way that warmth softens metals.

It is suggested that the name 'Fish Region' arose from the belly of the thumb looking like a fish. But there is also a tradition that speaks of the rarity and exceptional cost of the purple dye used for the Chinese emperors' clothing, having been made from the sea snail *Purpura lapillus*.

So this is a place of softening the frozen brittleness of metal with the warmth of the sun; of waiting for when the sun will not scorch or evaporate metal's delicate balance, but restore its fluidity and divine partnership with that which is most precious within us – our remembrance of the breath of life and the true quest of our soul.

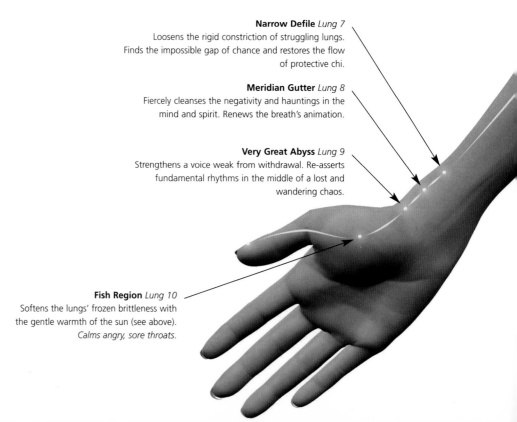

Narrow Defile *Lung 7*
Loosens the rigid constriction of struggling lungs. Finds the impossible gap of chance and restores the flow of protective chi.

Meridian Gutter *Lung 8*
Fiercely cleanses the negativity and hauntings in the mind and spirit. Renews the breath's animation.

Very Great Abyss *Lung 9*
Strengthens a voice weak from withdrawal. Re-asserts fundamental rhythms in the middle of a lost and wandering chaos.

Fish Region *Lung 10*
Softens the lungs' frozen brittleness with the gentle warmth of the sun (see above). *Calms angry, sore throats.*

Cloud Gate *Lung 2*
Transformation of oppressive grey clouds to the illuminated silver of mists. Parts the veil of separation between oneself and others.

Middle Palace *Lung 1*
Initiation of the breath of life. *Opens the shoulder and stops coughs.*

Heavenly Palace *Lung 3*
Shambhala. An ultimate opening to the canopy of Heaven. The capacity for living with inspiration and presence.

Valiant White *Lung 4*
Constant guardianship of our connection to heaven.

Outside Marsh *Lung 5*
Lubricates and moistens the lungs' capacity to be still. Lets the past fall away with grace. *Frees the arm.*

Greatest Hole *Lung 6*
Assuages the desperate void that can assault the lungs. Nourishes the meridian and brings movement.

chi kung
THE PRACTICE OF ENERGY

Guiding and Pulling Chart, excavated from the Mawangdui tombs, sealed in 168 BCE

Chi kung, meaning 'the practice of energy', encompasses a wide range of traditions:

Medical chi kung – chi is used to combat illness and promote longevity. Typically, this includes exercises, visualizations and the shaping of spiritual intention, as well as chi massage.

Iron shirt chi kung – an example of the use of chi kung in martial arts. The outer skin of the chi field is developed, making it impervious to injury.

Sexual chi kung – sensitivity and stamina are developed in spirit and body. An understanding of the rhythms and needs of ourselves and our partners helps us to become fully naked emotionally, spiritually and physically.

Internal/spiritual chi kung – the training of the 'shen', or consciousness, and its expansion within the energy body, freeing us from petty addictions and allowing a progression into enlightenment.

The term 'chi kung' dates back to the Ming Dynasty, and developed from gymnastic and meditation traditions more than 3,000 years old. Some chi kung lineages continue to hold shamanic elements, where a direct relationship with the guardians of various realms and places of power is a little too vivid for our contemporary world. Such vitality, however, is a potent link between people and the land. In China, the ley-lines of the Earth are called Dragon Lines, and 'riding the dragon' means to open oneself up to the energies of the Earth, standing as a guardian, and walking in service of the land.

The COLON Meridian

da chang **refinement**

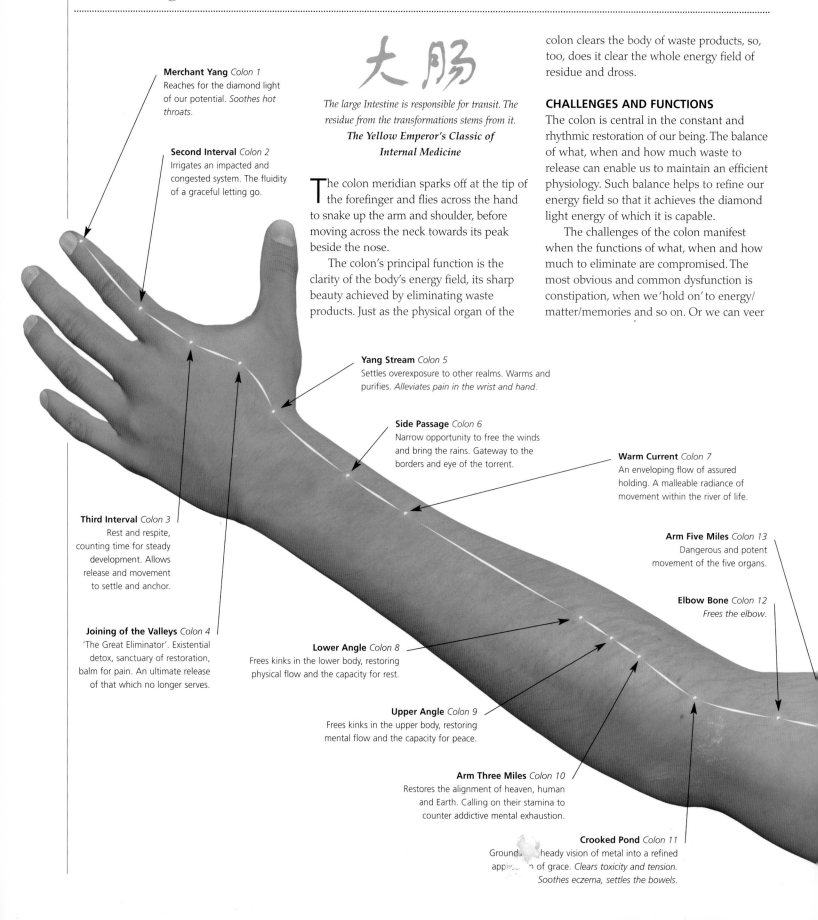

大肠

The large Intestine is responsible for transit. The residue from the transformations stems from it.
The Yellow Emperor's Classic of Internal Medicine

The colon meridian sparks off at the tip of the forefinger and flies across the hand to snake up the arm and shoulder, before moving across the neck towards its peak beside the nose.

The colon's principal function is the clarity of the body's energy field, its sharp beauty achieved by eliminating waste products. Just as the physical organ of the colon clears the body of waste products, so, too, does it clear the whole energy field of residue and dross.

CHALLENGES AND FUNCTIONS

The colon is central in the constant and rhythmic restoration of our being. The balance of what, when and how much waste to release can enable us to maintain an efficient physiology. Such balance helps to refine our energy field so that it achieves the diamond light energy of which it is capable.

The challenges of the colon manifest when the functions of what, when and how much to eliminate are compromised. The most obvious and common dysfunction is constipation, when we 'hold on' to energy/matter/memories and so on. Or we can veer

Merchant Yang *Colon 1*
Reaches for the diamond light of our potential. *Soothes hot throats.*

Second Interval *Colon 2*
Irrigates an impacted and congested system. The fluidity of a graceful letting go.

Yang Stream *Colon 5*
Settles overexposure to other realms. Warms and purifies. *Alleviates pain in the wrist and hand.*

Side Passage *Colon 6*
Narrow opportunity to free the winds and bring the rains. Gateway to the borders and eye of the torrent.

Warm Current *Colon 7*
An enveloping flow of assured holding. A malleable radiance of movement within the river of life.

Third Interval *Colon 3*
Rest and respite, counting time for steady development. Allows release and movement to settle and anchor.

Joining of the Valleys *Colon 4*
'The Great Eliminator'. Existential detox, sanctuary of restoration, balm for pain. An ultimate release of that which no longer serves.

Lower Angle *Colon 8*
Frees kinks in the lower body, restoring physical flow and the capacity for rest.

Upper Angle *Colon 9*
Frees kinks in the upper body, restoring mental flow and the capacity for peace.

Arm Five Miles *Colon 13*
Dangerous and potent movement of the five organs.

Elbow Bone *Colon 12*
Frees the elbow.

Arm Three Miles *Colon 10*
Restores the alignment of heaven, human and Earth. Calling on their stamina to counter addictive mental exhaustion.

Crooked Pond *Colon 11*
Grounds heady vision of metal into a refined application of grace. *Clears toxicity and tension. Soothes eczema, settles the bowels.*

towards an over-eager evacuation and let go what we actually need to retain for our wellbeing. More problematic is holding on to waste and eliminating nourishment. It is also a question of what we hold to be precious in our lives. Such a focus in itself can become addictive avarice rather than a clear choice for a sustaining way of life. But this focus also allows the pinpoint accuracy achieved from being able to be meticulous and exact. It is this that can be of prime importance within the practice of acupuncture, as the accuracy required during needling is demanded from the whole Body/Mind/Spirit of practitioners. This includes their intention as well as their knowledge of physical and energetic anatomy.

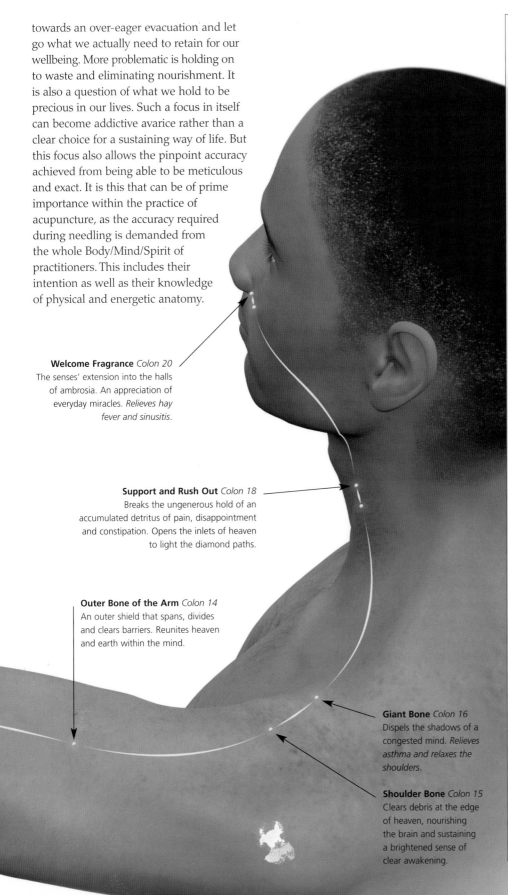

Welcome Fragrance *Colon 20*
The senses' extension into the halls of ambrosia. An appreciation of everyday miracles. *Relieves hay fever and sinusitis.*

Support and Rush Out *Colon 18*
Breaks the ungenerous hold of an accumulated detritus of pain, disappointment and constipation. Opens the inlets of heaven to light the diamond paths.

Outer Bone of the Arm *Colon 14*
An outer shield that spans, divides and clears barriers. Reunites heaven and earth within the mind.

Giant Bone *Colon 16*
Dispels the shadows of a congested mind. *Relieves asthma and relaxes the shoulders.*

Shoulder Bone *Colon 15*
Clears debris at the edge of heaven, nourishing the brain and sustaining a brightened sense of clear awakening.

ACUPUNCTURE

Acupuncture's mastery and elegance seeks the one point that transforms the whole

Acupuncture uses fine needles to balance the meridians and restore health. It is used across the world as a general medical technique as well as for specific medical contexts, such as childbirth, sports medicine and addiction.

It developed as a system of medicine around the 3rd century BCE in what is now eastern China. The diversity of weather systems in the region played its part in the process. The dry, elevated Mongolian deserts, for example, demanded a different approach to the damp lushness of the lands bordering Vietnam.

But there are indications that acupuncture may be far older. In the 1990s, a 5,000-year-old man was found preserved in the ice of the Italian alps near the town of Otzi. He was found to have tattoos corresponding to acupuncture points that treat arthritis of the lower back, a condition X-rays confirmed 'Otzi', as the man was named, did indeed have.

Needles are inserted into points on each of the meridians in patterns according to patients' presenting conditions and their underlying constitution. Needles are typically inserted 2–4 mm (about ⅛ in) below the skin. They rarely cause pain, but there is a sensation, often described as a 'dull ache', that most people recognize as therapeutic. Most patients seek treatment for specific complaints, but continue to use the therapy long after the initial symptoms have disappeared to maintain wellbeing.

Today, acupuncture remains an 'environmental medicine', encouraging a more harmonious balance between people and planet.

The STOMACH Meridian

wei appreciation

The spleen and the stomach are responsible for the storehouses and the granaries. The five tastes stem from them.
The Yellow Emperor's Classic of Internal Medicine

The stomach meridian starts at the height of the cheek and gently falls down the face to the edge of the mouth and side of the neck. As the main meridian dives over the torso, a separate branch reaches to the corner of the temple. At the lower abdomen, the meridian flips on to the side of the thigh and then descends the shin bone to the top of the foot, finishing at the outer edge of the second toe. The flow of energy down the meridian is both gentle and swift.

CAPACITY AND INCAPACITY

The stomach gives us the capacity to take in nourishment – food and experience. It enables us to be full with life, and abundant within who we are. In the same way that the Earth's rotation and transit around the sun provide a rhythm and season of its fruits, so, too, does the stomach provide us with the wisdom of generosity and appreciation. This rotational rhythm holds the essential dynamic of give and take, the mysteries of all that is given will be received back in abundance. But in imbalance this rhythm can descend into a painful tug of war, where the measure of what is given and taken arises from a mean-spirited exactitude. Physically this will manifest as a tightness throughout the abdomen and the range of the stomach meridian, and further manifest in the texture and body of the muscles. The flesh can lose its ripe abundance, turning rather to a strained poverty or an engorged slackness. As the stomach becomes full up, a stoniness will appear in our energy, and commonly our face will appear impervious to anything getting through.

The very first point of the stomach meridian – Receive Tears – rests just beneath the eye and it is the antidote to such stony blankness, melting any pettiness or pride, allowing us to receive the blessings that will nourish us. The ultimate challenge of the stomach is maintaining a sense of balance in the face of barrenness and rejection.

The dangers that face us from the stomach occur when pride overcomes us and our capacity to maintain the flow of exchange with the world becomes too much. Here is where our pettiness can retreat into a rejection of nourishment so that we close off to the gifts of the world. We can starve ourselves of food, comfort and all we know of as home. We can reverse the flow of blessings and regurgitate food and experience, either consciously or through the reflex reactions of an imbalanced stomach meridian. Should the stomach struggle to such an extent, all aspects of the Body/Mind will suffer. For the network of appreciation directs the staged digestion of nourishment for all levels of Mind/Body/Spirit.

Leg Three Miles *Stomach 36*
Near limitless stamina and fundamental restoration of sustenance. The simple magic of harvest.

Abundant Splendour *Stomach 40*
'Thunder.' The furthest swing of the Earth's circumference, clearing and restoring the imaginings of self and environment. A reacquaintance with one's face of beauty.

Released Stream *Stomach 41*
An authoritative calming of chaotic dispersal.

Branch Opening *Stomach 38*
An effortless renewal of fresh perspectives. Gently clears obstructions and discomfort.

Rushing Yang *Stomach 42*
Bedrock of stability and the foundation of life.

Lower Great Void *Stomach 39*
Restores vitality to a wasting Earth, burdened and vacuous. *Brings balance to the lower abdomen, legs and small intestine.*

Inner Courtyard *Stomach 44*
The stillness of solitude held in the embrace of community. A bringing of the understanding that quells anxiety and shyness, restlessness and suspicion.

Hard Bargain *Stomach 45*
Antidote to the hard veil of resentment. Culmination of the path of appreciation and the gifts of the covenant.

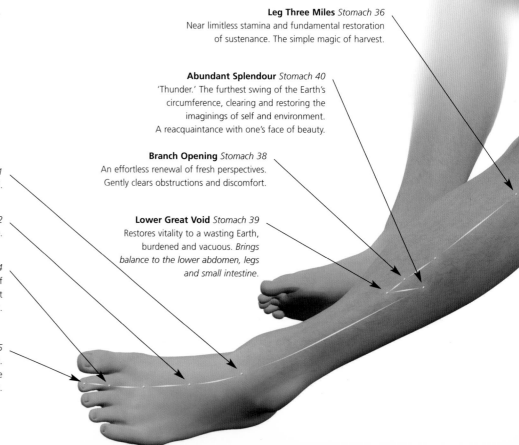

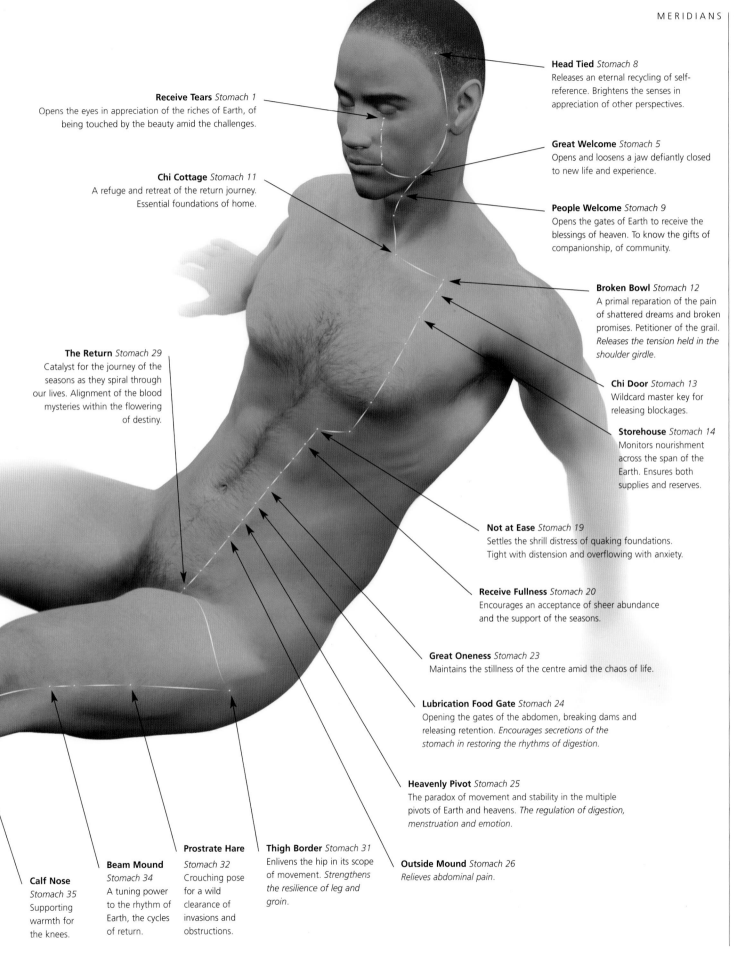

Head Tied *Stomach 8*
Releases an eternal recycling of self-reference. Brightens the senses in appreciation of other perspectives.

Receive Tears *Stomach 1*
Opens the eyes in appreciation of the riches of Earth, of being touched by the beauty amid the challenges.

Great Welcome *Stomach 5*
Opens and loosens a jaw defiantly closed to new life and experience.

Chi Cottage *Stomach 11*
A refuge and retreat of the return journey. Essential foundations of home.

People Welcome *Stomach 9*
Opens the gates of Earth to receive the blessings of heaven. To know the gifts of companionship, of community.

Broken Bowl *Stomach 12*
A primal reparation of the pain of shattered dreams and broken promises. Petitioner of the grail. *Releases the tension held in the shoulder girdle.*

The Return *Stomach 29*
Catalyst for the journey of the seasons as they spiral through our lives. Alignment of the blood mysteries within the flowering of destiny.

Chi Door *Stomach 13*
Wildcard master key for releasing blockages.

Storehouse *Stomach 14*
Monitors nourishment across the span of the Earth. Ensures both supplies and reserves.

Not at Ease *Stomach 19*
Settles the shrill distress of quaking foundations. Tight with distension and overflowing with anxiety.

Receive Fullness *Stomach 20*
Encourages an acceptance of sheer abundance and the support of the seasons.

Great Oneness *Stomach 23*
Maintains the stillness of the centre amid the chaos of life.

Lubrication Food Gate *Stomach 24*
Opening the gates of the abdomen, breaking dams and releasing retention. *Encourages secretions of the stomach in restoring the rhythms of digestion.*

Heavenly Pivot *Stomach 25*
The paradox of movement and stability in the multiple pivots of Earth and heavens. *The regulation of digestion, menstruation and emotion.*

Prostrate Hare *Stomach 32*
Crouching pose for a wild clearance of invasions and obstructions.

Thigh Border *Stomach 31*
Enlivens the hip in its scope of movement. *Strengthens the resilience of leg and groin.*

Outside Mound *Stomach 26*
Relieves abdominal pain.

Calf Nose
Stomach 35
Supporting warmth for the knees.

Beam Mound
Stomach 34
A tuning power to the rhythm of Earth, the cycles of return.

The SPLEEN Meridian

pi **the dancer**

Absorbing and moving: these are the essential actions which define the spleen/stomach network as the main source of the life-sustaining postnatal energy.

Traditional Diagnosis Compendium

The spleen meridian starts from the outer edge of the big toe and ascends the side of the foot to the ankle, where it tucks underneath the tibia to rise the length of the calf and inner thigh. Traversing the span of the outer abdomen, it rises to the apex of the breast and then retreats to the side of the chest at the master point of all the body's energetic junctions. It is assured and smooth in its ripe ascension of the body.

CAPACITY AND INCAPACITY

The spleen meridian gives us our capacity for smooth and rhythmic movement, both physically and spiritually. It is responsible for transporting the nutrients derived from our food to all parts of the body and is the spiralling dance of our energy field, whirling in equilibrium and balance. The health of this meridian reveals itself in the ease with which we achieve range and rhythm within our energy field.

The most common challenge for the spleen meridian is that of 'stuckness' and inertia. Here we can imagine the smooth, unending rotation of the Earth as the ideal model for the easy dance of the spleen, which spirals around our energy field in nourishment and communication, facilitating all aspects of movement.

As nourishment is transported around our energy field, the meridian becomes the cornucopia of abundance. It is in this way that the spleen meridian also becomes manifest in the mouth and lips, as the dancer tastes the fruits of life, the treasures of creation. Here, too, is the responsibility for the flourishing of everyday life, and the ease of movement the spleen oversees is seen in the vibrancy of muscles and the movement of limbs.

It is the slow quiescence of such ease and momentum that leads to an imbalanced spleen meridian, giving rise to lethargy and dull inaction. Digestion, circulation and so on will slow down, leading to tiredness and the pain of stagnation. Mentally we will suffer from memory loss as our access to archives grinds to a halt. Emotionally we will retreat into ourselves as we become stuck and unable to appreciate the rhythm of give and take with others. And spiritually, we will lose the connection to the rhythm of our lives in relationship to the Earth, the innate knowledge of our energetic magnetism to the Earth's rhythms and the holding and nourishment they provide. The slow grinding to a halt that dogs the spleen meridian can create a counterweighted spiral of worry. Lacking any rooting, this then spins out of control, frantic for movement and rhythm.

Just as the rhythm of the planets affects each other's orbits, so, too, does the spleen's rhythm reach out to the energy fields of its environment. In the same way that women's menstrual cycles can develop a synchrony, and pendulums in close proximity will come into harmony, so the spleen meridian seeks to know itself as part of a wider energetic community. Within the calm centre of life's myriad transformations the spleen enables us to reach beyond the spirals to the infinite freedoms that arise when dynamics resonate.

HERBAL MEDICINE

Ginko biloba **leaves and powder, master herb of love and long life**

here (see left). These are boiled up to make a concoction that typically tastes 'earthy'. While each part of the world has its own native herbal medicine traditions, oriental herbal medicine has travelled the world, as have its herbs, in the same way that aspirin is now also used within formulas and prescriptions of herbal medicine in contemporary China.

Herbal medicine has come under attack for using animal products from endangered species in some of its preparations. As the tradition comes into alignment with such concerns, other challenges remain, such as the efficacy of herbal medicine and, particularly, the logic of its diagnostic frameworks. Based on traditional theoretical structures, such as yin yang and the five elements (see page 152), herbal medicine resists analysis from Western pharmacology, and through the experience of patients continues to hold its place within pluralist healthcare systems across the world.

Herbs have been integral to oriental medicine and longevity practices for more than 2,000 years. Inseparable from food science and meditation, oriental herbal medicine uses mineral, vegetable and animal products to bring balance to the body. At the beginning of herbal medicine it was understood that there were three classes of medicine; first, there was remedial medicine for treating illness and disease; then there was the prevention of illness; and, finally, the higher class of medicines were understood to nourish our destiny. As a consequence, dietary advice and meditation were as much a part of this tradition as were the prescription of medicinal herbs.

Oriental herbs are today taken either in the form of preprepared pills or as loose herbs prescribed uniquely for each patient, as shown

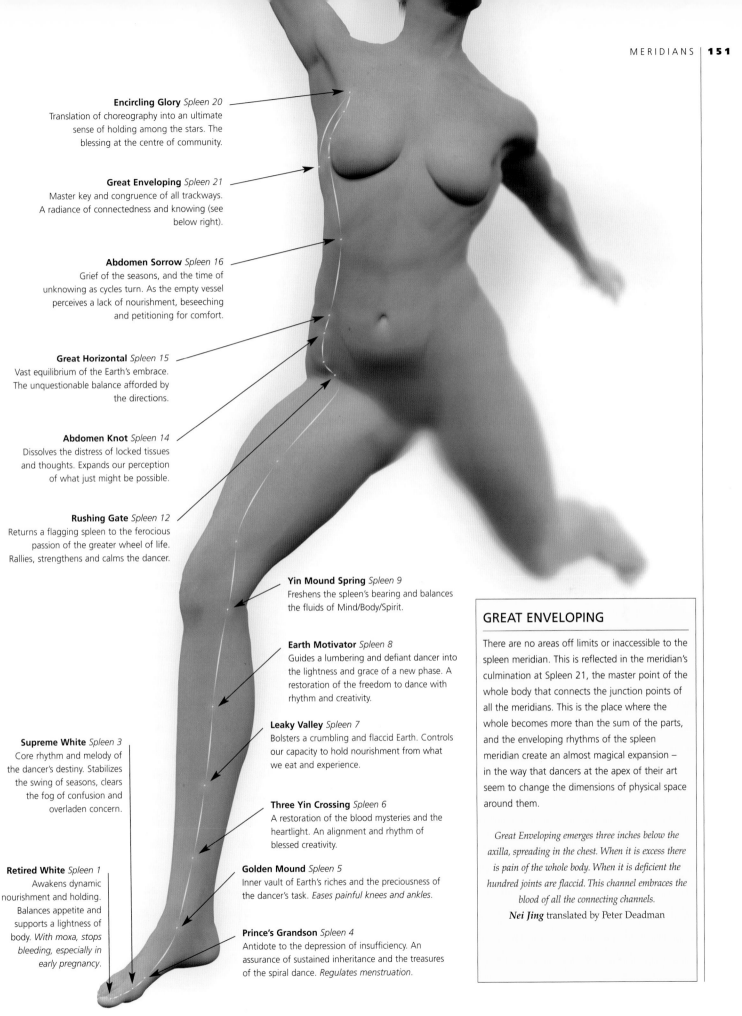

Encircling Glory *Spleen 20*
Translation of choreography into an ultimate
sense of holding among the stars. The
blessing at the centre of community.

Great Enveloping *Spleen 21*
Master key and congruence of all trackways.
A radiance of connectedness and knowing (see
below right).

Abdomen Sorrow *Spleen 16*
Grief of the seasons, and the time of
unknowing as cycles turn. As the empty vessel
perceives a lack of nourishment, beseeching
and petitioning for comfort.

Great Horizontal *Spleen 15*
Vast equilibrium of the Earth's embrace.
The unquestionable balance afforded by
the directions.

Abdomen Knot *Spleen 14*
Dissolves the distress of locked tissues
and thoughts. Expands our perception
of what just might be possible.

Rushing Gate *Spleen 12*
Returns a flagging spleen to the ferocious
passion of the greater wheel of life.
Rallies, strengthens and calms the dancer.

Yin Mound Spring *Spleen 9*
Freshens the spleen's bearing and balances
the fluids of Mind/Body/Spirit.

Earth Motivator *Spleen 8*
Guides a lumbering and defiant dancer into
the lightness and grace of a new phase. A
restoration of the freedom to dance with
rhythm and creativity.

Leaky Valley *Spleen 7*
Bolsters a crumbling and flaccid Earth. Controls
our capacity to hold nourishment from what
we eat and experience.

Supreme White *Spleen 3*
Core rhythm and melody of
the dancer's destiny. Stabilizes
the swing of seasons, clears
the fog of confusion and
overladen concern.

Three Yin Crossing *Spleen 6*
A restoration of the blood mysteries and the
heartlight. An alignment and rhythm of
blessed creativity.

Golden Mound *Spleen 5*
Inner vault of Earth's riches and the preciousness of
the dancer's task. *Eases painful knees and ankles.*

Retired White *Spleen 1*
Awakens dynamic
nourishment and holding.
Balances appetite and
supports a lightness of
body. *With moxa, stops
bleeding, especially in
early pregnancy.*

Prince's Grandson *Spleen 4*
Antidote to the depression of insufficiency. An
assurance of sustained inheritance and the treasures
of the spiral dance. *Regulates menstruation.*

GREAT ENVELOPING

There are no areas off limits or inaccessible to the
spleen meridian. This is reflected in the meridian's
culmination at Spleen 21, the master point of the
whole body that connects the junction points of
all the meridians. This is the place where the
whole becomes more than the sum of the parts,
and the enveloping rhythms of the spleen
meridian create an almost magical expansion –
in the way that dancers at the apex of their art
seem to change the dimensions of physical space
around them.

*Great Enveloping emerges three inches below the
axilla, spreading in the chest. When it is excess there
is pain of the whole body. When it is deficient the
hundred joints are flaccid. This channel embraces the
blood of all the connecting channels.*
Nei Jing translated by Peter Deadman

The HEART Meridian

xin **the one**

The heart holds the office of Lord and Sovereign. The radiance of the spirits stems from it.

The Yellow Emperor's Classic of Internal Medicine

The heart meridian begins in the depth of the axilla (the armpit). It slowly unfolds to descend the inner plane of the arm to the wrist and palm, finishing on the inside of the little finger.

The heart is the centre of our being. It allows self-coordination of other meridians by providing a central focus for their movement. The heart is linked to the role of emperor, who enjoyed a divine mandate on his rule. The virtues of this arise from an unobtrusive presence throughout the energy field or land, ensuring that every aspect of the Body/Mind/Spirit is held by the blessings that the heart itself receives from heaven.

BALANCE AND IMBALANCE

The heart's silent government is achieved by the radiance of its presence. It has no active role apart from 'being', and radiating its own divine nature. When that silence is lost, an anxiety can grow, doubting the intrinsic rightness of the Body/Mind/Spirit and the balance of forces within it. Typically, the heart will then further lose its own peace and attempt to control actively the organs and meridians, exerting a stifling influence that hinders rather than helps order to be restored.

In extremes, imbalances of heart energy can lead to the rise of an internal tyrant who prevents the meridians from getting on with their jobs. This is the corruption of power and the paranoia of never trusting one's circle of government. If we experience such challenges of trust and power, we are likely to become domineering and suspicious. More obviously, though, will be the lack of peace within our heart centre, so radiating anxiety and chaos, rather than peace.

In balance, however, the settledness of our heart will carry much of our charisma and the quiet communion shared with others. This is the sparkle in our eyes that speaks of our passion for life and the eternal flame of our spirits. This feeling of 'oneness' that the heart provides to the government of the Body/Mind/Spirit is a quality that can be experienced in our relationships. This again is characterized by a silent communion, a feeling of being at peace, in the right place at the right time.

YIN YANG AND THE FIVE ELEMENTS

Yin yang

Yang	Heaven	Day	Male	Speech	Chi energy	Outside	Increase
Yin	Earth	Night	Female	Silence	Blood	Inside	Decrease

The five elements

Element	Season	Classical description	Colour	Organs	Direction
Wood	Spring	Curves and straightens	Azure green	Liver and gall bladder	East
Fire	Summer	Blazes and ascends	Red	Heart and small intestine	South
Earth	Harvest	Takes seeds and gives crops	Golden yellow	Spleen and stomach	Centre
Metal	Autumn	Obeys and changes	White	Lungs and colon	West
Water	Winter	Soaks and descends	Blue	Kidneys and bladder	North

Yin yang and the five elements are the two schemas that describe the natural organization of the universe as perceived by Southeast Asian culture and medicine.

Yin yang is the fundamental axis of life, describing the balance of light and dark forces within the 'great unity' of the universe. Classically, these distinctions include the attributes above.

Yin yang is not the polar opposition of good and bad, for it is the way of balance between these two forces that is valued. For what worth is the fruit of summer without the germination of winter? And nor are they constant definitions, with all life being divided into yin or yang; rather, they are eternally relative to their context. The classical depictions of yin and yang were as the sunny and shady sides of a hill, and they described aspects of military strategy and divination as much as aspects of health and the body.

And with such balance of yin yang comes the paradox that within the heart of each is the seed of the other. At the height of summer comes the stillness of the evening, at the depth of winter the fire festivals of Christmas, Yule, Hanukkah.

The five elements are a further elaboration of the profoundly simple yin yang. They were used in the 1st millennium BCE to explain the seeming impossibility of dynastic succession. The replacement of one emperor with another was uncomfortable for the Chinese in their belief that each enjoyed a divine mandate, so the replacement of one emperor (or element) by another was observed as a natural phenomenon. The elements are aligned to the seasons and, as with yin yang, hold many correspondences that are also relative.

The elements, too, are not restricted to the body, but are integral to much of oriental cultural life, including astrology and architecture.

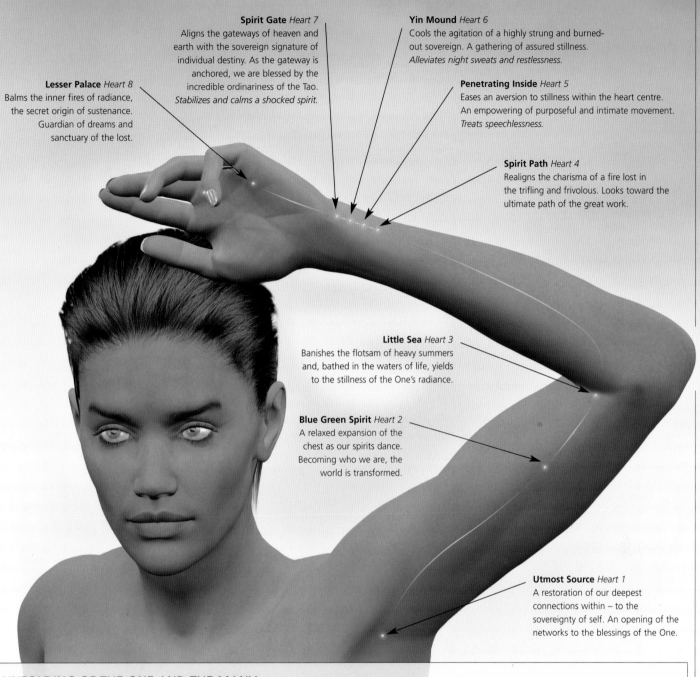

Spirit Gate *Heart 7*
Aligns the gateways of heaven and earth with the sovereign signature of individual destiny. As the gateway is anchored, we are blessed by the incredible ordinariness of the Tao. *Stabilizes and calms a shocked spirit.*

Yin Mound *Heart 6*
Cools the agitation of a highly strung and burned-out sovereign. A gathering of assured stillness. *Alleviates night sweats and restlessness.*

Lesser Palace *Heart 8*
Balms the inner fires of radiance, the secret origin of sustenance. Guardian of dreams and sanctuary of the lost.

Penetrating Inside *Heart 5*
Eases an aversion to stillness within the heart centre. An empowering of purposeful and intimate movement. *Treats speechlessness.*

Spirit Path *Heart 4*
Realigns the charisma of a fire lost in the trifling and frivolous. Looks toward the ultimate path of the great work.

Little Sea *Heart 3*
Banishes the flotsam of heavy summers and, bathed in the waters of life, yields to the stillness of the One's radiance.

Blue Green Spirit *Heart 2*
A relaxed expansion of the chest as our spirits dance. Becoming who we are, the world is transformed.

Utmost Source *Heart 1*
A restoration of our deepest connections within – to the sovereignty of self. An opening of the networks to the blessings of the One.

UNFOLDING OF THE ONE AND THE MANY

The ONE – the great unity

The TWO – yin and yang

The FIVE – water, wood, fire, earth and metal

The SMALL INTESTINE Meridian

xiao chang **discernment**

*The small intestine
is responsible for receiving and making things thrive.
Transformed substances stem from it.*
**The Yellow Emperor's Classic of
Internal Medicine**

This meridian begins at the little finger and traces the knife edge of the hand and arm to the shoulder, doglegging over the scapula and rising over the side of the neck to the front of the ear.

The small intestine's function of discernment ensures that only appropriately pure substances are admitted to the Body/Mind/Spirit. This discernment is the filtration of all phenomena and experiences as they approach our inner core, the separation and compartmentalizing of that which serves us and that which does not. In balance, this is the easy joy of everything in its place, naturally arising together. In distress, it is the breakdown of knowing elixirs from poisons, friends from foes.

PHYSICAL AND SPIRITUAL CHALLENGES

At a physical level, discernment operates through the separation of nutrients within the organ of the small intestine. Nutritional intolerances react mainly within this area of the digestive system. It is here that the wisdom of 'what is one person's meat is another's poison' bears out. The filtration system itself may be awry and not know the nature of what is needed. This confusion occurs not only at an individual level, but also in the collective, as we struggle to find the correct balance of what is 'good food'. With this arises the further challenge of not becoming too precious about what we ingest and experience. If our small intestine is too over-protective, then the heart never gets to experience the 'world outside'.

Spiritually, the challenges of the small intestine arise when the judgement needed in knowing what is nourishment and what is poison goes awry. In the governmental characterization of the meridians, the heart is the emperor and the small intestine the

NOURISHING THE OLD

Small Intestine 6 is the gateway to knowing the blessings and challenges of all the ages within us, of eternal youth, of our working potency and of our wisdom as elders.

In the power brought to us by the element of fire we have the capacity to mature and to know who we are between the poles of birth and death. And yet there is paradox here. The lineage master of Taoism is Lao Zi, author of the *Tao De Jing*, the book of virtue and the Tao. He is the epitome of Taoist wisdom. His name translates as 'Old Infant', reflecting the childlike state of natural and spontaneous wisdom (with a good dose of the ridiculous) that is the goal of Taoist spiritual practice. As an elder, he discovered the paradox that we return again to the innocence of who we are as a child.

Small Intestine 6 nourishes this wisdom within us all, bringing balance where it is needed; our gravitas and our ridiculousness, our maturity and our innocence.

emperor's secretary. It is the closest to the absolute centre of the body empire, intimate with the daily rhythms and needs of the heart emperor. The trust required for such a relationship is phenomenal, but so, too, is the capacity for betrayal, both real and imagined.

The meridian traces a path of discernment to end in front of the ear at Listening Palace, and a common challenge of the small intestine is of pre-judging what is appropriate rather than taking time to listen. The skills of a truthsayer are not dependent on mental clarity, but on a recognition of the threat posed by any circumstance or person. This is a deep trust in our own intuitive knowing of what is right, and while latent in some, for most of us it takes a great discipline of listening deep inside to the silent 'gong' of when something hits home, and is known to be true and pure.

Listening Palace *Small Intestine 19*
A release from paranoia into the embrace of dialogue and hearing the truth of the world. *Benefits deafness and tinnitus.*

Cheek Bone *Small Intestine 18*
Clears the countenance, relieving pain and inflammation, tension and sorrow.

Heavenly Appearance *Small Intestine 17*
The capacity to see the best in people.

Heavenly Window *Small Intestine 16*
Releases the oppression of tasks and tactics into the trust of service.

Shouldering the Centre *Small Intestine 15*
Supports the discernment of holding our backbone, of discomfort in the neck region and unease within oneself.

Grasping the Wind *Small Intestine 12*
Antidote to spiritual poison and appreciation of heavenly brilliance.

TUI NA

Typical pushing and grasping technique of tui na

Tui na literally means 'to push and grasp'. It is, in effect, Chinese massage and has been a medical discipline since about 600 CE. Archaeological evidence, however, tells us that it is even older, and was used more than 3,500 years ago.
Tui na is known to be very effective with muscular disorders and fertility problems and its 'pushing and grasping' techniques are based on the oriental diagnostic framework. Therefore, the five elements, eight principles and the meridians all feature in the training.

Tui na practitioners will also be trained in aspects of chi kung, allowing them to attend to the body's energy field as well as massaging the musculature. They may also use herbal lotions and oils according to the principles of Chinese medicine. Tui na goes further, however, and through a variable use of acupressure is able to bring a balance to the body energetically and physically.

Acupressure is often seen as an effective home treatment for various ailments. Some caution does need to be taken, however, with points such as Large Intestine 4. It is a very effective point for toothache, but one that is also used to induce labour, and so is forbidden during pregnancy.

Lesser Sea *Small Intestine 8*
A gentle grounding for the fires of heaven.

Upright Branch *Small Intestine 7*
The aligned embodiment of integrity as discernment joins illumination.

Nourishing the Old *Small Intestine 6*
Balances a maturity of presence with the looseness and vitality of youth (see left).

Yang Valley *Small Intestine 5*
Sheds glamour and stimulates the true flames of passion.

Shoulder Blade
Small Intestine 10
A potent elevation of spirits, held in the fluidity of the shoulders.

Heavenly Ancestor *Small Intestine 11*
A restoration of faith from the authority of our ancestors.

Wrist Bone *Small Intestine 4*
Caches of secret wisdom held in living bone.

Back Ravine *Small Intestine 3*
Dislodges the dysfunctions of repetition, Restores nourishment to a structure exhausted with emotion.

Forward Valley *Small Intestine 2*
The swelling momentum of open waterways, a sparkling brilliance of appropriate relationships. *Eases stiffness in the fingers.*

Lesser Marsh *Small Intestine 1*
The initiation of discernment. *Alleviates stiff necks and headaches.*

The BLADDER Meridian

pang guang **the archivist**

*The bladder is
responsible for the regions and cities.
It stores the body fluids. The transformation of chi
(the breaths) then gives out its power.*
**The Yellow Emperor's Classic of
Internal Medicine**

The bladder meridian starts in the hollow of the nose, beside the eye, and progresses up the forehead, across the scalp to the neck. Each side of the meridian then divides so that the back is mapped by four lines of the bladder's descent. The branches rejoin to descend the back of the leg and the outer edge of the foot, with the body's longest meridian ending up at the little toe.

The bladder meridian is responsible for our reserves, for the rhythmic exchange of water throughout the energy field and the overall irrigation of our tissues, minds and spirits. The physical problems of oedema, incontinence, dehydration and cystitis also have their spiritual counterparts, as we can both 'dry up' and 'flood' energetically. The comparison of water regulation in the natural world demonstrates the continuum of challenges that arise for the bladder – from dehydrated ground causing flash floods, to the erosion of boundaries, the barrenness of drought, the oppressiveness of endless rain, the destructiveness of tsunamis and the collective fear of great floods.

The more we can see the wisdom of how water can be managed effectively in our environment, the more we will be able to see how to manage not only our own body fluids, but also our energy reserves.

BALANCE AND IMBALANCE

Typically, if we have an imbalanced bladder meridian we will be concerned with energy reserves on an almost existential level – wondering if we have the strength to carry on. The nightmare that this can turn into for some is a parched and paranoid terror of fearing for our lives, so we can become frantic in seeking the barest scrap of refreshment and energy. But we can never

hold water actively – it literally slips through our fingers, and energetically there is a level of trust and surrender required in order to be able to form a vessel, a grail, to hold the waters of life. On the land, hard, dry earth will cause sudden rains to move on and pass by and we need a discipline of surrender and permeability in being able to hold this resource within our energy field.

ORGANS AND MERIDIANS

Yet the bladder meridian does not just store a neutral and bland stock of energy. Beneath its seemingly mundane role of tending the wells of the energy field is the uniqueness of those wells themselves. The pathway of the bladder meridian on the back either side of the spine comprises points where each of the internal organs/meridians are accessed very directly – the 'highway' of the bladder meridian visiting the 'cities' of the Body/Mind/Spirit.

These points can be used in the practice of acupuncture to restore, detox or nourish a whole organ/meridian system at a very deep level, reaching beneath the worldly formality of each meridian's pathway and going directly to the heart of each system. In this way, the bladder is responsible for memory, it is the archivist of the system and will betray its health and balance in how effective our memory is.

And the meridian does this twice, for as it returns to trace its way down the back for a second time, it revisits the 'cities' of the meridians. This time, however, at a level of transformation rather than of restoration. These points are all catalysts of potential – holding the beacon of each organ's/meridian's capacity to help us become who we are. The goal of this quest has been described in the Chinese classics and throughout the long span of Chinese history as the goal for longevity or immortality.

TAOIST PRACTICE

The 'transformation of wings' is a technical term used within Taoist alchemy. It is used to describes the process of refining one's energy body to such a degree that it becomes light enough both to fly and to phase in and out of what we perceive as normal existence. At the same time, it is the

EYES BRIGHT

This point, Bladder 1, is the beginning of the bladder meridian and the opening in the energy field to the realm of water and body fluids as they irrigate our soul's journey. Each of the 'entry' points of the meridians can operate as 'reset' buttons for the work of that meridian, and here, the blueprint held within the template of each drop of water. Eyes Bright offers the essential starlight of water that brings us the fluid and radiant sparkle in our eyes, the dewdrops of essence from our soul's vision. Physically, this point will reinitiate our hormonal balance, all of the internal physiological secretions that regulate our rhythms and hold the impeccable balance of risks and resources in sheer, existential courage. This is no less that a renewal of our seas, streams, waterfalls and lakes, the water mysteries of our soul's landscape.

most unspectacular magic of being human, and the Taoist paradox of remembering our own natural, divine state rather than striving for an artificiality that masks our inherent perfection.

Many of us will have dreams of flying and it is an almost universal human notion of going beyond everyday consciousness. Taoist alchemy sees the process as arising from a refinement of each of the five elements within so that we remember our original nature, rather than being dragged down by the weight and seriousness of living. The ethic of spontaneity, lightness and 'following the chi' within Taoist practice is this spectrum of remembering the original nature of the elements, which the outer bladder points hold, and which strangely trace the line on the back where wings might be attached to the human form.

Heavenly Pillar *Bladder 10*
The illuminated possibilities of water: assured strength, brightness of perception and freshness of faith.

Great Shuttle *Bladder 11*
Convoy of ancestry deep within the bones, shrugging off slights and winds.

Wind Gate *Bladder 12*
Master point of wind protection through the outer edges of the turtle's carapace.

Spiritual Soul Gate *Bladder 42*
The deepest renewal of the soul that we can call to.

Yang Net *Bladder 43*
Gathering network of yang's clear essence honed for clear and courageous action.

Thought Dwelling *Bladder 44*
Antidote to an endless recycling of thoughts and worries. A dwelling of deep peace for thought, intention and consciousness itself.

Stomach Granary *Bladder 45*
Secret source of the Earth's gift.

Equilibrium Middle *Bladder 54*
Holding balance amid the paranoid isolation of uncontained flow.

Supporting Muscles *Bladder 56*
Fluid and silent strength of a hydrated musculature. Adaptable responsiveness of the alert archivist.

Supporting Mountains *Bladder 57*
Alleviates the chronic discomfort of not knowing ones foundations. *Invigorates the bowels, calms menstrual pain, alleviates back pain.*

Foot Bone Yang *Bladder 59*
Banishing the remnants of dog days and smoothing the lithe movement of the limbs.

Kunlun Mountains *Bladder 60*
Lands the fires of Heaven onto the crests of Earth's peaks, blending frost and fire in the eternal dance of the axis of manifest life.

Servants Aide *Bladder 61*
Releases the entrapment of servitude, reclaiming the rhythms of universal service. Stirs courage, stills fear and engages movement.

Eyes Bright *Bladder 1*
First contact with the fluids, the sparkle of starlight and dewdrops in our eyes.

Soul Door *Bladder 37*
The capacity to be 'grounded' in physical existence while allowing an 'inner life' of spiritual richness, connection and reflection.

Rich for the Vitals Correspondence
Bladder 38
Macrocosmic nourishment of every cell in the body. A powerful gathering of completeness, deepest honouring of the blood mysteries.

Spirit Hall *Bladder 39*
The dignity of knowing the deep peace of boundaries, holding true to the words of guardians. Allowing the power of mystery to have a place in the world. Unassailable antidote to the enemy of power.

Ambition Room *Bladder 47*
Regulation of an excessively eager (or absent) need to manifest and achieve.

Womb and Heart Diaphragm *Bladder 48*
Restoration of the balances between sexuality, sex, love, sensation, passion and feeling.

Fly and Scatter *Bladder 58*
A harmonization and gathering of energy – fragmented and scattered by fear and timidity.

Extended Meridian *Bladder 62*
Resources beyond personal memory and templates. The numinous capacity to break the bounds of mental restriction.

Capital Bone *Bladder 64*
Absolute reassurance of touching the unique signature of one's own path.

Bone Binder *Bladder 65*
Invites participation in a greater dream. Moves things forward.

Penetrating Valley *Bladder 66*
Unfathomable momentum of glaciers, bores and tsunamis as they swathe through obstructions of depleted waterways.

Extremity of Yin *Bladder 67*
Far reach to the outer arc of yin's expanse, relaxing the treasures of inversion and offering seeds of stillness.

The KIDNEYS Meridian

shen **the keeper**

The kidneys are responsible for the creation of power. Skill and ability stem from them.
The Yellow Emperor's Classic of Internal Medicine

The kidneys meridian rises from a position at the sole of the foot, spirals around the ankle and onto the calf and then ascends the inner aspect of the leg before rising across the abdomen and chest to finish tucked under the collar bone.

THE ROLE OF THE KIDNEYS

The kidneys' principal function within the Body/Mind/Spirit is to act as the storehouse of the ancestral energy that governs our progress through each stage of life. Good kidney energy will entail a strong presence in each of these stages, and enable smooth transitions through both the transitions of puberty and menopause.

The kidneys also provide us with the necessary constitution to help us to be potent within our lives and live them to their full potential. This energy that we receive from our ancestors is given directly through our parents and it also contains the mysteries of destiny that are present at both our conception and incarnation. These mysteries are held throughout life within the kidneys' networks, waiting to be uncovered as the treasure of who we are. Should we fail to

manifest our essential nature, then we will perish rather that live long and then die with illumination. Here, the kidneys are the repositories of the wisdom required for us to know what is important within life to give energy to, holding firm to the authenticity of who we are.

As the foundation of our strength, the kidneys' deep power is responsible for producing the bones and the marrow of the body, which are the contrasting hard and soft manifestations of our stature. The vibrancy of the kidneys can also be seen in the silkiness and strength of the head hair. The integrity and balance of all the body's fluids illustrate the equilibrium of the kidneys, and their capacity to hold the balance of opposites gives rise to both reproduction and sexuality.

ILLUMINATED SEA

Kidney 6 describes the stillness of a body of water so calm that it acts as a mirror for the moon and stars. This stillness goes beyond merely sitting quietly. It can be a silence so potent that it becomes almost magical. It is the experience we might have when entering a temple, mosque or grove, a place where the atmosphere is so strong and still that we feel cautious of speaking loudly. Such a stillness and blessing are key gifts of the kidneys in their role within the body. Stillness holds mysteries, clues as to who we are. But we need to be silent enough to be able to listen.

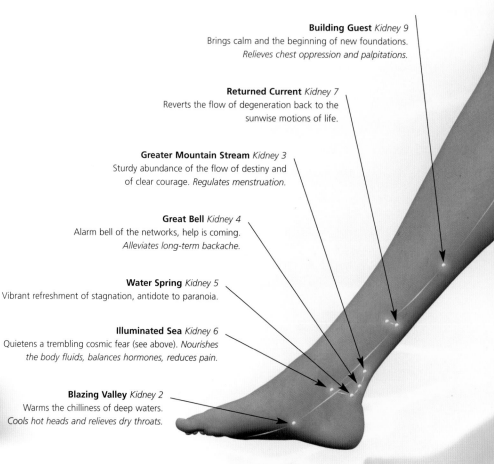

Building Guest *Kidney 9*
Brings calm and the beginning of new foundations.
Relieves chest oppression and palpitations.

Returned Current *Kidney 7*
Reverts the flow of degeneration back to the
sunwise motions of life.

Greater Mountain Stream *Kidney 3*
Sturdy abundance of the flow of destiny and
of clear courage. *Regulates menstruation.*

Great Bell *Kidney 4*
Alarm bell of the networks, help is coming.
Alleviates long-term backache.

Water Spring *Kidney 5*
Vibrant refreshment of stagnation, antidote to paranoia.

Illuminated Sea *Kidney 6*
Quietens a trembling cosmic fear (see above). *Nourishes
the body fluids, balances hormones, reduces pain.*

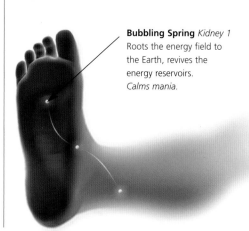

Bubbling Spring *Kidney 1*
Roots the energy field to
the Earth, revives the
energy reservoirs.
Calms mania.

Blazing Valley *Kidney 2*
Warms the chilliness of deep waters.
Cools hot heads and relieves dry throats.

Amid Elegance *Kidney 26*
A summoning of the magical when all is ready, and at peace.

Spirit Storehouse *Kidney 25*
Sanctuary and nourishment for worn spirits.

Spirit Burial Ground *Kidney 24*
Resurrection of the light in our eyes, and our power to pray.

Through the Valley *Kidney 20*
Gateway of danger and death, the advent of healing.

Vitals Correspondence *Kidney 16*
Ecstacy of the inner marriage, vibrancy of the essences.

Door of Infants *Kidney 13*
The life caller, gateway to a dialogue of incarnation.

Yin Valley *Kidney 10*
The heart of mid-winter. The purification of solitude. *Alleviates urinary problems.*

Storehouse *Kidney 27*
Flourishing power of the all and the everything. *Relieves asthma.*

Spirit Seal *Kidney 23*
The signature of our soul, the quest of who we are.

Walking on the Verandah *Kidney 22*
The convalescence of woundings, the promise of restoration.

Dark Gate *Kidney 21*
The restoration of shade and the shielding off of nightmares.

Great Brightness *Kidney 12*
Refreshes the waters. *Aids conception.*

Transverse Bone *Kidney 11*
Supports sperm production, nourishes the genitals.

AN INTERACTION OF MERIDIANS

The kidney points that are found across the chest are some of the most important on the entire body. Many of us struggle at some stage with questions of happiness, of who we are, and of what our existence is about. It is these types of question that the kidney chest points hold a map for. The chest's principal energetics are those of the heart. The journey of the kidneys meridian over the heart's sphere now brings an interaction between the elements of water (the kidneys) and fire (the heart). This is an interaction of opposites, and an alchemical meeting.

The kidneys hold the mysteries of destiny for each one of us, and the presentation of these mysteries to the court of the internal emperor (the heart) is one of the most crucial internal dialogues we can engage in.

The sense organs associated with the kidneys are the ears. Hearing extends to spatial awareness and particularly to knowing what is around and behind us. Kidney energy is associated with the emotions of fear and courage, from which arise the skills of knowing exactly the layout of our environment.

The HEART MASTER Meridian

xin zhu **the emissary**

The centre of the breast (the heart master) has the charge of resident as well as envoy. Elation and joy stem from it.
The Yellow Emperor's Classic of Internal Medicine

The heart master meridian begins on the breast and flows down the side of the arm to trace across the centre of the forearm and onto the wrist and palm.

The function of this meridian is to stand as protector and envoy of the heart emperor. It operates within the Body/Mind/Spirit as the gatekeeper of both blood flow and intimacy.

BALANCE AND IMBALANCE

When we are warm, joyful and enlivened, our heart master is standing in service. The heart carries the light of the eternal flame, the heart master carries the beacon fires, lighting the way and the festivals, banishing darkness, ensuring safety and celebration throughout the realm. The light and warmth that the heart master brings allows us the fluidity to be able to navigate the inevitable challenges and slights of relationships and to cultivate the networks of friendships that support a settled ease for the truth of the heart. In balance, the heart master is the graceful warmth of gentle joys; in imbalance we can sink towards the shrill pain of a shattered heart.

With such imbalance of the heart master meridian we will invariably feel vulnerable, emotionally and physically, as if our chest wall were transparent and our inner world available for all to see. This is the failing of our energetic shield that should stand before our heart, and the substance of our natural defences. Equally, the responsiveness of this meridian can become impaired so that instead of becoming transparent and vulnerable, our flexible shield of appropriately judging the friend/foe quotient becomes rigid, and we build walls around us, sealing the outside world out – but, more tragically, ourselves in.

HEART CENTRE

But not only is the heart master the protector of our heart, it is also the envoy, carrying the presence, messages and blessings of the heart emperor throughout the realm. This is the sphere of the heraldic seals carried by ambassadors and emissaries.

It is here, too, that we can come to know the blessings of forgiveness that is at the heart of the near global traditions of the 'king's pardon'. Compassion softens the hardness of slighted hearts, and allows us to release the accretions of hurt that harden our heart centre. But the polarity of such generosity of spirit are the seductions of revenge that insist on perpetuating conflict and seeking revenge. The gift of compassion is not the capitulation of all boundaries– this would be as much an aspect of imbalance for the heart master as would the vehemence of revenge. Rather, it is the letting go of the coiled tension within the breast of an arrow waiting to be released, darts and daggers spat out from our own hurts. Instead, there is a discipline of joy and humour, of releasing hurt and seeking always the path of love.

SHENMING

The love of the heart protector will carry the essence of the heart's oneness and the mystical union that can be known when we touch the truth of our heart. So, too, will it hold the love of sexual passion, the discernment of navigating appropriately our sexual landscape. As humans it is important that we each have 'shenming' (radiance of the spirits) within our eyes, as a way of seeing the world, of blessing it with our gaze. Classical Taoist medicine has been described as seeing a sexual universe, one of energetic interchange between all forms of life. The heart master enables us to be fully present with all those held strongly within our energy field, and to shield or radiate such presence as is appropriate.

---

nei jing
THE YELLOW EMPEROR'S CLASSIC OF INTERNAL MEDICINE

Chinese medicine achieved a tremendous level of sophistication more than 2,000 years ago. This was documented in the *Huang di nei jing* – 'The Yellow Emperor's Classic of Internal Medicine'. The text was split into the *Su Wen* (Simple Questions), dealing with matters of cosmology and the theory of medicine, and the *Ling Shu* (Spiritual Pivot), dealing with acupuncture and moxibustion. Specific chapters dealt with appropriate behaviour for each season to avoid illness, on the progression of each stage of life for men and women and on the coming and going of the spirits of the body. Each of the meridians described in this atlas was explained in terms of its specific function within the working of the body-empire, and how, between them, they maintained health and promoted wellbeing.

Three centuries later the *Nan Jing* 'Classic of Difficulties' posed and answered 81 questions that arose from challenging issues within the *Nei Jing*. Pulse diagnosis and the complexities of the balance of fire and water energies in the body were further discussed and elaborated. These texts continue to be the bedrock of oriental medicine, and it is the nature of written Chinese and the logic and poetry of its construction that analysis of ancient texts is a valued way to study medicine and the transformations of the body.

The physician-anthropologist Elisabeth Hsu in her book *The Transmission of Chinese Medicine* identified three ways that medicine continues to be taught to this day:

1 The transmission from master to student, as exemplified in some chi kung lineages, where direct transmission from the spirit of the master to the spirit of the student forms the basis of the training.
2 The training of the scholar physician, who, by careful analysis of classical texts, discovers the universal transformations of energy present within human health and illness.
3 The recent development of curriculum-based schools, where knowledge becomes more standardized and less holistic in practice.

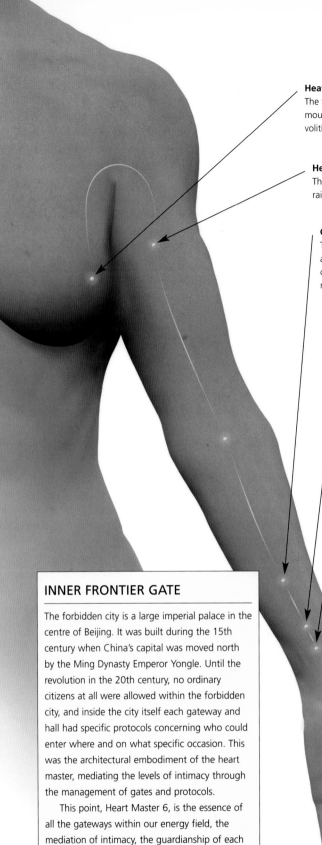

Heavenly Pond *Heart Master 1*
The vitality of heaven's elixirs held within mountain pools. A return to relationship and volition in the heart centre.

Heavenly Spring *Heart Master 2*
The excited beauty of gushing springs. A raising of spirits in refreshment and freedom.

Gate of Chi Reserve *Heart Master 4*
Turns around the experience of habitual attrition. Reassures the emissary's capacity to maintain appropriate relationships.

The Intermediary *Heart Master 5*
A clearing of the trackways of the chest as messengers of the emissary. Travel with the blessing of the heavenly officials.

Inner Frontier Gate
Heart Master 6
(See below left).

Great Mound *Heart Master 7*
Expanded vision of a higher vantage point, a centredness and perspective. Absorption of frantic and fearful fire. Touchstone of the emissary's destiny, of the words of the champion.

Palace of Weariness
Heart Master 8
A deep well of true warmth where the path has yielded stability but no joy, centredness but no passion. A restoration of sanctuary and the spark of life.

INNER FRONTIER GATE

The forbidden city is a large imperial palace in the centre of Beijing. It was built during the 15th century when China's capital was moved north by the Ming Dynasty Emperor Yongle. Until the revolution in the 20th century, no ordinary citizens at all were allowed within the forbidden city, and inside the city itself each gateway and hall had specific protocols concerning who could enter where and on what specific occasion. This was the architectural embodiment of the heart master, mediating the levels of intimacy through the management of gates and protocols.

This point, Heart Master 6, is the essence of all the gateways within our energy field, the mediation of intimacy, the guardianship of each hall, temple and courtyard within the landscape of who we are in this particular moment. Not only do we have the protection of a well-tended heart, we also have a relationship with ourselves.

I CHING

Casting coins for the I Ching's hexagrams

Chinese medicine, together with most traditional forms of knowledge, arises from oral histories that weave mythological symbolism as a basis for imparting wisdom and complex sciences. As well as the written sources of the *Nei Jing* and the *Nan Jing*, Chinese medicine comes from the same source as the I Ching, the first revelation of yin yang as both a complex system of divination and a map of the 64 phases of the universe's rhythms.

The I Ching, one of the four Confucian classics, is said to have been presented to the legendary Emperor Fu Xi, who saw it in a vision on the back of a 'dragon-horse' rising from a river. This is an emblem of the basic structure and organization of life being represented as various combinations of the two elementary forces of nature; yin and yang. In the I Ching, these forces are depicted graphically as either a broken line (yin) or a solid line (yang). Sets of three of these lines form trigrams, of which there are eight combinations that form the ba gua, or eight trigrams.

The ba gua continues to underlie both geomancy (feng shui) and martial arts as well as aspects of oriental medicine. The doubling of trigrams yields six-lined figures called hexagrams and it is these which are 'cast' during I Ching divination. Interpretation of the result is always ambiguous, and is always different in the hands of a master.

The THREE HEATER Meridian

san jiao **the harmonizer**

San Jiao is responsible for the opening up of the passages and irrigation. The regulation of fluids stems from it.

The Yellow Emperor's Classic of Internal Medicine

The three heater meridian begins on the ring finger and rises across the outer aspect of the arm, scaling the height of the shoulder towards the back of the ear, whose outline it traces on the side of the head, to finish at the tip of the eyebrow.

FUNCTION AND DYSFUNCTION

The function of the three heater meridian is to regulate the internal environment of the body so that all the other organs have the right conditions within which to work. It is unique throughout the meridian network in that it has no obvious counterpart within the internal organs, but instead describes a function within the energy field. Even the heart master, the other 'function' meridian, holds tenuous links to the pericardium, the sheath that surrounds the heart.

The three heater meridian not only moderates the response of the Body/Mind/ Spirit to the external environment, but it also regulates the relationships between all the other meridian/organ networks. If the temperature of the internal environment is regulated effectively, then the capacity for teamwork within the various aspects of the energy field is enhanced.

From the perspective of Chinese embryology, this regulatory function is one of the first to develop after conception – it prepares the way for all the other functions and organs within the Body/Mind/Spirit. Should the temperature of our environment vary beyond tolerable extremes, our system will begin to shut down.

When this part of who we are becomes imbalanced, we will invariably 'blow hot and cold' and be unable to maintain an even context for our relationships. We may, for example, go from a state of wild passion to one of cold withdrawal in a matter of just moments. We can lose the discernment of

social relationships that support who we are and fail to listen to the internal promptings of how we should relate to others.

The three heater meridian is so named because it regulates the 'three burning spaces' of the upper chest and middle and lower abdomens. Each of these has a different quality of energy and fluids to them and are known, respectively, as housing the mists, seas and marshes. Within Chinese medicine it is seen as important to care for each of these areas of the body appropriately and specifically to ensure that the lower 'jiao', or burning space, is always protected from the cold. This will then allow the three heater meridian – in association with the kidneys – to maintain an even temperature.

Such wisdom is used by Japanese dockers working in freezing fish markets, dressed only in shorts, but with a thick wrap insulating their lower abdomen, keeping the burner of their internal central heating system well tended. This is an image well contrasted with transient Western fashions, in which the midriff is sometimes bared while the rest of the body is well insulated – a fashion that not only threatens the regulation of the body's temperature, but also the vibrancy of its fertility.

MOXIBUSTION

Moxa roll brings blood and chi to the surface of the skin

The therapeutic technique of using the herb *Artemisia* (mugwort) to warm and nourish the energy field is known as moxibustion. It is a key component of acupuncture practice and the early descriptions of its use actually referred to 'acumoxa' therapy. It is used in its pulped form and resembles a tan-coloured cotton wool that is:

- Rolled into small cones, placed on top of specific points and then lit. The cone burns halfway down (until the patient feels the heat) and the practitioner removes it.
- Moxa can also be used in relation to specific points by wrapping the top of an inserted acupuncture needle with moxa, which is then lit.

- Loose moxa wool is lit in a box with a grid base. It is then located above the skin in order to heat an area of body.
- A tightly wrapped moxa cigar-shaped roll is lit at one end and traced slowly 2.5 cm (1 in) above the skin.

The actual herb used in moxibustion is very specific. Each herb has its own energetic signature that is distinct from its pharmacological or homeopathic descriptions. Acumoxa therapy developed out of a shamanic culture, and the spirit of the herb itself can become active in the healing process. In applying moxa directly, where cones are applied and removed over a number of minutes, the steady process of warming the point, particularly the rise of the smoke from the moxa cone, and the necessary concentration of both patient and practitioner mean the technique can become ritualistic. In Western traditions, another variety of the *Artemisia* family is dried and placed under pillows to bring blessed dreams.

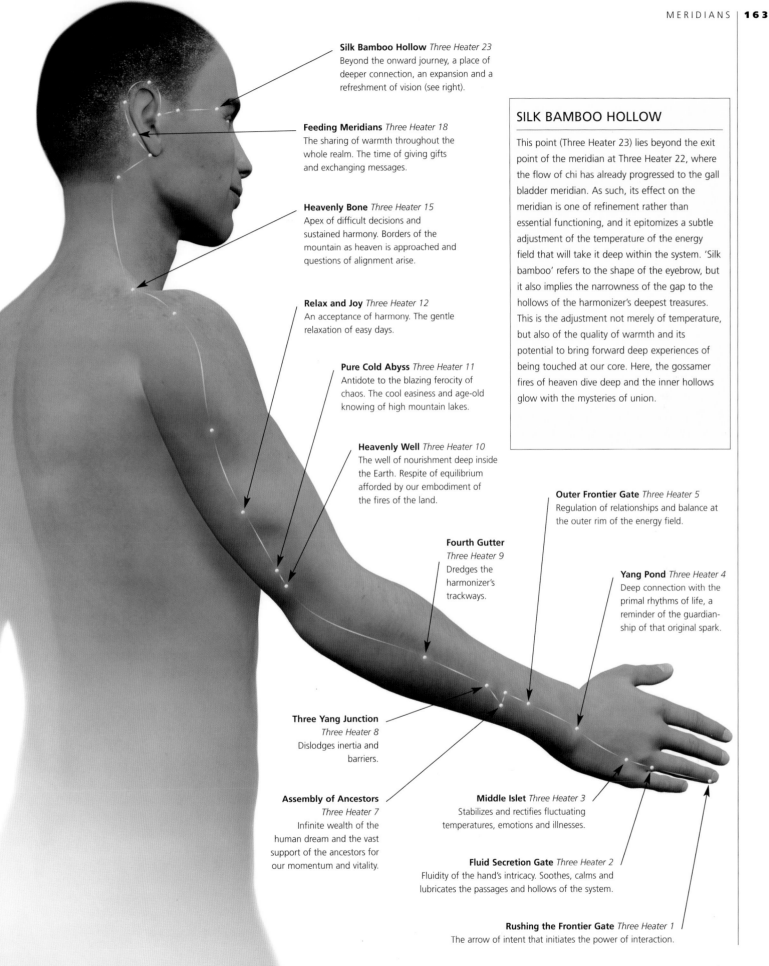

Silk Bamboo Hollow *Three Heater 23*
Beyond the onward journey, a place of
deeper connection, an expansion and a
refreshment of vision (see right).

Feeding Meridians *Three Heater 18*
The sharing of warmth throughout the
whole realm. The time of giving gifts
and exchanging messages.

Heavenly Bone *Three Heater 15*
Apex of difficult decisions and
sustained harmony. Borders of the
mountain as heaven is approached and
questions of alignment arise.

Relax and Joy *Three Heater 12*
An acceptance of harmony. The gentle
relaxation of easy days.

Pure Cold Abyss *Three Heater 11*
Antidote to the blazing ferocity of
chaos. The cool easiness and age-old
knowing of high mountain lakes.

Heavenly Well *Three Heater 10*
The well of nourishment deep inside
the Earth. Respite of equilibrium
afforded by our embodiment of
the fires of the land.

Fourth Gutter
Three Heater 9
Dredges the
harmonizer's
trackways.

Three Yang Junction
Three Heater 8
Dislodges inertia and
barriers.

Assembly of Ancestors
Three Heater 7
Infinite wealth of the
human dream and the vast
support of the ancestors for
our momentum and vitality.

Outer Frontier Gate *Three Heater 5*
Regulation of relationships and balance at
the outer rim of the energy field.

Yang Pond *Three Heater 4*
Deep connection with the
primal rhythms of life, a
reminder of the guardian-
ship of that original spark.

Middle Islet *Three Heater 3*
Stabilizes and rectifies fluctuating
temperatures, emotions and illnesses.

Fluid Secretion Gate *Three Heater 2*
Fluidity of the hand's intricacy. Soothes, calms and
lubricates the passages and hollows of the system.

Rushing the Frontier Gate *Three Heater 1*
The arrow of intent that initiates the power of interaction.

SILK BAMBOO HOLLOW

This point (Three Heater 23) lies beyond the exit
point of the meridian at Three Heater 22, where
the flow of chi has already progressed to the gall
bladder meridian. As such, its effect on the
meridian is one of refinement rather than
essential functioning, and it epitomizes a subtle
adjustment of the temperature of the energy
field that will take it deep within the system. 'Silk
bamboo' refers to the shape of the eyebrow, but
it also implies the narrowness of the gap to the
hollows of the harmonizer's deepest treasures.
This is the adjustment not merely of temperature,
but also of the quality of warmth and its
potential to bring forward deep experiences of
being touched at our core. Here, the gossamer
fires of heaven dive deep and the inner hollows
glow with the mysteries of union.

The GALL BLADDER Meridian

dan **the ranger**

The gall bladder is responsible for what is just and exact. Determination and decision stem from it.
The Yellow Emperor's Classic of Internal Medicine

The gall bladder meridian begins at the outer edge of the eye and zig-zags across the side of the head to jump down the side of the body, legs and feet to end at the fourth toe. It is swift, lithe and darting in its movement. Its 44 points trace the gall bladder's visionary skill in scanning the territory ahead, in both time and space, and having the strength, flexibility and courage to leap across obstacles.

The gall bladder is the decisive courage of our stepping out into the world, and manifests itself in the body's tendons and ligaments. It is essential that ligaments and tendons remain well hydrated and flexible. They need the correct amount of tension and elasticity in order to be able to spring into action appropriately and without injury. Such flexibility can be cultivated by staying hydrated, exercising, and ensuring that we do not become rigid, mentally or spiritually. The elastic tension they hold is literally that of a spring, swift and immediate, necessary both physically during exercise and mentally in terms of decision-making.

BALANCE AND IMBALANCE

The network of the gall bladder governs the storage and secretion of bile. If it is deficient and the efficiency of bile storage and secretion is disrupted, digestion is likely to be troublesome, with nausea and belching. But bile is also known in oriental medicine as the purest of the body fluids, and as such forms the sap of our soul's vision, nourishing the intricate rigging of tendons in their coordination of movement throughout the world. The gall bladder masters our vision. This is the capacity to see into the distance of our lives, to scout out strategies for the liver and then to make appropriate decisions in the immediacy of the present moment.

Receiving Spirit *Gall Bladder 18*
The capacity for grace and the power to pray. The ranger's call in the wilderness for visions of the way forward. The enchanted simplicity of a spiritual home.

Upright Living *Gall Bladder 17*
A strong stance of vigilant calm reaching high within the ranger's form. Balanced vision and appropriate decisions for the nurturing of life.

Head Over Tears *Gall Bladder 15*
Brings perspective for the despairing and the stability needed for a smooth release of tears.

Heaven Rushing
Gall Bladder 9
Raises the Gall Bladder's capacity for vision and courage. *Calms trembling spasms.*

Root Spirit *Gall Bladder 13*
Locates a hub of connection in the middle of the most disparate storms. Brings the spirits in to land.

Floating White
Gall Bladder 10
Loosens and lightens the neck, head and stride.

Yang White
Gall Bladder 14
Brightens the eyes and clarifies the vision.

Brain Hollow *Gall Bladder 19*
Clears the sensory organs and stabilizes frantic chaos in the head.

Orbit Bone *Gall Bladder 1*
Laser-sure insight of the ranger's infinite gaze, the dare-all courage to see what needs to be seen. *Lightens the eyes and clears the head.*

Wind Pond *Gall Bladder 20*
Still mountain waters and the calm of a weathered constitution. *Unlocks tensions, pains and chills.*

Head Hole Yin *Gall Bladder 11*
Opens the senses in restoring an aligned trajectory of vision.

Loathsome Jaws *Gall Bladder 4*
Moves the clenched distaste of jaws locked in disgust and revulsion. Restores the ranger's capacity to laugh.

Final Bone *Gall Bladder 12*
Calms the mania of exhausted chi. *Settles the channels, relieving neck and head pain.*

Crooked Hair on the Temple *Gall Bladder 7*
Alleviates headache, toothache and readjusts a distorted face.

The challenge of the gall bladder is the discipline of remaining balanced between being too decisive and not decisive enough. In deficiency, we are wilted and hidden, apologizing to others when they tread on our feet, having a lack of projection that means we can hardly be heard. In excess, the gall bladder leads us to being bullying, issuing challenges indiscriminately and causing chaos and friction. Timidity within oriental medicine is typically referred to as arising from a small gall bladder.

In making decisions and executing plans for the liver, the gall bladder can best be likened to a hunter, in the skills needed for tracking, or a seer, in the skills needed for expanded vision. The challenges of the gall bladder are the traps of wandering through life making idle decisions that take us off course, ensnaring us in blinkered timidity or overgrown and untended paths. It is the sensitive courage to hold true to our visions that gives us the flexibility and initiative to steer skilfully through the terrain of our lives.

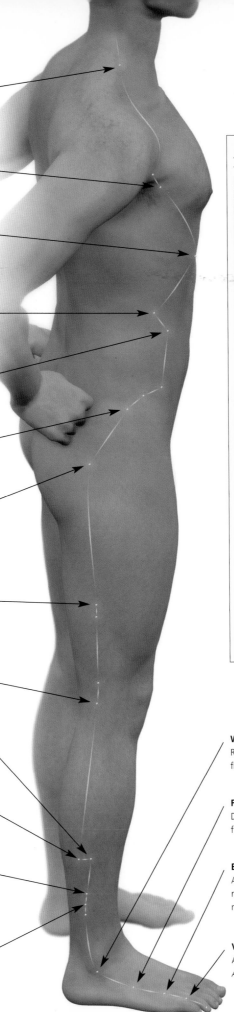

Shoulder Well *Gall Bladder 21*
Allows the interchange of heaven and earth.
Abundance of body and inspiration of spirit.*Relaxes and opens the shoulder girdle.*

Neglected Muscles *Gall Bladder 23*
Sees the hidden pain of determination. Balms deep-seated stagnations of denial, resilience and despair.

Sun and Moon *Gall Bladder 24*
Moves beyond opposites to the alliance of rhythmic alchemy. *Promotes balanced emotions and movement.*

Capital Gate *Gall Bladder 25*
Heralds renewal of the ranger's mandate, a geometric folding into new phases of movement.

Belt Vessel *Gall Bladder 26*
Surrounds the equator of the chi field, regulates the integrity of the fibres.

Dwelling in the Bone *Gall Bladder 29*
Balances the body's infrastructure.
Releases a twisted lower torso and one-sided sciatica.

Jumping Circle *Gall Bladder 30*
A flourishing kick of life, snapping into the wide arc of the outer extent of the chi field (see right). *Alleviates hip and leg pain and rouses consciousness.*

Wind Market *Gall Bladder 31*
Dislodges wandering weaknesses, smoothes the flow of upright chi.

Yang Mound Spring *Gall Bladder 34*
Relaxes and smoothes the movement of knees, legs and ankles.

Outer Mound *Gall Bladder 36*
Restores the momentum of a sustainable rhythm and achievable pace.

Yang Crossing *Gall Bladder 35*
Calms a frantic clamour for distracted action. Realigns the networks into meaningful endeavour.

Bright and Clear *Gall Bladder 37*
Immerses the ranger in the intoxicating web of life, enabling the blending of vision and service. *A respite for networks overloaded with drugs.*

Yang Support *Gall Bladder 38*
Regulates the intensity of hope and desire, calms fever. Rallies the heartwood's radiance of human kindness.

JUMPING CIRCLE

Bruce Lee – master of adaptation

The ranger's challenges of flexibility and suppleness are epitomized within Gall Bladder 30. The power and beauty of Jumping Circle is demonstrated in the kicks and leaps of martial arts, where the legs provide the most extended boundary of who we are, as well as our grounding and movement. This is particularly so in the kicks of many kung fu styles, which demand incredible flexibility in this joint. Its rotation should be smooth and swift within our physical capacities to run, jump and turn as well as our energetic and spiritual flexibility to adapt to circumstances. One of homeopathy's definitions of health is simply this capacity of being able to adjust ourselves to experience.

Wilderness Mound *Gall Bladder 40*
Rallies the most timid of spirits and bolsters the most flaccid flows of energy.

Foot Above Tears *Gall Bladder 41*
Detonates spring's vision, clarifying the eyes, and freshening the heart with tears of honest release.

Earth Five Meetings *Gall Bladder 42*
Assured control of appropriate boundaries, decisions, relationships. Assembly of the five elements and restoration of the implicate order.

Valiant Stream *Gall Bladder 43*
A turquoise embodiment of calm and fluid courage.
Assuages anxiety and a heavy, constricted chest.

The LIVER Meridian

gan **the shaman**

The liver holds the office of general of the armed forces, and assessment of circumstances and conception of plans stem from it.
The Yellow Emperor's Classic of Internal Medicine

The liver meridian starts at the outer edge of the big toe and ascends the top of the foot to the ankle, where it tucks underneath the tibia to run the length of the calf, rising quickly to the groin and on to the lower borders of the ribs. A deep pathway ascends from the organ of the liver itself up the centre of the body to One Hundred Meetings, Governer Vessel 20 (see page 170). It is short, direct and purposeful.

IMBALANCE

The liver meridian is classically described as being a general, the martial strength of defending the boundaries and highways of the realm. When it is imbalanced, energy flows within the body will become stuck or constrained as the healthy fury of passion ceases to rage through us. Anger, when it is embodied and balanced, is not damaging either to ourselves or to others. This is the assertion of fully knowing who we are and is as destructive and violent as a daffodil, bamboo or redwood, all natural expressions of the wood element, which is represented within us by the liver. When it is suppressed, this energy can become embroiled in convolutions that stem its fluid rhythm and either quash its momentum or twist its expression. The positive expression of this power is held within our central core, and is seen particularly in martial artists, who, by virtue of just standing still, appear like an immovable mountain. This strength arises from a deep connection with the energy of the Earth that is rooted in their bodies, and an undeniable knowledge of who they are, without rancour or quarrel.

When the strength of such presence is not available to us, then the middle sections of our abdomen can become stagnant and the channels that should be free-flowing

become entangled with each other, leading to pain and distention and anger physically, frustration and resentment emotionally. Typically, menstruation will become heavy and painful as the liver struggles, for it is the liver that stores the blood and a coming and going of ease is of great importance for healthy periods. Equally, weak and convoluted liver energy will lead to impotence and a lack of passion. One of the classical herbal remedies for a healthy liver is called 'Free and Happy Wanderer'.

Energetically, the capacity to dream can also become disturbed when the liver is in distress. It is the home of that aspect of our spirit that journeys each night as we sleep, into the dreamtime in order to quest for vision for each day and the overall meaning of our lives. The smoothness of this coming and going is what the liver oversees, and should this function become disturbed we can become devoid of hope, as the beacon of each day is not nourished by the dreams of who we are and what our path ahead is.

SYNCHRONIZATION

A further complication of our dreaming spirit is the timing and embodiment of its return. We need to be synchronized with ourselves, and it is important that the liver looks ahead – indeed, does its job and finds in the future beacons to walk towards – or the coordination of our everyday consciousness and strategist of our future can become disrupted.

Here, we can become out of synch with ourselves, and while it is reasonably natural to have some sense of what is around the corner and occasionally have prophetic dreams, this capacity can become exaggerated to the extent that we are always ahead of ourselves. This might be caused by trauma or an unacknowledged destiny, but more commonly occurs through drug and alcohol abuse. This arises when the rest of the energy field is not sufficiently strong to contain the visions and expansions that have been gleaned from turbo-fuelled and unmapped journeys into the dreamtime.

Such imbalance will often mean a descent into depression as the vivid liqueurs of the shaman's repertoire become coagulated and toxic. When aligned with the rest of the energy field, however, such elixirs can

regulate and choreograph our consciousness with a degree of ease and freedom.

BALANCE

In balance, the assured control of the liver will ensure a smooth flow of energy around the body as the trackways are kept clear. It is the warrior and dreamer, the loose-limbed roll of freedom within. It is the ultimate strategist of courage and timing who has won the game before it begins, the embodiment of our own individual shaman.

In the nine provinces there is not room enough:

I want to soar high among the clouds,
And, far beyond the Eight Limits of the compass,
Cast my gaze across the unmeasured void.
I will wear as my gown the red mists of sunrise,
And as my skirt the white fringes of the clouds:
My canopy – the dim lustre of Space:
My chariot – six dragons mounting heavenward:
And before the light of Time has shifted a pace
Suddenly stand upon the World's blue rim.
Cao Zhi (3rd-century poet from Lo Yang, northern China), translated by Arthur Waley

---

GATE OF HOPE
THE TRANSCENDENT DRAGON

Liver 14 is the culmination of the liver meridian and the point at which the energy dives into the depth of the ribs and lungs to emerge once again at the beginning of the meridian cycle, at Middle Palace, Lung 1 (see page 145). Physically, the point will alleviate tension in both the abdomen and chest. But this is also a pivot of existence for the shaman and the emergence onto the surface of the body of the blue-green dragon that is the emblem of the liver and the wood element. It is here that our florid enjoyment of exploration and the relentless optimism of our inner child experiences total freedom and remembers the magic of believing that anything just might be possible.

Chapter Gate *Liver 13*
So gather the vessels in readiness of rebirth. As revolution's gateway opens its riches. And change is called to the stage of renewal.

Gate of Hope *Liver 14*
Blue-green hues of the final gateway. The transcendent dragon soars with heaven in its eyes. Beyond the clouds, the eternal returns.

Yin Angle *Liver 11*
Relaxes the folds of generation at the height of the cradle's ridge, as boundaries of birth are held in cleansing clarity.

Five Miles *Liver 10*
Clears the dankness of stagnation in the lower abdomen. Realigns spring's low swing towards the centre.

Hasty Pulse *Liver 12*
Calms the frequency of the shaman's functioning. A return to the power of slow success, as potency diluted by frantic dispersion is reclaimed by depth and the coursing power finds its fertility.

Yin Wrapping *Liver 9*
Clothes rhythms of the hidden in the care of cycles and the reassurance of spirals.

Crooked Spring *Liver 8*
In the misty stillness of high frost's stark watch, far-off streams come forward and stand for the spring. The seedbed of winter offers up its charge and the embattled are bathed in emergent jade.

Knee Border *Liver 7*
Nourishes the knees and protects a soft grace of motion.

Middle Capital *Liver 6*
Clears the flow of energy and blood as an invigorating thrum of power beats from the hub and the cradled vessels are awash with the vibrancy of awakened yin.

Supreme Rushing *Liver 3*
The centred and steady power of rebirth, holding emergent destiny in a vast torrent of calm vision.

Insect Ditch *Liver 5*
Transformation of irritation, frustration, infestation. The excited chatter of insects as they herald extension and clarity throughout the networks, harmonizing levels of consciousness and being.

Walk Between *Liver 2*
Relaxes the liver and calms aggression.

Great Esteem *Liver 1*
A smooth and gentle explosion of spring, as the shaman takes the first essential steps to the vision of the dream.

Middle Seal *Liver 4*
The mark of heaven on the shaman's quest, as the chest is refreshed and uplifted with self-recognition.

SUN SI MIAO

Sun Si Miao, the Yao Wang – King of Medicine

Sun Si Miao is one of the great ancestors of Chinese medicine. Born in 581 CE in Shanxi Province, northern China, he mastered the classics before he was 20 years old and travelled widely, learning all he could from physicians across China. He settled to live in the remote caves of Wubai Mountain, treating patients and researching the mysteries of alchemy (the science of consciousness through herbs and meditation). Sun declined the invitations of three emperors to serve as a court physician, and was insistent in his writings on medical ethics that all patients should be treated equally, regardless of their rank.

In art he is often shown mastering the forces of yin and yang, the tiger and the dragon. In the White Cloud Monastery in Beijing, Sun is honoured as Yao Wang, 'King of Medicine', a Taoist Immortal. A painting of him there depicts the legend of a young Dragon Prince who left the ocean, and while ashore in the form of a snake was injured. Sun saved his life, and to reward him the Dragon King offered Sun great riches, which he refused. But he did accept two great works of medical knowledge, including the *Qianjin Yaofang*, 'Prescriptions Worth a Thousand Gold Pieces'. In the *Qianjin Yaofang* he detailed herbal formulas and the 13 'Ghost Points', used in acupuncture to dispel hauntings and demons. This text was so comprehensive that it is considered to be the first Chinese medical encyclopaedia.

Within Sun's lifetime he saw the unification of north and south China under the Sui Dynasty. As an alchemist he was concerned with longevity and lived himself to an age of 101.

The CONCEPTION Vessel

ren mai **creation**

The conception vessel is the vast reservoir of birth. Cradled in the Earth's caverns, it is the cosmic mother of life . . . and the holder of all seeds.
Paul Hougham

The pathway of the conception vessel rises from the depths of the perineum to the midline of the abdomen, across the central chambers of the chest and throat, to finish below the soft outcrop of the lower lip. A deeper pathway then swings down within the body, looping in the pattern of infinity to join the power of navigation, the governer vessel, at the coccyx (see pages 170–1).

VESSELS AND PATHWAYS

Ren Mai and Du Mai are both 'vessels', not meridians, and they share characteristics predating the 12 main meridians in our embryonic development. They belong to a total of eight vessels that hold the energy we inherit from the cosmos, ancestors and our soul rather than the everyday processing of food, air and fluids. The other six vessels share points with the standard meridians, but Ren Mai and Du Mai enjoy their own pathways within the body.

The conception vessel has deep connections to the uterus and genitals, nourishing all functions of fertility and reproduction. This operates not only in regard to conception and childbirth itself, but also the birthing of passion and vision for our lives. As primal force of creation, the conception vessel is the manifestation of yin within us, regardless of our gender, the polarity of who we are as mother, as earth. These qualities of yin are those dark and moist places of nurturing and conception, and the germination of each of our seeds, whether those of children or of dreams. Earth energy rises from the vast reservoirs of birth cradled in her caverns, softly held in the mossy freedom of dragon lines and dreams. The texture of the energy is dark, soft, moist and fertile. The structure of dragon lines are the ley-lines that snake across the land, the electromagnetic field of the Earth undulating and yielding according to the energetic contours of the land. The yielding that is held in such an observance of the close flow of the Earth's matrix allows us to cultivate equally our own energy field, and develop the necessary sensitivity to give birth to our own dreams, and have our destiny sated as they achieve their freedom from within us.

DEPLETION AND FULFILMENT

The types of demands and challenges that confront us when the conception vessel is depleted are the exhausted depressions of abandonment, a loss of connection with the source of who we are and from where we came. The centrality of Conception Vessel 8 (Spirit Deficiency) at the umbilicus is the watchtower of the self as we continue to be nourished by the cosmos throughout our lives. In acupuncture traditions, to stimulate this point it is often levelled with salt and then heat applied through the use of moxa, a herbal substance burned just above the skin (see page 162). This is deeply nourishing and informs and reminds the Body/Mind/Spirit of the integrity that is the birthright of each lifeform, clearing through any memories in the energy field that hold the pain and trauma of the inner child.

ELIXIRS

The blessings of the conception vessel unfold across the chest, as the highest qualities of jade used in the names of these points convey the rarefied energy of this part of the body. It is as the vessel arrives at the face, however, that the culmination of its journey holds the essence of yin brought to the height (the yang) of the body. This is comparable to the elixir sought by alchemists that would transform consciousness and extend life.

While most of the conception vessel is concerned with the transformation of fluids at some stage or another, the final points around the throat and mouth cultivate those special fluids of the saliva. In the practice of chi kung, there is often a stage when a pool of saliva will gather in the mouth. This should be swallowed and is seen as being highly favourable as it indicates a return of yin qualities to the body's energy field. Indeed, the whole of the body can be seen as a network of such elixirs, transforming themselves and refining the hidden fluids of the energy body that hold the destiny and magic of who we are.

In the ancient Chinese scripture the *Tao Te Ching*, it is written:
The spirit of the valley never dies.
This is called the mysterious female.
The gateway of the mysterious female
Is called the root of heaven and earth.
Dimly visible, it seems as if it were there,
Yet use will never drain it.
Tao Te Ching, verse 6, translated by D C Lau

ESTABLISHED MILE

The point Conception Vessel 11 is the pause along the vessel's elevation across the torso, where the achievements of rising yin can be held and stabilized. It is a staging post of creation where the ledges on the path up the mountain can provide a perspective on the path walked so far and the work yet to come. The points ahead embody the rise towards the pagodas of the heart and heaven – and this is the base camp before the final ascent. Through its deeper connections with the organs and the meridians of digestion, this point will provide support for the nutritive matrix that extends throughout the body and, especially, the middle of the abdomen – the capacity to rest and restore. This is an often forgotten aspect of the process of birth, where the infrastructure of our life is made fast and held steady.

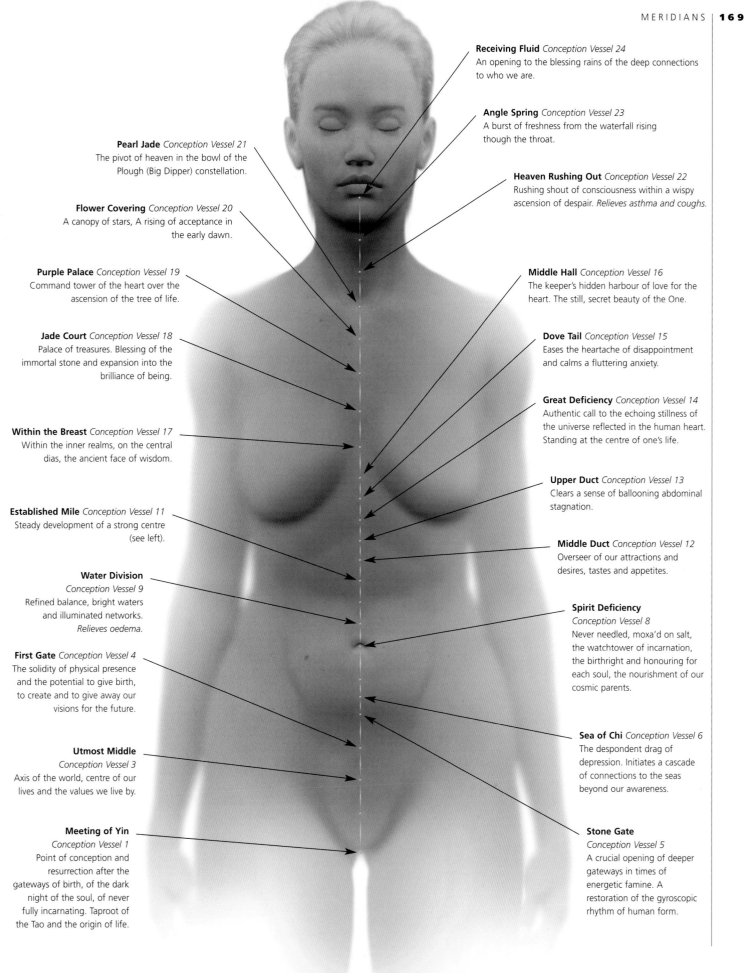

Receiving Fluid *Conception Vessel 24*
An opening to the blessing rains of the deep connections to who we are.

Angle Spring *Conception Vessel 23*
A burst of freshness from the waterfall rising though the throat.

Pearl Jade *Conception Vessel 21*
The pivot of heaven in the bowl of the Plough (Big Dipper) constellation.

Heaven Rushing Out *Conception Vessel 22*
Rushing shout of consciousness within a wispy ascension of despair. *Relieves asthma and coughs.*

Flower Covering *Conception Vessel 20*
A canopy of stars, A rising of acceptance in the early dawn.

Purple Palace *Conception Vessel 19*
Command tower of the heart over the ascension of the tree of life.

Middle Hall *Conception Vessel 16*
The keeper's hidden harbour of love for the heart. The still, secret beauty of the One.

Jade Court *Conception Vessel 18*
Palace of treasures. Blessing of the immortal stone and expansion into the brilliance of being.

Dove Tail *Conception Vessel 15*
Eases the heartache of disappointment and calms a fluttering anxiety.

Great Deficiency *Conception Vessel 14*
Authentic call to the echoing stillness of the universe reflected in the human heart. Standing at the centre of one's life.

Within the Breast *Conception Vessel 17*
Within the inner realms, on the central dias, the ancient face of wisdom.

Upper Duct *Conception Vessel 13*
Clears a sense of ballooning abdominal stagnation.

Established Mile *Conception Vessel 11*
Steady development of a strong centre (see left).

Middle Duct *Conception Vessel 12*
Overseer of our attractions and desires, tastes and appetites.

Water Division
Conception Vessel 9
Refined balance, bright waters and illuminated networks. *Relieves oedema.*

Spirit Deficiency
Conception Vessel 8
Never needled, moxa'd on salt, the watchtower of incarnation, the birthright and honouring for each soul, the nourishment of our cosmic parents.

First Gate *Conception Vessel 4*
The solidity of physical presence and the potential to give birth, to create and to give away our visions for the future.

Sea of Chi *Conception Vessel 6*
The despondent drag of depression. Initiates a cascade of connections to the seas beyond our awareness.

Utmost Middle
Conception Vessel 3
Axis of the world, centre of our lives and the values we live by.

Stone Gate
Conception Vessel 5
A crucial opening of deeper gateways in times of energetic famine. A restoration of the gyroscopic rhythm of human form.

Meeting of Yin
Conception Vessel 1
Point of conception and resurrection after the gateways of birth, of the dark night of the soul, of never fully incarnating. Taproot of the Tao and the origin of life.

The GOVERNER Vessel

Du Mai **navigation**

*The governer vessel is the vast reservoir of direction.
Suspended across the face of the stars, it is the
cosmic father of life, the origin of strength and
the holder of all initiations.*

Paul Hougham

The pathway of the governer vessel begins at the tip of the coccyx and rises up the spine, across the mountains of the back and the midline of the neck, head and face, to finish beneath the overhang of the upper lip. A deeper pathway then swings down within the body, looping in the pattern of infinity to join the conception vessel.

AN ACTIVE PRINCIPLE

Du Mai is the sea of all yang channels. It is the source from which the active power of yang arises. It is literally our backbone. The path of the vessel begins at the coccyx. The nature of this starting point is conveyed in the sense we can sometimes have of needing to give ourselves a 'kick up the backside' should our resolve falter during life.

This active principle continues to unfold throughout the vessel, traversing each of the areas of the internal organs. The brilliance of the governer vessel finally unfolds as it traverses the top of the head and face, bringing the power of the deep pistons of our being to the heights of consciousness.

BALANCE AND IMBALANCE

Clinically, the points on this vessel are used to treat the spine, brain and mind, sedating mania and settling chaos throughout the system. The points on the head enjoy connections to the heavenly chi of sun, moon and stars and, with such proximity to the expansiveness of the sky, can help settle our energy should we become disproportionately enamoured by the lure of the stars.

In balance, however, the governer vessel continues to transport the essence of yang across the head to the face and mouth, where the gap with the conception vessel can be bridged by the tongue during meditation: breathe in – tongue to the

roof of the mouth; breath out – tongue behind the lower teeth.

This bridging of yin and yang is similar to the joining of yin and yang that can occur during sex, where the 'polarity' we hold in these vessels can cascade into a reversal and equalization. This is the same dynamic as that within a lightning storm, the cosmic sex of heaven and earth, where the energies of the positive and negative ions within the thunderclouds are in that moment equalized and brought together. In sex, the cascading of our own yin yang can be enhanced if synchronized with that of our partner. So, while yin and yang are often characterized as female and male, we each hold these polarities within us.

One of the most significant energy blocks can occur when the flow through these vessels becomes dammed, whether through trauma along the pathway (during childbirth, for example) or a development of inertia. This is the core of our energetic structure and needs to be clear, for the governer vessel is the web of focus we have in directing our lives. It is the navigation of consciousness through the intricacies of the starweb. This is not so much the understanding of astronomy, but an energetic appreciation of the magnetic attraction of our guiding star, felt rather than understood, known by the physical experience of gravity rather than the intellectual subtleties of a concept.

One Hundred Meetings *Governer Vessel 20*
A gathering of focus and vision. Gateway of the spirits, calming overexposed psychic mania.

Anterior Summit *Governer Vessel 21*
Anticipation. A gathering of the unity of being, averting a fragmentation of the officials from divergent directions.

Skull Meeting *Governer Vessel 22*
Regulation of the skull's web and restoration of reins to the navigator.

Upper Star *Governer Vessel 23*
The stars in our eyes and the peace of dawn in our hearts.

Spirit Court
Governer Vessel 24
The stroking calm of the original face of our soul. A sweeping away of the winds and distractions of illusory claims.

Plain Bone
Governer Vessel 25
The clarity and uncomplicated lightness of breath.

Middle of Man *Governer Vessel 26*
Restoration of consciousness amid a drifting integrity of being.

Correct Exchange *Governer Vessel 27*
Rectification of fluids and freshening of the chi of the nose, mouth and teeth.

Mouth Crossing *Governer Vessel 28*
(Located underneath upper lip.) Blast of awakening in the restoration of the Tree of Life. Soothes and settles the spirits. A place of simple choices, simple freedom.

Posterior Summit *Governer Vessel 19*
A reflection of the unity of being, calming the chaotic dissipation of a fragmented system not knowing who it is or where it is going.

Wind Palace *Governer Vessel 16*
Cache of commitment to ourselves. Secret treasures and renewed motivation.

Gate of Dumbness *Governer Vessel 15*
Delicate release of the pathways to the head.

Great Hammer *Governer Vessel 14*
A shimmer of strength, bracing and clarifying, expanding the vision. *Frees the neck and shoulders, strengthens the voice, clears the head.*

Kiln Path *Governer Vessel 13*
Convergence of opposed trajectories in the ascent to heaven. The alchemical firing of consciousness (see right).

Body Pillar *Governer Vessel 12*
Spreads wide our sails into the expanse of history and hope, a strong masthead and a kaleidoscopic casting forward. Backbone.

Spirit Path *Governer Vessel 11*
A recollection of centred stillness, an unfolding of the path – free from the illusions of divided loyalties, of self and others, the path and life.

Utmost Yang *Governer Vessel 9*
Rising shout of assertion in the face of a crumbling backbone and a wavering will.

Contracted Muscle *Governer Vessel 8*
Releases layers of locked thoughts, prejudices, fluids, tissues. *Alleviates spasms, headaches and depression.*

Middle of the Spine *Governer Vessel 6*
Holds together a fragmenting spirit, torn in different directions. Gathers a central rhythm that can encompass a wider interaction, and strengthens our capacity to go the distance.

Kiln Path
THE INITIATION OF FIRE

Taoist alchemy is a spiritual tradition that seeks to transform consciousness through meditation exercises that can be compared with chemical reactions. Through purposefully altering the make-up of our internal energies, we can seek to refine and develop who we are. Fire and water are the most typical substances that can affect our energy, either through the hydration and washing of water or the firing and purification of fire. Kiln Path (Governer Vessel 13) is the stage in the journey where we can be usefully 'cooked'. This is entering the flames of transformation, as if we were a clay pot needing to be 'fired' and made functional, and to bring out the vibrancy of our colours. Clinically, this point can clear heat from the body and it is for this reason that it is effective in the treatment of malaria.

Gate of Destiny *Governer Vessel 4*
Gateway of the void where all things are possible. Balance of primal and eternal fires. The renewal of every dawn.

Loins Yang Border *Governer Vessel 3*
Fortification, focus and flexibility for the back and spirits, A revision of regions and reassessment of balances. *First-aid for concussion, fractures, insensibility, spinal injury and sprains.*

Loins Correspondence *Governer Vessel 2*
A reinforcement of the lower abdomen and deep resource of reserves.

Long Strength *Governer Vessel 1*
Reinitializes the pillar of light. A strengthening of stamina to weather the storms of existence.

Nommo

Initiation body map of the Dogon ancestors

Nommo, eternal ancestor of the Dogon peoples, and the semi-aquatic origin of life itself

The Dogon, West Africans living around the Bandiagara Cliffs, Mali, and famed for an intricate knowledge of the path of the star Sirius B before European astronomers were even aware of its existence. Such an idea is so alien to modern notions of progress that many have tried to suggest means by which the Dogons could have come by such knowledge, other than by the tales they tell.

The story is of Nommo, a half amphibian from the stars who divided his body in order to create modern humanity. Perhaps French explorers took the findings of 19th-century European astronomers deep into West Africa where the Dogon integrated them into their own stories of origin. But then we note that they also possess stories of a third star (Sirius C). The mystery deepens.

We focus on the lore of the Dogon, in part, because it is their wisdom that has been most effectively communicated to a wider world, thanks to French anthropologist Marcel Griaule and Dogon elder Ogotemmêli. Griaule lived for long periods among the Dogon before he was invited to hear the deeper knowledge of the tribe. This he published in 1948. His *Conversations with Ogotemmêli* charts the 33 days in which the Dogon elder imparted the progress of human society from our origin within Nommo, the first ancestor. Both semi-aquatic and divine, teaching weaving and agriculture while occasionally returning to the stars for updates of the human design, Nommo's form and fascination have been echoed in other cultures across the globe in the deification of fish and half-fish humans. Recently, Nommo's watery power over spaceflight and creation have led to more contemporary speculation of longevity and DNA design.

Such creativity and resonance is justified as the potency of Nommo, and the whole Dogon civilization resonates with the integrated body knowledge of other traditions within this atlas. Each map on the human body charts complex relationships within the social, spiritual and sexual aspects of our lives. As the continent harbouring the oldest human life, Africa holds our longest secrets, and we attempt here to pay some level of respect to the depth of Dogon experience.

Kinndou-Kinndou
soul-soul, social body of the human village

Such was man and woman, different yet alike, inseparable but divided, thanks to whose fusing and reaction humanity was able to survive.
Basil Davidson

As we have seen throughout the story of the world, each people has encountered the diversity and polarity of gender in various ways. Traditions have tended either to a patriarchal or matriarchal creation myth that often justifies the perpetuation of social hierarchies. Bodily modification has frequently challenged us, from the circumcision of boys and girls to the gender assignment of intersex children and cosmetic piercing and scarification. There are many debates about this issue from points of view of healthcare, culture and religion, and we struggle to find the right course of action within increasingly diverse waters.

IN THE BEGINNING
The creation story told by Ogotemmêli (see page 173) tracked the sexual history of the gods. Amma, the creator, had flung clay into the stars and created the flatness of the earth. In his solitude, he sought her for love, but the termite hill/clitoris of his creation barred his way until he 'reduced' it.

From this ill-fated union was born the jackal, 'symbol of the difficulties of God'. But further union, and the giving of Amma's water to his wife's earth, gave to the cosmic parents twins who were: 'green in colour, half human beings and half serpents. Their arms were flexible and without joints, their bodies green and sleek all over.' Such beings retained the divine essence of water, and even though they were a pair, they still retained the singular name, Nummo.

The Nummo returned to earth to repair some of the disorder created by their parents' first coupling, taking bunches of plant fibres with which to clothe their mother and bring order to the ongoing creation of the new humans that Amma persisted with. The birth of eight primal humans brought further order to the world, but it was the gentle rocking rhythm of the comings and goings of celestial beings to and from the stars, the celestial granary, that gradually created the potential for a complete world populated by all its creatures.

And yet these eight ancestors, although they walked as four bonded pairs of male and female, retained the hermaphroditic divinity of their origins. Even as we went on to develop solid limbs, joints, and began to know death, still, for the Dogon, each child is born both male and female – physically and spiritually. The process of gender differentiation begins with the twin souls that mirror the hermaphroditic nature of our divine ancestor Nommo.

GENDER ASSIGNMENT
Amma had in the beginning modelled humans in this way to echo the great design of the amphibious Nommo, who then drew outlines in the sand for the new human to absorb the twin souls of male and female. The task at the initiation into adulthood is for the emerging adult to take the gender best suited to them, achieved through the surgical removal of the part of the child that carried the remaining aspect of the twin soul. For the male, this was the 'female' foreskin; for the female, the 'male' clitoris.

Today, heated debate rages about the ethics of such practices. However, Dogon vision correlates with those who suggest that our physiology betrays a time when we not only emerged from the waters, but also spent time as semi-aquatic beings.

Whether such a stage occurred and if it were mediated by star visitors, the innate intelligence of DNA or a guiding divine presence (be these the same or different), is beyond our present wisdom. But it may be no great stretch of imagination to consider that the ancestral memory of the Dogon reaches so far back into our history that it engages a time when our physiology bore more aquatic qualities, particularly a tendency to hermaphroditism and the switching of gender throughout a life cycle.

The twin soul of each human is further represented in the layout of a traditional Dogon village, which is mapped out along the plan of a hermaphroditic human with representations of both male and female genitalia. It is widely suggested that the role of the women huts arose from the supposed needs of men to track their wives' fidelity, but, as with most traditions, the mysteries of the actual interaction of male and female parts of society is fraught with often purposeful misunderstanding. However we understand such a layout, and whatever its truth, the Dogon village-body is a potent reminder of the meeting of both genders.

Divination PATH OF THE PALE FOX

This was destined to affect the course of things forever; from this defective union there was born, instead of the intended twins, a single being, the jackal, symbol of the difficulties of God.
Ogotemmêli

In some tellings of the Dogon creation story (there are many villages and many elders – when Ogotemmêli spoke, he would often pause to refer to other elders) the path of the jackal from the womb of Amma came about because he tried to mate with his unborn twin. However the tale is told, the jackal, or pale fox, is a singular being rather than the perfect twin of the Nummo. To this day, he is able to perform divination in order to assist humans to find a way through the complexities of life.

At dusk, a diviner will trace in the sand outside the village compound an intricate drawing of a grid of six squares populated by symbols, and accompanied by raised holes and sticks. Each aspect of this architecture conveys an aspect of village life and concerns.

Overnight, the fox is attracted by offerings of millet and, in the morning, the diviner interprets his paths in the sand. In this way, the creature outside the natural balance of creation, the single-souled being of the pale fox, offers the Dogon ways through the labyrinth.

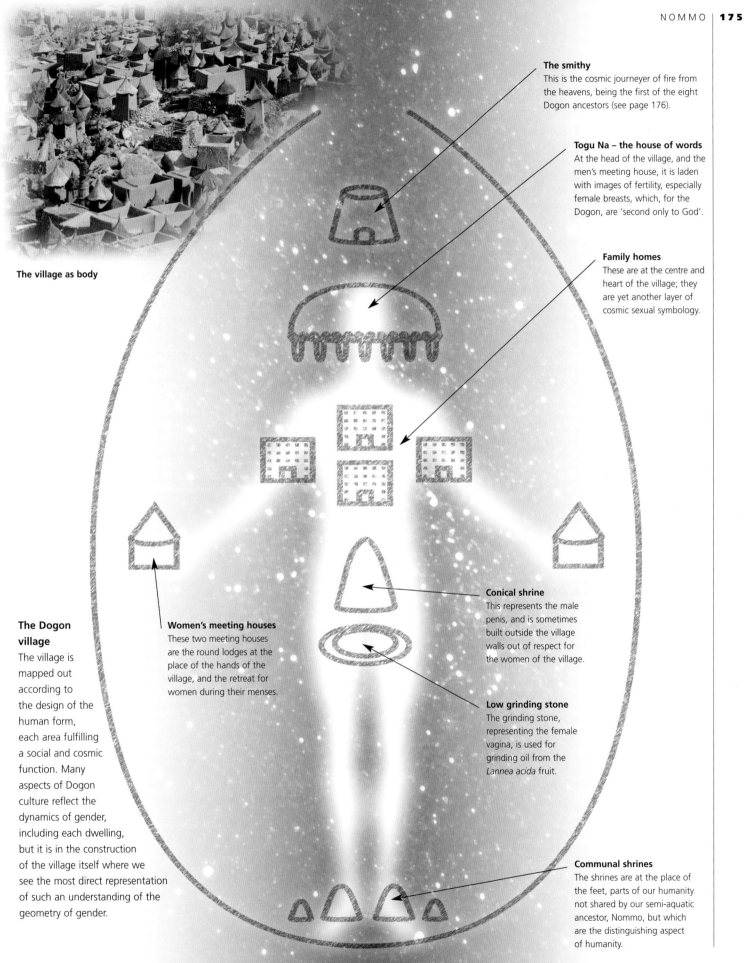

The village as body

The smithy
This is the cosmic journeyer of fire from the heavens, being the first of the eight Dogon ancestors (see page 176).

Togu Na – the house of words
At the head of the village, and the men's meeting house, it is laden with images of fertility, especially female breasts, which, for the Dogon, are 'second only to God'.

Family homes
These are at the centre and heart of the village; they are yet another layer of cosmic sexual symbology.

Conical shrine
This represents the male penis, and is sometimes built outside the village walls out of respect for the women of the village.

Low grinding stone
The grinding stone, representing the female vagina, is used for grinding oil from the *Lannea acida* fruit.

Communal shrines
The shrines are at the place of the feet, parts of our humanity not shared by our semi-aquatic ancestor, Nommo, but which are the distinguishing aspect of humanity.

Women's meeting houses
These two meeting houses are the round lodges at the place of the hands of the village, and the retreat for women during their menses.

The Dogon village
The village is mapped out according to the design of the human form, each area fulfilling a social and cosmic function. Many aspects of Dogon culture reflect the dynamics of gender, including each dwelling, but it is in the construction of the village itself where we see the most direct representation of such an understanding of the geometry of gender.

Gouyo

celestial granary of the stolen nothing

He remembered that, two days before, when he asked what was in the granary, the old man replied: 'Wolo!' which being interpreted means 'Nothing!'
Marcel Griaule

During the movements of the Nommo twins between the stars and earth and the path of the eight human ancestors as they discovered the 'words' of awakening (making iron and weaving), there came a time when two of the ancestors were no longer able to conform with the customs of the heavens. All ancestors then came to earth in Gouyo, the 'celestial granary' that contained the whole future population of the planet.

The Gouyo travelled to earth along the rainbow, with the first of the eight ancestors, the smith, standing on top of its roof. With his anvil and hoe, he defended it from the attacks of the Nummo as all eight of the first humans attempted to flee heaven. But the thunderbolts that were thrown at the smith and the granary were deflected, apart from those fragments that remained to form both male and female fire.

As the granary crash-landed, its citizens were thrown to the four corners of the earth, but its form persisted as a practical design for the storage of grain as well as the eternal model of the world itself. For the granary essentially offers an organization of life from the directions of the compass to the internal harmony of our organs. It is as cosmically conceptual as it is immediately pragmatic. In another world view, it would be foodstore as cathedral. Even though some interpretations have had the Gouyo as an extra-terrestrial craft, Ogotemmêli explained that the concept of each species having a place on its steps came from a figurative telling, for the whole of earth and space was contained here.

EARTHLY INHERITANCE
To the east are Venus and the birds; to the south is Orion and all domestic animals; in the west are wild animals, vegetables and insects with the 'long-tailed star'; whereas in the north, in the place of the Pleiades, are both fishes and men. All the beings of the world had a place here, a different 'file leader' for each step, each aspect of the world plan. But in the north was a unique story.

On the lower two steps of the northern wall were two men umbilically connected to a fish. On the third and fourth steps was each a woman, connected similarly to a fish. The fifth step saw a human woman, with no fish, and above her, on the last five steps, there was nobody. We may speculate that this progress of human-fish, to human, to nothing indicates to the Dogon that we are yet but half way to our full potential; that we are as far from this as we are from our aquatic origins. But we still have, on the seventh stair, the opening and doorway to the granary itself.

What is the relevance to us of a body map derived from the celestial granary? Where do we find the resonance of our fish-like and even serpentine origin? For the double meaning of Gouyo (granary) in Dogon is 'stolen', an indication that all human civilization is a result of spirit shared with that of the Greeks as we steal knowledge from our divine antecedents, the power of the smith.

Today, iron is mostly reclaimed from old cars and disused railway lines rather than through the knowledge of the smith of the temperatures and timing that produce the best iron from ore. The granaries are still a central part of Dogon life, the presence of mythological wonder of the first smith's flight with it along the cosmic rainbow as much as it is a testament to agriculture in poor conditions. It is a living relic that speaks still of our aquatic origins, the pragmatism of our survival, and the potential for our future – for where else do the next five steps of the north face lead us? Such open mystery echoes the teaching given by Ogotemmêli, that inside the granary is 'nothing'. This is the return to the void, the path of our future.

SACRIFICE

What is eaten is the sunlight. What is excreted is the dark night. The breath of life is the clouds, and the blood is the rain that falls on the world.
Ogotemmêli

Sacrifice is involved in many African sacred rituals, the letting of animal blood as a part of an honouring of life. Marcel Griaule speaks of how his understanding of the role of sacrifice came only after many years, when a Dogon man spoke to him of how it was a 're-ordering' of the forces of life and the universe. Sacrifice is one aspect of African life that has perhaps created more alienation between the continent and the rest of the world. And yet most peoples have their own customs about the right way to treat animals.

Yoruba priests and priestesses suggest that the chickens they keep and sacrifice live better lives and have better deaths than those of their battery-farmed cousins. But sacrifice moves too into the sphere of blood magic, and the instinctive awareness we have that the blood carries spirit.

Kosher and halal meat is predicated on correctly blessing and killing an animal, an aspect of our relationship with animals that spans vegetarianism and the ways of the Masai, who drink the blood of live cattle in a sustainable, symbiotic relationship.

From a purely health perspective, the high animal fat content in the diet of some African peoples would collapse the arteries of those elsewhere on the planet, but the feats of physical endurance (especially running) that such tribes engage in have expanded their arteries and created thicker arterial walls.

In terms of ritual, just as the spilling of blood is seen as being in service of the cosmic order, so too might it be used for more harmful purposes – just as we can pray for both goals. African historian Basil Davidson cites the Christian eucharist as an act of blood magic, which can be a ceremony of blessing or bondage.

Some traditions choose not to partake in blood magic at all, cognizant of its dangers should our prayers stray from the sacred, a tendency of which we all are capable.

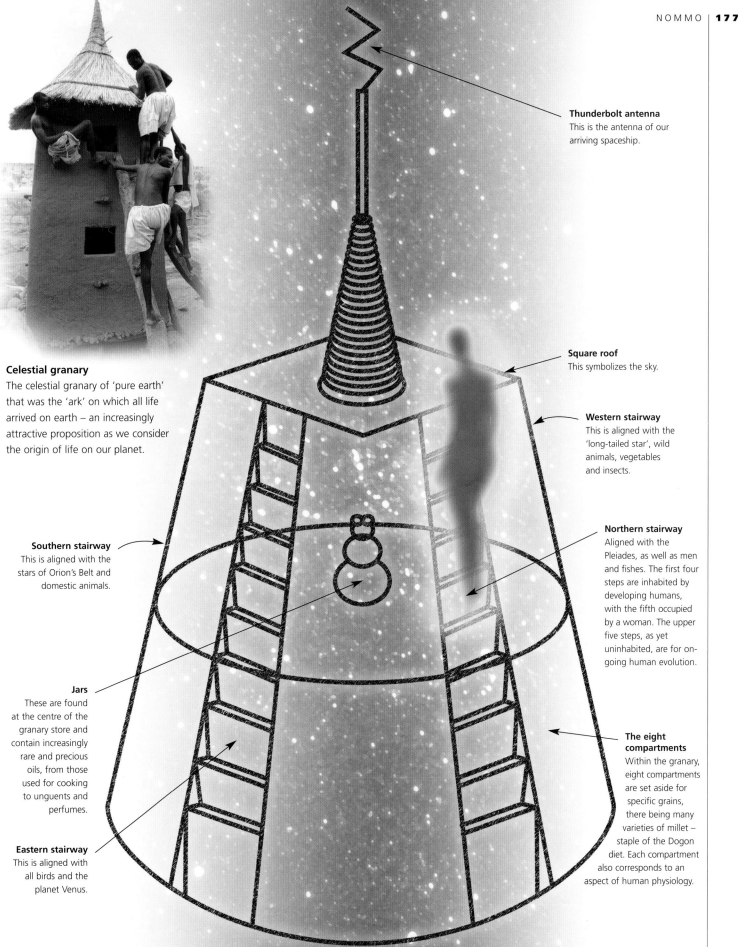

Thunderbolt antenna
This is the antenna of our arriving spaceship.

Celestial granary
The celestial granary of 'pure earth' that was the 'ark' on which all life arrived on earth – an increasingly attractive proposition as we consider the origin of life on our planet.

Square roof
This symbolizes the sky.

Western stairway
This is aligned with the 'long-tailed star', wild animals, vegetables and insects.

Southern stairway
This is aligned with the stars of Orion's Belt and domestic animals.

Northern stairway
Aligned with the Pleiades, as well as men and fishes. The first four steps are inhabited by developing humans, with the fifth occupied by a woman. The upper five steps, as yet uninhabited, are for on-going human evolution.

Jars
These are found at the centre of the granary store and contain increasingly rare and precious oils, from those used for cooking to unguents and perfumes.

The eight compartments
Within the granary, eight compartments are set aside for specific grains, there being many varieties of millet – staple of the Dogon diet. Each compartment also corresponds to an aspect of human physiology.

Eastern stairway
This is aligned with all birds and the planet Venus.

Dougué
covenant stones of lebe – the first ancestor

There are various reasons for the silence that is generally observed on the 'deep knowledge' [including] a natural reserve before strangers who, even when sympathetic, remain unconsciously imbued with a feeling of superiority. [But] every grown-up person responsible for some small fraction of social life can acquire knowledge on condition that he has the patience and, as the African phrase has it, 'he comes to sit by the side of the competent elders' over the period and in the state of mind necessary.

Germaine Dieterlen

Initiation is the process by which we pass from one state of knowledge and perception into another. Around the world there are specific ceremonies and rituals that mark these transitions, when a person is seen to leave one world and then be welcomed into another. Most crucially, these are the transitions into life itself and then into the world of the adult.

In the Western world, most initiations happen by accident and default, events moulded by ground-breaking experiences, such as our first taste of alcohol, sex, change of school or job of work, rather than the ceremonial crafting by the ancestors, adults and elders of the new being that will emerge out of childhood to be honoured as a full member of society.

Initiation, however, is a powerful current running through the African continent, enabling its people to navigate life's patterns and challenges. Until the end of the 20th century this was largely seen from outside as being a 'primitive' practice, tethering Africa's peoples to ways of superstition and ignorance. Slowly now, though very slowly, the wisdom of the modern West is beginning to acknowledge the deep human power of initiation and the essential component of mystery that imbues it.

But initiation is no automatic gateway, no egalitarian right. It is through the petitioner's commitment and patience and the mercy of the spirits that a successful transition is achieved. The transmission of Dogon wisdom to Marcel Griaule himself was undertaken only after careful preparation and discussion. The elders of the region had previously met to decide to reveal to Griaule the deeper layers of wisdom beyond the 'simple knowledge' that was told to casual inquirers. While this deeper knowledge was not esoteric in that is was purposefully kept secret from outsiders, let alone the wider population, the price of its telling was the commitment of the listener. It is this exact same patience that is shown by all cult leaders as they seek a deeper initiation into the mysteries of their tribe, as they search for the 'douge' covenant stones of the first elder, the first 'joints' that were known by humans-who-were-once-fish.

HUMANITY'S INITIATION
In the undulating birth of humanity between the earth and the stars, it was not until the advent of the smith and iron making that humans took on the solid form and joints that brought them away from their amphibious ancestors. It was to the sound of the smith's rhythm that the seventh ancestor descended to the tomb of the body of Lebe, the oldest man of the eighth family. With the rippling dance of his half-serpent form, he swallowed his relative, bone by bone, and immersed each in the waters of his womb, only to expel them again with all the order of the fivefold human with joints, for the joints, as Ogotemmêli said, 'are the most important part of a man'.

The subsequent laying down of cowrie shells as the ribs, bones, fingers and toes of the new human was to form the basis of Dogon mathematics based on a complex system of alignment between the 8, 80 and 640 of cowrie counting, which was then translated into the customs of arranging marriages according to the eight families of the first humans.

The swallowing of Lebe's bones by the seventh ancestor is a deep immersion into the mysteries of initiation. Death, burial and a watery rebirth through being swallowed and emitted by a spiritual cousin, reordered at a very basic level in order to survive and manage the environment he faced. Joints and bones are needed to wield a hoe.

INITIATION

Go and let yourself be swallowed. Your ancestors will do the rest. You must remember. Remembering means submitting to your fate. Once you have obeyed, the ancestors will intervene in all the good ways they can. That includes helping you with all the things you cannot know about until you have allowed yourself to be swallowed into the wilderness.

Malidoma Patrice Some

Malidoma Patrice Some is a man of many worlds. Having been born to the Dagara people of Burkina Faso, just south of Mali, he was captured by French missionaries when a young boy and raised a Catholic. When he eventually escaped and returned to his village, his experiences marked him as different, and his subsequent initiation as an adult was, in some ways, more challenging than it would have been for one who had not lived outside the realm of the spirits for so long.

His initiation was a great success, and the elders recognized that there was a task for him to do – speak to the world about the depth of African spirituality.

Malidoma Patrice Some now travels between the two worlds of the modern West and his home in Burkina Faso helping to extol the insight and wisdom of Africa. As the Dogon have held close to their cultural power, and Malidoma Some has found a bridge between worlds, other African tribes have fared less well in the post-colonial world. The author Basil Davidson has even suggested that the very existence of nation states in Africa, inherited from colonialism, is the *Black Man's Burden*.

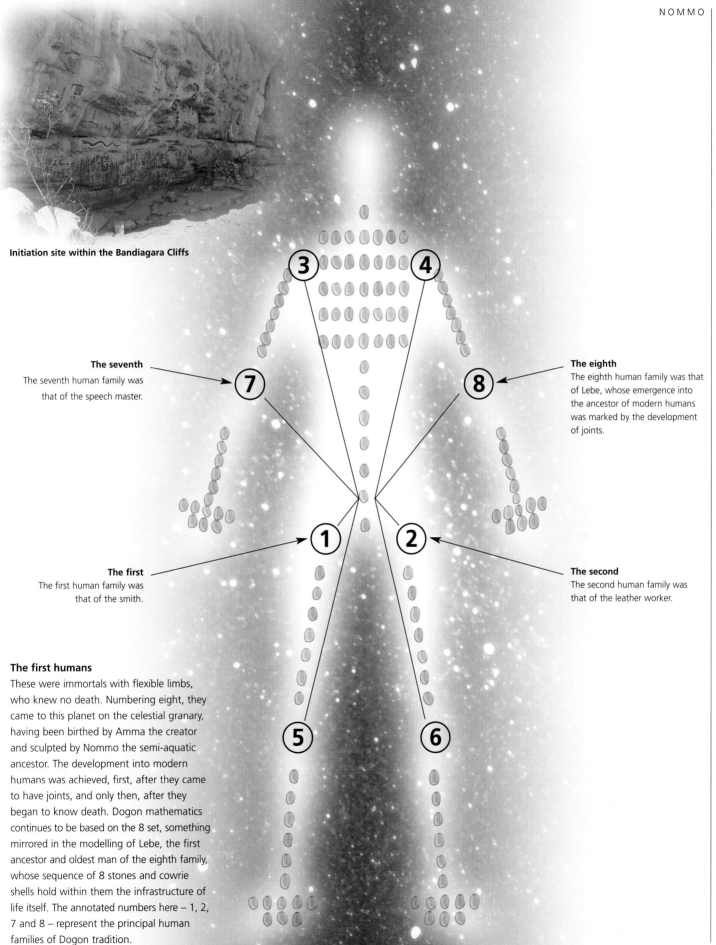

Initiation site within the Bandiagara Cliffs

The seventh
The seventh human family was
that of the speech master.

The eighth
The eighth human family was that
of Lebe, whose emergence into
the ancestor of modern humans
was marked by the development
of joints.

The first
The first human family was
that of the smith.

The second
The second human family was
that of the leather worker.

The first humans
These were immortals with flexible limbs,
who knew no death. Numbering eight, they
came to this planet on the celestial granary,
having been birthed by Amma the creator
and sculpted by Nommo the semi-aquatic
ancestor. The development into modern
humans was achieved, first, after they came
to have joints, and only then, after they
began to know death. Dogon mathematics
continues to be based on the 8 set, something
mirrored in the modelling of Lebe, the first
ancestor and oldest man of the eighth family,
whose sequence of 8 stones and cowrie
shells hold within them the infrastructure of
life itself. The annotated numbers here – 1, 2,
7 and 8 – represent the principal human
families of Dogon tradition.

Yalu Ulo

the spiral star systems of sirius

The Dogon have an 'internal system of stars' that corresponds to the stream of blood and the functioning of vital force and organs in the human body.
Germaine Dieterlen

Spirals shapes and designs occur within many different aspects of Dogon craft and mythology denoting, among other things, the essential life-giving power of the womb, the sun and the stars.

As we saw with the Gouyo, the celestial granary coming to earth to populate the planet (see pages 176–7), life travels in this way both in its internal organization and its external pathways. For the spiral is key to Dogon star lore, both during those first crucial steps of creation as well as within the intricate knowledge of the Sirius star system so vigorously debated – knowledge that was known to the Dogon in advance of Western astronomy (see page 173). As Teresea Vergani has commented: 'This spiral movement expresses a holistic understanding of the world and all things, symbolic of deep and harmonious knowledge, the "good word" from which comes music, kindness, pleasure and poetry – a feminine word linked to the loving nature of woman and the solar light.'

Sirius A is the brightest star visible in the night sky from our planet, and it is sometimes known as the Dog Star held as it is with the constellation Canis Major. Most stars exist in groups, affecting each other's gravitational fields and dancing around each other as they progress through space. While Sirius B is too small to be seen with the unaided eye, the long-term observation of its progress can be deduced by the undulation of the path of Sirius A – something that would occur only if another, heavy but unseen, stellar mass was in gravitational orbit with it.

ANCIENT CONNECTIONS

In the 1960s, author Robert Temple spent time with the Dogon, retracing the steps of Marcel Griaule and delving specifically into their star-lore. In his 1975 book, *The Sirius Mystery*, he develops an argument for extra-terrestrial visitations to earth based on the Dogon stories, suggesting that since the Dogon had not had telescopes, their access to such intricate knowledge of the stars and their movements can only have been through the tutelage of a more advanced, and particularly stellar, civilization. Widely celebrated and criticized, Temple's work certainly drew attention to the path of Sirius and its companion stars.

The Dogon teachings speak of three stars, however, with Sirius A (Sigu Tolu), Sirius B (Po Tolu, and the seed of the Milky Way) and Sirius C, which is the female star as yet undiscovered by astronomers. It has also been suggested that the Dogon fascination with Sirius arises from a connection with Egypt, where the narrow aperture running all the way from the Queen's chamber to the outside of the Great Pyramid at Giza is aligned with Sirius (the aperture of the King's chamber is aligned with Orion).

Such teachings may have come through either the migration of peoples or of the knowledge itself. In more recent years, more voices claim the whole affair to be a fraud, even back to the pioneering work of Griaule himself, citing the lack of any widespread knowledge among the Dogon people of these mysteries.

Yet proof is often fickle, and our challenges here are perhaps not to miss the subsequent flights of imagination that have arisen in how they reflect our dance with belief, proof, civilization and the stars. For it is the essence of Dogon practice to hold an internal alignment with all the forces of the universe. Since these forces spiral within our bloodstreams and in the heavens themselves, we still have to regulate and respond to them, regardless of their narrative drama. Such vital roles are principally fulfilled by the three ceremonial cults of the Dogon – the Awa, the Lebe and Binu.

CULTS OF THE AWA, LEBE AND BINU

The Awa are a cult of the dead whose role does not have the connotations that a European might ascribe to a priest of the dead; rather the Awa hold the responsibilities of bringing to order and balance the spiritual forces that were disrupted by the creation of life. The Awa ceremonies involve the dancing of the 78 ritual masks that chart the ordering of Dogon society. These include the Kananga masks representing the first humans, which have become an icon for the Dogon people as a whole. The highest official of the Awa cult is Olubaru, who governs during the ceremonial, while at all times is responsible for the maintenance of the women's huts, the sacrifice and eating of animals and all death rites. The appropriate rituals for guiding a dead person are an essential part of Dogon life.

In charge of the tribe at all times apart from those noted above are the Hogons, leaders of the Lebe cult – that of agriculture.

As the Awa are known as the 'impure' or 'dead' men, those of the Lebe cult are the 'pure' men responsible for the fertility of the land. Each village of the tribe has an altar dedicated to Lebe, the earth deity, which holds within it pieces of earth to bless this ongoing fertility.

The Hogons lead the tribe for all agricultural ceremonies and they are responsible not only for the fertility of the soil, but also for its purity. It is the Hogon that Lebe, earth deity and eighth of the first ancestors, visits at night, taking the form of the serpent of the earth, licking his high priest with the gift of fertility for the benefit of all the tribe.

Before death walked for the Dogon, the ancestors walked the planet, still immortal expressions of Nummo's twin divinity. The Binu cult is responsible for this ongoing relationship with these primal ancestors who speak to modern man through the spirits of animals and birds. Binu shrines mark this deep bonding with the ancestors before death and of Nummo's gradual descent to earth to help shape his people.

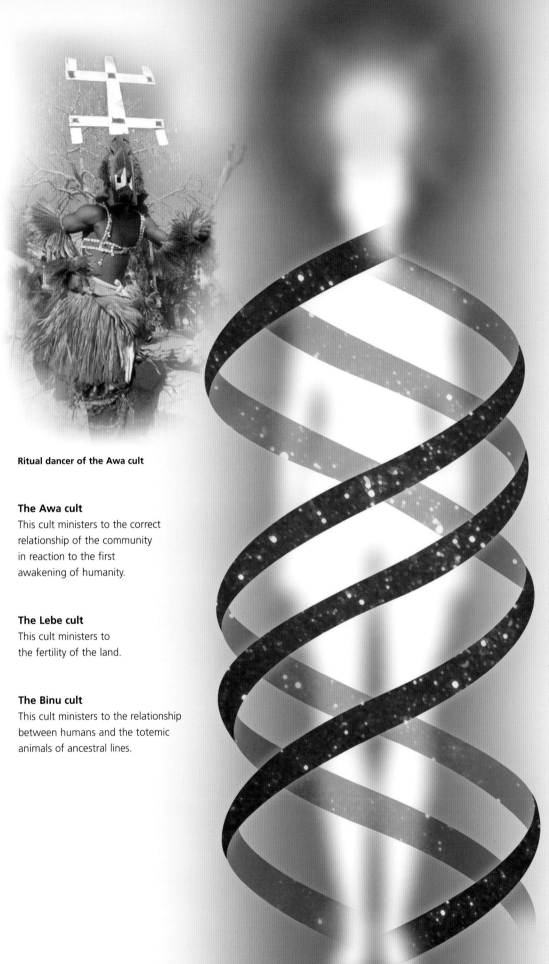

Ritual dancer of the Awa cult

The Awa cult

This cult ministers to the correct relationship of the community in reaction to the first awakening of humanity.

The Lebe cult

This cult ministers to the fertility of the land.

The Binu cult

This cult ministers to the relationship between humans and the totemic animals of ancestral lines.

Spiral star system

Yalu Ulo are 'spiral star systems' and there are many throughout the universe, including that of our own sun. This essential spiralling motion of the stars is central to the mystery concerning the Dogon's star lore and their insight into Sirius B, and potentially Sirius C. Such triplicity is reflected in human society, with the three religious cults of the dogon ministering to the seasons of the spirits and the community.

LightWheels

Earth–Sky centres of consciousness

I think of the Medicine Wheel as a Cosmic Blueprint, a Mandala of the Greater Medicine Wheel of the Universe, where everything created has its appropriate place, all things moving inward from the circumference to the Centre.

Mahad'yuni

Way Shower (Evelyn Eaton)

(Métis medicine woman)

The LightWheels are centres of energy within the human form that build the totality of the energy body and serve as gateways to other forms of life and realms of consciousness. Each is an expression of the interconnectedness of people to the environment, energized by our linkings with other beings and spiritual forces.

Every LightWheel corresponds to a realm of consciousness, an aspect of life, from the worlds of plants and animals to the spheres of gods and goddesses. There is a constant flow between the human being and the universe itself. This inter-active relationship with the energies of life's manifestations and rhythms is the heart of the medicine wheel and shamanic practice of the holy people of Turtle Island (see pages 184 and 186).

The mapping of the LightWheels corresponds to the 'Twenty Count' of Meso-american civilizations. It is a mapping of the journey of consciousness in our universe, with each aspect of life bearing a correspondence with a particular number. In this way, the Four is the place of the animals, the Seventeen the place of dragons, the Twenty the place of Great Spirit. As each number describes stations of consciousness, each LightWheel describes aspects of human potential. Most of the first seven LightWheels are similar to the chakras. The subsequent three complete the vision of the One to the Ten presented in this chapter – the 'so below' of the tonal

(everyday) world – while those of the Eleven to the Twenty correspond to realms commonly inaccessible to most of us. This second layer is the 'as above' of the nagual (the extraordinary), which, in the following pages, is cited as the cosmic reflection and guardian of our everyday world. In this way, the stars of the Eleven guard and guide the spirits of our One, the dragons of the Seventeen guard and guide the Seven of our Sacred Dream.

The Twenty Count is an aspect of the medicine wheel developed by the Mayans. DayKeepers of the Quiche Maya people today still practise a form of divination using the Twenty Count's system of mnemonics and sound associations.

The Twenty Count was to travel north with traders and medicine people, the knowledge blending with other civilizations. As the Mayans fell, the Toltecs gained ascendancy, and while their warriors had a fierce reputation, the Toltec era also held peaceful trade relations reaching into the southern region of what is now the USA.

The teachings presented here come from many such trade routes across Turtle Island, but especially from the Navajo Grandfather Tom Wilson, the métis (mixed blood) medicine man Hyemeyohsts Storm and, in particular, the métis medicine woman Arwyn DreamWalker. To what extent other sciences remain protected is unknown: some tribes jealously guarded their traditions and knowledge; with others, the teachings have always been there for those who would hear.

Each of the LightWheels has its own appearance and alchemy, but they change as we grow, showing both balance and imbalance, distress and brilliance. The images in this chapter describe Light-Wheels as they might appear to those who can see energy fields.

The ONE
sun fire and gifts of grace

What is life? It is the flash of a firefly in the night. It is the breath of a buffalo in the wintertime. It is the little shadow which runs across the grass and loses itself in the sunset.

Crowfoot
(19th-century chief of the Blackfoot Tribe)

The teachings of the medicine wheel (see right) present the vastness of creation through which life emerges from nothing and returns to nothing. The One is our explosion of passion into the playground of the universe, the tumbling ball of fire that is alive with the infinity of lights and colours. This is fire, our light, our spirit and our sexuality. For life itself is the fruit of sex, from our own form to the cosmic union of creator and creatress, ever present in nature's own bawdy sacredness, her perpetual creativity.

It is such arcs of conscious lightning that we coax and blaze towards a climax of celebration at any moment of any day, wherever we are, whatever we are doing. This encompasses the sex we share with lovers as much as it does the awe of sunsets and sheer power of the natural world as it inspires and enriches us. It is awe and wonder that enlivens our spirits to charge the creative imagination of the relationship we share with our world. This is the spark of who we are, the sexual presence of our life, which, at essence, reaches out to touch all aspects of creation.

FIRE MEDICINE
As yogic teachings on the chakras might focus more on a linear development through each of the realms they govern, teachings on the LightWheels encourage a maturation that similarly includes refinement, but also finds an emphasis on ongoing flowering. In this way the appearance of each LightWheel will grow and develop beyond the basic starting point of their formulation, their shape and colour. As each comes into balance with its corresponding Earthrealm and forms bondings and connections with that world, it will take on the textures, patterns and blessings of that world. Fire medicine will, in this way, often appear in the spontaneous and playful textures of flame and heat hazes as much as it will manifest in blazing brilliance, steady flickers or dead embers.

In balance, it is essential that there is a level of constancy so that our eternal flame keeps burning, and that too much or too little fire does not cause us to die away or burn out.

Equally, however, there are the mysteries of fire's purification and the surrender to conflagration of the spirit that gives rise to new life. Such freshness of perspective is the joy that fire brings, the youthful visitation of the powers of grace and the sheer wonder of spirit as the power of divinity enters into our space within unexpected ferocity and love.

STARFIRE
In the medicine wheel of the Twenty Count, the One is in the place of the east, of the rising sun and the emergence of the cycles of life from the depths of the underworld. This is the new dawn, the half light of the realm of the Morning Star. This is the passion and activation of the positive principle within life that lights the way. As grandfather sun lights our way throughout the daytime, so too do his brothers light our way during the night. For the great nations of the starweb are the perennial beacons of all people, whether in the tribal wonder of those who honour the Earth–Sky alliance, the technological fascination of astronauts or the concerned interest of ufologists. And just as their brother, our sun, is the origin of all our life force, so do the streams of solar and cosmic storms feed and affect our energy bodies.

Our starfire is a shared journey into the spark of life that perpetually burns, and like our sun, frequently erupts with the charged power of a lover's touch, the rejuvenating excitement of life itself.

THE MEDICINE WHEEL

The medicine wheel at Big Horn, Medicine Mountain, Northern Wyoming, USA

The medicine wheel maps the sacredness of creation into the geometry of the wheel and is part of the sacred sciences of Native America. Arising from the basic directions of the compass, the rhythms of life are understood as they emerge from the passage of the seasons – rhythms that can be applied widely as a universal template of change.

Archaeologists tend to limit their own studies to the representation of medicine wheels as laid down in physical monuments, such as the wheel at Big Horn (see above). In actuality, the medicine wheel is a living sacrament within the embrace of all life, all of our relations on the Earth. It is multi-dimensional in that each direction holds reflections of many wheels. In this way the east will hold the human world, the sun, the element of fire, the starweb, the grandfathers. It will also hold the animals and plants each people hold sacred to that direction.

While the common thread of unity permeates Native American spirituality, the form of the medicine wheel is by no means universal, and each people employ a wide variety of associations and correspondences. Such diversity might seem contradictory to those concerned with standardized bodies of knowledge, whereas the essence of the wheel itself asks for an authenticity of connection to the worlds themselves. Each teacher of the sacred traditions will employ the unifying essence of the sacred hoop with the allies and correspondences of their tribe and medicine.

The first LightWheel
This takes the basic form of a scarlet sphere,
evolving and changing as we come into a deeper
relationship and reciprocity with the element of
fire, adopting the patterns, colours and flames
of light itself. It is the ignition of our energy
body and life-path, the brilliance of fire at
our sexual core.

The alchemy of our Tree of Life
The first LightWheel is our ignition and inspiration
from Grandfather Sun.

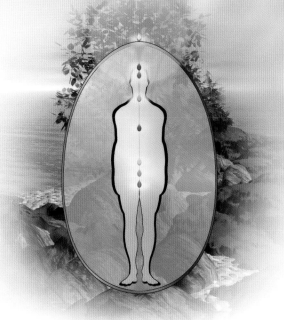

**Enemy: old age
Virtue: grace**

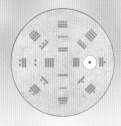

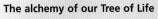

The One – initiation of sun fire

Fires of spirit	
Twenty Count *(as above, the nagual)*	The Eleven, the star nations
Twenty Count *(so below, the tonal)*	The One, Grandfather Sun
EarthRealm	Humanity
Human aspect	Spirit
Medicine wheel	East
Dynamic	Determining, choosing
Element	Fire
Tendency	Blazing, explosive
Balance	Equanimity, equilibrium
The way of . . .	Enlightenment

The TWO
earth home and the touchstone of body

In the East, creation was planned: in the West, creation was fulfilled.
Sakuruta (Coming Sun)
(Kurahu priest of the Morning Star Clan, Pawnee Tribe)

The Two is our embodiment of the element of earth and the realm of the minerals. The earth element gives us the form with which to receive the spark of fire, to anchor and mould for ourselves a body to receive the inspiration of spirit. In the teachings of the medicine wheel, the Two is in the west, a placing shared with Grandmother Earth, and here we have the parallel teachings of our body being the home for our spirits, just as Earth has offered herself as home for us.

The second LightWheel begins as a two-pointed starflame; its symbol, two orange spinning spheres tracing an orbit within the pelvic cradle. The earth element provides us with the qualities of grounding, holding and substantiation. In it, we find the solidity and strength of our bodies. This element allows us to draw things to us in the same way that a planet exerts an influence of gravity.

This gathering and accumulation is echoed in the physical body where the second LightWheel emerges. The pelvic cradle is itself our own container of energy, a basket within which we might harvest the fruits of our fertility. This is also the place of our ability to give birth to new ideas, as well as our young.

Whereas the fires of our first LightWheel have ignited new life and passion, here we have the holding and reflection of harbouring such seeds. But the blessing of going deep in this way can also polarize into an inability to 'sink' or an excessive tendency to go so deep that one becomes immobile.

SANDSTONE OR GRANITE
Our own balance of the earth element will appear both in terms of our levels and qualities of its presence within our energy field. Of the many manifestations of rocks, stones, mountains, sands, soils, gems, crystals, caves, sand dunes and ores there will be ones that represent the substance of our bodies and our overall energy field. Most of us will be able to glance around a group of people and have a sense of which mineral each one reminds us of. Is this person more granite or sandstone; the other, more slate or quartz? For most, these associations are symbolic; for the medicine person they may be the core rhythm of their reciprocal engagement with the mineral world.

As our alignment and development of earth within ourselves is expanded and blessed by such alliances with the minerals, the appearance of our second LightWheel will change. Its most basic appearance is the twin orange spheres circling each other in orbit. The bonding of minerals will develop the LightWheel's texture, weight, colour and patterns, as well as affecting the whole of our energy field. While earth is focused here, its influence is cast throughout every aspect of our substance and stillness, regardless of where it is in the body.

Alongside such a discernment of the nature of our earth element, it will also manifest to a specific degree. Some people will manifest more of the earth element than others, being more grounded, more able to accumulate. Such skills can become as imbalanced as any, and the challenges of earth are neither to accumulate too much nor become too fixed in that accumulation.

Such caveats can be seen in the movements of the Earth herself as a planet, in that she manifests the energy she accumulates as fruits for those who dwell on her. We need to be able to find generosity within our accumulation lest it pile up and overwhelm us. We also need to be able to know the rhythms of our earth, to hear the drumbeat of our own cycles of manifestation that will yield the innate wisdom of the body that we know of as our gut feelings. This is the 'touchstone' of the body's truth-sense by which traditional medicine people are able to hear the gong of truth in their own bodies, and know clarity from a place other than the mind.

Sweat lodge WOMB OF THE GRANDMOTHER

Skin-covered temporary sweat lodge

The sweat lodge is a sacred ceremony of the people of Turtle Island. Celebrated in many ways, it is essentially a retreat into the womb of the Grandmother and is held as a purification before major sacraments, but also as a ceremony in its own right for restoration, healing and vision.

The form and method of the sweat lodge varies. Universally there is an enclosed space, constructed from stone or logs and earth for a permanent lodge, or blankets, skins and branches for a temporary one. Every aspect of the sweat lodge's construction is conducted as part of the ceremony, from the cutting of branches to the building of the fire. The inside of the lodge is heated in various ways – the Navajo and Sioux use hot rocks; the Inuit direct fire. The symbolism is the power of the east and the sun coming into the heart of the west and the earth.

Herbs such as sweetgrass, sage and cedar are sprinkled on the hot rocks or fire to act as a blessing and a protection. Prayers are held constantly throughout the ceremony, in the silence and the hearts of the people, and spoken out loud so that the spirit may hear the song of our hearts and our cry for vision.

There is typically a certain number of prayer 'rounds' where healing and vision are called for others, ourselves, the earth and all our relations, the Earthrealms. The Lakota prayer of *mitakuye oyasin* is that for 'all my relations', and holds the essence of the lodge's purpose.

The second LightWheel

This takes the basic form of two orange spinning spheres, evolving and changing as we come into a deeper relationship and reciprocity with the element of earth, adopting the patterns, colours and textures of the mineral world. It is the form with which we receive the spark of life.

The alchemy of our Tree of Life

The second LightWheel is the vessel of our holding and welcome from Grandmother Earth.

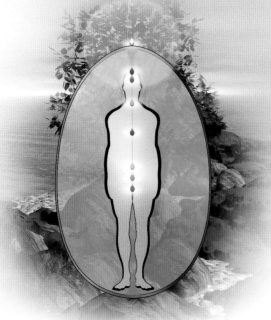

Enemy: clarity
Virtue: deep peace

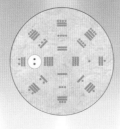

**The Two – holding of
the minerals**

Stillness of body	
Twenty Count *(as above, the nagual)*	The Twelve, the sisterhood of planets
Twenty Count *(so below, the tonal)*	The Two, Grandmother Earth
Earthrealm	Mineral world
Human aspect	Body
Medicine wheel	West
Dynamic	Holding
Element	Earth
Tendency	Accumulation, banking up
Discipline	Generosity of spirit, abundance
The way of . . .	Introspection and intuition

The THREE
soul-will and the give-away

Four nights after she vanished, the child had a dream of her, in which White Shell Woman said she was well and happy. 'The holy people have built me a house of white shell that is beautiful,' she said. 'I will live in that house forever. I don't think I will be seeing you again, nor will you see me in this form. But I won't be far. Look for me when it rains. The soft falling female rain, the corn that grows because of that rain will encompass me.'

Paula Allen Gunn
(Laguna Pueblo and Sioux)

The third LightWheel begins as a three-pointed starflame, its symbol the golden yellow triangle of the Three. This is our link with the element of water and the Earthrealm of the plant world. Our balance within water can determine whether we have the will to manage water's instinctive merging with the world and sculpt a direction for our growth. This helps us navigate the realm of the waters as they manifest in our emotions, where they can appear with all the resonance that water does in the natural world. Each of us will vary according to the levels and character of water within us, whether we resemble a lake or a stream, in drought or in flood, with clear or toxic waters.

Each of the LightWheels embodies an aspect of the energy field by virtue of its reciprocal interchange with the natural world and the dynamics of her realms. In this way, the Three is the expression of our water and emotions, where we can find a place of equilibrium along the spectrum of trust and fear.

The flourishing of our emotional life provides the energy and movement to offer the world our own flowering, our Give-Away, the purpose of which, according to medicine woman Jamie Sams, is sharing: 'If one cannot give without strings attached, there is no true release and the sacredness of giving without expectations has been destroyed.'

FOCUS AND INTENT

The freedom and trust held by the Give-Away ceremony is the quality that should be present at the third LightWheel. It is here that we know the central vine of our soul and how we 'braid' the many aspects of our lives. From this LightWheel emerges the luminous fibres of our energy body, linking us to all that we are attached to in life.

Various spiritual disciplines and healing practices are designed to release those links that do not serve us and restore the lost energy to the integrity of our energy field. Equally, vision quest and ceremony aid us in making the links to those places and beings with which we form reciprocal connections of blessing. Unless we bring a focus to what our links are within the world, our third LightWheel and the fibres of our energy body can become alternately floppy or knotted, neglected by a lack of honouring of emotion, allowing us to be pulled this way and that without the conscious celebration of intent that is the gift the plant world brings to us.

PHARMACOPOEIA

Plants are a central part of many healing traditions. Native American tribes possessed a rich and sophisticated pharmacopoeia, including black nightshade (a Comanche tuberculosis remedy), Indian turnip (a Pawnee headache cure) and spruce cones (a Cree sore-throat soother). But within the ways of the medicine people of Turtle Island, plants are also distinct allies and totems as well as mere ingredients of sustenance or healing. An 'ally' in this context is a being of one of the other worlds of the Grandmother (mineral, plant or animal) that becomes part of one's own personal 'medicine'.

WHITE BUFFALO CALF WOMAN

Sacred white buffalo, Arizona, USA

The goddess appears in many forms across the world. To the Lakota (western Sioux) of the mid-western plains of the USA, her principal manifestation is that of White Buffalo Calf Woman. She came to the people of the Lakota more than 19 generations ago, and she brought with her the medicine pipe, as the ways of prayer had been forgotten. She taught the way of the sacredness of the circle, of the unity of all people and their relations of all the worlds of the Grandmother. In her coming, she challenged the braves of the nation to see the sacredness of her beauty, and in her leaving she transformed into a buffalo.

As an avatar of Great Spirit, she said she would come again in the 'end times' as an envoy of hope, and that she would come not in human form – for we would have grown too arrogant to hear her words – but as a buffalo, a white buffalo.

For more than a century there were no white buffalo born across Turtle Island. There is something like a one in 10 million chance of a buffalo being born white, and the last one of modern times was killed by the Cheyenne in 1833, during the time of the Leonid meteor shower ('The Night the Stars Fell'). Many false white buffalo have emerged as either cattle hybrids or albino buffaloes. In 1997, however, Miracle Moon was born – a true white bison – and became the beginning of a herd that is now seven in number. They are now living at Spirit Mountain Ranch in Flagstaff, Arizona, where their guardians struggle to care for these sacred beings amid a paucity of funding for their care, but where their beacon of hope is brilliant, and shines with the radiance of the goddess they represent.

The third LightWheel

This takes the basic form of a golden saffron triangle, evolving and changing as we come into a deeper relationship and reciprocity with the element of water, adopting the patterns, colours and flows of the plant world. It is our path of intention within our emotions.

The alchemy of our Tree of Life

The third LightWheel is the expression of our Give-Away through the trees and plants.

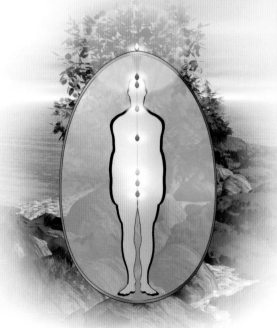

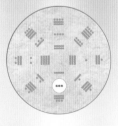

Enemy: fear
Virtue: beauty

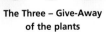

**The Three – Give-Away
of the plants**

Waters of the will	
Twenty Count *(as above, the nagual)*	The Thirteen, Quetzal, spirit of all the plants, mother of all, many faces of the goddess
Twenty Count *(so below, the tonal)*	The Three, The Plants
Earthrealm	The plant kingdom
Human aspect	Emotions
Medicine wheel	South
Dynamic	Giving
Element	Water
Tendency	Merging, converging
Balance	Definition, focus
The way of . . .	Trust and innocence

The FOUR
expansion of the heart-mind

*If you talk to the animals they will talk with
you and you will know each other.
If you do not talk to them you will not know
them and what you do not know, you will
fear. What one fears, one destroys.*

Geswanouth Slahoot (Dan George)
(Salish Band Chief)

The fourth LightWheel is a bright emerald flame at the heart. It is the breath of our lives and connection to the wind element. The character of wind is that of limitless expansion – we commonly employ the symbolism of the 12 winds to denote the full spectrum of our environment. It is in this way that as water becomes uncontained in its flow into the world, so the wind finds no limit to its range of exploration. But while the winds expand our hearts so, too, do they expand our minds.

The excitability of wind is often echoed in the flightiness of our minds seen when we soar off into the realms of abstract fantasy. And this with little connection or bonding to other people or other aspects of ourselves, whether emotion, spirit or body. This is the archetype of the rigid bureaucrat or abstracted boffin. The discipline with which we counter such tendencies is that of constancy of heart, and remembering that it is the heart-mind that dwells at our fourth wheel, and that heart and mind are connected. Here is the way of wisdom, as the great halls of intellect find a balance and loyalty within themselves.

ANIMAL WORLD
The dynamic of this LightWheel is our capacity to 'receive', to take others into our hearts, and it is for this reason the allies that come along the shamanic or medicine path are initially those of the animal world. For even in homes with little knowledge of earth medicine it is know that those animals who live with us, whether as pets or medicine companions, allow us to open our hearts. We more naturally receive animals into our hearts than either those of our own kind or those from the other worlds of the Grandmother, such as trees or stones. Each of us will hold our own medicine, our own ally that is neither separate from us nor ours to command. To begin to take on the reciprocal dance of

medicine allies is to become more than we are as humans. For while it is the role of the human as the Five (see pages 192–3) to determine, to bring change and to catalyse the other worlds, such a deep medicine bonding with other beings starts to extend us beyond the sphere of who we are.

It is natural to go beyond ourselves and as we asked in relation to the rocks and stones of our bodies, here at the fourth LightWheel we consider who our reflections are in the animal world. And just as medicine people enter very specifically into such alliances, it is something we lean towards naturally, for the impulse to identify with our animal brothers and sisters arises as much in street slang across the world as it does with national emblems. For Turtle Island it is the bald eagle, the grizzly, the hummingbird and the condor that carry the totems of the tribes, symbols of the nation and the land.

CONNECTIONS
The vibrancy of our fourth LightWheel often determines the health of our heart and lungs and the resilience of the bone and muscle of our chest wall. It is here that we can become either walled off or energetically transparent if we have experienced sustained pressure on our heart-bondings, or if we have never made such connection out into the world. The development of this wheel and area of the body is to be found less in the cosmetic enhancement of breasts for women, the bulking of pectorals for men or the loading of weight for either, but rather in the opening of the heart to the love of other beings.

This is not an indiscriminate offering of our inner selves, but a genuine communication that respects our own truth as much as another's wisdom. The challenges of the wind and mind often lead to power battles within this sphere as we try to dominate others lest they hurt us, or see us for who we fear we are. The blessings of this place is the settledness of the winds within our heart that enables a relationship of equals.

KOKOPELLI

Kokopelli – piper of fertility

Kokopelli, the hump-backed flute-player, plays his song across much of Turtle Island. He is the sacred seed-carrier and fertility deity who travelled north from the Mesoamerican region of the Maya and Aztecs to settle in the American southwest amid the Hopi and Pueblo tribes. As this humped-back figure plays his flute, lines of light stream from his head – a horned halo – and he is commonly represented with an inhumanly sized phallus.

His origins may hark back to the Aztec traders, who came north with their wares slung across their backs, announcing their friendly presence by the playing of a flute. In recent years, the silhouette of Kokopelli (without phallus) has been adopted as a symbol by the whole area of south-western America. But his ceremonial role was that of trickster, trader and lover, and he is seen in the ancient petroglyphs of the Anasazi as he is still seen in the katchina dolls of the Hopi.

His pipe is the song of the heart that beckons us towards a greater expansion of our own song. His humped back holds the seeds that will grow corn. His phallus is the irrepressible creativity of our own sacredness. The strands of his hair light the antennae of his own divinity and connection with Great Spirit, asking us to extend our own antennae, to grow our own horns, to know our own magic.

The fourth LightWheel

Our fourth LightWheel takes the basic form of an emerald diamond, evolving and changing as we come into a deeper relationship and reciprocity with the element of wind, adopting the patterns, colours and heart of the animal world. It is our breath of life and the heartbeat of our bondings.

The alchemy of our Tree of Life

The fourth LightWheel is our openness of heart through our animal brothers and sisters.

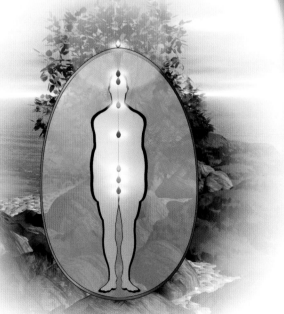

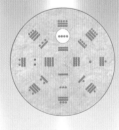

Enemy: power
Virtue: heart

**The Four – embrace
of the animals**

Breath of the heart-mind	
Twenty Count *(as above, the nagual)*	The Fourteen, Coatl, spirit of all the animals, father of all, many faces of the god
Twenty Count *(so below, the tonal)*	The Four, The Animals
Earthrealm	The animal kingdom
Human aspect	Heart-mind
Medicine wheel	North
Dynamic	Receiving
Element	Wind
Tendency	Scattering, expansion
Balance	Constancy, loyalty
The way of . . .	Wisdom

The FIVE
sacred human and the blending of worlds

I do not see a delegation for the Four Footed.
I see no seat for the Eagles.
We forget and we consider ourselves superior.
But we are after all a mere part of creation.
And we stand somewhere between the
mountain and the Ant.
Somewhere and only there as part and
parcel of creation.
Chief Oren Lyons, Iroquois
(Turtle Clan faith keeper)

The fifth LightWheel begins as a five-pointed starflame at the throat. Its symbol is the electric blue pentagram that is our link to our own humanity, our bonding with our own species and our own soul. Here the LightWheels mirror the progression of the chakras, as within both traditions the fifth energy centre is to be found at the throat and corresponds with a fifth element of unity. For the Vedic lineages it is Aether; for the Mayan, Void. Is the 'kultalini' of the Maya related to the 'kundalini' of the yogi?

Our discipline here is one of pragmatic and holistic science and, as such, these questions can remain unanswered without halting our quest for the authenticity and power of the insights that remain. For this dance of Void at the fifth LightWheel is the first of four steps into the centre of the medicine wheel that will be followed by

the Ten, the Fifteen and the Twenty. This is the core of 'self' at the centre of who we are. Unsullied by self-reflection or awareness, but suspended between the four worlds and elements both in command and union.

WISDOM OF THE GARDENER
The sacred mathematics of the Maya describe a universe of progression and sequence that is reflected in the spiritual potency that each being possesses. This potency is a fusion of awareness, sentience and spiritual presence. A human would 'mark' as a five, an animal four, a plant three. This is no hierarchy of dominion that was understood by the pyramid of being within medieval Christendom, where the flora and fauna was humanity's to command. For the potency of the five and the role of the human within creation is that of the 'determiner'. This is the decisive direction and weaving of all the other worlds, the transformer and the catalyst.

Here is the wisdom of the gardener who tends the planet with a deep insight into its rhythms, so that we might sustain and nourish life rather than dominate it. For that which we do not understand we will usually try to destroy. It is in this way that contemporary humanity cannot seem to cope with untamed power and unexploited resource of forests and animals. We domesticate wilderness and raze trees. We cannot collectively cope with

the sharing of resources, and as we lose the sacredness of our charge, our potency decreases, dropping below the 'Five' of a Sacred Human. Equally though, it can rise, and for the tree or animal that walks beyond its natural scope of blessing it will become more than that one expression of a tree or animal. Trees and rocks who have woken up, through their own spontaneous calling or the prayers of birds and people, will journey into a sustained community of wakening.

POWER OF THE FIVE
As humans, our power is that of forming our world, shaping and interpreting it and making it anew. Here we come into the skills of all of our facets and the uses to which we put our intelligence, creativity, vision and understanding. This is typified in the expression of our voices and the complexity of language with which we communicate with each other. For this is our relationship with ourselves as a human being as well as the whole of humanity. As the LightWheels develop, the fifth is likely to both deepen and brighten its colours and patterning and also its melodies, rhythms and harmonies.

LIGHTNING IN THE BLOOD

Momostenanago in Guatemela, home of the guardian being 'Lightning in the Blood'

Mayan Daykeepers are the mediators of the community and the spirit world. By counting chips of seeds and crystals they echo the counting of yarrow stalks by their divinatory cousins across the Pacific who cast the I Ching. Birth charts are divined for children, their birth day holding resonances with other themes within the environment and dreamtime of the rainforests.

The history and richness of such traditions are held close within the integrity of lineage teachers, but during the 1970s two anthropologists from New York, Dennis and Barbara Tedlock, themselves became Daykeepers. Dennis went on to translate the *Popul Vuh*, one of the principal Mayan sacred texts. Barbara Tedlock's book of 1982, *Time and the Highland Maya*, describes a deep aspect of

Mayan divination that involves a somatic sensitivity that can be interpreted and decoded as messages.

Here, the Daykeeper will experience 'Lightning in the Blood' sensations moving swiftly through and over the body, akin to lightning or serpents, rippling or flashings. Part of the Daykeeper's training is to interpret these sensations, apportion to whom they apply and what the message is. Each part of the body will hold a meaningful correspondence; the front and back of the body will translate as descendants and ancestors respectively.

The fifth LightWheel

This takes the form of an electric-blue pentagram, evolving as we come into a deeper relationship and reciprocity with the element of void, adopting the patterns, colours and expression of who we are as a sacred human. It is our path of balance and reconciliation.

The alchemy of our Tree of Life

The fifth LightWheel is our balance of the elements and of male and female principles through the sacred expression of our humanity.

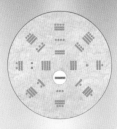

**Enemy: death
Virtue: freedom**

**The Five – sacred voice,
Sacred Human**

Freedom song of the soul	
Twenty Count *(as above, the nagual)*	The Fifteen, collective soul of all humans
Twenty Count *(so below, the tonal)*	The Five, The Sacred Human
Earthrealm	The human world
Human aspect	Soul
Medicine wheel	Centre
Dynamic	Catalysing
Element	Void
Tendency	Boredom
Balance	Self-command
The way of . . .	Transformation

The SIX
ancestors and the pool of reflection

*Sisiutl, the fearsome monster of the sea. Sisiutl who
sees from front and back. Sisiutl the soul searcher.
When you see Sisiutl you must stand and face him.
Face the horror. Face the fear. If you break faith with
what you know, if you try to flee, Sisiutl will blow
with both mouths at once and you will begin to spin.
Before the twin mouths of Sisiutl can fasten on your
face and steal your soul, each head must turn towards
you. When this happens, Sisiutl will see his own face.
He who sees the other half of Self, sees Truth.*

Nootka tale, Anne Cameron
(Coastal tribe of west Canada)

The sixth LightWheel begins as a six-
pointed starflame at the brow, its symbol
the purple hexagram – gateway to knowing
our ancestors and the earth guardians. For
this is the place of all our sensory faculties, our
ability to see, hear and smell not only in the
realm of the Sacred Human, but also now in
the other realms of the earth, usually unseen
and unacknowledged. This is the realm of
the Tohliloquai, the earth guardians, known
in many ways as the little people, sprites,
fairies and for all the cultural filters of names
and appearance, beings of great ancientness
and eternal youth.

EXPANDED PERCEPTION
The sixth LightWheel holds the potential of
an expanded perception into the wider realms
of the Grandmother, the beginning of other
ways of seeing and being. For we are now at
the Six, past the basic unit of human counting
– the five of each hand/foot, and have moved
on to the second level of our humanity. We
have crossed the bridge of our basic constitution, and now begin to piece together the
components of our lives so that we might
yield something greater than we are.

This bridge is formed by the capacity to
look within ourselves, along the Sword of
Truth, and see past the illusions of self-concept
into a balanced perspective of our place
within an historical stream of evolution. This
LightWheel will become activated and strong
to the extent to which we accept this gateway,
discovering who we are and what the world
is. It will shine by virtue of its acceptance of
both ancestors and Tohliloquai, the sheen
of its realm as vibrant and intricate as such
connections yield.

FUTURE DREAMS
At the Six, the gateway is that of going beyond
ourselves to realize not only that we are who
we are by virtue of our bonding with the
ancestors and earth guardians, but also that
we can affect those along this continuum. Our
actions are powerful in how we bequeath a
heritage and accept a lineage. This is not the
inheritance of monetary estates or family
trees, but the riches of dreams and memories,
the wider acts of who we seek to be in life
and the offering of that belief to the inner
vision of our people. And, indeed, it is not
only in the care of our own children that
we leave a mark on the world – of crucial
importance are the dreams, ethics and
passions that we either accept or reject.

Part of the vision of the Navajo Grandfather Tom Wilson was that there would be
a spiritual lineage to leave to the next seven
generations. This, too, includes the clearing
from our consciousness the taints of our
nightmares. For inasmuch as dreams carry
for seven generations, so do nightmares and
hauntings. At any point, a generation is able
to make a choice to stop the nightmares or
to seed the dreams, and to sustain that choice
for such a span of time that it then becomes
the default position of who we are. The healing done in any one generation has the power
of retrospective blessing, releasing the
shadows of memory from those still suffering
with such blights. Equally, the reinforcement
of pain and habitual abuse serves to anchor
such trackways, and it is into such a milieu
that those not of our genetic line can stand
as beacons, as encouragement to understand
further what it means to be human.

Who we are when we look into the
mirror is often as much a question of choice
as it is of chance and heritage. For just as
the ancestors hold our history so, too, do we
hold their dreams, and cultivate our own
seeds for all of the world's children.

Popul Vuh THE BOOK OF ADVICE

The *Popul Vuh* is a sacred book of the Maya that
was translated into Spanish in the 18th century to
stop it falling victim to the Spanish quest to destroy
the native Quiche Maya culture. A Franciscan friar
translated it into Spanish from the romanized
Quiche script it had been written in two centuries
earlier by the Mayan nobility.

The text is a creation story telling of the expanse
of the sky and the waters at the absolute beginning
of all things, inhabited only by Gucumatz, the
Sovereign Plumed Serpent and Huracan, the Heart
of Sky. Their very conversation gave rise to the
Earth and all life on it. It tells, too, of the creation
of humanity, and the failed attempts of the hero
twins as they made numerous attempts to sculpt
humanity, aborting versions made from wood; with
other early attempts that then lived on as monkeys.

There are a number of other key Mayan texts
that have survived, including the Dresden codex
from the 13th century that charts the movements
of the planet Venus. Contemporary reconstructions
of the Tzolkin, the Mayan calendar, have extended
the range of the Mayan ancestors beyond their direct
descendants, with the Harmonic Convergence of
1987 gathering people across the planet in an
assertion of peace.

The origins of the Twenty Count are yet debated
by anthropologists, but remain as integral tools of
Mayan Daykeepers, shaman-priests of the surviving
peoples in Guatemala and Venezuela. Among its
many complex and intricate roles of mathematical
sophistication, it forms one of the many numerical
cogs in the calculations of the Mayan calendar.
Remarkable within this calendar is the 'long
count' of our current galactic cycle, which began
on 11 August 3114 BCE, its culmination being
21 December 2012 CE. Classical Mayan teachings
speak of ours being the 'fourth world', the first
three of which the creator discarded, and of the
coming of a fifth world when ours will end. Some
cite this as 2012; others suggest that the calendar
actually indicates an end date of 4772 CE.

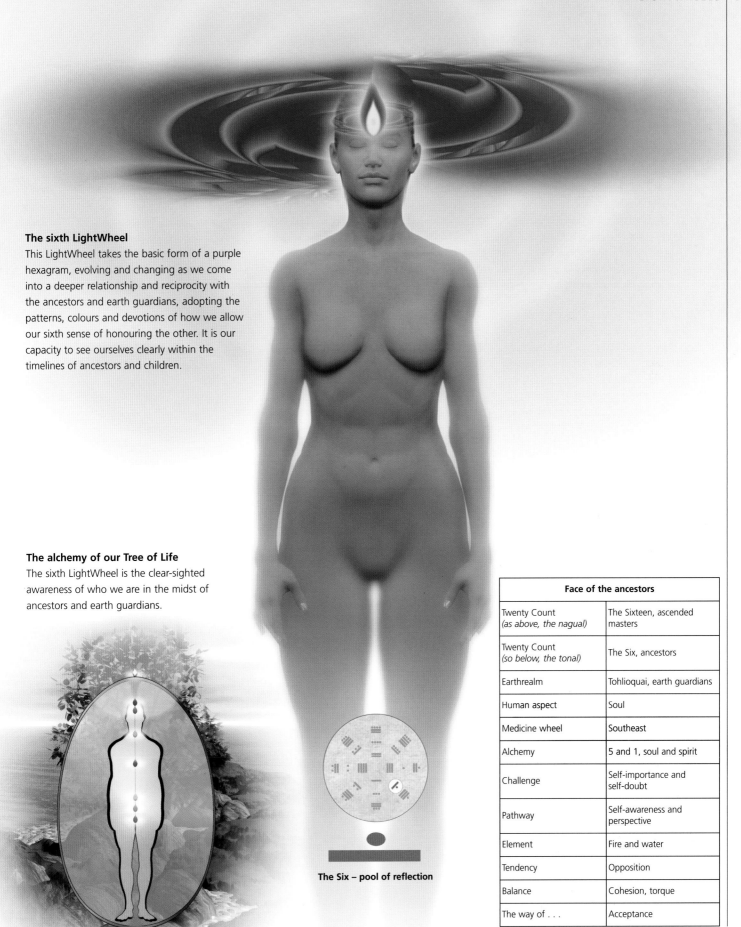

The sixth LightWheel

This LightWheel takes the basic form of a purple hexagram, evolving and changing as we come into a deeper relationship and reciprocity with the ancestors and earth guardians, adopting the patterns, colours and devotions of how we allow our sixth sense of honouring the other. It is our capacity to see ourselves clearly within the timelines of ancestors and children.

The alchemy of our Tree of Life

The sixth LightWheel is the clear-sighted awareness of who we are in the midst of ancestors and earth guardians.

The Six – pool of reflection

Face of the ancestors	
Twenty Count *(as above, the nagual)*	The Sixteen, ascended masters
Twenty Count *(so below, the tonal)*	The Six, ancestors
Earthrealm	Tohlioquai, earth guardians
Human aspect	Soul
Medicine wheel	Southeast
Alchemy	5 and 1, soul and spirit
Challenge	Self-importance and self-doubt
Pathway	Self-awareness and perspective
Element	Fire and water
Tendency	Opposition
Balance	Cohesion, torque
The way of . . .	Acceptance

The SEVEN
the dreamer and the dreamwheel

The Dreamer takes on the hero's quest, as those who have gone before: Merlin, Christos, Mara Gautama, Quetzalcoatl, Einstein, Navajo Grandfather Tom Wilson, Grandfather Dan and Grandmother Caroline of the Hopi, and today, Dreamers like Stephen Hawking, who search for the songs of the universe and the essence of God, the Dalai Lama seeking liberation for all sentient beings; Nelson Mandela, Lion of the Morningstar, who seeks freedom for his people. It is the Dreamer's search for, and manifestation of, the Core of the Universe and the Heart of the World.
Arwyn DreamWalker
(Métis medicine woman)

The seventh LightWheel is our Dreamwheel – a perpetual gateway in a landscape of communication. The seven-pointed starflame at the crown of the head is an expansion into myriad webs of consciousness shared by other beings – an appreciation that we exist within a great sea of many and varied expressions of sentience, constantly interacting, developing – creating and streaming within the vastness of the Dreamtime itself.

Here at the Seven are the blending of the elements of water (south) and earth (west), not in the muddiness of a swamp, but in the flow of the 'songlines' of the land – rivers of consciousness streaming through rocks, plants, animals, humans and all the great aspects of life.

The streaming of such songlines finds expression in the care and form of dragons, kachinas, yei; guardians of the dream who span the vast chasms of potentiality and possibility. And so they carry seeds, chant songs, guard treasures, preserving and embodying the essence of life itself.

For after the development of insight at the sixth LightWheel into our place among the ancestors and on the earth, the seventh is the gateway to open to and develop a dialogue with our own soul as to the purpose of our lives. The seventh opens up not only to the symbolic creativity of our nightly sojourns but it also experiences the stream of symbolic life in which we are immersed on a daily basis. With eyes wide open we absorb and transmit the subtle languages of symbol and aspiration. To what do we steer the totality of our energy field; to what signals on the Earthweb do we

attune ourselves? The person who awakens this LightWheel is one who will become devoted with a passion to a sacred dream, a cause greater than themselves.

SYMBOLS . . .
The Seven permeates the whole of the energy field. As each of the LightWheels is both locally specific to an area of the body and energy field, it also exerts an influence over the whole. The first LightWheel is located at the base of the spine and radiates its passion through the whole human landscape. So, too, does the Dreamwheel of the seventh open at the crown of the head, emerging through the imagination and creativity of the consciousness and cognition held within the brain, blossoming also within each cell, thought and feeling. Through each minutiae of form, the organization and patterning of our energy will convey the level to which we have embodied the Seven as it manifests in the vibrancy of the symbols and their impact at every level of consciousness.

. . . AND DREAMS
Dreams, too, are places of rich omens, teachings, warnings, and guidance from the holy ones. If we take the path of awakening in the Dreamtime then the substance of our seventh LightWheel takes on a vibrancy and activation of its own.

Its intensity of radiance will increase, shining more brightly and increasing in size. Its colour will develop from the basic lavender/violet shade of its standard form and include patterns and symbols of the Dreamtime itself. The symbolic languages of cultural, historical and geographical waves throughout human and non-human civilization emerge at this LightWheel, so it may stream with runes, glyphs or letters of human languages, phases of lunar imagery, the infinity of flower forms. It is within each of these symbols that an infinity of consciousness can be accessed.

Vision quest
THE CRY FOR A DREAM

Each person lives a vision quest on a daily basis. The key is to be aware of it. To seek the signs and omens that allow humans to make proper decisions, then act upon those signs is a part of the quest for life. The goal is to reach that place of inner-serenity so that the inner-world is equal to the outer world. When the two worlds are one, we become the living dream.
Midnight Song
Hancoka Olowampi (Jamie Sams)
(Métis medicine woman)

In most native tribes there are ceremonies of transition, initiation into the different worlds of adulthood, manhood, womanhood. Each will differ according to the tradition and the transition called for.

Of almost universal presence is the vision quest ceremony, during which the adolescent will journey, most commonly to the top of a mountain or deep within a cave, to seek a vision for their lives, a dream whose banner can light their way and give through them to the people and the earth. Often going without food and water, certainly isolated from mobile phones, and often within the sphere of animals who prowl and prey at night, this is as much a test of both resolve and stamina as it is a test of whether there is indeed a dream that we might carry through life.

Often, the visions gained are also messages for the people, and the ones who comes down from the mountain are forever changed, gifted with a geas (magical obligation) from spirit, carrying the blessing of the vision throughout their lives, no matter how many more ceremonies may be done, however many more experiences may test their resolve.

Such initiations anchor within the energy body a link with the soul and spirit that serves as a signpost throughout the white noise of the collective Dreamtime.

The seventh LightWheel

This takes the basic form of a lavender, seven-pointed star, evolving and changing as we come into a deeper relationship and reciprocity with the dreamtime, adopting the patterns, colours and hope of our sacred dream. It is a flowering of our humanity as we go beyond the realms of our prescribed roles.

The alchemy of our Tree of Life

The seventh LightWheel is our awakening into the greater realms of consciousness and reality held within the Dreamtime.

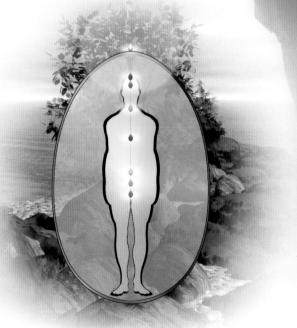

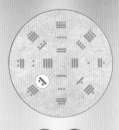

The Seven – visions of the dream

Symbols of the dream	
Twenty Count *(as above, the nagual)*	The Seventeen, great sleeper dreamers, dream guardians, katchinas and dragons
Twenty Count *(so below, the tonal)*	The Seven, the symbols of the dream
Earthrealm	Dreamtime, songlines of the land
Human aspect	Sacred dream
Medicine wheel	Southwest
Alchemy	5 and 2, soul and body
Challenge	Despair
Pathway	Hope
Element	Water and earth
Tendency	Swamp
Balance	Assisted flow
The way of . . .	Awakening

The EIGHT

cycles and patterns of the book of life

Let us keep these customs.
Keep the tradition.
Let us keep it.
We respect the Mother Earth.
Mama (elder) of the Kogi Tribe
(Colombian Highlands)

The eighth LightWheel begins as an octagon enclosing the physical body in a deep, black chamber of healing. It holds the blueprints and archives of our lives, our alignment with the sacred laws of this earth and this universe, our resonance with our own soul's signature. Here, we depart from the known and near universal territory of seven energy centres and begin the first of thirteen commonly uncharted spheres of energy.

This is a contained implosion revealing the soul's memory, an intimate understanding of the interaction of the elements on the earth, of the consequence of our actions and the impact of how we walk on the earth. Here, each word spoken, each meal eaten, each book read networks into the database of alignment that is a mirror for who we are.

THE SOUL'S SACRED COVENANT

Physically, within our own bodies, this wheel will manifest in our alignment, how balanced we are in our posture, how centred we are in our bodies. If we pursue actions not in alignment with our soul, then a vacancy of expression can result, a vacuity within the energy body as we distance ourselves from that which our souls know to be right.

These are not the ethics of human laws, but the sacred covenant many peoples know as their link and bonding with the divine. These laws arise from the very dynamics of life rather than any cultural mores. Of varying origin and expression, they congregate around the three sacred laws of the earth: nothing shall be done to harm the children; everything is born of woman; all there is, is love.

SIGNATURE OF BEING

Should any such expression of sacred law calcify, they are then ripe for exploitation. Whether the righteous anger of the zealot or the vindictive anger of revenge, anger taints the energy body. This is not the flash of affront from the emotions that is light, expressed and gone. This is, rather, the knot of pain with the weight of soul behind it that tries to control another being. The antidote and pathway of such wounding is a return to our own context, our own choices, and which aspects of our deep-seated rhythms of soul are struggling to make themselves manifest.

The Eight is the meeting of our soul (the Five) and our intention (the Three). It is the follow-through from those meetings at source in how we planned this incarnation. It is the repository of any contracts we made with ourselves as we prepared for incarnation, the profiling of those gifts we would bring and the lessons we would both learn and teach. Here there is the weaving of all these aspects of preparation with the accrued glitches necessarily accompanying us of our own unfinished soul business, together with those pathways inherited by the genetic and tribal line we were born to.

In the way that Buddhist traditions describe fear and shame as guardians of the universe, at this LightWheel any inclination to hide who we are, particularly from ourselves, causes infolds in the energy body within which our light and our seeds fester. The Eight is our healing temple of sound within which resonates our particular song, our signature of being that keeps us 'on key' throughout any of our lives. In some teachings it has come to inherit the Vedic terminology of both Karma and Dharma, for it does mutually bear the patterns and teachings of our incarnating soul.

MEDICINE WAMPUM BELTS

Wampum medicine belt – bodies of knowledge spanning politics, history, medicine and spirituality

'Much of what we know about the Medicine Wheels has been kept on Medicine Belts or the Wah-Palm-Atl-Shee-aey-Hel-am,' Ammie began. 'Of the Great Belts, around two hundred still exist. Some of these Belts were carved on wood, others exist on wool, leather or burned clay. Many are painted. All of them are called the Great Belts, even though only about eleven of them are actually belts.'
LightningBolt (Hyemeyohsts Storm)
(Métis medicine man)

Amulets and talismans have been made from wampum (quahog clam shell) by native Americans for more than 4,000 years.

In more recent centuries, they were formed into beads and crafted into 'wampum belts', or 'medicine belts', that commemorated treaties or held whole bodies of knowledge. The peace treaty of the Iroquois confederacy between the Oneidas, the Cayugas, the Onondagas, the Mohawks and the Senecas in 1701 was marked by the giving of such a medicine belt.

Laws within the traditions of the first peoples were held as such sacred items, linked through story to the commemoration of a meeting of the holy ones and the people, a place always held for the presence of the numinous, the sacred.

These traditions are not those of archived text, but of relationship and symbol passed in oral teachings, where the multimedia spiritual context of the lessons could be imparted to apprentices and the people.

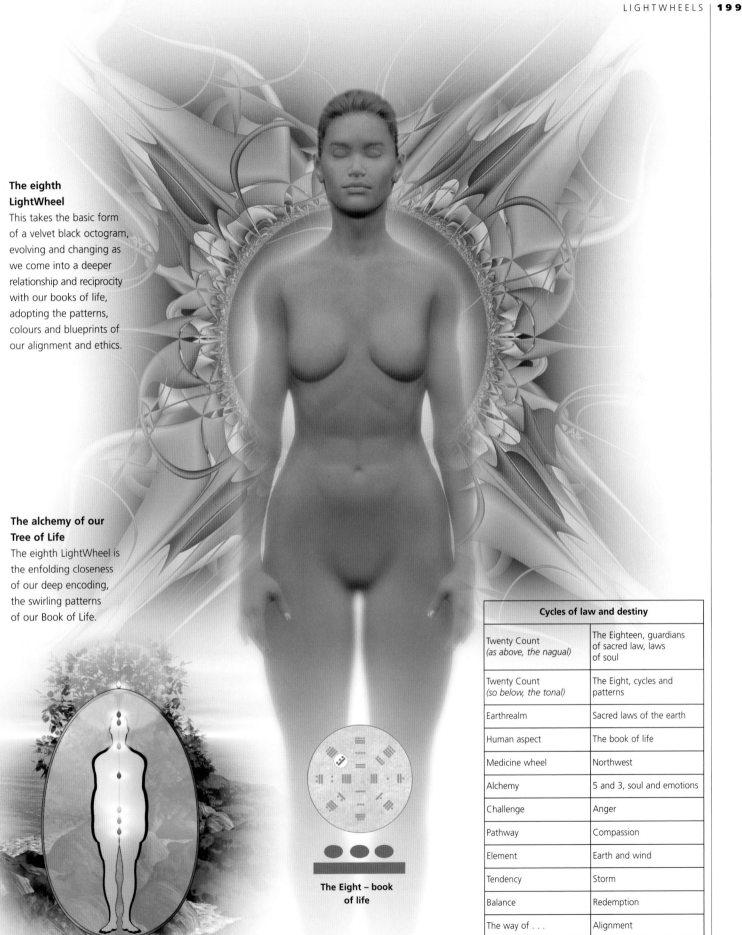

The eighth LightWheel

This takes the basic form of a velvet black octogram, evolving and changing as we come into a deeper relationship and reciprocity with our books of life, adopting the patterns, colours and blueprints of our alignment and ethics.

The alchemy of our Tree of Life

The eighth LightWheel is the enfolding closeness of our deep encoding, the swirling patterns of our Book of Life.

The Eight – book of life

Cycles of law and destiny	
Twenty Count *(as above, the nagual)*	The Eighteen, guardians of sacred law, laws of soul
Twenty Count *(so below, the tonal)*	The Eight, cycles and patterns
Earthrealm	Sacred laws of the earth
Human aspect	The book of life
Medicine wheel	Northwest
Alchemy	5 and 3, soul and emotions
Challenge	Anger
Pathway	Compassion
Element	Earth and wind
Tendency	Storm
Balance	Redemption
The way of . . .	Alignment

The NINE
the design of our lives

Whatever befalls the Earth, befalls
the sons of the Earth.
Man did not weave the web of life –
he is merely a strand in it.
Whatever he does to the web, he does to himself.
Chief Seattle (via Ted Perry)

The ninth LightWheel is the cascade of light that forms the whole of the energy field, emerging to encompass every strand of awareness within which we dwell. Here, each aspect of our lives is choreographed, held together as we would drive a team of horses, conduct an orchestra, lead an army. It is how we apportion and relate given amounts of attention and time to different aspects of our lives, and assess and follow through with right action. The Nine governs whether there is smooth interconnection and dialogue between head and heart, or if we partition and compartmentalize aspects of our history and internal drama, who we are as adult and child, man and woman.

FINDING A VOICE
The ninth LightWheel begins as a sphere of rainbow light that is in constant motion and balance, a giant gyroscope yielding more, not less, energy. In health, this is not merely a perpetual-motion machine, but a living contradiction of entropy (that all systems lose energy) and an embodiment of syntropy (co-creative systems that can generate energy).

This is a cosmic timetabling determining whether or not we bounce around like a pinball or whether there is some form of internal truce between the many aspects of our being so that they might work co-operatively together. From the perspective of the Nine, there is a concern for the integration of all aspects, enabling each to have its own voice, lest there be unacknowledged internal skeletons.

Our balance within the Nine is mirrored within our lives as we weave together the complex aspects of what it is to be human, to defy the impulse to conform and find the peaceful balance of expressing individuality with smooth elegance, a balance that neither jars with the collective nor disallows our uniqueness.

PREPARING FOR THE TEN
Within the rhythms of the Nine, any unacknowledged or unintegrated aspects of the energy field will create a sustained limp in the design of our lives. Chronic fatigue and lassitude will usually arise from a sustained imbalance, where tension sets up a resonance of deep-seated and unresolved internal conflict. This is the stress dynamic of internal rhythms wound to a level that is fundamentally incompatible with sustained health, the frenzied anxiety of inefficient work and application.

At the other end of the spectrum, we experience the mastery of time in both our everyday schedules and in the graceful weaving of seemingly incompatible strands. This is the much celebrated multi-tasking of the mother or the peacemaker and visionary who draw together seemingly incompatible elements into some type of strange harmony.

The blending of grace and heart held by the dancers of Turtle Island, where the minimum of action holds vast potency in the tread where the delicate feather touch yields a cascade of response from the worlds. These are the Hoop, the Yei, the Katchina Dancers. This is the dynamic of healing where the justly placed and subtly chosen intervention has much more power than the clumsy shifting of whole planes of being.

The power of the Nine is that of the master conductor who, through the intimacy of movement, is able to drop a pebble in the pond and watch everything ease. This is the preparation for the work of the higher self at the Ten, and its formulation through clearing the space in order for it to manifest. For the Ten will only come into an empty space where the Sacred Human has matured and stepped back enough to let the sheer being-ness of the Ten be present.

SpiderWoman WEAVER OF WORLDS

SpiderWoman is the deity of the Navajo and Hopi, whose realm reaches widely across Turtle Island and who is honoured, too, within the glyphs of the Mayans. Her story is that of the saviour mother of all the people. For during the time when monsters roamed the earth, she so loved her people that she showed the way for the hero twins (Monster Slayer and Child Born of Water) to find their father, the sun god, who taught them how to destroy earth's monsters.

Her story is that of the Earth herself, as she is the World Soul, who invited the 12 star tribes to come to the earth, the thirteenth, to share her soil and waters and to make new life. Of constant concern to SpiderWoman are those, of any tribe, who eschew the offer of coexistence and attempt to sabotage the web, the unity of the many diverse expressions of humanity. It is the mastery of the circle and the whole that SpiderWoman holds, the spirit trail out of the web that prevents entrapment and ensures that the circle is a home.

It is said that SpiderWoman resides at Spider Rock, in Canyon de Chelly in Arizona. Talking God Yei remains her confidant as to the progress of each of her children, and it is from here that she continues to weave the earth's web.

Weaving and beadwork are core aspects of the sacred knowledge of the women's societies. Teachings of the loom and the subtleties of prayer infuse much Navajo weaving. At the centre of each weaving, a small hole used to be left as an honouring of SpiderWoman. More commonly this is now represented by a 'spirit trail' of thread that breaks the main pattern and provides an avenue from the edge of the weaving into the main pattern. Just as SpiderWoman listens, weaves and holds her centre, she holds, too, a deep knowing of each of us, encouraging us to become our own dancers, weavers, choreographers, to make a place for the stranger, to welcome the 'spirit trail' of freedom in our own lives.

The ninth LightWheel

This takes the basic form of a rainbow-coloured, swirling canopy cascading over the head. The whole of the aura evolves and changes as we come into a deeper relationship and reciprocity with the organization and energy of life itself, adopting the patterns, colours and velocity of who we are as we choreograph our lives and our environment. It is our mastery of movement and energy.

The alchemy of our Tree of Life

The ninth LightWheel is the rainbow aura of our interactive web of life that we weave around us.

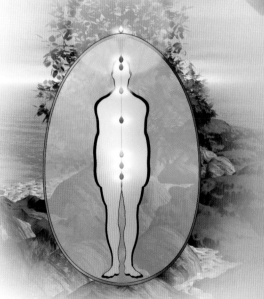

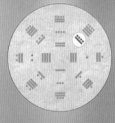

The Nine – design of energy

Dances of life	
Twenty Count *(as above, the nagual)*	The Nineteen, masters of the universe
Twenty Count *(so below, the tonal)*	The Nine, energy movement
Earthrealm	Day, moon and sun cycles
Human aspect	Choreography of energy
Medicine wheel	Northeast
Alchemy	5 and 4, soul and heart
Challenge	Stress and anxiety
Pathway	Harmony
Element	Wind and fire
Tendency	Chaos
Discipline	Feather touch
The way of . . .	Right action

The TEN

dome of the higher self

Ten is the number for Pure Intellect and Measure. Creation gave humans the power of Reason and Self Choice. Ten is also the number of the humans' Higher Self, their Sacred Twin. What can give better measure than this Spirit-Knowing? Come, Children, have you met your Self and Known Existence?

LightningBolt (Hyemeyohsts Storm)

(Métis medicine man)

The tenth LightWheel is the canopy of consciousness. It lights our way just as the DreamWheel of the Seven does, but this is the cascading illumination of the higher self, an access point to higher realms of consciousness. It appears as a spinning sphere, radiant with the blue-white hue of starlight. This is our uplink, where the blessings of the 'as above' are known and blended with those of the 'so below'.

Here there is the reflection in human form of the earth–sky alliance, the spirits of heaven and earth, union of changing woman and the sun god. It is now that as humans we begin literally to bridge heaven and earth and our 'uplink' and expand into the realms of knowledge held by a community of heart-mind that both inspires and connects us.

SACRED SPACE

The Ten is the actualization of the 'twice energy' of the Sacred Human. The Five is now doubled in its potential, expanded in on itself. Of the four quarters of the universe described by the Twenty Count (1–5, 6–10, 11–15, 16–20) this is the culmination of the second leg of our development of consciousness, extending us beyond the limitations of the singular human and beginning to prepare us as a shelter and a refuge, a sacred space. For the dome of the Ten is a sacred enclosure, offered to the earth–sky alliance as a holding for the prayers and beings of the earth. As such, we have the central pole of the world within us by which to navigate our ongoing journey. This is the Axis Mundi (world tree) of Western alchemy, the Tree of Life that appears in Mayan, Celtic, African and Hindu traditions.

Here, the sacred space created by the tenth LightWheel expands out to allow not only the blessings from above, but also the emergence of the run of consciousness throughout the whole Tree. As the Light-

Wheels are sequentially linked and we trace our development along them, they begin to expand their axis of energy through which our power rises, changing and developing each phase of who we are.

The Ten in this capacity is both a staff of law and a sphere of power and, as we seek to approach its anchoring, there will often come an ally who reflects and holds the upright strength of our spine, the axis in the centre of our luminous egg of awakened consciousness.

TRANSCENDENT GATEWAY

This gateway holds death and communion, the surrender of petty callings and the magnetism of our higher selves as we open to the channelling of heavenly energy that fills us. Such paradox of communion and death is held across Turtle Island by the power of the snake. For Mesoamerican civilizations the plumed serpent was the primal ancestor of all cosmic forces, and within the tribes of the eastern woodlands the serpent guarded the underworld and secrets of healing, symbols and powers echoed across the whole of the Americas.

One of the most potent incarnations of this divine power is the diamond-backed rattlesnake, the continent's most venomous snake. It is understandable that this predator is seen as the gateway to many of the shamanic mysteries held by the holy people, as its bite can either kill or change forever our consciousness.

Having run the gauntlet of death and undertaken the initiation that the snake offers, our remaining 'medicine' is transmutation – the antidoting of poisons. This is the power held by those who, by virtue of their heavenly qualities, are able to counter deadly poison. While the power of our sacred presence can journey further along the Twenty Count and open the doors of the LightWheels from the Ten to the Twenty, it is only once we have mastered acceptance of ourselves as more than who we are that we can safely surf the halls of the centre of the Mayan universe, Hunab Ku.

SACRED SPACE

Tipi of the Plains Tribes – home and temple

With Beauty before me, I walk.
With Beauty behind me, I walk.
With Beauty below me, I walk.
With Beauty all around me, I walk.
Navajo prayer

The Navajo word *hozho* is often translated as 'beauty', but as with all translations across cultures, its telling requires the embellishments of context in order to carry something of it import, its truth. For hozho is also harmony, blessing, prayer. It is a potency of presence wherein all things have their alignment arising from a simple and spontaneous essence of rightness. This is the harmony of communion brought by the Ten, where one becomes a dome of power exerting a radiance of sanctuary within our orbit.

Such a sacred presence is echoed in the form and symbolism of dwellings across Turtle Island, from the hogans of the Navajo, the igloo of the Inuit to the tipi of the Plains Tribes.

Each construction is aligned to the directions, each protocol echoes the balance of cosmic proportion, the role of the men, the role of the women, all bringing an alignment with the sacred marriage of heaven and earth. So the home literally becomes a dome of blessing, a place of the Ten where we can receive the blessings from above.

The tenth LightWheel

This LightWheel takes the basic form of a blue-white, ten-pointed star. It is a beacon of the halo above our head, evolving and changing as we come into a deeper relationship and reciprocity with both our higher self and the collective knowledge of all beings in all times. It is our Tree of Life standing between heaven and earth, the actual tree of our medicine, whether oak, cedar, birch or frangipani.

The alchemy of our Tree of Life

The tenth LightWheel is the radiant halo of our higher self, the star of our Tree of Life.

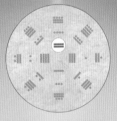

The Ten – one mind, all mind

The staff of law and sphere of power	
Twenty Count (*as above, the nagual*)	The Twenty, great mystery, great spirit
Twenty Count (*so below, the tonal*)	The Ten, all knowledge of all times and spaces
Earthrealm	Earth–sky alliance (*kajulew*, in Quiche Mayan)
Human aspect	Higher self
Medicine wheel	North of centre
Alchemy	5 and 5, soul and soul
Element	Void upon void

HUNAB KU
prophecy at the crossroads

Astronomy, divination and prophecy are close cousins within the Mayan universe and continue to help each generation of native tribes navigate the web of life. Teachings of the ancestors are commonly interwoven with the words of the gods and essential guidance on the 'right way' to live. This is no archaeological relic, but a living part of an Earth-centred spirituality that has rekindled the power of prophecy for many.

For the Hopi, it is the ways and words of Masau, the creator, who taught the people the ways of living in harmony with the Earth. For the Hopi, we live now in the place of *koyaanisqatsi*, meaning 'world out of balance', which can be rectified only by the coming of the 'fifth world'. It is said that the end of the fourth world and the beginning of the fifth will be marked by upheaval and disaster. But a choice is offered to humanity – to live with the Earth or abuse it.

HARMONIC CONVERGENCE

This Hopi crossroads of choice is echoed in the Mayan prophesies. On 17 August 1987 people across the world met to celebrate the 'Harmonic Convergence'. The timing and import of this event suggested an alignment of cosmic forces that would begin the count-down of a 25-year cycle ending in 2012, itself the ending of a phase of the 'long count' of the Mayan calendar that began in 3114 BCE. The uneven axis of the Earth around which

it spins changes slowly over time, altering its trajectory. During the winter solstice of 2012 it will align astronomically with the dark rift at the centre of the Milky Way, known by the first peoples in its many names as the Road of Xibalba, the Black Road, the Crossroads, the Hunab Ku.

SYMBOLS, PROPHESIES AND PORTENTS

The Hunab Ku is a mystery symbol of many origins and meanings. The inverted black and white spiralling 'G', so akin to the yin/yang icon, is now indelibly linked to the contemporary renaissance of Mayan cosmology and prophecy.

The symbol's link with Hunab Ku is both disputed and celebrated – but the Mayan Daykeeper Hunbatz Men speaks of it as being given to him on weavings inherited from his elders. It is likely that the growing emphasis within Mesoamerican culture on the Hunab Ku was the result of Spanish missionary activity in its quest for a 'one god' with which to engage the native religion. It was Hunab Ku as an aspect of the Mayan creator god Itzamna that was recruited into such a campaign, but given that the whole pantheon and culture of native spiritual politics was so fluid, it was perhaps inevitable that such a focus would have surprising consequences.

As all of the prophesies and portents converge towards 2012, commentators offer many versions of the great transition that

may occur. Most range between the extremes of a destructive cataclysm and the return of a golden age. Many attempt to track the vast cycles of astronomical complexity and the very 'weather' of our planet's destiny.

For millennia we have been changing the face of our planet. When it comes to an awareness and insight into the effects of our collective consciousness on the state of the earth, we are generally dismissive of any such link. Into this context, suggestions that we might not want to 'litter' space with either our space-faring garbage and defunct satellites, our cacophony of electromagnetic noise or squabbling negativity, is likely to receive little attention.

In the ways of Mesoamerican peoples, traditions, deities, festivals and sciences were accrued and blended rather than opposed and fought. It is perhaps these skills that are called for in navigating the current multitude of scientific hypotheses regarding the stability of our planet's climate and the sustainability of industrialized civilization as we know it. Perhaps within the renaissance of Mayan sciences there may be themes that can harness our imagination more effectively rather than the strictures of economic self-interest and isolationism.

Nagual CELESTIAL CROSSROADS AND THE UNSEEN DOOR

We cannot understand the Nagual, we can only see for ourselves that it exists.
Don Juan Mateus

Within Aztec and Mayan mythology, each deity walked with a nahualli (nagual) animal form of their sacred presence. Quetzalcoatl walked as a quetzal bird, Huitzilopochtli as a hummingbird, Tezcatlipoca as a jaguar or coyote.

Meanings and usage of the term 'nagual' continue to range between the guardian animal of a person (similar to the familiars of European witches and wizards) and the guardian holy person of a particular village. Such themes continue in the shamanic lineages, where any medicine person

who walks as a shapeshifter becomes the form of their ally. This is more than a co-creation of beings under the canopy of the earth–sky alliance, but an immersion into the inter-regnum world that borders creation itself, and engages with a facet of our universe unencumbered by the rules of reality with which we normally structure our lives.

This is the nagual as an experience of the world where we go beyond an everyday consciousness. It is the realm offered by the hallucinogenic plants of ayahuasca, peyote, datura, mescaline, fly agaric and psilocybin. These great teacher plants allow us to flex our consciousness in ways that might otherwise be inaccessible, unless we have a natural facility with stepping through the looking

glass of reality and staying afloat within an infinity of possibilities. It is such stability within infinity, the ability to navigate a constantly shifting universe that is at the heart of the path of the nagual. For some medicine people, it is the path of an awakening humanity in harmony with our galactic environment, an ability to develop a multiple and expanded awareness of who we are and where we are going.

Hunab Ku

This is the centre of the universe, heart of
the Milky Way and aspect of Great Spirit, the
culmination of the Twenty Count at the Twenty.
It is the dark gateway to our knowing the
unknowable, beyond both time and space,
beacon for our evolution beyond and within
the realms of the Tree itself.

And this will go on for us, as if we were being slowly lifted,
and filled and washed by a soft singing wind that clears our sad muddled minds,
and holds us safe and heals us, and feeds us with lessons we never imagined.
And here we all are together. Here we are . . .
Doris Lessing

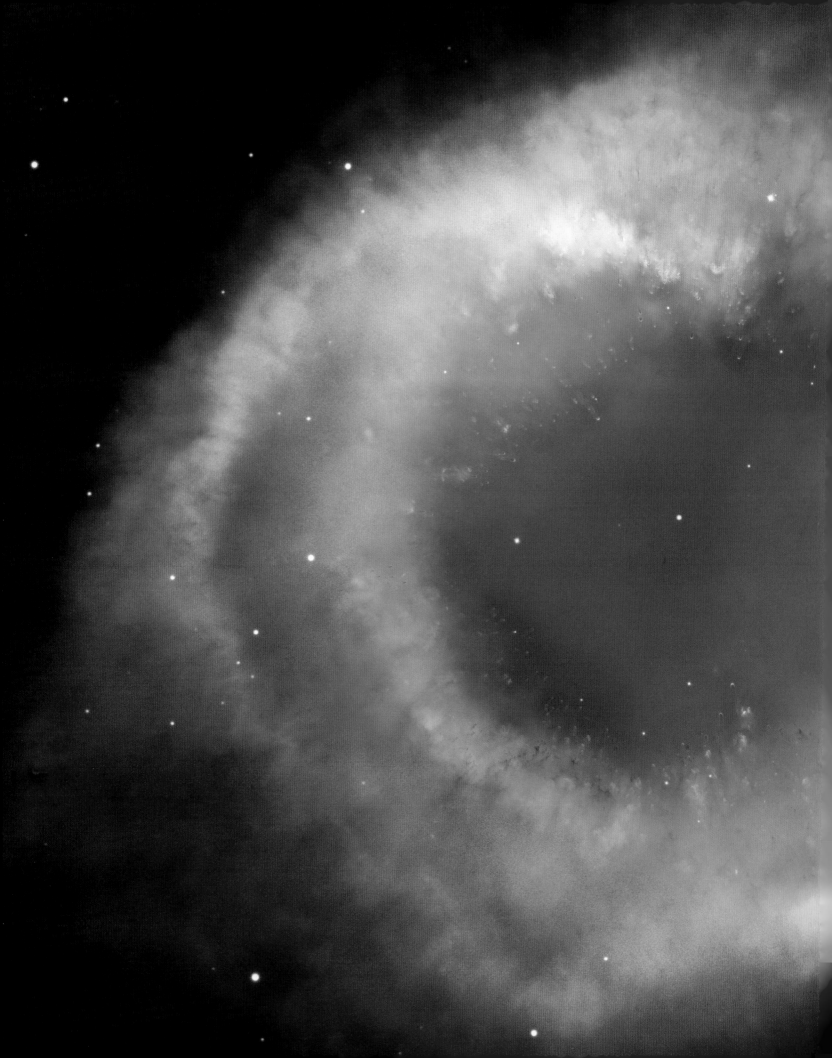

Remembering the future

Landscaping the developing human

As we have surveyed these maps of humanity that have arisen across history, our perceptual skills have been of multiple vision and of self-perspective. For these are the skills of the human surveyor, the holistic astrolabe, essential aspects of perspective that are needed just to engage this material without being ensnared by the cultural filters determined by our time and place of birth, by the agenda of our glands, our addictions and our collective and personal mythology. But these skills embody paradoxes – what we see depends on where we stand; just by looking at or thinking about something, we change it; nothing is solid; energy is life; we are powerful – and were the subject of discussion in the first chapter.

This final chapter turns the handle of the kaleidoscope one more time, shifts perspective yet again and suggests how the skills of the human surveyor might evolve into faculties that help steer and construct our future. In this way, the surveyor's skills become the developer's tools.

- We're lightening up
- We're misbehaving
- We do it together, or not at all
- We don't discover, we create

While these may combine aspects of who we have always been as humans with a self-awareness of the dynamics involved, they may yet emerge as the dials and switches of our next phase of evolution.

While this next phase of evolution is likely to involve a technological future, projections that future humans might be disincarnate intelligences are overstated. Even the cyborg future that is already here – replacement hips and heart valves – can reach only so far into the fire-making, tool-using ridiculousness of human existence.

Just as we are able to engineer our tools to take on some of our characteristics and skills, it is likely that we will extend our frontiers into dimensions not accessible to the linear logics of machines. Surgeons have gazed into the 'grey mush' inside our heads wondering how consciousness is held within its complexity of neurons, chemical messages and lightwaves. But however much they are programmed to imitate random choices and the effects of chaos, digital-binary systems of intelligence don't quite reach the intuitive realms of 'being-ness' of DNA-based, human life-forms.

Whether or not our origins were within an eruption of life inside some primordial soup or whether we were created by an external agency, we carry a seed of mystery. Whether we call such consciousness sacred or scientifically complex, it is remarkable.

The following pages suggest how some of these paradoxes might collapse in on one another, building the skills of the developer, and mapping the horizon of our next phase of evolution. William Blake said of his quest that it was not one of discovery, but of creation. It may be that this is the path of the developing human.

Cosmic jokes
switters is lightening up

The Hopi clown is not like a comedian or a rodeo circus performer. He is a Perfect Fool, showing the people that man can never be perfect . . . He opens a door into a greater reality than the ebb and flow of everyday life. Pueblo clowns, in the course of the contribution to the katsina ritual, might, for example, engage in sexual displays which are normally quite taboo. This breaks down the ordinary round of everyday existence, shocks people out of their petty daily concerns, opening the mind to greater considerations than mere humour . . .

Stewart Lee

The alchemical task of refinement has for centuries been relegated to the realms of passé superstition and kitsch illustration. But across the world, and particularly in China and Europe, alchemy has been the precursor of modern chemistry, from whose perspective it might now seem a ragbag of experimental chemical analysis (transformation of metals), philosophical speculation (evolution of consciousness as symbolized by these metals) and sympathetic magic (gold used in spells as a symbol of divinity).

But throughout the alchemical traditions there is a common thread of transformation, most commonly symbolized by the transformation of lead into gold by virtue of the mythical 'philosopher's stone', which was both an extraordinary chemical catalyst, able to turn base metals to gold, and an enlightening elixir capable of transforming consciousness from the most mundane to the most sacred.

ASPECTS OF REALITY

In its capacity to alter totally the nature of consciousness, the 'philosopher's stone' has been compared with the life-giving and restorative qualities of the grail, whether the Druids' Grail of the 'All and the Everything', the Christians' Holy Grail or the Persians' Grail of Djemscheed. The philosopher Nicholas Roerich even painted the Grail as a stone rather than a cup, closing the circle of its aspects as a philosopher's stone.

Each of these extraordinary objects share not only the capacity to provide a cornucopia of nourishment, but also the en-lighten-ing catalyst whereby either the consciousness or substance is transformed into something more rarefied. It is this ability to lighten up

that Tom Robbins' character Switters (in *Fierce Invalids Home from Hot Climates*) identifies as the growing edge of humanity – a blended ability to see the ridiculousness of life while navigating the multiple levels of reality afforded by a shamanic consciousness.

Even politically, the power of satire has a potent tempering impact on the excesses of those in positions of power; it is the essence of the court jester, able to speak the truth to the unreachable heights of kingship. So it is within out internal world as we desperately seek to bring our own inner sovereign back into contact with all the other parts of who we are, during times of blind governance. The danger of taking ourselves too seriously can bring a rigidity and tension to the energy field that restricts the flow of energy through us, at all levels of Body/Mind/Spirit.

Typically, it will reflect in our physical systems, either making us constipated or so stolid that we need massage rather than exercise. Mentally and spiritually, we can tyrannize ourselves to the extent that we have no slack, no give in who and what we allow ourselves to be. It is a sobering thought that those who ruthlessly harass and oppress other people are likely to be acting far more harshly to themselves in their own inner world.

While an increase in sadomasochism has met with a level of prurient disdain from some, it may involve no less a lack of humour than the knots we tie ourselves up in every day. The clown dissolves such knots, releases the oppression of the powerful and the nightmare of the victim. For the Taoist, the practice was to ridicule the sacred, and sages have been shown riding backwards on donkeys, baring their backsides to the moon. Laughter helped in the quest for longevity and enlightenment, but these were more side effects. Blasphemy, needless to say, doesn't enter into the vocabulary.

WALK GENTLY UPON THE EARTH

Moccasins of a native American dancer

Within each of the traditions profiled in this atlas, the task of refinement has been offered giving various routes. Diet, meditation and the invigoration of the elements all contribute to clearing the energy body of heaviness, so that we are able still to find our centre, but inhabit more fully that region between heaven and earth. The sacred dances of the first peoples of Turtle Island echo this cushioned walk, stepping as they do, first, with the ball of the foot, bringing the heel down gently, on the back-beat, and never with the full weight of the body. It is such conscious elevation that allows us to find a more balanced place within ourselves and upon the planet.

We're lightening up.

~

It's the ridiculousness of humour that is one of the masters'
most badly kept secrets, in its irrepressible power to refine
the energy of the Body/Mind/Spirit, extend life,
and beckon us towards enlightenment.

Wildfire

surfing the laws of the universe

It is said that soon after his enlightenment, the Buddha passed a man on the road who was struck by the extraordinary radiance and peacefulness of his presence. The man stopped and asked, 'My friend, what are you? Are you a celestial being or a god?'

'No,' said the Buddha.

'Well then, are you some kind of magician or wizard?'

Again the Buddha replied, 'No.'

'Are you a man?'

'No.'

'Well, my friend, what are you?'

The Buddha replied, 'I am awake.'

Christina Feldman and Jack Kornfield

It is our nature to go above and beyond the limitations we believe are there for us, to map the universe we find and then to throw out those very same maps lest they limit our perception and progress. In his science-fiction epic *Dune*, author Frank Herbert spans a history of hundreds of thousands of years as he speculates about the path of humanity through a future where its technological and ethical restraints have been unleashed by reckless expansion.

Through the course of our adventures, Herbert skilfully leads us to a place where the erstwhile hero, a cloned man trained as a human computer and honed to the apex of sexual proficiency, flees from the remnants of yet another bitter and costly war. But he flees not only from his friends and allies, he also flees from the shimmering web of destiny woven by the cosmic gods of his time. These are beings evolved over many thousands of years from genetically modified humans, existing within dimensions unseen by his peers, but glimpsed by him at the edges of his awareness. He succeeds in his escape only through dumping the navigational cores of his computers, the star maps that lock him and his crew into one time and space, freeing them from the imprisonment of what they think they know of where and when they are.

BEYOND BOUNDARIES

For us, in this time and space, it is only though the suspension of our addictions to certainty that we find balance within the unsteady surface of our universe. By giving up the battles with ourselves and others

to win and conquer territory of ground, resources or ideas. Such battles tether us to the fixity of our limitations. Just as the alpha monkey will have twice the levels of the feel-good neurotransmitter serotonin in his system than his minions, so, too, do we still thrive on dominance and gratification. Our next rewiring task as a species is to reroute our neurology to pathways where we reward ourselves for philosophical somersaults that most of our forebears would probably have considered blasphemy.

This we will turn into a navigational quest of who, where and why we are. A rhythm echoing between the collective and the individual as the third point of morphic resonance itself attempts to surf rather than understand reality. Within the alchemical wisdom of Europe, it is only through a deep knowledge of the elements themselves that people are then able to construct a grail strong enough to transcend the elements. Only then to find that beyond the limitations of this time and space, beyond the bounds of our gods and creators, still lies the simple truth of the elements themselves.

While many medieval European knights were somewhat maverick in their ways, and were necessarily committed to a fiercely independent experience of the word of god, their code of chivalry also called for a sensitivity to the customs of the places that they found themselves. The anarchic necessity of the wildfire at the centre of our humanity is also that of a gentle humour and a sensitive chaos. It is the fire that transforms rather than burns.

MORPHIC FIELDS

Quantum learning of the wisdom monkey

Morphic fields are part of the radical ideas developed by British scientist and visionary Rupert Sheldrake to describe the phenomena displayed by DNA-based life to grow into the form that it does. This is the imprint in the universe that we each follow to take the form that we do, and offers an explanation for how DNA itself actually unfolds. It is also a model of 'universal learning' and the way in which a level of critical mass is often reached within the society of any life-form to be able to anchor any new learning and make it accessible. This is similar to the 100th-monkey syndrome, where once enough of any population take a particular leap in learning, then the whole population has access to this learning, stored not in any recorded medium or biological code, but in the morphic field shared by that species.

It is in this way that the ethical life of humanity copes with the wildfire of its expansiveness. The mundane necessity of regulations and laws never even come close to the intuitive understanding of ethics each of us has. It is rather in the interactive mass of consciousness that we find approximate answers to how to navigate this swirling sea of confusion we exist in. Commandments and codes have been useful stabilizers and fodder for philosophers, but it is within the collective conscience existing in our midst that ethics lie.

We're misbehaving.

~

Given our tendency towards conformity, our spark of
brilliance is the eternal call to misbehave,
steal fire from the heavens and find the power of ethics in
collective resonance rather than regulated mediocrity.

The inner planes
doors of perception and the perennial philosophy

The perennial philosophy is the metaphysic that recognises a divine reality substantial to the world of things and lives and minds; the psychology that finds in the soul something similar to, or even identical with, divine reality; the ethic that places man's final end in the knowledge of the immanent and transcendental ground of all being – the thing is immemorial and universal.

Aldous Huxley

We have approached the plentiful chaos of how we see the world and what it is made of, and attempted to view these relativities into active skills of surfing reality. In so doing we need also to reveal the interlacing web that connects our experience if such skills are to hold any cohesion.

As we have seen, such a synthesis needs to avoid the sureties that held back our initial dive into plurality, resist fundamentalism and objectivity as much as romanticism and subjectivity. Any synchrony needs equally to avoid any patina of unity that is merely a rehash of the pseudoscientist's interpretation of life and diversity from within their own prejudices. For it is in this way that the Marxist views all history as an expression of class war and the Freudian as aspects of repressed sexual urges. Each philosophical movement tends to jockey for the position of a meta-system that explains away other systems and casts itself as the one that tidily assembles and organizes the chaos of philosophical competition.

PERENNIAL PHILOSOPHY

The 'perennial philosophy' is an approach that could be accused of such an assimilating strategy, depending on which of its versions we examine. Its first exposition in the modern world was by the 17th-century German philosopher Gottfried Leibniz, who suggested that at the heart of all religions was a shared mystical vision of interconnectedness.

His perspective largely derived from his aspirations to blend together the vast diversity of his other philosophical and scientific explorations, and is said to have discovered the term in the writings of the 16th-century theologian Augustine Steuch. For Steuch, the perennial philosophy's defining feature was the knowledge available to mankind before our fall from grace. As such, this soul knowledge bore much in relation to the soul remembrance described by Plato as anamnesis – the process by which any accruing of knowledge was in actual fact a mere remembrance by our ordinary minds of the infinite knowledge of our souls.

While the perennial philosophy has found many articulations and facets within different times and in different places, its contemporary articulation was made by Aldous Huxley in his description of the world's mystical philosophies, and primarily that of Hinduism's Vedanta, the idea that reality is, at its core, a single principle.

For Huxley, a number of key principles characterized his understanding of the perennial philosophy. Essentially, these came down to his belief that our experience of life and, particularly, of our shared consensus of ordinary reality, is just the tip of the iceberg in terms of any ultimate sense or understanding of the universe.

Here, Huxley paints a classically mystical vision, citing the higher virtues of ethics, intellect and the direct knowledge of the soul as those perceptual faculties that extend our everyday senses into the occult realms of a universe hidden from everyday sight and sound. This is the culmination of all that we have examined in relationship to the neurophysiology of perception and the unavoidable contamination of inter-subjectivity, and can be expressed in the lines from William Blake that Huxley was to borrow for one of his later works: 'If the doors of perception were cleansed, everything would appear as it is, infinite and holy.'

THE INNER SANCTUM

Multi-faceted universality

The perennial philosophy is also to be found in the many mystery schools of esoteric traditions. These are less the mystical enclaves of hermits and meditators, but more the active realms of magicians and warrior societies. Such places have been called the 'inner planes'. These places are not so much articulated as philosophies and doctrines, but rather the actual and phenomenological experience of those realms on the inner planes, the spiritual realms of expanded vision.

Whereas the innermost mysteries and secret treasures of many temples and cathedrals are often perceived to be the distinguishing myth that demarcates them from other religions and schools, at the heart of their insights is the realization that each is but a facet of the central core of our existence. It is a strange truth that the honour of all manner of classes, from warriors to thieves, will at times transcend the immediate agenda of their individual goals and discover a shared experience.

This is the spontaneity of the Christmas day football match in the no-man's land of the First World War. It is the shared experience, often anticipated and aspired to by corporations and governments, where our differences suddenly melt and we tap into the well of myth that can shape our world. It is where experiences can claim a universal applicability and the great quest of humanity is no longer the domain of difference but of collective possibility. Spontaneity and intention in active collusion.

We do it together, or not at all.

~

Just as the next Buddha will be the consciousness of a collective, our next jump is the collapsing paradox of the individual and the collective, and the fine web of possibility in between.

Top of the world
our dance with spiderwoman

At the top of the world, in mountain retreats, river villages and suburban enclaves, are lone individuals and circles of people who consciously dream with the path of our planet. A virtual community of people who, through some of the landscapes described within this atlas, have awakened the potential of their consciousness to the extent that they are able not only to perceive the wider energetic grid of themselves, the Earth, her worlds and peoples, but also steer its progress. In this way, the simple passion of prayer imbues the heart of the planet's consciousness with those adepts and masters guiding her passage though the galaxy, joining with her in the journey of our questions as to who we are and where we are going.

COMMUNION

Such a vision may seem for some a romantic gloss on the deep-green politics of environmentalism. And, indeed, perhaps it is. But it intrinsically holds within it the disciplines and stabilizers described within these last few pages, the perspective and caveats of an embodied understanding of the limitations of our knowledge and the preparation for the next stage of our evolution.

Constantly is the gaze cast forward to the time when the circle turns and those rhythms and philosophies that might seem irrevocably alien come into a relationship with the dreaming web that they tend. For one of the central disciplines of any circle of dreamers, any initiate of the inner planes, is that the notion of 'I' becomes communal.

As I hold within me the seeds of the other there is no feeling or experience so alien that I do not bear its potential. It is from this place that I find the compassion not to alienate, but to encircle. Not in restriction, but in the discipline of not seeing myself as separate, and the other as less. Within such communion there is still the questing sense of the consequences of our actions, the ripples of our thoughts and the responsibilities we can choose.

Here, ethics becomes a dance of dynamics rather than judgement, as each intention, action and internal transformation moulds and shapes our own energy field, those of others, and the collective energetic context within which we live. This maturity of perspective in the consequence of our actions is the bedrock of rehabilitation programmes, truth and reconciliation systems. It is in such a science of dynamic systems that ethics might once again find a universality of application.

LANDSCAPES OF THE BODY, MAPS OF THE MIND

But just as for some the knowing of spiderwoman might seem to be a romanticized pastoralism, for others its implications will be an outdated and irresponsible perpetuation of superstition – remnant of a prescientific era that refuses to wither. Most of the landscapes of the body described within this atlas are still viewed by mainstream science as out-dated superstitions.

It is no doubt true that within many spiritual disciplines the flourishing interface of traditions meeting each other, free from the indoctrination of a mediating priesthood, has led to a diluted, fuzzy sense of discipline and focus. Within such a fertile and unfettered spiritual environment such freedom has led to other, more subtle abuses of power, as education is sidelined for evangelism and freedom sacrificed for the hollow surety of shallow prophesy and hypnotic prescriptions.

But just as the spiralling milieu of spirit encounters its own challenges in a deregulated world of personal exploration, so too does science now face its own challenges. For as spiritual disciplines lose their focus, scientific traditions are losing their perspective. Some of the discoveries of quantum physics and holographic systems are terribly slow in following through to an everyday appreciation of their implications. The notions that the universe is one great mass of knowledge with which we can interact could have prompted a cascade of research programmes investigating how exactly we can develop such interactions, and even exploring some of the ways in which we have already been doing so.

This is a blind spot of modern science, where the mechanics of our own self-management of consciousness and intentionality and its interface with the infinity of creation has been sidelined, presumably because of the fear of superstition. But then again, it is somehow more comforting to consider the gods and goddesses that walk with thunder and lightning as aspects of the electrical regulation of the atmosphere, or even from the archetypal well of collective humanity. Far safer then to consider them as some kind of separate, self-motivated beings or patterns of consciousness. For such a reductionist rationalization somehow dilutes the instinctive understanding of the interactive arena of our energy fields with our environment, and dulls the passionate conjuration of thunder and lightning that might hold essential clues to the nature of human beings' evolutionary context.

This atlas is an attempt to recast our net of potential research into the nature of our own evolution, reclaiming some of those traditions that have been excluded from the scientific quest. To overview with a depth of authentic engagement some of the themes within the great constructions of our world, and as they lie together, between them, and upon the web of spiderwoman, to contribute to the blended emergence of our next phase of understanding our world.

A PRAYER OF BLESSING

For as the Druids greet the sunrise across the heel stone at Stonehenge, they are not just enacting outdated ritual, but participating in the vast choreography of consciousness of the life that teems on our planet.

This is no attempt at order or control, but simply a prayer of blessing that, within the swirling patterns of absolute chaos displayed by the infinite number of interactions, patterns of harmony can be sown that will then echo and create more consciousness, more beauty, more exploration, and more understanding.

The questions we now face as a global people are whether we will embrace this quest, and whether it will be embodied not only by circles of dreamers at the top of the world, but by the vast mass of humanity, collectives who have languages and cultures at seeming odds, but who nonetheless share in a sense of belonging and participation in the co-creation of the world.

We don't discover, we create.

~

The neutrality of our participation in life is a mere limiting ruse;
we inevitably create the texture of our lives.

References
sources and further reading

The following references are those works that have served as text sources for the material presented within this Atlas, as well as suggestions for further reading. All effort has been taken to cite the appropriate information for each of the sources.

A BODY OF KNOWLEDGE

Anderson, WT (ed), *The Fontana Postmodernism Reader*, Fontana, London, 1996

Bear, G, *Songs of Earth and Power*, Tor, New York, 1994

Donaldson, S, *The Chronicles of Thomas Covenant*, Del Rey, New York, 1977–83

Freire, P, *Pedagogy of the Oppressed*, Seabury, New York, 1973

Lessing, D, *The Golden Notebook*, Simon & Schuster, New York, 1962

McTaggart, L, *The Field – The Quest for the Secret of the Universe*, HarperCollins, London, 2001

Merleau-Ponty, M, *The Primacy of Perception*, Northwestern University Press, 1964

Neihardt, JG (ed), *Black Elk Speaks*, William Morrow, New York, 1932

Palmer, P, *To Know as we are Known – Education as Spiritual Journey*, HarperCollins, San Fransisco, 1983

Rucker, R, *The Fourth Dimension*, Houghton Mifflin, Boston, 1984

Schlesinger, A, *Address to the Indian Council of World Affairs*, 1962

Tansley, DV, *Subtle Body – Essence and Shadow*, Thames and Hudson, London, 1996

Watson, B, *Chuang Tzu: Basic Writings*, Columbia University Press, New York, 1964

FORM

Fausto-Sterling, A, *Sexing the Body, Gender Politics and the Construction of Sexuality*, Basic Books, New York, 2000

Hesse, H, *The Glass Bead Game*, Fretz & Wasmuth Verlag AG, Zurich, 1943

Juan, S, *The Odd Body*, Collins, London, 1995

Porter, R, *Blood and Guts – A Short History of Medicine*, Penguin, London, 2002

Sarup Singh Alag, S , *Hair Power*, self-published, 1996

Tortora,GJ, & Grabowski, SR, *Principles of Anatomy and Physiology*, HarperCollins, California, 1996

Wallis Budge, EA, *The Egyptian Book of the Dead*, 1895

Wilson, KJW. & Waugh, A, *Anatomy and Physiology in Health and Illness*, Churchill Livingstone, New York, 1996

FUNCTION

Abd Al-Sabour, S (O'Grady, D ed), *Fragments of a Common Tale. From Ten Modern Arab Poets*, Dedalus Press, 1992

Allison, D, *Bastard out of Carolina*, Plume, New York, 1993

Bear, G, *Darwin's Radio*, HarperCollins, London, 1999

Dickinson, E, *Complete Poems*, Roberts Brothers, Boston, 1890

Foster, R, & Kreitzman, *Rhythms of Life, The Biological Clocks that Control the Daily Lives of Every Living Thing*, Profile Books, London, 2004

McKenna, T, *Food of the Gods: The Search for the Original Tree of Knowledge*, Bantam, New York, 1992

Murphy, M, *The Future of the Body, Explorations Into the Further Evolution of Human Nature*, Jeremy P Tarcher/Putnam, New York, 1992

Narby, J, *The Cosmic Serpent. DNA and the Origins of Knowledge*, Phoenix, London, 1998

Pert, C, *Molecules of Emotion*, Touchstone, New York, 1997

Pinchbeck, D, *Breaking Open the Head: A Visionary Journey From Cynicism to Shamanism*, Flamingo, London, 2002

Pratchett, T, *Mort*, Victor Gollancz, London, 1987

Thomas, L, *The Lives of a Cell: Notes of a Biology Watcher*, Bantam, New York, 1974

Watson, L, *Dreams of Dragons: Ideas on the Edge of Natural History*, Hodder and Stoughton, London, 1986

Wells, HG, *The War of the Worlds*, Books of Wonder, New York, 1898

FREEDOM

Berne, E, *Transactional Analysis in Psychotherapy*, Grove, New York, 1961

Byatt, AS, *How We Lost Our Sense of Smell*, Sightlines (Royal National Institute of the Blind), London, 2001

Campbell, J, & Moyers, B, *The Power of Myth*, Doubleday, New York, 1988

Chatwin, B, *Songlines*, Jonathan Cape, London, 1987

Chelsom, P, *Hear My Song* (Film released 1992)

Descartes, R (Veitch, J trans), *Meditations*, Open Court Publishing Company, La Salle, Illinois, 1962

Foucault, M, *The History of Sexuality*, Penguin, Harmonsworth, 1978

Fuller, M, *Truth, Value and Justification*, Avebury, Aldershot, 1991

Graves, R, *The Larousse Encyclopedia of Mythology*, Hamlyn, New York, 1959

Harding, D, *On Having no Head – Zen and the Rediscovery of the Obvious*, Arkana, London and New York, 1961

Joines, V, & Stewart, I, *Personality Adaptations*, Lifespace, Nottingham, 2002

Jung, CG, BBC Interview with John Freeman, 1959

Krupp, EC, *Echoes of Ancient Skies*, Oxford University Press, Oxford, 1983

Lawrence, DH, *The Plumed Serpent*, Alfred A Knopf, New York, 1926

Maslow, A, *A Theory of Human Motivation*, Collier, New York, 1943

Nesse, RM, & Williams, GC, *Evolution and Healing: The New Science of Darwinian Medicine*, Weidenfeld & Nicolson, London, 1995

Robbins, T, *Jitterbug Perfume*, Bantam, New York, 1984

Robertson, I, *Mind Sculpture: Your Brain's Untapped Potential*, Bantam, London, 1999

Reid, DP, *The Tao of Health, Sex and Longevity*, Fireside, New York, 1989

Sagan, C, *Can We Know the Universe?*, in The McGraw-Hill Reader, *Issues Across the Disciplines* by Gilbert Muller, McGraw-Hill Higher Education, Columbus, 2002

Scott-Mumby, K, *Virtual Medicine, A New Dimension in Energy Healing*, Thorsons, London, 1999

Sheldrake, R, *The Sense of Being Stared At, and Other Aspects of the Extended Mind*, Arrow, London, 2003

Steiner, G, *In Bluebeard's Castle: Some Notes Towards the Redefinition of Culture*, Faber, London, 1971

MIRRORS

Albrecht-Buehler, G, *Cell Intelligence*, 1998

Blake, W, *Collected Poems*, Routledge, London, 1863/1905

Bridges, L, *Face Reading in Chinese Medicine*, Churchill Livingstone, London, 2003

James, A, *Hands On Reflexology*, Hodder Arnold, London, 2002

Jensen, B, & Bodeen, D, *Visions of Health*, Avery, New York, 1992

Lama Govinda, *The Way of the White Clouds*, Rider & Co, London, 1966

Lenaghan, R, *Aesop's Fables: The Fox and the Mask*, Harvard University Press, Cambridge, 1967

Ovason, D, *The Zelator – The Secret Journals of Mark Hedsel*, Arrow, London, 1999

CHAKRAS

Eliade, M, *Yoga – Immortality and Freedom*, Princeton University Press, 1958

Iyengar, B K S, *Light on Yoga*, George Allen & Unwin, London, 1966

Johari, H, *Chakras: Energy Centres of Transformation*, Destiny, Vermont, 2000

Mookerjee, A, *Kundalini – The Arousal of the Inner Energy*, Thames and Hudson, London, 1982

Sivananda, SS, *Kundalini Yoga: Divine Life*, Sivanandanagar, New Dehli, 1935

Turlington, C, *Living Yoga – Creating a Life Practice*, Michael Joseph (Penguin), London, 2002

Woodroffe, J, *The Serpent Power – The Secrets of Tantric and Shaktic Yoga*, Luzac & Co, London, 1919

Yogananda, P, *The Autobiography of a Yogi*, Rider, London, 1950

SEPHIROTH

Blumenthal, D, *Understanding Jewish Mysticism – The Philosophic-Mystical and Hasidic Tradition*, Ktav, New York, 1982

Fortune, D, *The Mystical Qabalah*, Weiser, Boston, 1935

Kaplan, A, *The Bahir Illumination*, Samuel Weiser, Maine, 1979

Levine, S, *Healing into Life and Death*, Doubleday, New York, 1989

Lorde, A, *Collected Poems*, Norton, New York, 1997

Parfitt, W, *The Complete Guide to the Kabbalah*, Rider, London, 1988

Regardie, I, *A Garden of Pomegranates, Skrying on the Tree of Life*, Llewellyn, Minnesota, 1932

Regardie, I, *The Tree of Life, An Illustrated Study in Magic*, Llewellyn, Minnesota, 1932

Scholem, G, *Zohar, The Book of Splendour*, Schocken, New York, 1949

Wanless, J, *Voyager Tarot, Way of the Great Oracle*, Merrill-West, Carmel, 1985

MERIDIANS

Bertschinger, R, *The Secret of Everlasting Life*, Vega, London, 2002

College of Traditional Acupuncture, *Acupuncture Point Compendium*, CTA, Leamington Spa, 1999

Deadman, P, *et al*, *A Manual of Acupuncture, Journal of Chinese Medicine*, Hove, 1998

Ellis, A. *et al*, *Grasping the Wind: An Exploration of Chinese Acupuncture Point Names*, Paradigm, Mass, 1989

Frantzis, B K, *The Great Stillness: The Water Method of Taoist Meditation*, Clarity Press, California, 1999

Jarrett, L, *The Clinical Practice of Chinese Medicine*, Spirit Path Press, Stockbridge, 2003

Johnson, JA, *Chinese Medical QiGong Therapy*, International Institute of Medical QiGong, California, 2000

Kohn, L (ed), *Taoist Meditation and Longevity Techniques*, University of Michigan Press, Ann Arbor, 1989

Larre, C, & Rochat, E, *Rooted in Spirit*, Station Hill Press, Barrytown, 1981

Loewe, M, *Ways to Paradise, the Chinese Quest for Immortality*, George, Allen & Unwin, London, 1978

Macciocia, G, *The Foundations of Chinese Medicine*, Churchill Livingstone, Edinburgh, 1989

Worsley, J R, *Traditional Five Element Acupuncture: Volume 1: Meridians and Points*, Element, Shaftesbury, 1993

NOMMO

Davidson, B, *The African Genius*, Little, Brown & Co, Boston, 1969

Dieterlen, G, & Griaule, M, *The Pale Fox*, Institut d' Ethnologie, Paris, 1965

Griaule, M, *Conversations with Ogotemmêli*, OUP, London, 1948 (reprinted 1978)

Some, PM, *Of Water and the Spirit*, Penguin Compass, New York, 1994

Temple, R, *The Sirius Mystery*, Inner Traditions, Rochester, 1977

LIGHTWHEELS

Allen, P G, *Grandmothers of the Light, a Medicine Woman's Source Book*, Women's Press, London, 1992

Cameron, A, *Daughters of Copper Woman*, Harbour, Madeira Park, 2002

Castaneda, C, *Tales of Power*, Simon & Schuster, New York, 1974

Curtis, N, *The Indians Book – Songs and Legends of the American Indians*, Dover, New York, 1907

Eaton, E, *The Shaman and the Medicine Wheel*, Quest, Madras, 1982

Ereira, A, *The Elder Brothers*, Alfred A Knopf, New York, 1992

Lame Deer, J, & Erdoes, R, *Lame Deer Seeker of Visions*, Washington Square Press, New York, 1972

Mails, T E, *The Hopi Survival Kit*, Penguin, New York 1997

Philips, C, *The Lost History of Aztec and Maya*, Hermes House, London, 2004

Sams, J, *Sacred Path Cards – The Discovery of Self Through Native Teachings*, Harper, San Fransisco, 1990

Storm, H, *Lightningbolt*, One World, New York, 1994

Tedlock, D (trans), *Popul Vuh – The Mayan Book of the Dawn of Life*, Touchstone, New York, 1985

Zimmerman, L, *American Indians, the First Nations*, Duncan Baird, London, 2003

REMEMBERING THE FUTURE

Bly, R, *A Little Book on the Human Shadow*, Harper & Row, New York, 1979

Capra, F, *The Turning Point*, Flamingo, London, 1982

Feldman, C, & Kornfield, J, *Soul Food: Stories to Nourish the Spirit and the Heart*, Harper, San Fransisco, 1996

Huxley, A, *The Perennial Philosophy*, Harper & Bros, New York, 1945

Lee, S, *The Perfect Fool*, Fourth Estate, London, 2001

Lessing, D, *Shikasta*, Jonathan Cape, London, 1979

Robbins, T, *Fierce Invalids Home from Hot Climates*, Bantam Books, New York, 2000

Glossary

Akasha

The Sanskrit word for 'aether', which is the fifth element that unites the other four (fire, water, earth and air).

Akashic records

Libraries of soul knowledge perceived, particularly by Theosophists and prophets such as Edgar Cayce, to store the knowledge of each soul. Similar to the Books of Life referred to in the Old and New Testaments.

Alchemy

Precursor of modern chemistry that seeks to transform consciousness. Both Western and Eastern forms of alchemy continue to see no difference between inner and outer alchemy.

Ari

Honorary calling of Rabbi Isaac Ben Solomon Luria (1534–72), who contributed vast amounts of scholarship and insight into the Kabbalah. *Ari* is literally 'lion' in Hebrew.

Aromatherapy

Ancient wisdom of using scents and odours to heal. In the last part of the 20th century it was developed as a distinct therapeutic discipline by combining massage with aromatic oils.

Astral body

One of the aspects or layerings of our Body/Mind/Spirit that has been variously described by different traditions. Often placed within a hierarchy that includes physical body, mental body, emotional body, spirit body and soul, its exact meaning depends on whether it is referred to from a predominantly Buddhist, Hindu, Theosophist, Kabbalistic or New Age perspective, where it is linked to 'astral travel' – a journeying of part of our non-conscious self.

Avatar

A sanskrit term meaning 'divine incarnation' and refers to an aspect of a divine being who takes incarnate form. Krishna and Rama were avatars of Vishnu. Originally Hindu, the term has also been used by other religions and philosophies, particularly Theosophy, to denote ascended masters.

Ayurveda

From the Sanskrit meaning 'knowledge of life', this Indian form of medicine employs a wide variety of therapeutic techniques to balance the qualities of nature within a human being.

Chakra

Sanskrit word for 'wheel' (pronounced *chukruh*) that refers to centres of energy in the subtle body, typically numbering seven. A term widely adopted by other traditions such as theosophy.

Chi (qi)

A Chinese term commonly translated as 'energy', but perhaps more accurately meaning 'breaths', it is the substrata of Taoist philosophy, underlying, penetrating and manifesting all life. The Japanese for this concept is *Ki*.

Dreamtime

A perspective of the universe where consciousness is shared by many aspects of the earth, including humans, ancestors, mountains, animals, plants and spirits. It is primarily an Australian Aboriginal term, but is now used widely in reference to shamanic cultures across the world where the prevailing consciousness is interactive rather than human-centred, and is typically beyond limiting perceptions of time and space.

Earthwalk

A Native American term used for our current personal incarnation.

Entropy

Model of dynamic systems in which components and participants compete rather than cooperate, and so eventually exhaust all the available energy within a system ('It's a dog eat dog world out there'). Opposite of syntropy. It is derived from the work of Italian mathematician Luigi Fantappie.

Epistemology

A central branch of philosophy, Eastern and Western, and an area in which different ideologies compete for their versions of routes to knowledge. A fluid epistemology is argued for throughout this Atlas, which balances and finds flexibility between varying approaches.

Ets Chayim

Hebrew for 'Tree of Life'.

Five elements

Chinese cosmology of all life being aspects of five essential dynamic processes – wood, fire, earth, metal and water. Each element is highly dependent on context and perspective and so resists definition, but operates on correspondences such as those of the seasons – spring, summer, harvest, autumn and winter.

Fractal

Complex computer diagrams developed by mathematical equations, and employing the functions of infinity. From the Latin *fractus* – meaning 'rough' or 'uneven'. Widely used to illustrate chaos theory and dreamtime visions.

Grail

Many-faceted talisman of transcendent consciousness, appearing in various traditions: the Holy Grail of Christ, the Philosopher's Stone of the Alchemists and the 'all and the everything' of the Druids.

Granthi

Sanskrit word for 'knot', denoting bundles of energy in the 1st, 4th and 6th chakras where the illusions of incarnation have to be traversed in order to expand into a deeper seeing of life.

Hologram

Light sculptures and memory banks created from the interfacing of light beams.

Ida

One of the three main nadi channels of the subtle body, carrying lunar energy and spiralling around the chakras, reuniting with its opposite nadi, pingala, at the brain.

Katchina

Elemental forces that are 'danced' by the Hopi tribe in ceremonies of seasonal renewal.

Kundalini

Sanskrit word for 'coiled' and meaning the latent energy bundled at the base of the spine that is activated by meditation.

LightWheel

Centre of energy within American shamanism that embodies links within the human being to the other realms of earth and sky.

Lingum

A Sanskrit term symbolizing the god Shiva, and the penis.

Maaseh Merkabah
Hebrew for the 'throne chariot' Ezekiel saw in his vision and which described the workings of the divine universe.

Mandala
Sanskrit for 'circle', meaning 'sacred diagram'. Often honouring the four directions and the unity of the circle, so symbolizing the virtual temples of consciousness encountered in meditation.

Medicine wheel
Foundation of much of Native American wisdom, with the directions of the compass holding a different reflection of Great Spirit, and paths for human beings to come into balance with the natural world.

Meridian
Channel of chi flowing throughout the human body, corresponding to internal organs and physiological and spiritual processes.

Metis
Mixed race, typically used to describe people of mixed European and native origin, particularly in the Americas and some areas of Southeast Asia.

Morphic field
The virtual mould of each species within which DNA instructs life to grow.

Nadi
Streams of subtle energy. Numbering many thousand throughout the body the principal ones are the sushumna, ida and pingala.

Nagual
Realm of consciousness and being extending to shapeshifting, being in many spaces at one time and changing the collective consciousness of groups. Complex etymology including Mexican Spanish and native Mayan.

Non-locality
Paradoxical theory within quantum mechanics that describes particles that 'know' what others are doing across great distance and with no perceivable 'cause' or 'locality' between them.

Order of the Golden Dawn
Western magical tradition that developed at the end of the 19th century. Based in London, it blended aspects of Egyptian, Greek and Masonic ritual and philosophy.

Pantheism
Doctrine that identifies god/divinity with the manifest universe.

Pingala
One of the three main nadi channels of the subtle body, carrying solar energy and spiralling around the chakras, reuniting with its opposite nadi, ida, at the brain.

Sacred hoop
Native American appreciation of the interconnectedness of life, and the sovereignty of the people and the land.

Samadhi
Sanskrit word for the absorption into the essence of beingness within the universe that is achieved at a certain stage of meditation.

Sanskrit
Language of the Vedic civilization, more than 4,000 years old, and integral to Hindu, Buddhist and Jain religions.

Sarira
Sanskrit for 'sheath', it describes the various layers of the human form within yogic traditions.

Sephiroth
Hebrew for 'number' and 'emanation', the spheres of consciousness that count down the cosmic incarnation of humanity from the crown of the head and the godhead to the soles of the feet and the earth.

Spiderwoman
Aspect of the great goddess in Mesoamerican cultures. Particularly linked with Spider Rock in Arizona and the Navajo telling of creation.

Subtle body
In a Hindu context, the suksma sarira that corresponds to the sixth chakra, but gives rise to all of them. More widely, loosely used to denote the non-physical body.

Sushumna
Central nadi of yoga traditions flowing from the sacrum along the spine to the brain.

Syntropy
Model of dynamic systems in which components and participants cooperate rather than compete, and so yield more total energy as a result.

Tao (Dao)
Often translated as 'the way', the essential state of beingness of the universe itself that famously resists definition. Core rhythm of Taoism (Daoism), one of the main religions/philosophies of China, together with Buddhism, Confucianism and Maoism.

Theosophy
Religious philosophy that developed towards the end of the 19th century, seeing the commonality between each of the world religions.

Toltec
Mexican civilization that succeeded the Mayan and laid the seeds of the Aztecs. Warrior society that had its capital at Tula, central Mexico, where carved statues of Toltec warriors still stand guard.

Tree of Life
Near global icon and theme that is the central energy channel of the planet, and also symbolic of the links between earth and sky. Many times mirrored within the human being as the central energy channel of the spine.

Twenty count
Mathematical construct of the Mayan civilization that expresses the totality of creation.

Tzolkin
The calendar of the Mayan civilization that tracks the development of days and eras according to the twenty count.

Yantra
Religious symbolic diagram, similar to mandalas, but often more simple and geometric.

Yoga Sutras
Scriptures of yoga.

Yogi/yogin
One devoted to the practice of yoga.

Yoni
Sanskrit term symbolizing the goddess Shakti, and the vagina.

Acknowledgements

Executive editor	**Patrick Nugent**
Executive designer	**Nick Harris**
Editor	**Jonathan Hilton**
Project editor	**Camilla Davis**
3D illustration and montage	**Nick Harris**
Additional design and illustration	**Rebecca Painter**
Anatomical and chakra illustration	**Bill Donohoe**
Picture research	**Emma O'Neill**
Production manager	**Louise Hall**

AUTHOR'S ACKNOWLEDGEMENTS

Most works are compilations of effort, constellations of shared dreams. This Atlas is no exception and has emerged through the generosity of many people. The team at Gaia have worked above and beyond all sense of duty in a production that has pushed the boundaries of anything so far in this genre, and I have deeply appreciated the skills and commitment of Camilla Davis, Nick Harris, Jonathan Hilton, Patrick Nugent, Emma O'Neill and Rebecca Painter. While production has spanned just three years, the seeds of this book for me personally reach back at least twenty, and touch on a very wide variety of adventures and periods of study. But for this particular phase, from providing space and inspiration to offering critical feedback about structure, argument, insight and presentation, I would like to thank Ruth App, Gig Binder, Evelyn Carter, Master Chan, Elisabeth Christie, Lyn and Graham Clarke, Arwyn DreamWalker, Mike Fuller, Tim Gordon, Else and Reinhold Herbich, Nancy Holroyde-Downing, Mary Hoptroff, Clive Koerner, Myron Kofman, Ri Palmer, Elisabeth Rochat de la Vallee, Judy Rose, Regina Schultz, Suzanne Shale, John Wheeler, Colin Wilson, Wang Zhi Xing, Ben Yeger, Pam and Simon Young.

In addition are those teachers who have opened the doors to the traditions that lie within this book, handed me the keys to know how I, too, might honour the ancestors, mountains and gatekeepers of the sacred sciences. And while I have sought a suitable rigour and accuracy and acknowledge all errors as my own, I hope that I have remained true to the motivating spirit of each lineage.

Finally, and especially, I thank Richard Hougham with whom I know the wealth of brotherhood, my parents, Jean and Peter Hougham, who continue to provide the love and stability for me to take such wild rides, and my daughters Maia and Anu, who seem to be taking them further.

ACKNOWLEDGEMENTS

Key: t top, b bottom, c centre, l left, r right, bg background
akg-images 117, 202/Binder 80/British Library 143 insert/Hervé Champollion 123 l/Gérard Degeorge 137 l/François Guénet 119 l /Erich Lessing 14; **Alamy**/Bryan & Cherry Alexander Photography 175 tl & 177 tl/Amazon-Images 52/ArkReligion.com 105 tl /Atmosphere Picture Library/Bob Croxford 38 t/Marco Brivio 114 /Danita Delimont 179 tl/Mike Hill 210/North Wind Picture Archives 79 tr/Phototake/Dennis Kunkel 57 tr/Robert Harding Picture Library Ltd/Omri Stephenson 188/david sanger photography 208/Mikael Utterstrom 99 bg; **The Art Archive**/Musée Guimet Paris/Dagli Orti 101 tl; **Art Directors & Trip**/Itzhak Genut 130, 128; **Bridgeman Art Library**/Bibliothèque Nationale, Paris, France 79 tl/Fitzwilliam Museum, University of Cambridge, UK 75 bl/Private Collection 79 br; **Christie's Images** 8–9, 75 br, 79 bl, 107 tl, 121 l/Jack Tjakamarra 77; **Richard Collier, Department of Wyoming State Parks & Cultural Resources** 184; **Corbis UK Ltd**/Bettmann 78, 147, 186/Mark A Johnson 38–39 bg/Danny Lehman 182–183, /David Lees 116–117 /Reuters 123 r/Sandro Vannnini 172–173 main picture/Michael S. Yamashita 215/Zefa/Jens Nieth 85; **Arwyn DreamWalker** 2 t, 185, 187, 189, 191, 193, 195, 197, 199, 201, 203; **Mary Evans Picture Library** 136; **Getty Images**/AFP 12/Angelo Cavalli 213/Georgette Douwma 209/Don King 211/John & Lisa Merrill 96–97/Peter Samuels 95/SMC Images 42–43/David Trood 14-15/Jochem D Wijnands 99 tl/Toyohiro Yamada 18–19; **Nick Harris** 23 bg; **Yoram Kahana** 192; **Photodisc** 54, 150/C Sherburne/PhotoLink 109 tl/StockTrek 107 bg, 125 r, 129 r, 135 r, 137 r, 170-171, 175; **Octopus Publishing Group Ltd** 11, 13, 30-31 bg, 58-59, 63 t, 63 c, 101 bg, 103 bg, 105 bg, 109 bg, 111 bg, 115 bg, 145 bg, 157, 158–159/Ian Parsons 161/Russell Sadur 100; **NASA** 32 l, 81 br, 121 r/A. Caulet St-ECF, ESA 81 bg, /ESA/ H. Bond (STScI) and M. Barstow (University of Leicester) 181 bg /Akira Fujii 142–143/JPL 81 tl, 127 r/JPL/Caltech 139 r/JPL/University of Arizona 131 r/Johnson Space Center 20–21, 60–61, 119 r/NOAO, ESA, The Hubble Helix Nebula Team, M. Meixner (STScI) and T. A. Rector (NRAO) 206-207; **North Wind Picture Archives**/Nancy Carter 81 bl, 190; **Onasia**/Yannick Jooris 106; **Photos12.com**/Jean Guichard 125 l, 139 l/Institut Ramses 127 l/Oasis 64; **Photolibrary Group**/Botanica/Romerein Lisa 102/Bsip/May 22/OSF/David Fleetham 115 c/Phototake Inc/Dennis Kunkel 28; **Rex Features** /Everett Collection (EVT) 165; **Reproduced by permission of Nicholas Roerich Museum, New York** 44; **Science Photo Library** /ArSciMed 16–17/BioPhoto Associates 27 tl/Steve Gschmeissner 27 cl /Roger Harris 32 c/Innerspace Imaging 27 bl/Philippe Plailly 82–83; **SuperStock** 94, 212/Lisette Le Bon 162/Newberry Library 198; **Tips Images Ltd**/Luca Invernizzi Tettoni 155/Antonello Lanzelloto 181 tl; **topfoto.co.uk**/Arena/PAL 90/Fortean 84/Topham Picturepoint 131 l, /Charles Walker 108; Wellcome Photo Library/Mark de Fraeye 167, /Welcome Library 145 t; **Pieter Weltevrede/ www.sanatansociety.com** 103 tl; **Werner Forman Archive**/86, 129 l /The Egyptian Museum, Cairo 135 l/Fuhrman Collection, New York 173 insert/Philip Goldman Collection, London 111 tl.